THE FLASH

THE FLASH AGE

VOL. 14

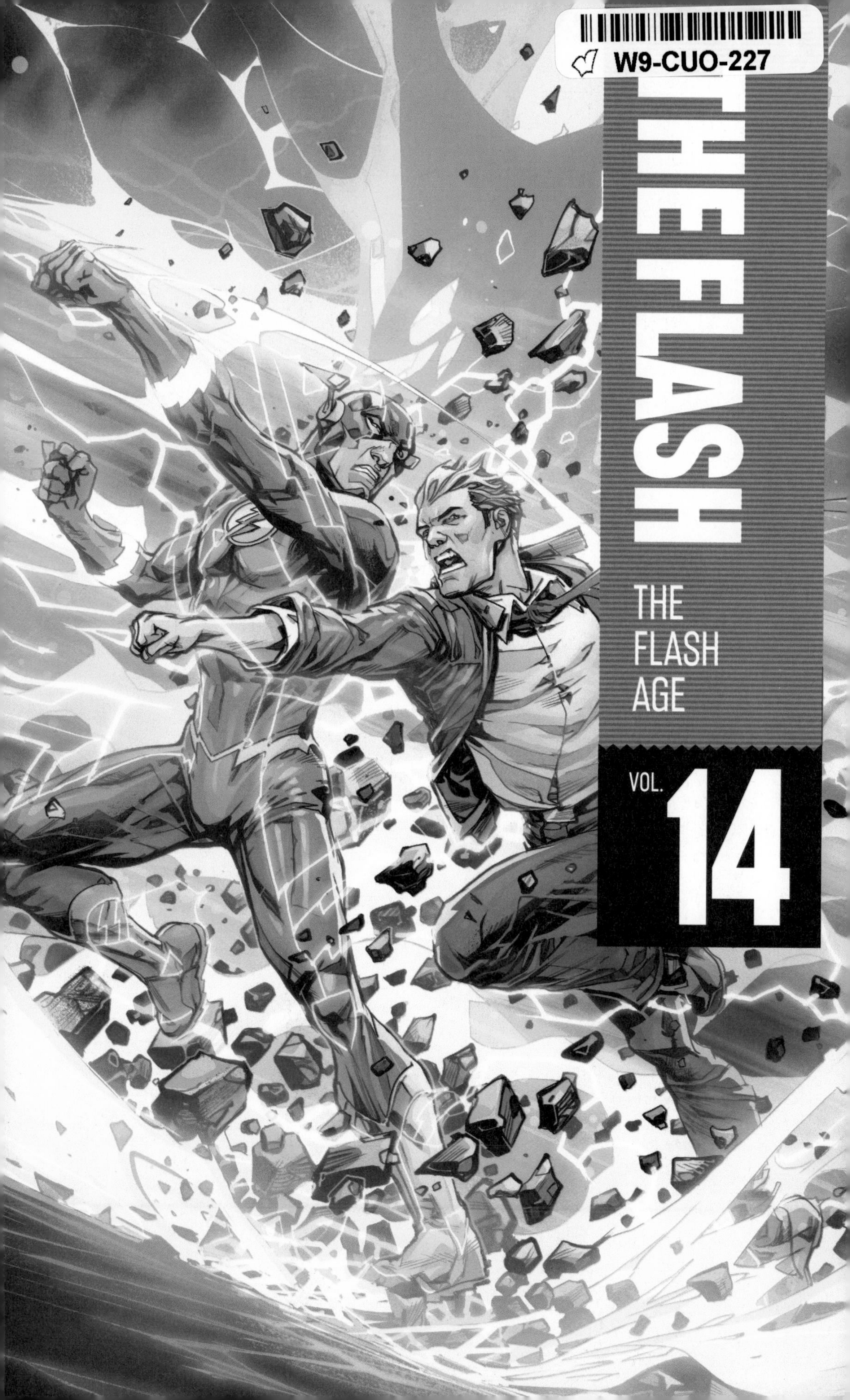

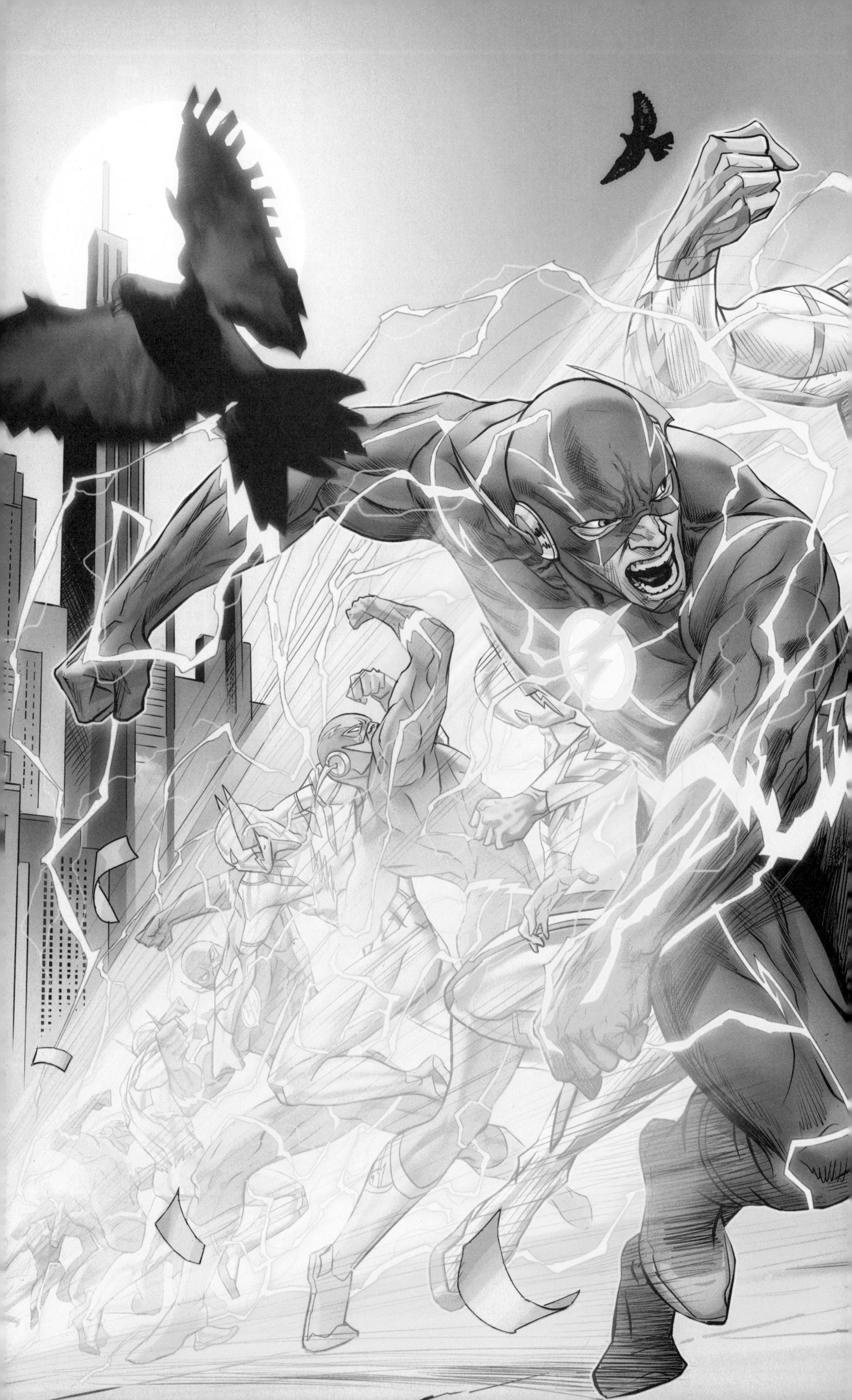

THE FLASH
THE FLASH AGE

writer

JOSHUA WILLIAMSON

artists

HOWARD PORTER
RAFA SANDOVAL
JORDI TARRAGONA
CHRISTIAN DUCE
STEVEN SEGOVIA
BRANDON PETERSON
CARLO PAGULAYAN
JASON PAZ

colorist

HI-FI
ARIF PRIANTO

letterer

STEVE WANDS

collection cover artists

RAFA SANDOVAL,
JORDI TARRAGONA,
and ARIF PRIANTO

VOL.

14

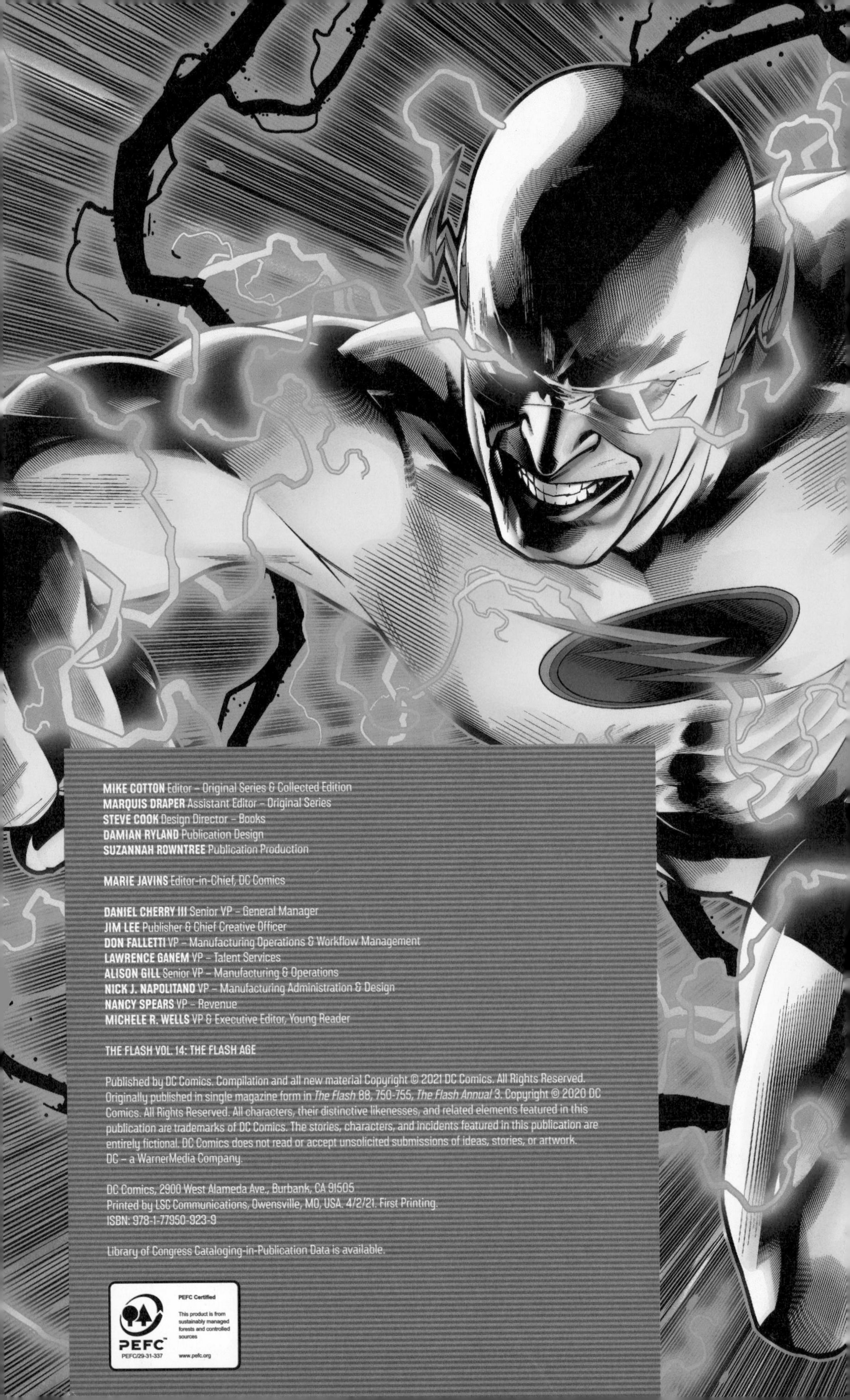

MIKE COTTON Editor – Original Series & Collected Edition
MARQUIS DRAPER Assistant Editor – Original Series
STEVE COOK Design Director – Books
DAMIAN RYLAND Publication Design
SUZANNAH ROWNTREE Publication Production

MARIE JAVINS Editor-in-Chief, DC Comics

DANIEL CHERRY III Senior VP – General Manager
JIM LEE Publisher & Chief Creative Officer
DON FALLETTI VP – Manufacturing Operations & Workflow Management
LAWRENCE GANEM VP – Talent Services
ALISON GILL Senior VP – Manufacturing & Operations
NICK J. NAPOLITANO VP – Manufacturing Administration & Design
NANCY SPEARS VP – Revenue
MICHELE R. WELLS VP & Executive Editor, Young Reader

THE FLASH VOL. 14: THE FLASH AGE

DC Comics, 2900 West Alameda Ave., Burbank, CA 91505
Printed by LSC Communications, Owensville, MO, USA. 4/2/21. First Printing.
ISBN: 978-1-77950-923-9

Library of Congress Cataloging-in-Publication Data is available.

PEFC Certified
This product is from sustainably managed forests and controlled sources
PEFC
PEFC/29-31-337
www.pefc.org

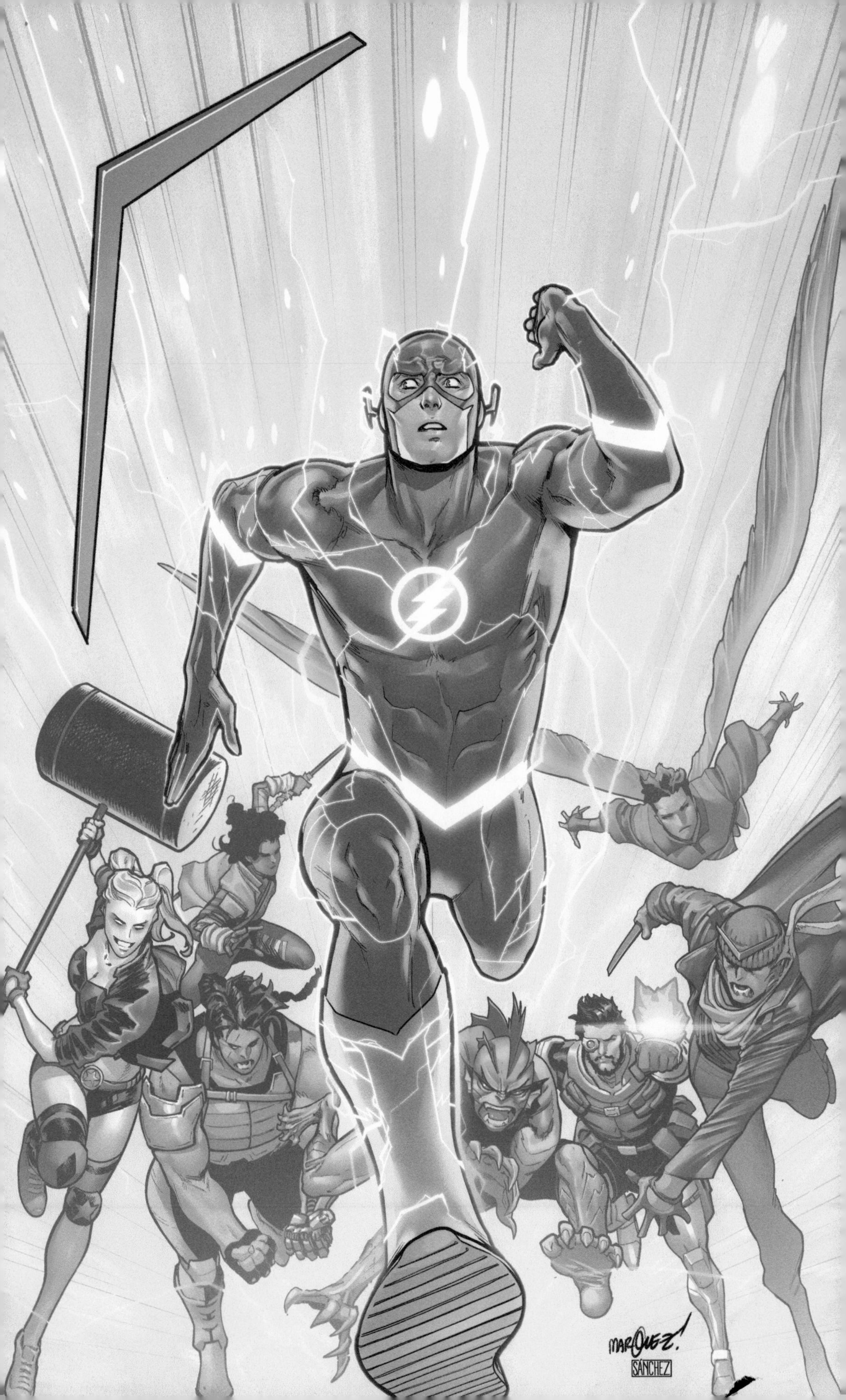
SÁNCHEZ

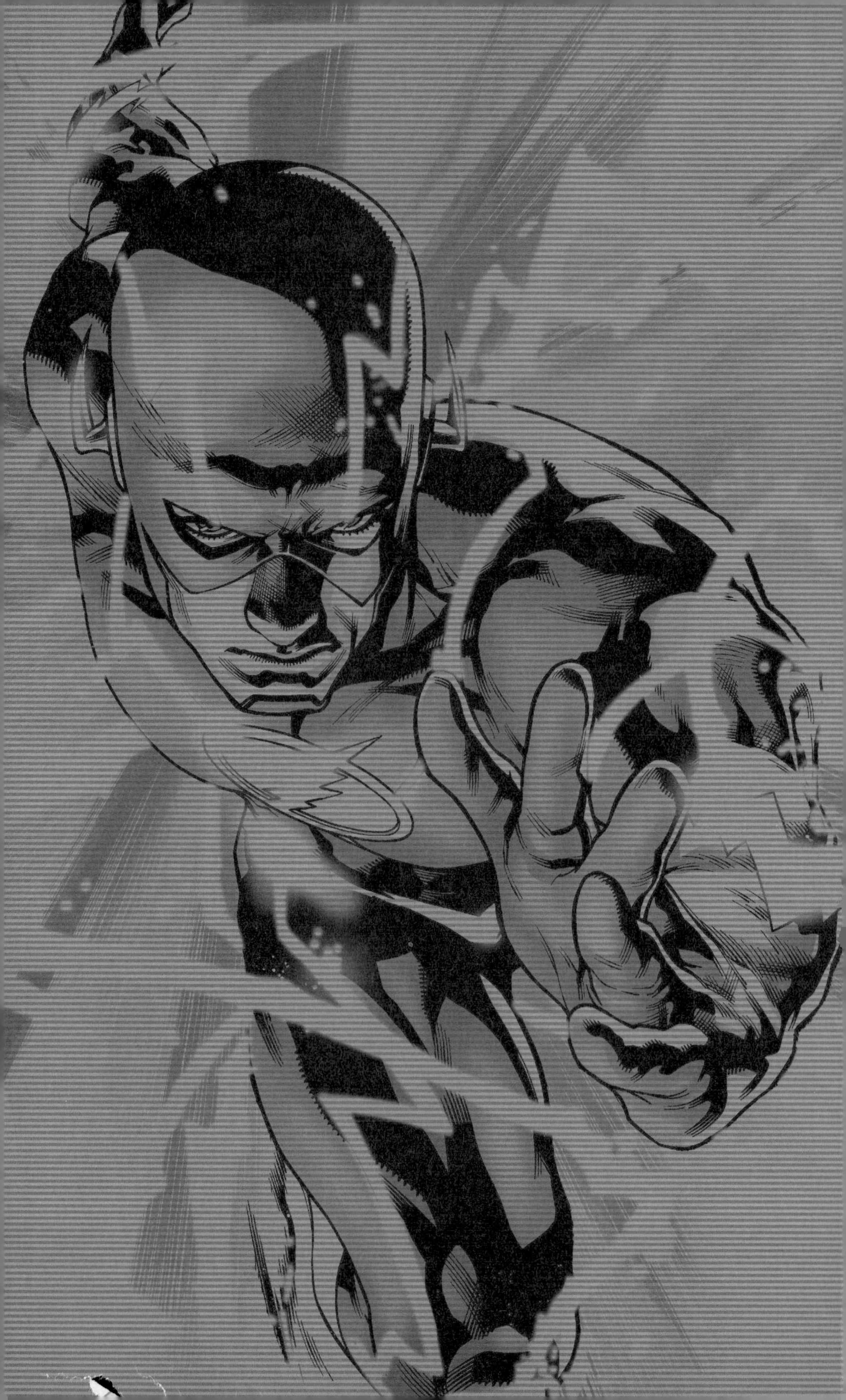

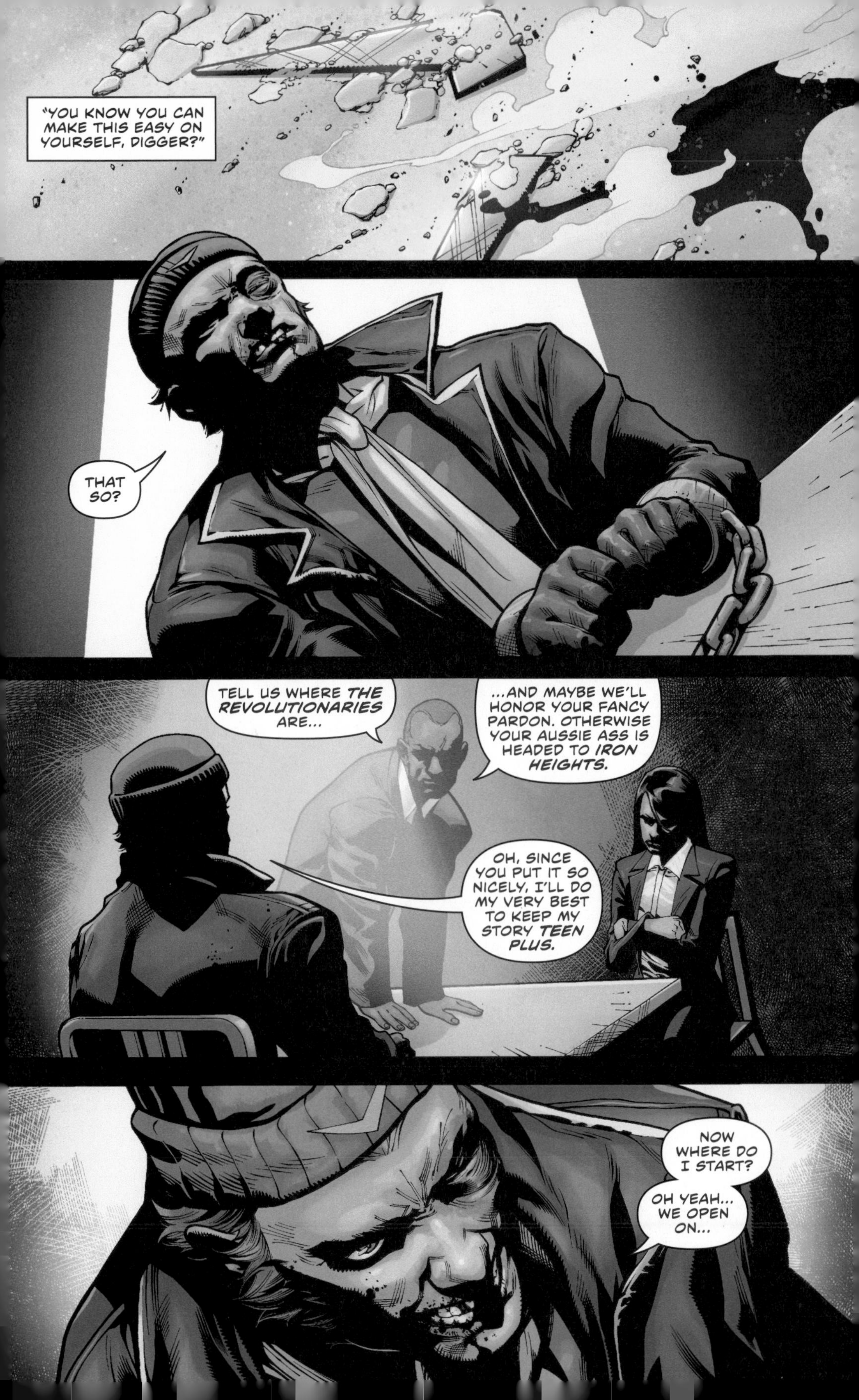
"YOU KNOW YOU CAN MAKE THIS EASY ON YOURSELF, DIGGER?"
THAT SO?
TELL US WHERE THE REVOLUTIONARIES ARE...
...AND MAYBE WE'LL HONOR YOUR FANCY PARDON. OTHERWISE YOUR AUSSIE ASS IS HEADED TO IRON HEIGHTS.
OH, SINCE YOU PUT IT SO NICELY, I'LL DO MY VERY BEST TO KEEP MY STORY TEEN PLUS.
NOW WHERE DO I START?
OH YEAH... WE OPEN ON...

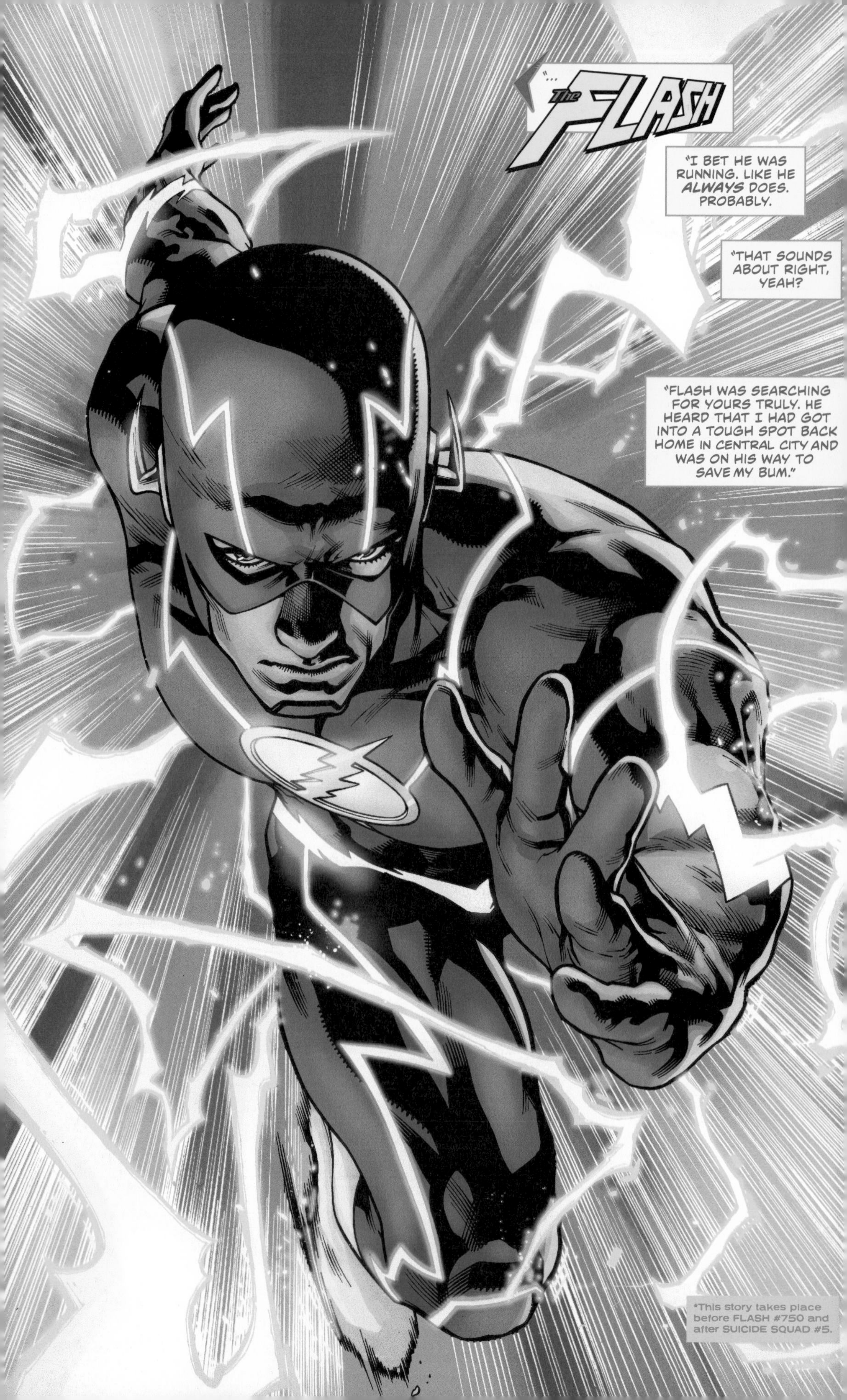
"...The FLASH
"I BET HE WAS RUNNING. LIKE HE *ALWAYS* DOES. PROBABLY.
"THAT SOUNDS ABOUT RIGHT, YEAH?
"FLASH WAS SEARCHING FOR YOURS TRULY. HE HEARD THAT I HAD GOT INTO A TOUGH SPOT BACK HOME IN CENTRAL CITY AND WAS ON HIS WAY TO SAVE MY BUM."
*This story takes place before FLASH #750 and after SUICIDE SQUAD #5.

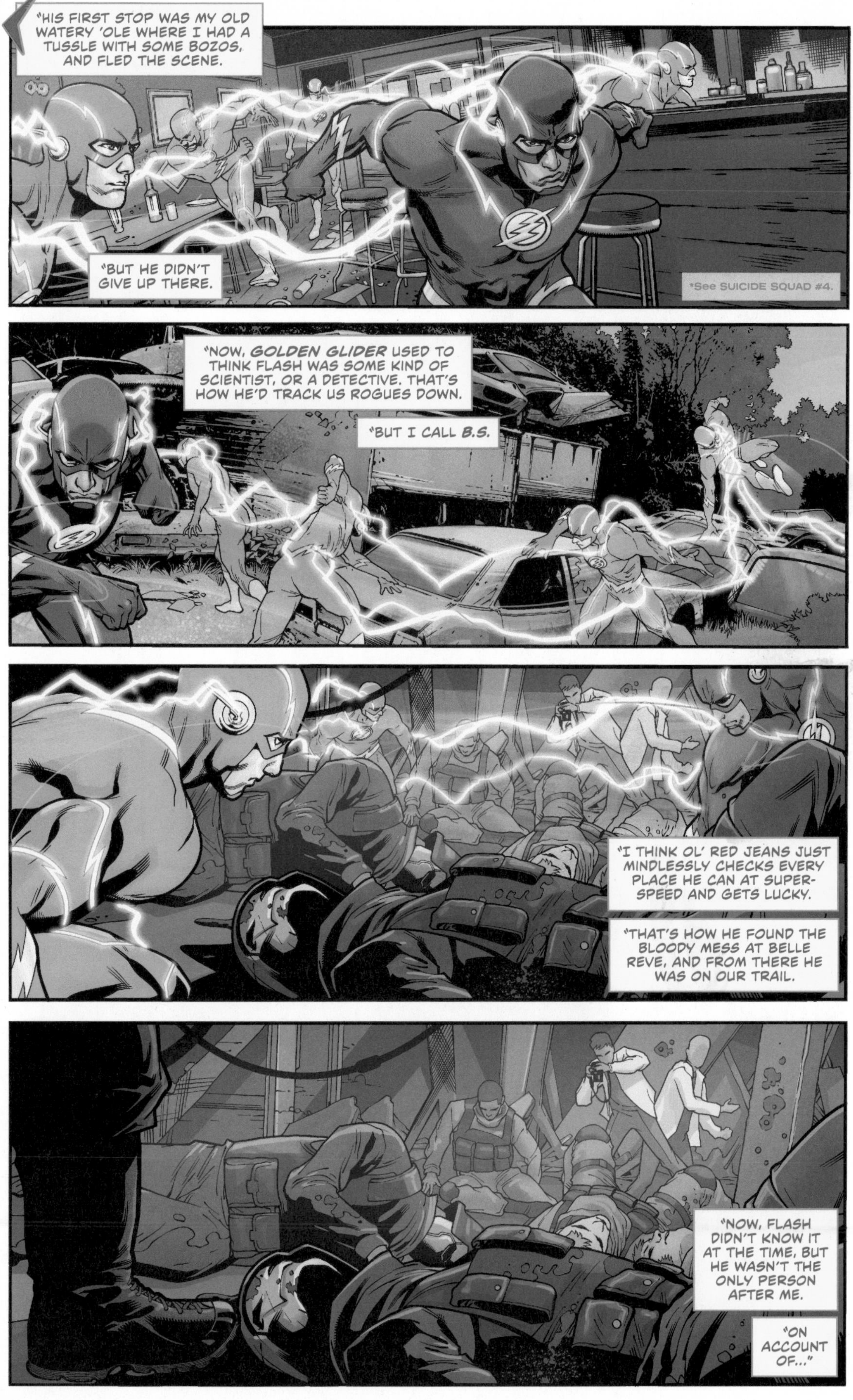
"HIS FIRST STOP WAS MY OLD WATERY 'OLE WHERE I HAD A TUSSLE WITH SOME BOZOS, AND FLED THE SCENE.
"BUT HE DIDN'T GIVE UP THERE.
*See SUICIDE SQUAD #4.
"NOW, GOLDEN GLIDER USED TO THINK FLASH WAS SOME KIND OF SCIENTIST, OR A DETECTIVE. THAT'S HOW HE'D TRACK US ROGUES DOWN.
"BUT I CALL B.S.
"I THINK OL' RED JEANS JUST MINDLESSLY CHECKS EVERY PLACE HE CAN AT SUPER-SPEED AND GETS LUCKY.
"THAT'S HOW HE FOUND THE BLOODY MESS AT BELLE REVE, AND FROM THERE HE WAS ON OUR TRAIL.
"NOW, FLASH DIDN'T KNOW IT AT THE TIME, BUT HE WASN'T THE ONLY PERSON AFTER ME.
"ON ACCOUNT OF..."

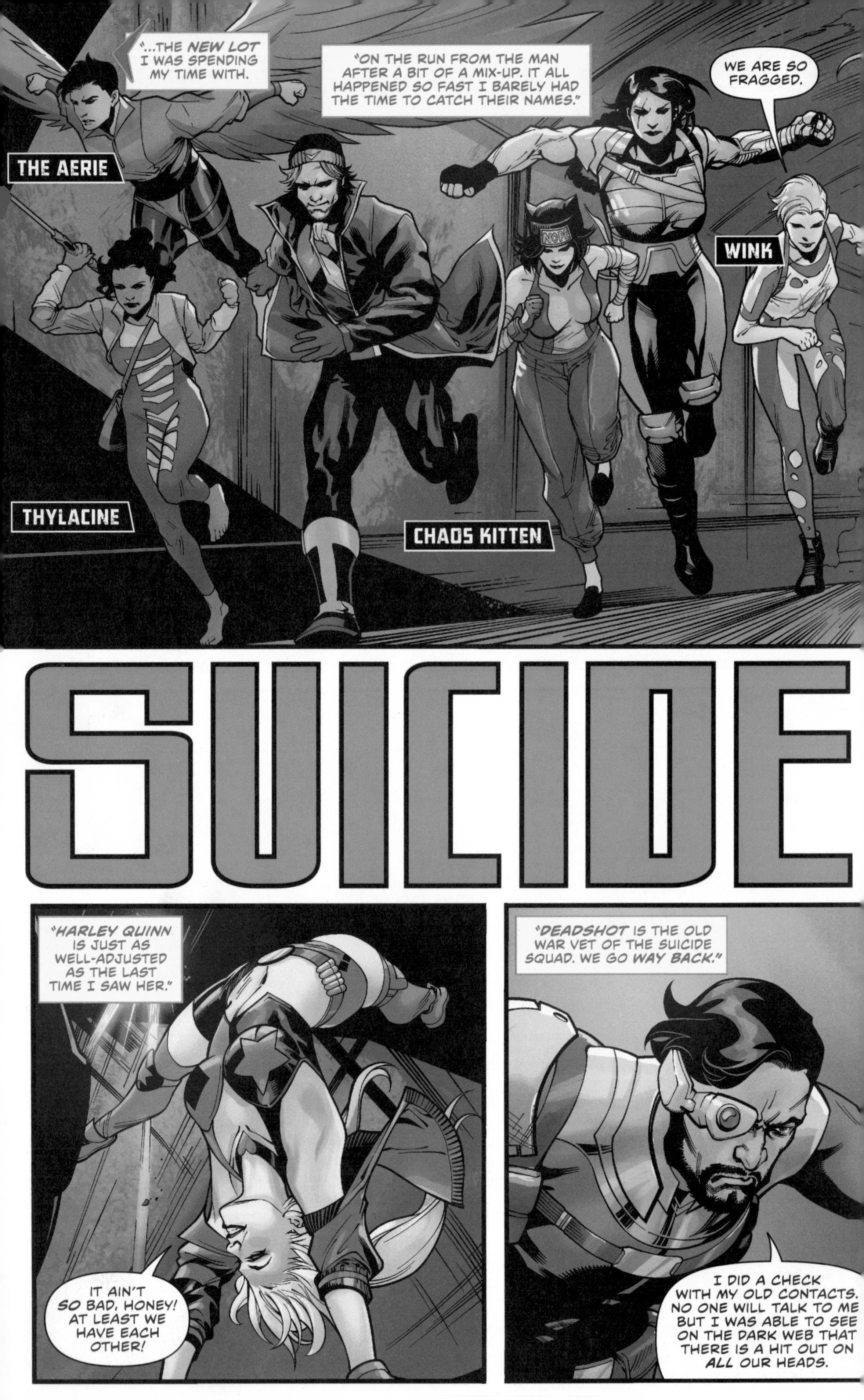
"...THE NEW LOT I WAS SPENDING MY TIME WITH.
"ON THE RUN FROM THE MAN AFTER A BIT OF A MIX-UP. IT ALL HAPPENED SO FAST I BARELY HAD THE TIME TO CATCH THEIR NAMES."
WE ARE SO FRAGGED.
THE AERIE
WINK
THYLACINE
CHAOS KITTEN
NOPE
SUICIDE
"HARLEY QUINN IS JUST AS WELL-ADJUSTED AS THE LAST TIME I SAW HER."
IT AIN'T SO BAD, HONEY! AT LEAST WE HAVE EACH OTHER!
"DEADSHOT IS THE OLD WAR VET OF THE SUICIDE SQUAD. WE GO WAY BACK."
I DID A CHECK WITH MY OLD CONTACTS. NO ONE WILL TALK TO ME BUT I WAS ABLE TO SEE ON THE DARK WEB THAT THERE IS A HIT OUT ON ALL OUR HEADS.

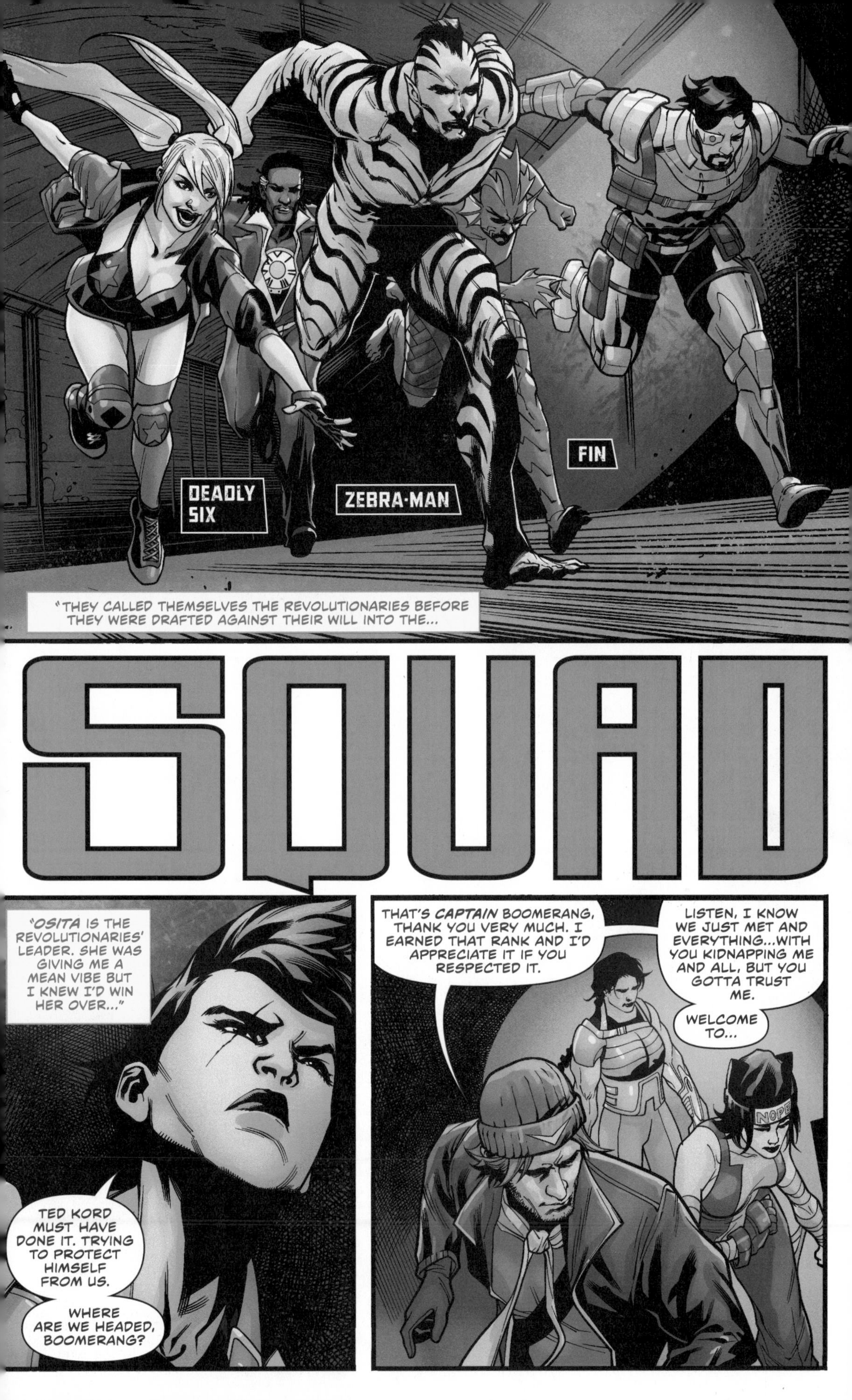
DEADLY SIX
ZEBRA-MAN
FIN
"THEY CALLED THEMSELVES THE REVOLUTIONARIES BEFORE THEY WERE DRAFTED AGAINST THEIR WILL INTO THE...
SQUAD
"OSITA IS THE REVOLUTIONARIES' LEADER. SHE WAS GIVING ME A MEAN VIBE BUT I KNEW I'D WIN HER OVER..."
TED KORD MUST HAVE DONE IT. TRYING TO PROTECT HIMSELF FROM US.
WHERE ARE WE HEADED, BOOMERANG?
THAT'S CAPTAIN BOOMERANG, THANK YOU VERY MUCH. I EARNED THAT RANK AND I'D APPRECIATE IT IF YOU RESPECTED IT.
LISTEN, I KNOW WE JUST MET AND EVERYTHING...WITH YOU KIDNAPPING ME AND ALL, BUT YOU GOTTA TRUST ME.
WELCOME TO...
NOPE

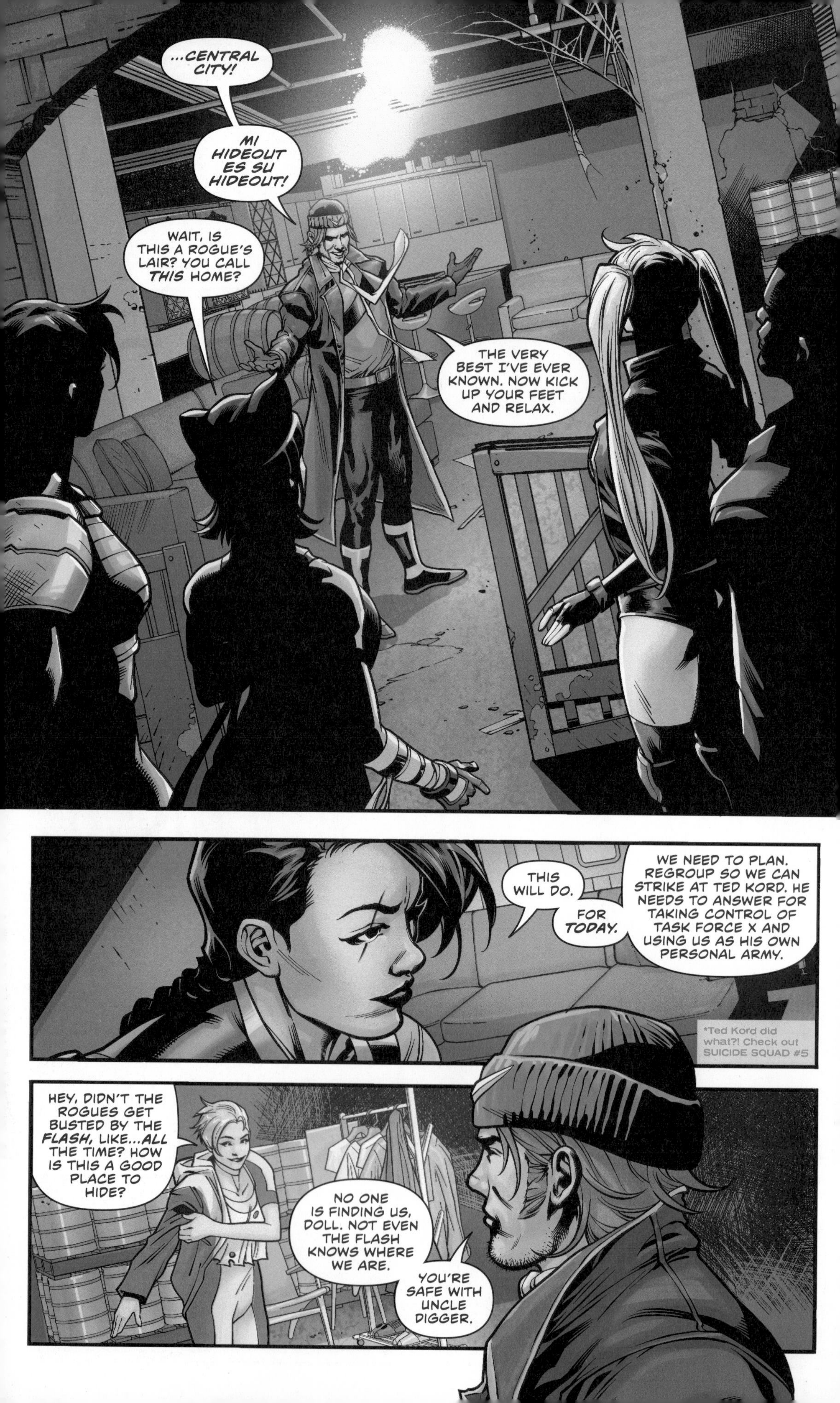
...CENTRAL CITY!
MI HIDEOUT ES SU HIDEOUT!
WAIT, IS THIS A ROGUE'S LAIR? YOU CALL THIS HOME?
THE VERY BEST I'VE EVER KNOWN. NOW KICK UP YOUR FEET AND RELAX.
THIS WILL DO.
FOR TODAY.
WE NEED TO PLAN. REGROUP SO WE CAN STRIKE AT TED KORD. HE NEEDS TO ANSWER FOR TAKING CONTROL OF TASK FORCE X AND USING US AS HIS OWN PERSONAL ARMY.
*Ted Kord did what?! Check out SUICIDE SQUAD #5
HEY, DIDN'T THE ROGUES GET BUSTED BY THE FLASH, LIKE...ALL THE TIME? HOW IS THIS A GOOD PLACE TO HIDE?
NO ONE IS FINDING US, DOLL. NOT EVEN THE FLASH KNOWS WHERE WE ARE.
YOU'RE SAFE WITH UNCLE DIGGER.

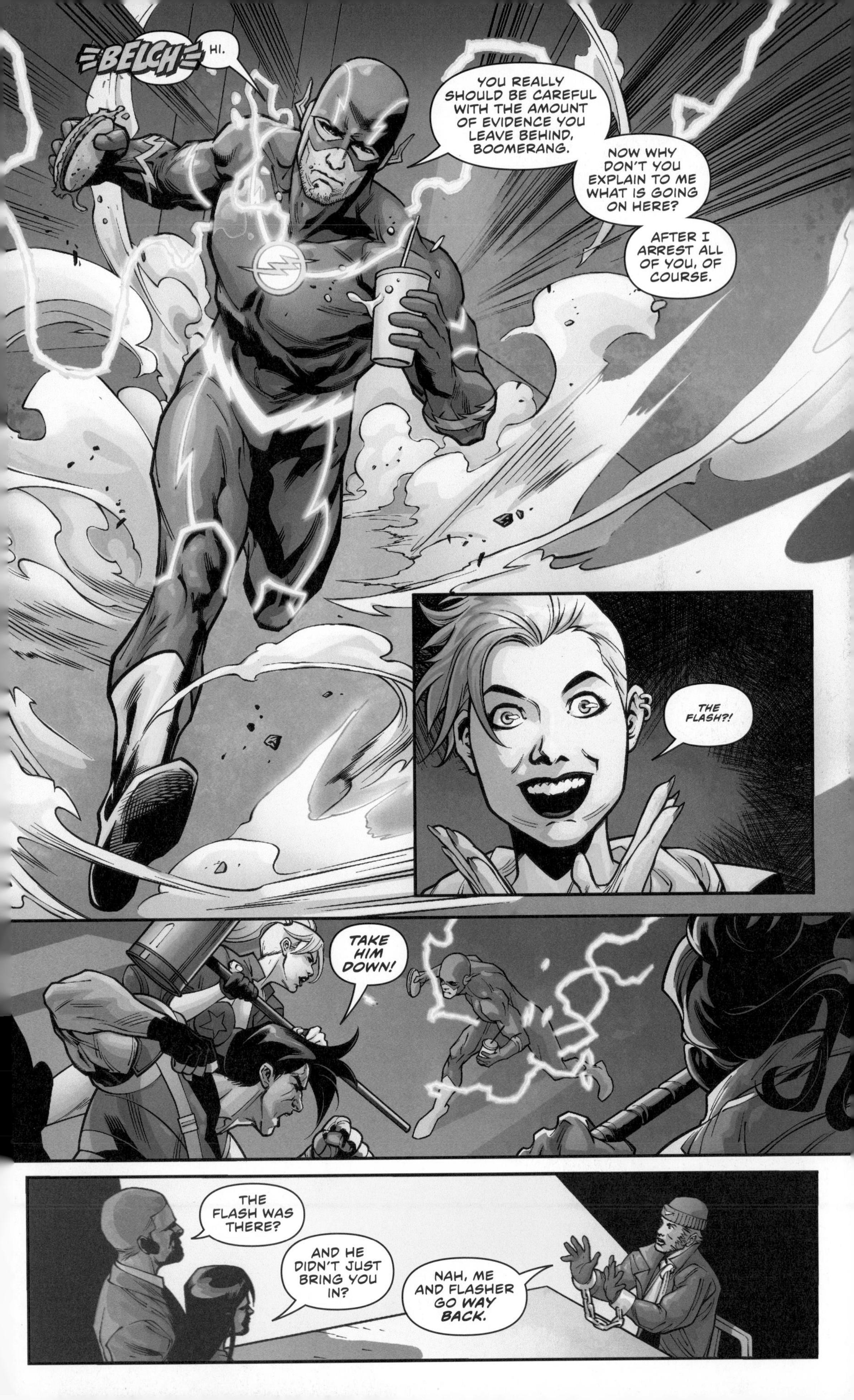
BELCH
HI.
YOU REALLY SHOULD BE CAREFUL WITH THE AMOUNT OF EVIDENCE YOU LEAVE BEHIND, BOOMERANG.
NOW WHY DON'T YOU EXPLAIN TO ME WHAT IS GOING ON HERE?
AFTER I ARREST ALL OF YOU, OF COURSE.
THE FLASH?!
TAKE HIM DOWN!
THE FLASH WAS THERE?
AND HE DIDN'T JUST BRING YOU IN?
NAH, ME AND FLASHER GO WAY BACK.

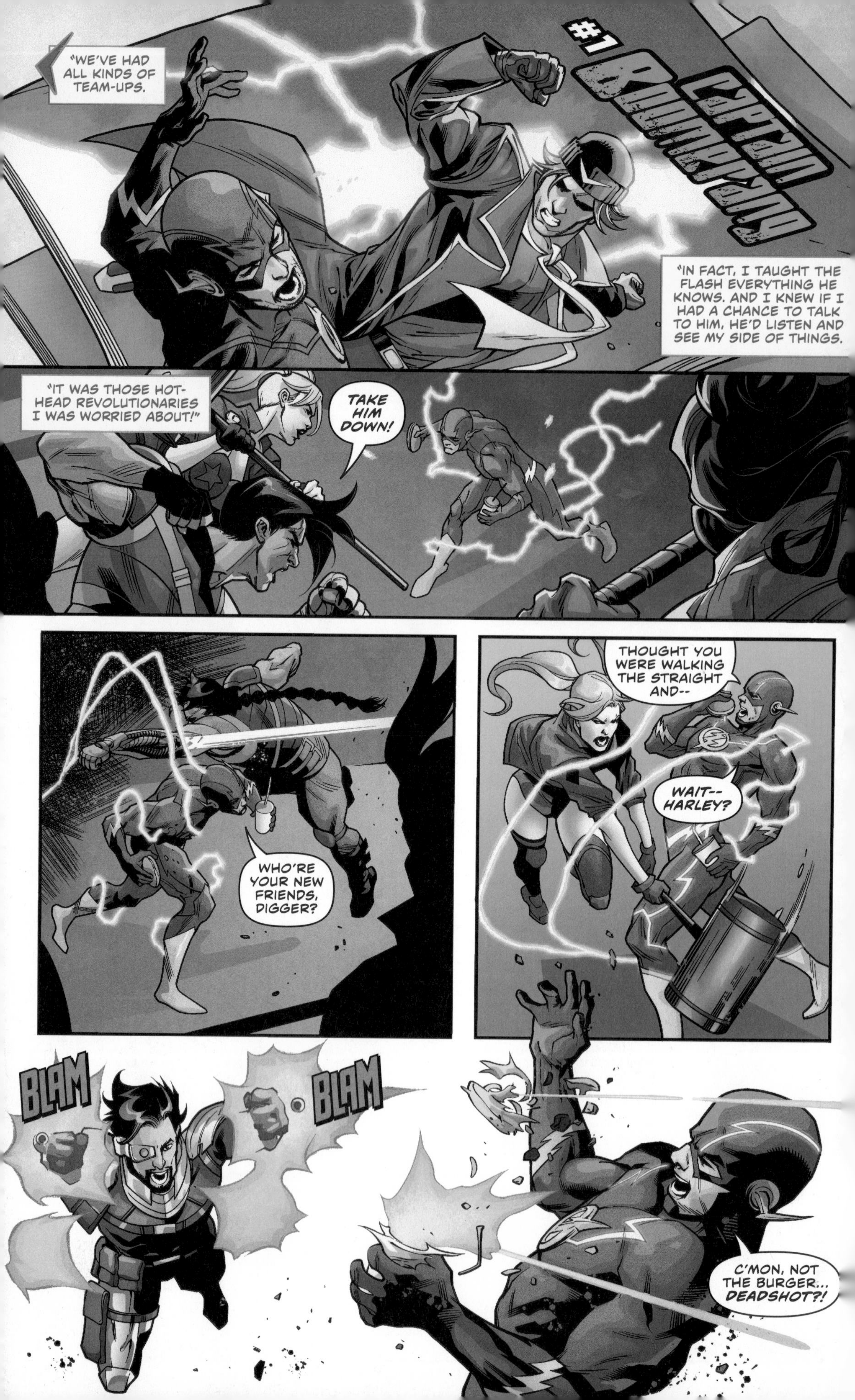
"WE'VE HAD ALL KINDS OF TEAM-UPS.
#1 CAPTAIN BOOMERANG
"IN FACT, I TAUGHT THE FLASH EVERYTHING HE KNOWS. AND I KNEW IF I HAD A CHANCE TO TALK TO HIM, HE'D LISTEN AND SEE MY SIDE OF THINGS.
"IT WAS THOSE HOT-HEAD REVOLUTIONARIES I WAS WORRIED ABOUT!"
TAKE HIM DOWN!
WHO'RE YOUR NEW FRIENDS, DIGGER?
THOUGHT YOU WERE WALKING THE STRAIGHT AND--
WAIT-- HARLEY?
BLAM
BLAM
C'MON, NOT THE BURGER... DEADSHOT?!

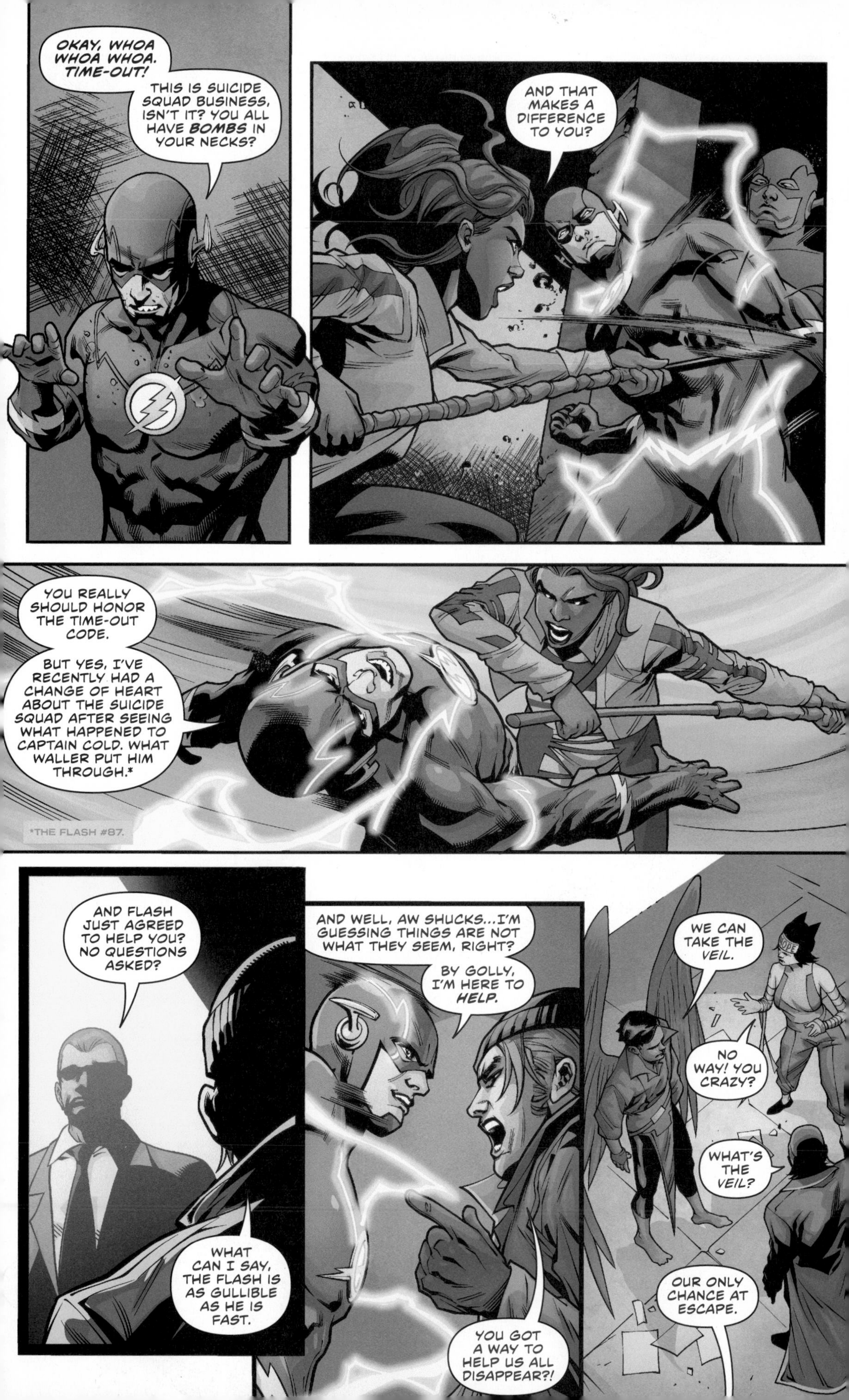
OKAY, WHOA WHOA WHOA. TIME-OUT!
THIS IS SUICIDE SQUAD BUSINESS, ISN'T IT? YOU ALL HAVE BOMBS IN YOUR NECKS?
AND THAT MAKES A DIFFERENCE TO YOU?
YOU REALLY SHOULD HONOR THE TIME-OUT CODE.
BUT YES, I'VE RECENTLY HAD A CHANGE OF HEART ABOUT THE SUICIDE SQUAD AFTER SEEING WHAT HAPPENED TO CAPTAIN COLD. WHAT WALLER PUT HIM THROUGH.*
*THE FLASH #87.
AND FLASH JUST AGREED TO HELP YOU? NO QUESTIONS ASKED?
WHAT CAN I SAY, THE FLASH IS AS GULLIBLE AS HE IS FAST.
AND WELL, AW SHUCKS...I'M GUESSING THINGS ARE NOT WHAT THEY SEEM, RIGHT?
BY GOLLY, I'M HERE TO HELP.
YOU GOT A WAY TO HELP US ALL DISAPPEAR?!
WE CAN TAKE THE VEIL.
NO WAY! YOU CRAZY?
WHAT'S THE VEIL?
OUR ONLY CHANCE AT ESCAPE.

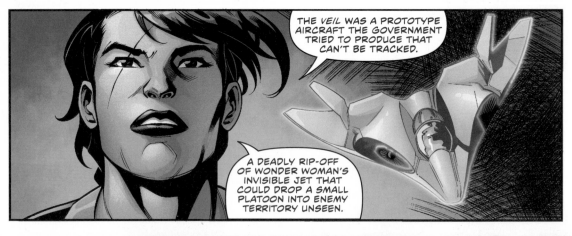

THE *VEIL* WAS A PROTOTYPE AIRCRAFT THE GOVERNMENT TRIED TO PRODUCE THAT CAN'T BE TRACKED.

A DEADLY RIP-OFF OF WONDER WOMAN'S INVISIBLE JET THAT COULD DROP A SMALL PLATOON INTO ENEMY TERRITORY UNSEEN.

"WE STOLE IT AND PARKED IT IN A SAFE SPOT SO NO ONE WOULD FIND IT.

"IN THE MIDDLE OF DEATH VALLEY.

ONCE WE'RE AIRBORNE, WE'LL BE ABLE TO GET AWAY.

BUT IF WE GO AFTER IT, WE EXPOSE OURSELVES.

SITTING DUCKS.

THEN I'LL COVER YOU.

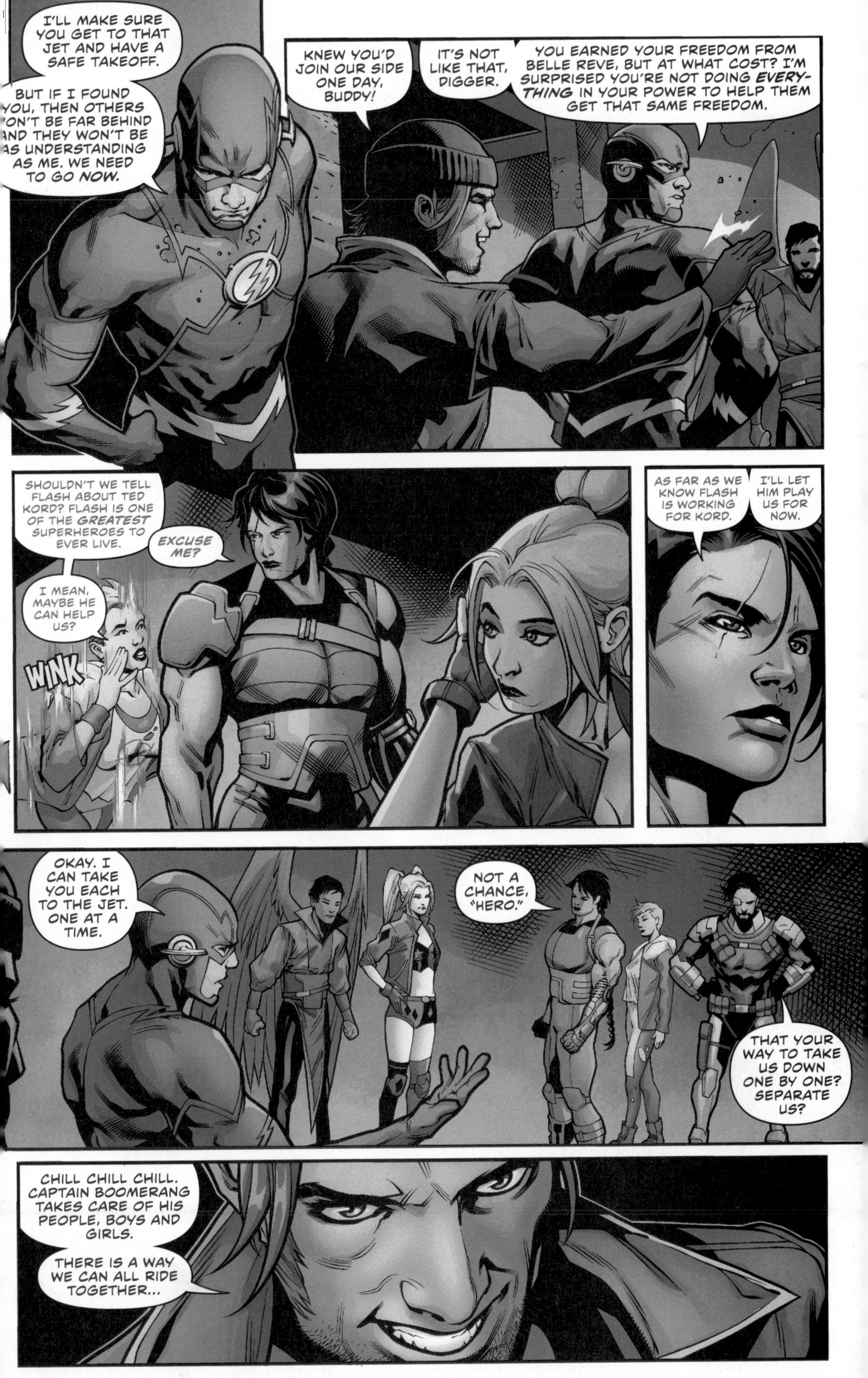

I'LL MAKE SURE YOU GET TO THAT JET AND HAVE A SAFE TAKEOFF.
BUT IF I FOUND YOU, THEN OTHERS WON'T BE FAR BEHIND AND THEY WON'T BE AS UNDERSTANDING AS ME. WE NEED TO GO *NOW*.
KNEW YOU'D JOIN OUR SIDE ONE DAY, BUDDY!
IT'S NOT LIKE THAT, DIGGER.
YOU EARNED YOUR FREEDOM FROM BELLE REVE, BUT AT WHAT COST? I'M SURPRISED YOU'RE NOT DOING *EVERYTHING* IN YOUR POWER TO HELP THEM GET THAT SAME FREEDOM.
SHOULDN'T WE TELL FLASH ABOUT TED KORD? FLASH IS ONE OF THE *GREATEST* SUPERHEROES TO EVER LIVE.
EXCUSE ME?
I MEAN, MAYBE HE CAN HELP US?
WINK
AS FAR AS WE KNOW FLASH IS WORKING FOR KORD.
I'LL LET HIM PLAY US FOR NOW.
OKAY. I CAN TAKE YOU EACH TO THE JET. ONE AT A TIME.
NOT A CHANCE, "HERO."
THAT YOUR WAY TO TAKE US DOWN ONE BY ONE? SEPARATE US?
CHILL CHILL CHILL. CAPTAIN BOOMERANG TAKES CARE OF HIS PEOPLE, BOYS AND GIRLS.
THERE IS A WAY WE CAN ALL RIDE TOGETHER...

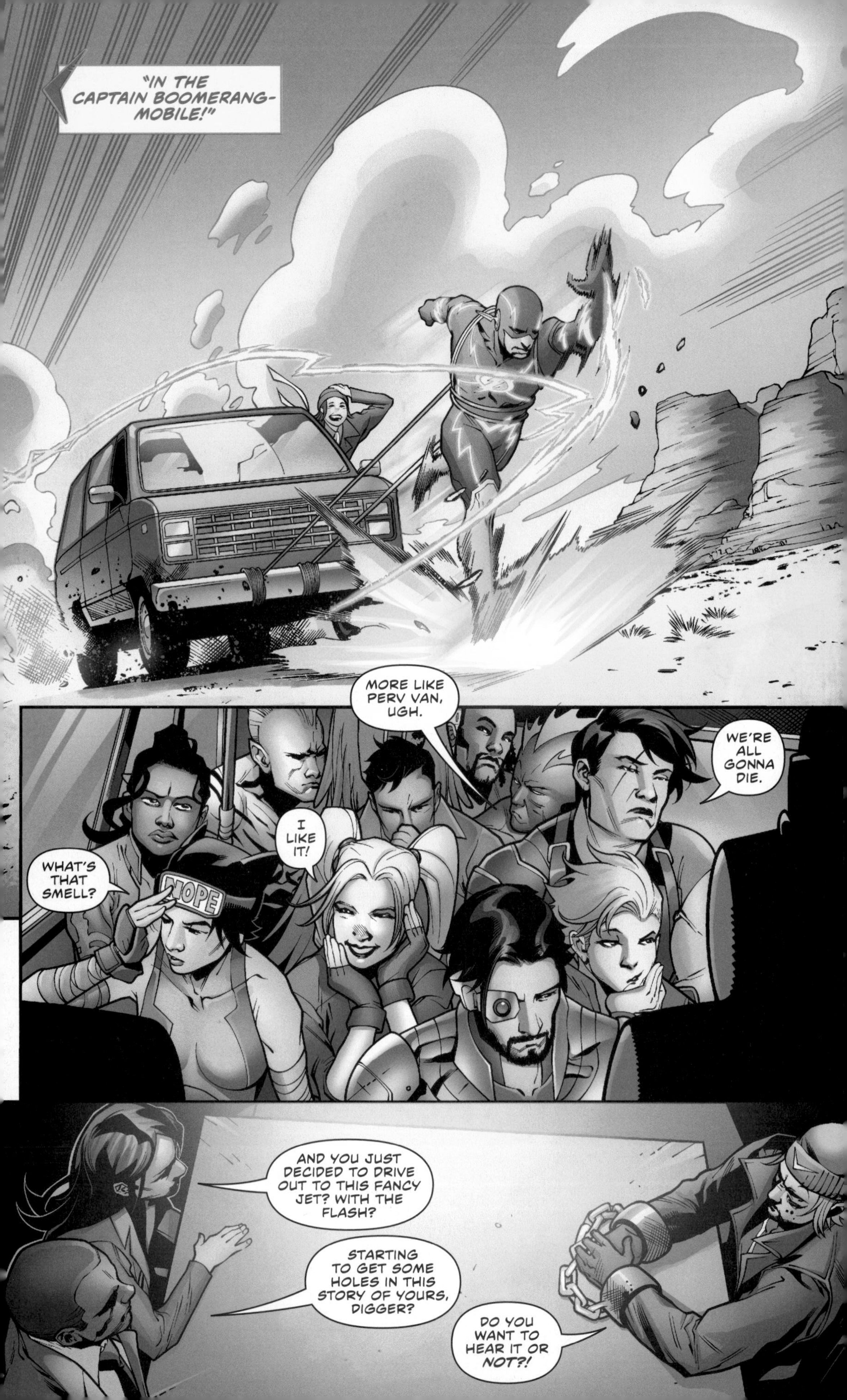
"IN THE CAPTAIN BOOMERANG-MOBILE!"
MORE LIKE PERV VAN, UGH.
WE'RE ALL GONNA DIE.
I LIKE IT!
WHAT'S THAT SMELL?
NOPE
AND YOU JUST DECIDED TO DRIVE OUT TO THIS FANCY JET? WITH THE FLASH?
STARTING TO GET SOME HOLES IN THIS STORY OF YOURS, DIGGER?
DO YOU WANT TO HEAR IT OR NOT?!

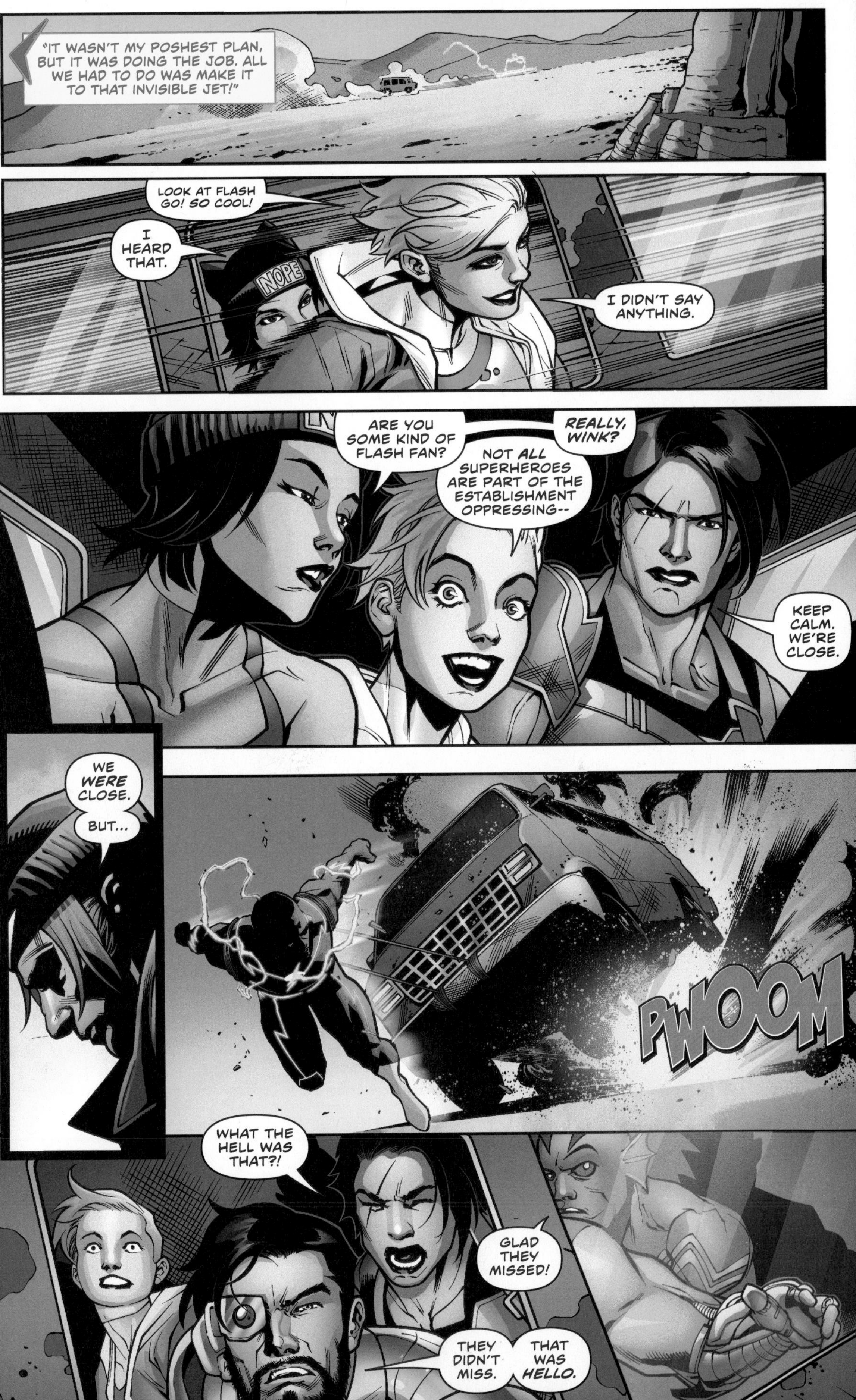

"IT WASN'T MY POSHEST PLAN, BUT IT WAS DOING THE JOB. ALL WE HAD TO DO WAS MAKE IT TO THAT INVISIBLE JET!"
LOOK AT FLASH GO! SO COOL!
I HEARD THAT.
NOPE
I DIDN'T SAY ANYTHING.
ARE YOU SOME KIND OF FLASH FAN?
REALLY, WINK?
NOT ALL SUPERHEROES ARE PART OF THE ESTABLISHMENT OPPRESSING--
KEEP CALM. WE'RE CLOSE.
WE WERE CLOSE.
BUT...
PWOOM
WHAT THE HELL WAS THAT?!
GLAD THEY MISSED!
THEY DIDN'T MISS.
THAT WAS HELLO.

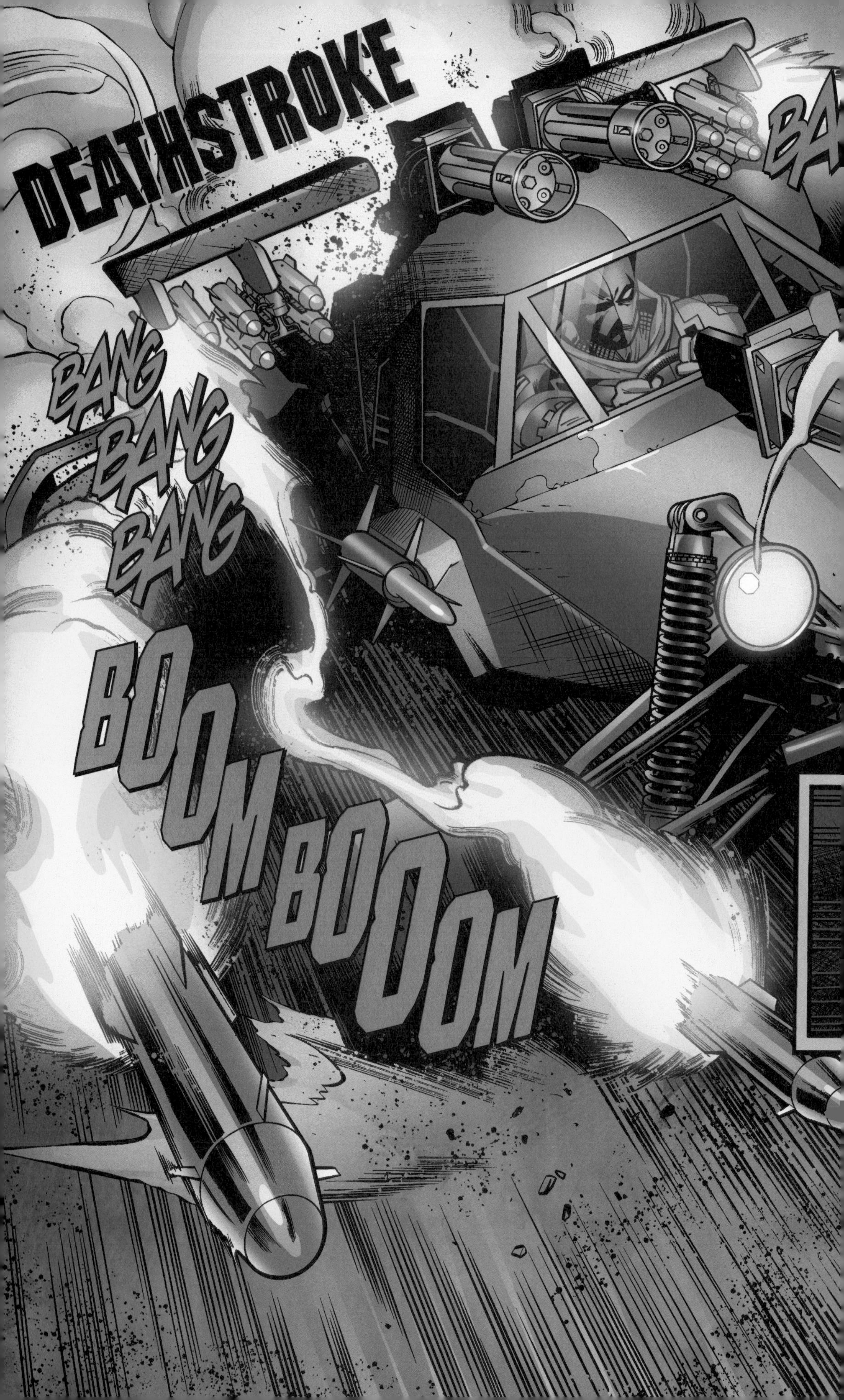
DEATHSTROKE
BANG
BANG
BANG
BOOM
BOOOM

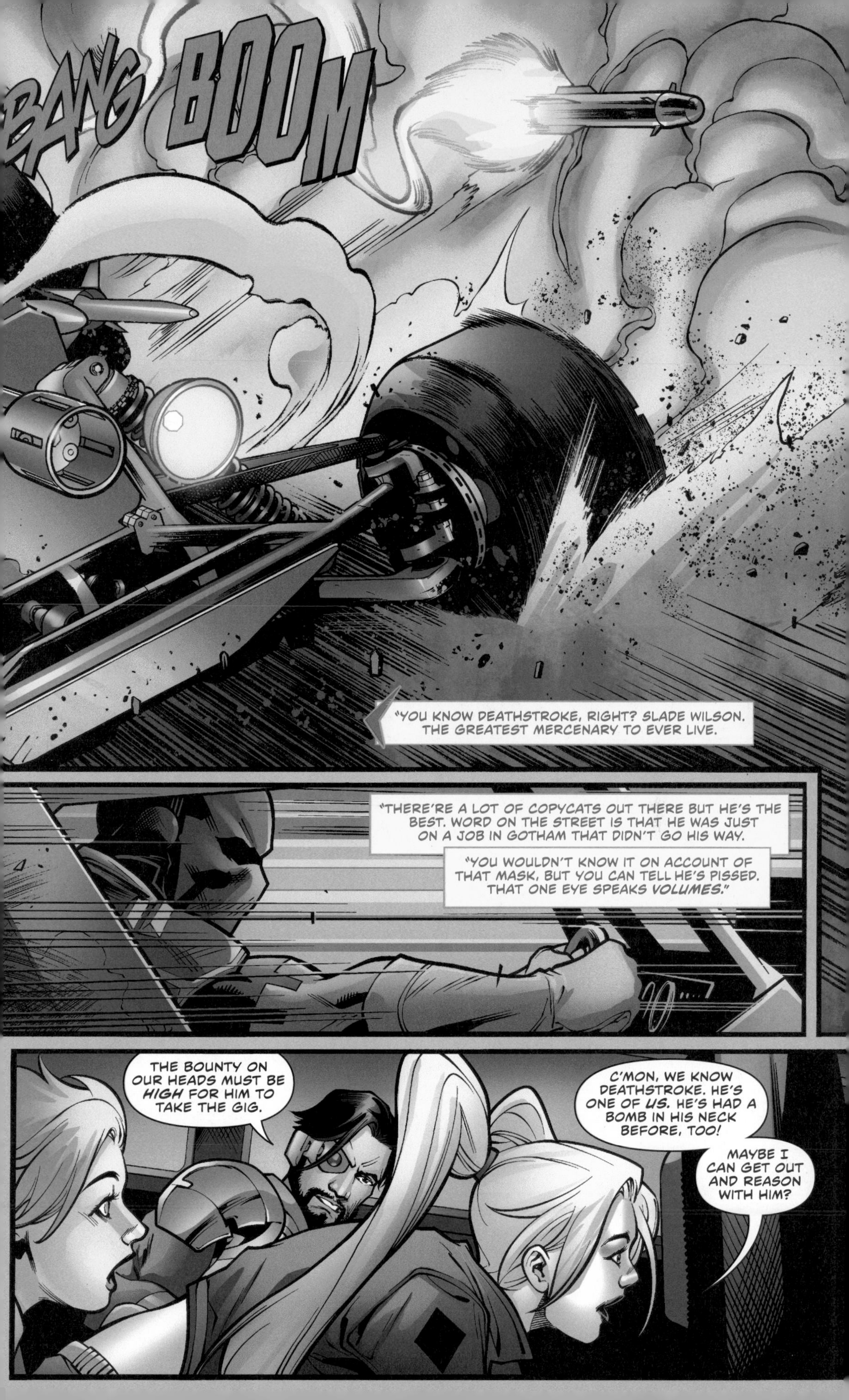
BANG
BOOM
"YOU KNOW DEATHSTROKE, RIGHT? SLADE WILSON. THE GREATEST MERCENARY TO EVER LIVE.
"THERE'RE A LOT OF COPYCATS OUT THERE BUT HE'S THE BEST. WORD ON THE STREET IS THAT HE WAS JUST ON A JOB IN GOTHAM THAT DIDN'T GO HIS WAY.
"YOU WOULDN'T KNOW IT ON ACCOUNT OF THAT MASK, BUT YOU CAN TELL HE'S PISSED. THAT ONE EYE SPEAKS *VOLUMES*."
THE BOUNTY ON OUR HEADS MUST BE *HIGH* FOR HIM TO TAKE THE GIG.
C'MON, WE KNOW DEATHSTROKE. HE'S ONE OF *US*. HE'S HAD A BOMB IN HIS NECK BEFORE, TOO!
MAYBE I CAN GET OUT AND REASON WITH HIM?

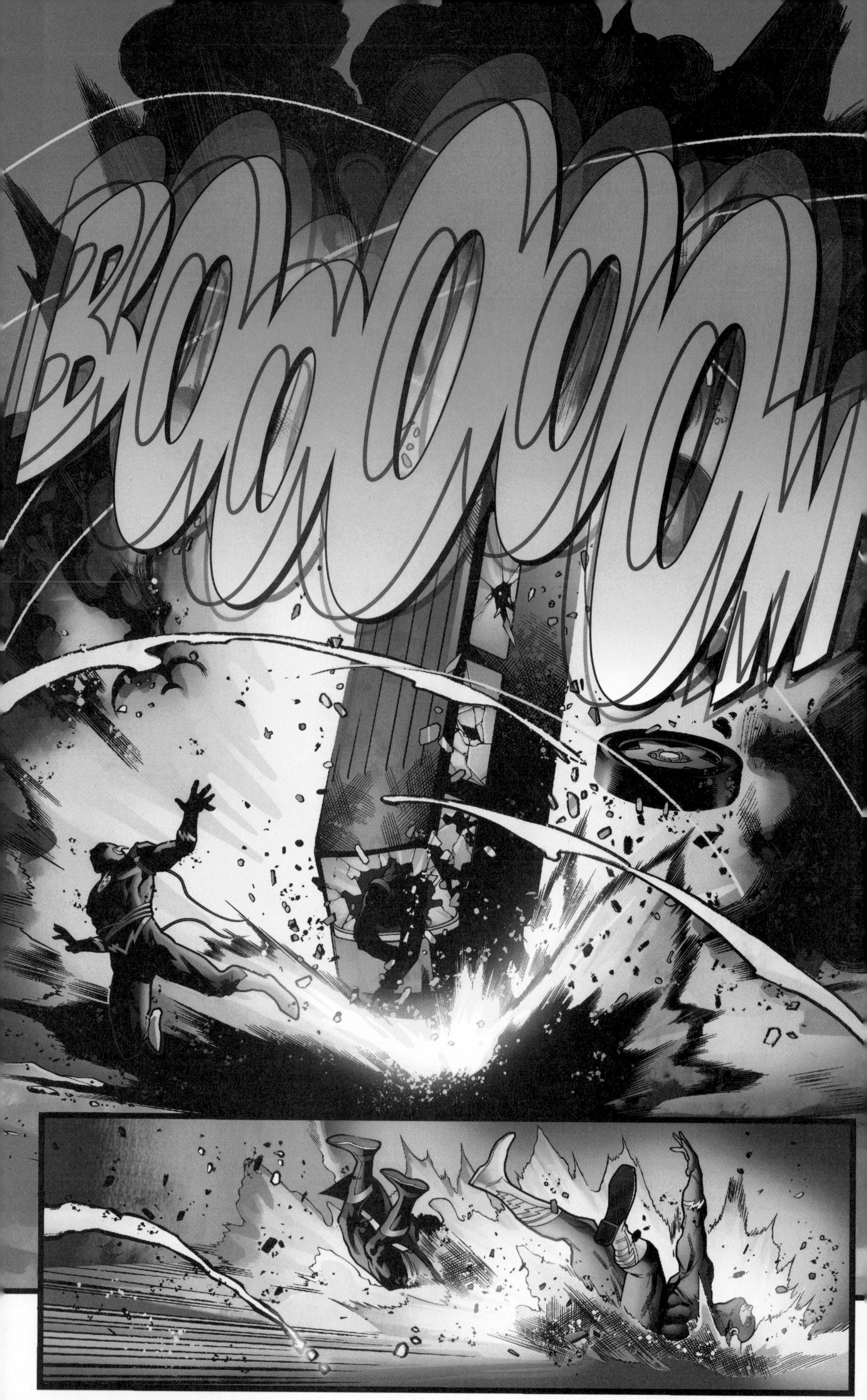
BOOOOOM

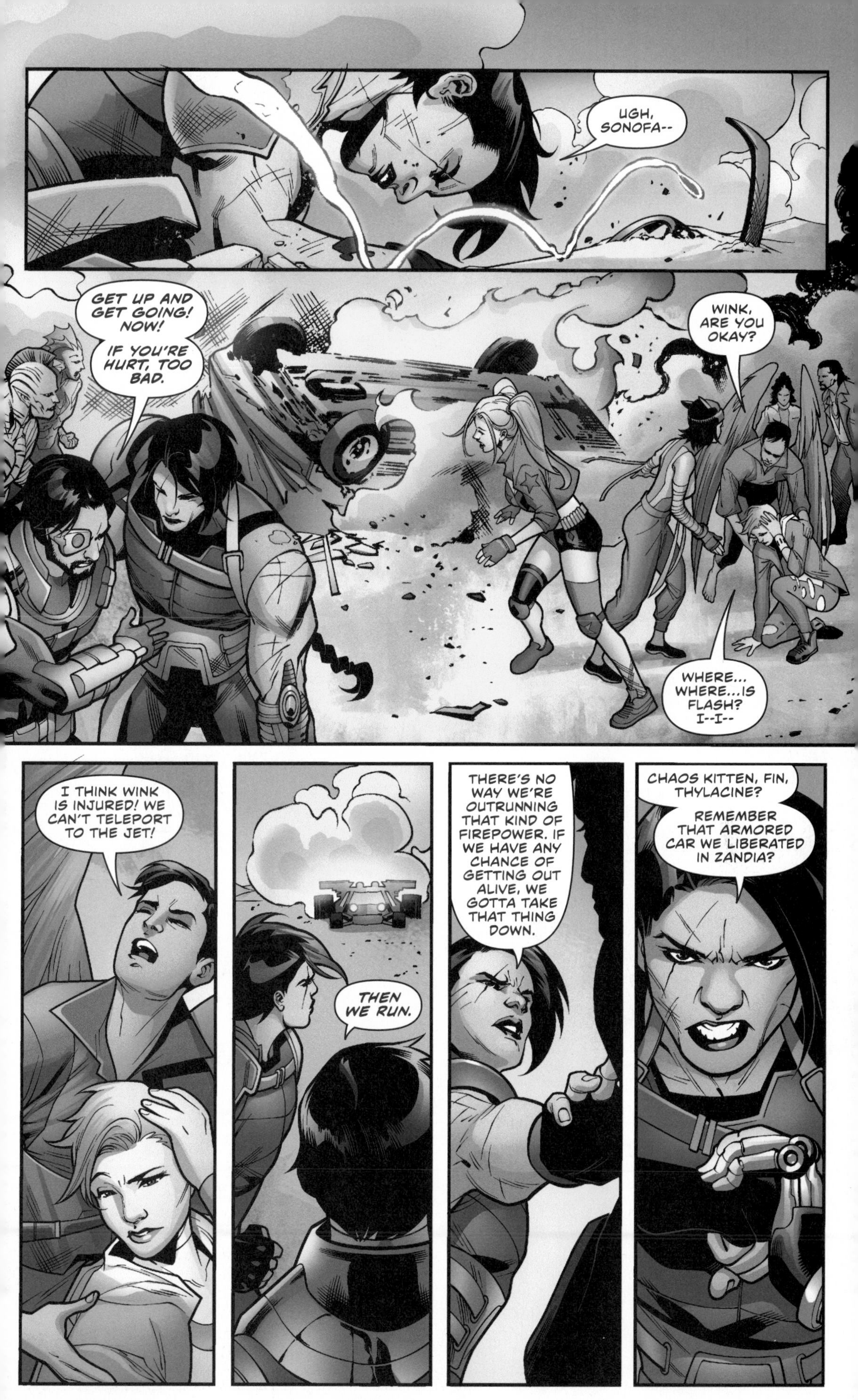
UGH, SONOFA--
GET UP AND GET GOING! NOW!
IF YOU'RE HURT, TOO BAD.
WINK, ARE YOU OKAY?
WHERE... WHERE...IS FLASH? I--I--
I THINK WINK IS INJURED! WE CAN'T TELEPORT TO THE JET!
THEN WE RUN.
THERE'S NO WAY WE'RE OUTRUNNING THAT KIND OF FIREPOWER. IF WE HAVE ANY CHANCE OF GETTING OUT ALIVE, WE GOTTA TAKE THAT THING DOWN.
CHAOS KITTEN, FIN, THYLACINE?
REMEMBER THAT ARMORED CAR WE LIBERATED IN ZANDIA?

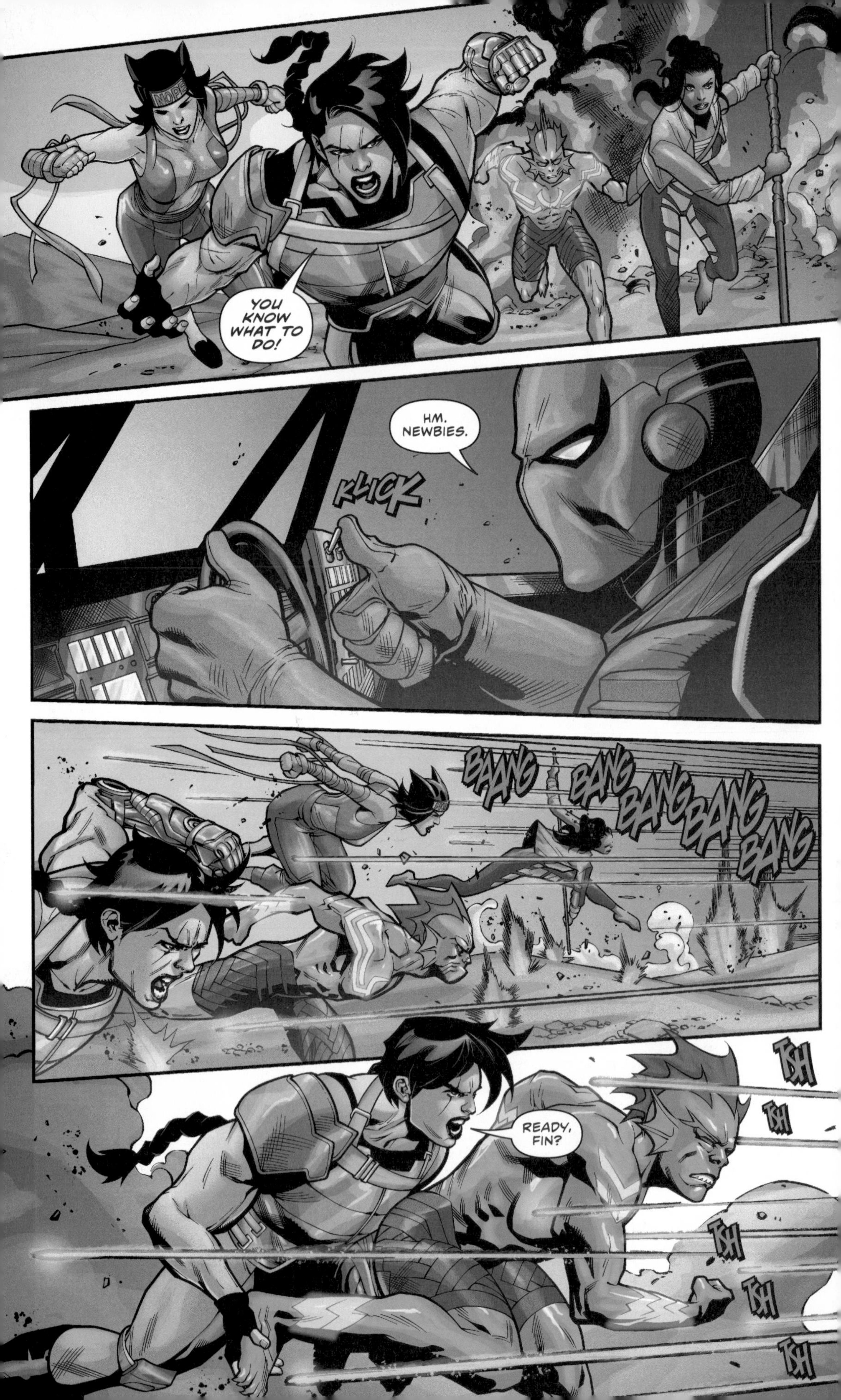
NOPE
YOU KNOW WHAT TO DO!
HM. NEWBIES.
KLICK
BAANG BANG BANG BANG BANG
READY, FIN?
TSH TSH TSH TSH TSH

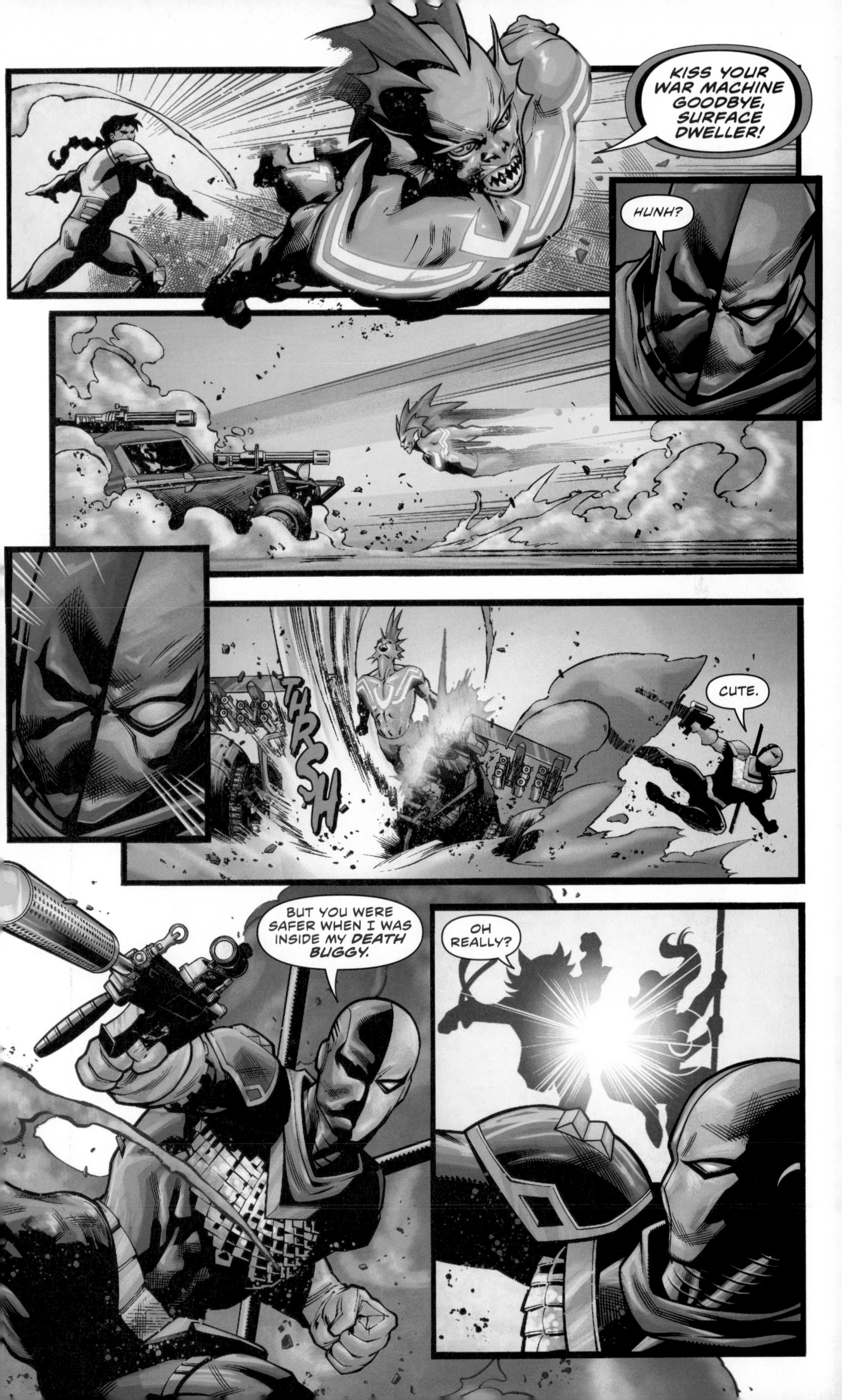
KISS YOUR WAR MACHINE GOODBYE, SURFACE DWELLER!
HUNH?
THRSH
CUTE.
BUT YOU WERE SAFER WHEN I WAS INSIDE MY DEATH BUGGY.
OH REALLY?

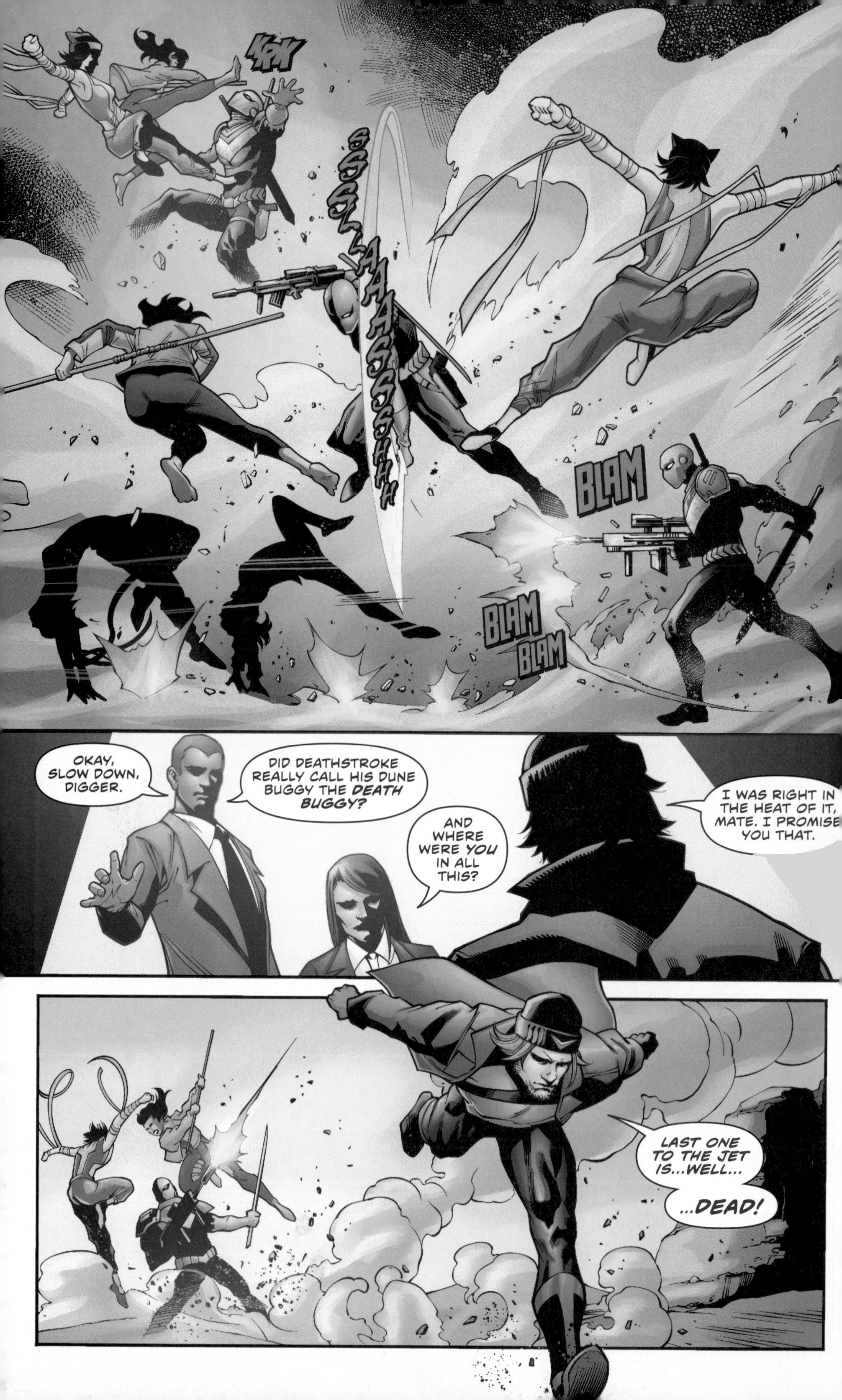
KRK
SSSLLAAAASSSSHHH
BLAM
BLAM
BLAM
OKAY, SLOW DOWN, DIGGER.
DID DEATHSTROKE REALLY CALL HIS DUNE BUGGY THE DEATH BUGGY?
AND WHERE WERE YOU IN ALL THIS?
I WAS RIGHT IN THE HEAT OF IT, MATE. I PROMISE YOU THAT.
LAST ONE TO THE JET IS...WELL...
...DEAD!

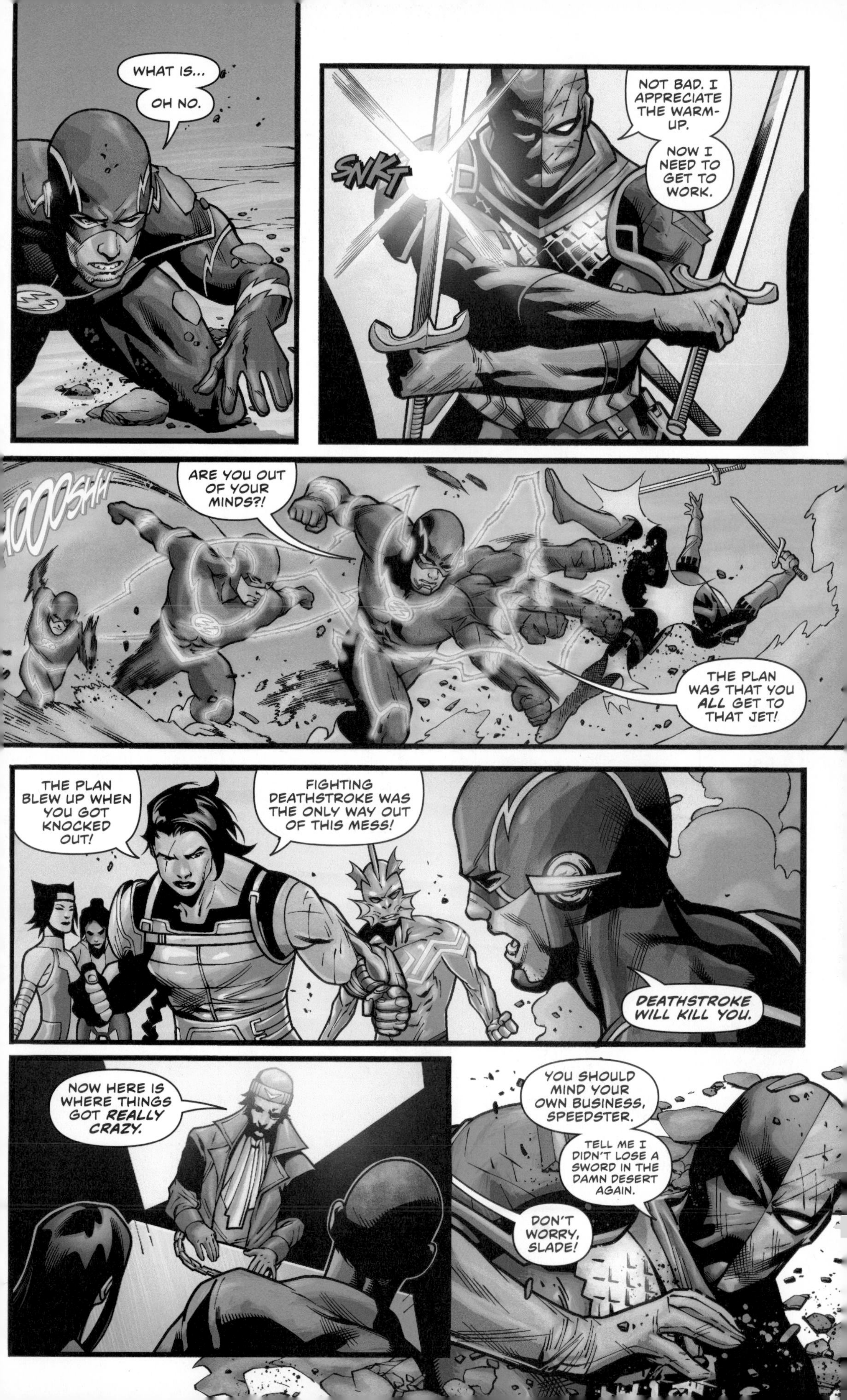
WHAT IS...
OH NO.
SNKT
NOT BAD. I APPRECIATE THE WARM-UP.
NOW I NEED TO GET TO WORK.
HOOOSHH
ARE YOU OUT OF YOUR MINDS?!
THE PLAN WAS THAT YOU ALL GET TO THAT JET!
THE PLAN BLEW UP WHEN YOU GOT KNOCKED OUT!
FIGHTING DEATHSTROKE WAS THE ONLY WAY OUT OF THIS MESS!
DEATHSTROKE WILL KILL YOU.
NOW HERE IS WHERE THINGS GOT REALLY CRAZY.
YOU SHOULD MIND YOUR OWN BUSINESS, SPEEDSTER.
TELL ME I DIDN'T LOSE A SWORD IN THE DAMN DESERT AGAIN.
DON'T WORRY, SLADE!

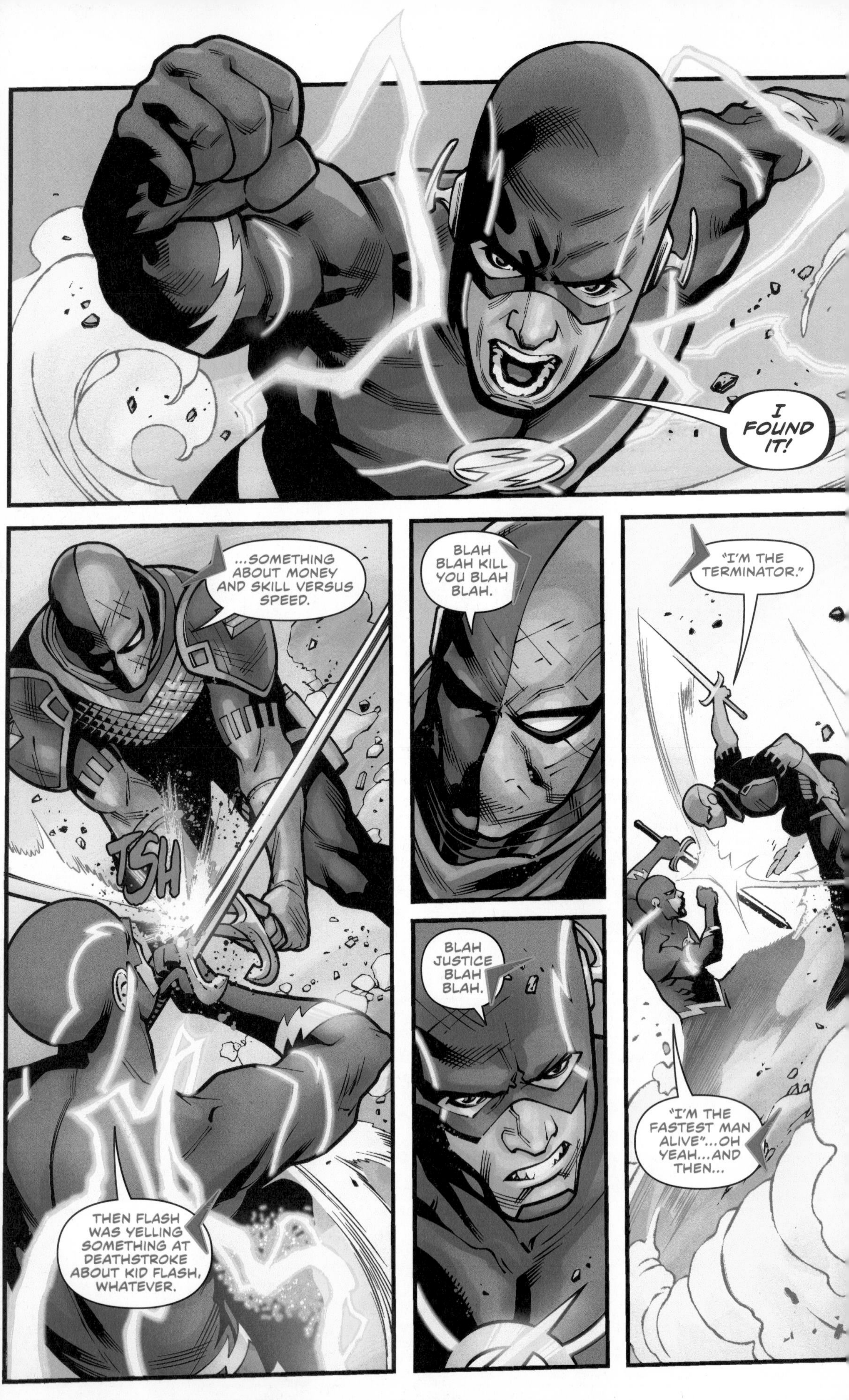
I FOUND IT!
...SOMETHING ABOUT MONEY AND SKILL VERSUS SPEED.
TSH
THEN FLASH WAS YELLING SOMETHING AT DEATHSTROKE ABOUT KID FLASH, WHATEVER.
BLAH BLAH KILL YOU BLAH BLAH.
BLAH JUSTICE BLAH BLAH.
"I'M THE TERMINATOR."
"I'M THE FASTEST MAN ALIVE"...OH YEAH...AND THEN...

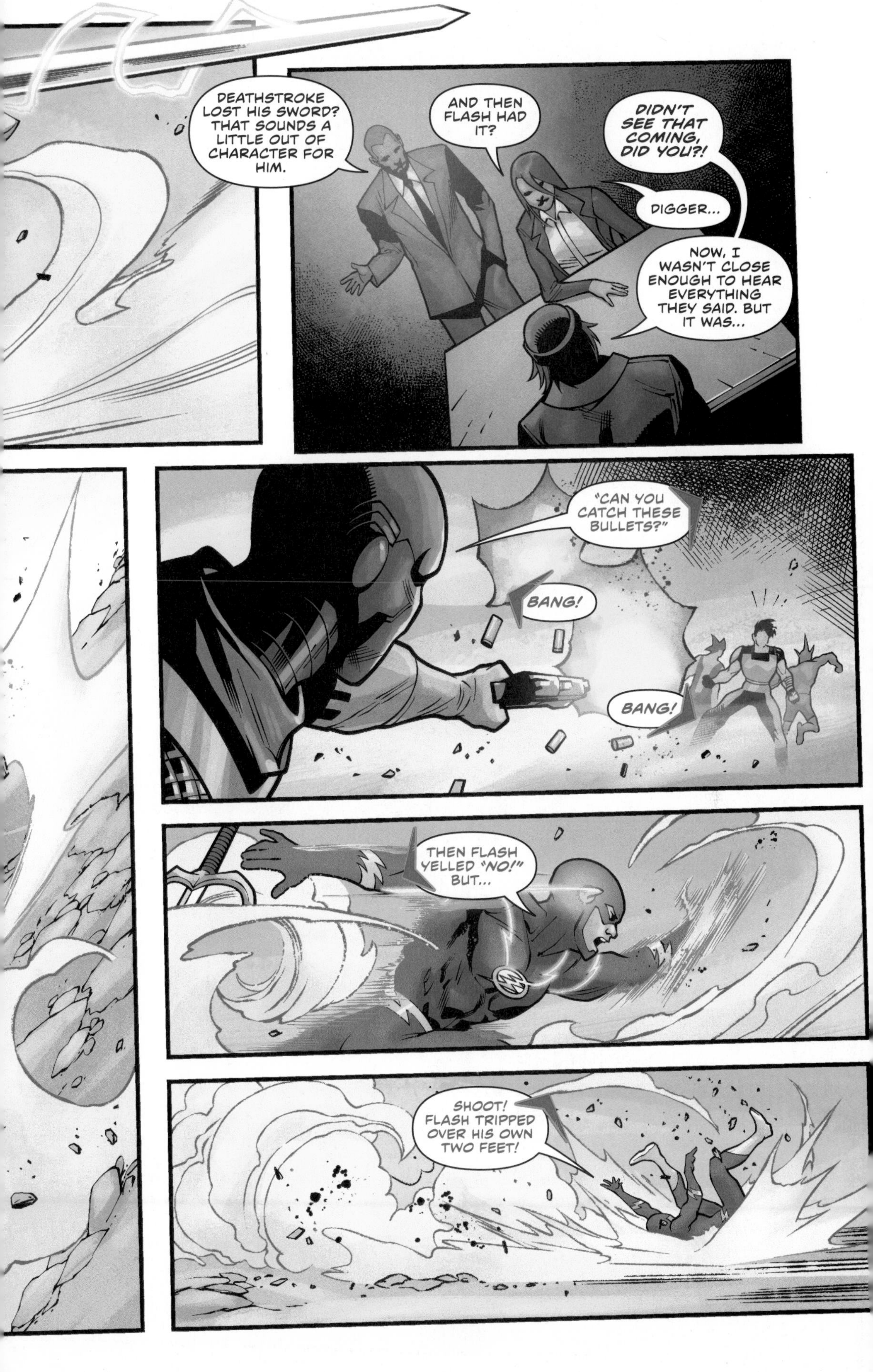
DEATHSTROKE LOST HIS SWORD? THAT SOUNDS A LITTLE OUT OF CHARACTER FOR HIM.
AND THEN FLASH HAD IT?
DIDN'T SEE THAT COMING, DID YOU?!
DIGGER...
NOW, I WASN'T CLOSE ENOUGH TO HEAR EVERYTHING THEY SAID. BUT IT WAS...
"CAN YOU CATCH THESE BULLETS?"
BANG!
BANG!
THEN FLASH YELLED "NO!" BUT...
SHOOT! FLASH TRIPPED OVER HIS OWN TWO FEET!

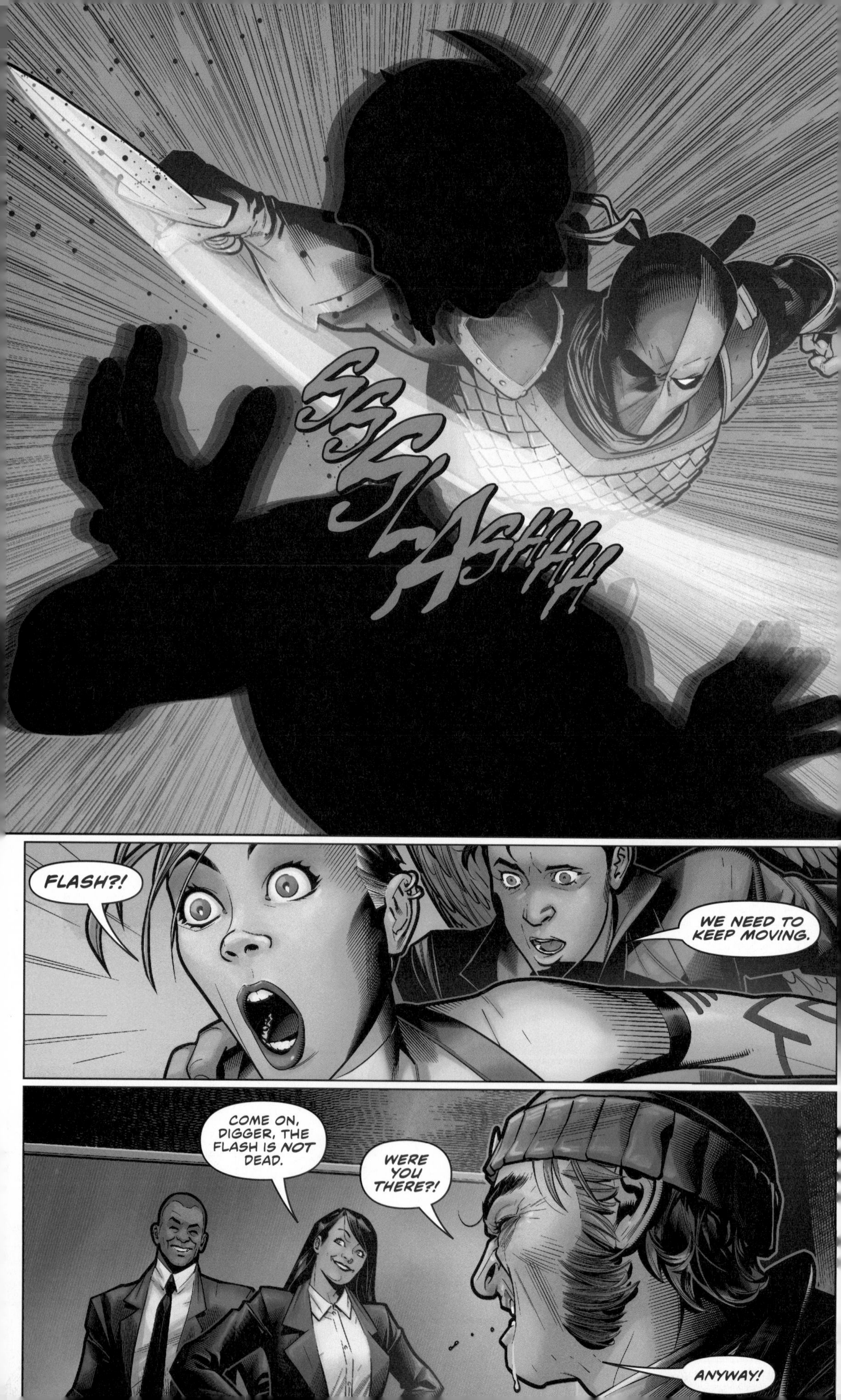
SSSLASHHH
FLASH?!
WE NEED TO KEEP MOVING.
COME ON, DIGGER, THE FLASH IS NOT DEAD.
WERE YOU THERE?!
ANYWAY!

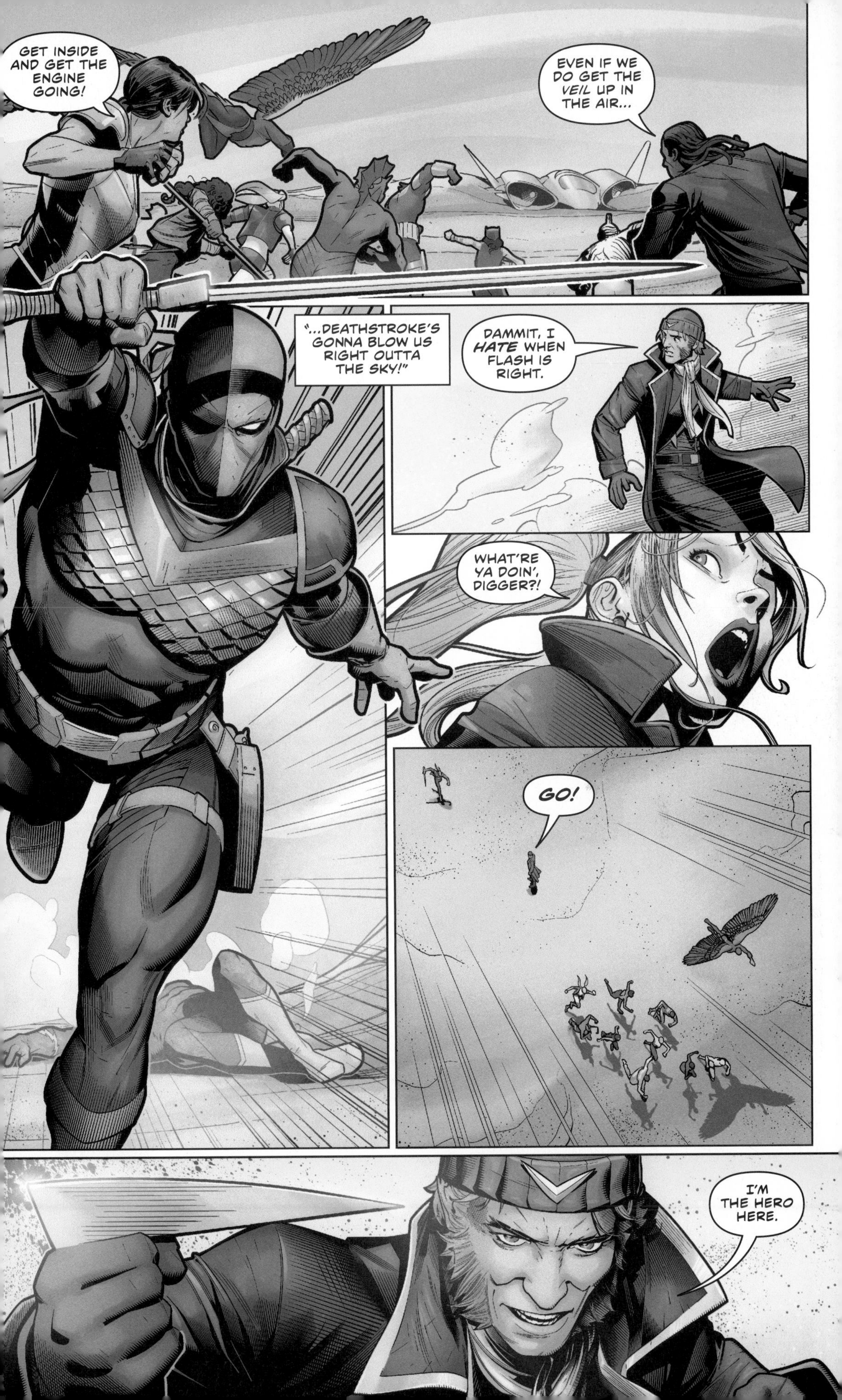
GET INSIDE AND GET THE ENGINE GOING!
EVEN IF WE DO GET THE *VEIL* UP IN THE AIR...
"...DEATHSTROKE'S GONNA BLOW US RIGHT OUTTA THE SKY!"
DAMMIT, I *HATE* WHEN FLASH IS RIGHT.
WHAT'RE YA DOIN', DIGGER?!
GO!
I'M THE HERO HERE.

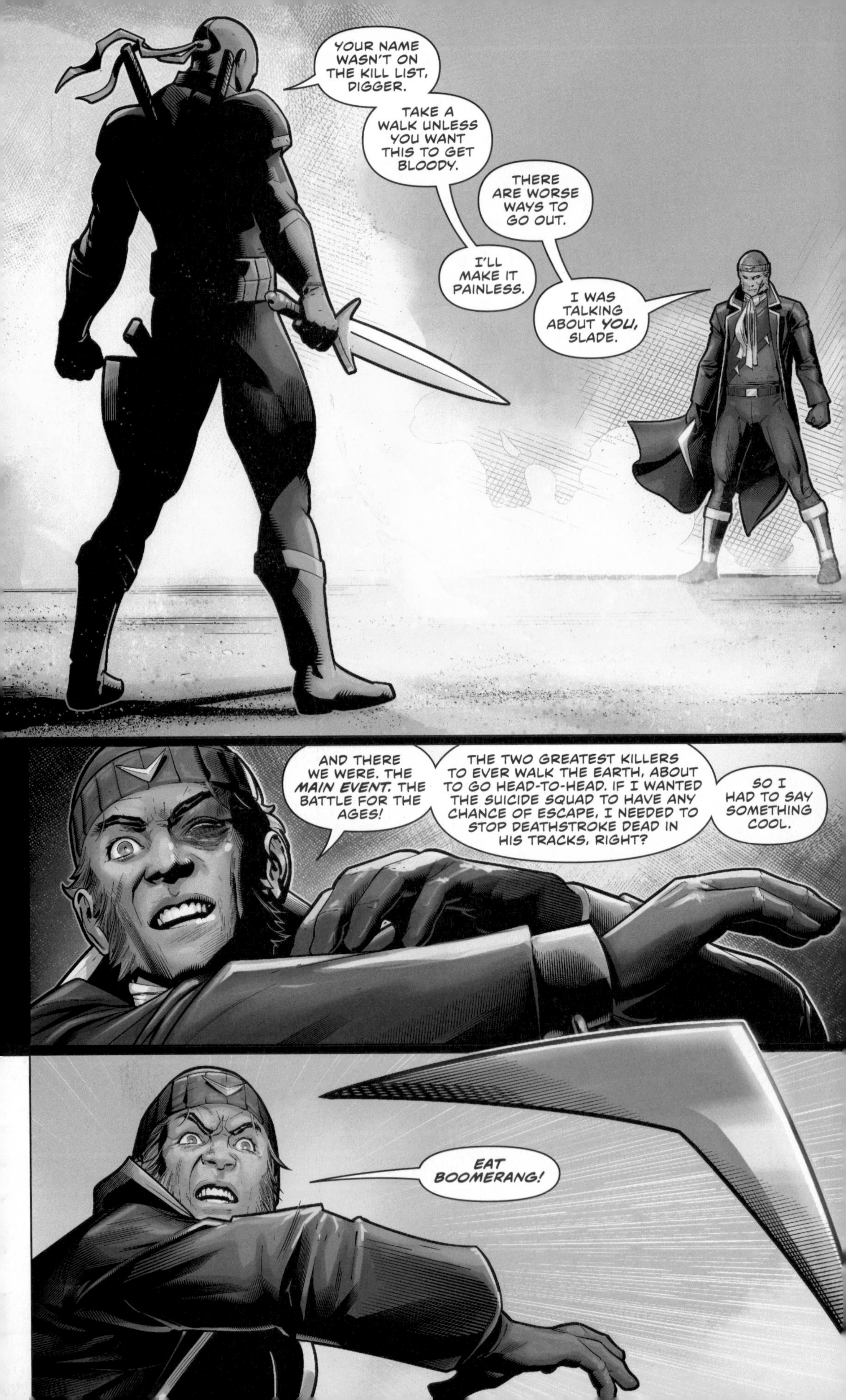
YOUR NAME WASN'T ON THE KILL LIST, DIGGER.
TAKE A WALK UNLESS YOU WANT THIS TO GET BLOODY.
I'LL MAKE IT PAINLESS.
THERE ARE WORSE WAYS TO GO OUT.
I WAS TALKING ABOUT *YOU,* SLADE.
AND THERE WE WERE. THE *MAIN EVENT.* THE BATTLE FOR THE AGES!
THE TWO GREATEST KILLERS TO EVER WALK THE EARTH, ABOUT TO GO HEAD-TO-HEAD. IF I WANTED THE SUICIDE SQUAD TO HAVE ANY CHANCE OF ESCAPE, I NEEDED TO STOP DEATHSTROKE DEAD IN HIS TRACKS, RIGHT?
SO I HAD TO SAY SOMETHING COOL.
EAT BOOMERANG!

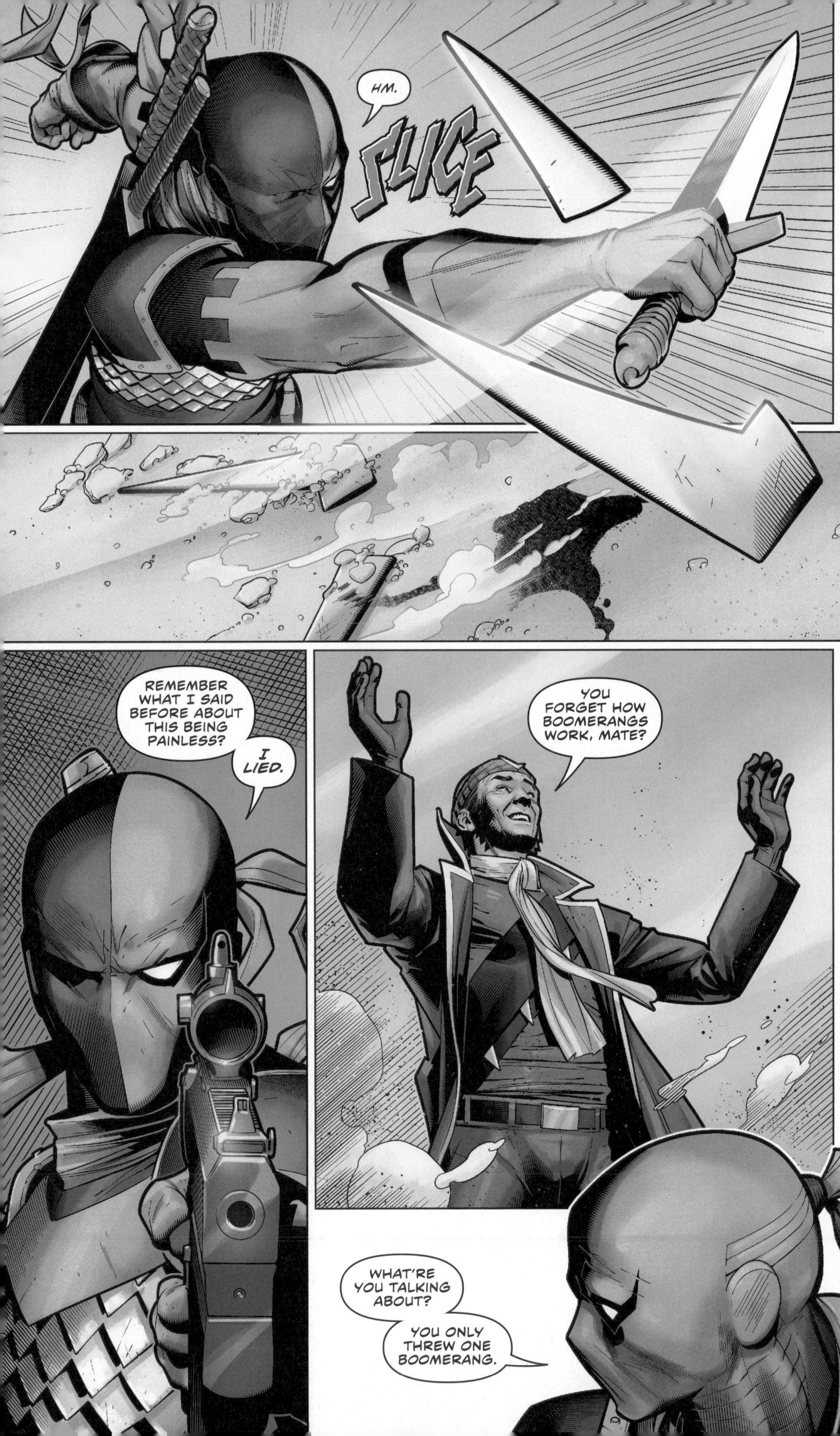
HM.
SLICE
REMEMBER WHAT I SAID BEFORE ABOUT THIS BEING PAINLESS?
I LIED.
YOU FORGET HOW BOOMERANGS WORK, MATE?
WHAT'RE YOU TALKING ABOUT?
YOU ONLY THREW ONE BOOMERANG.

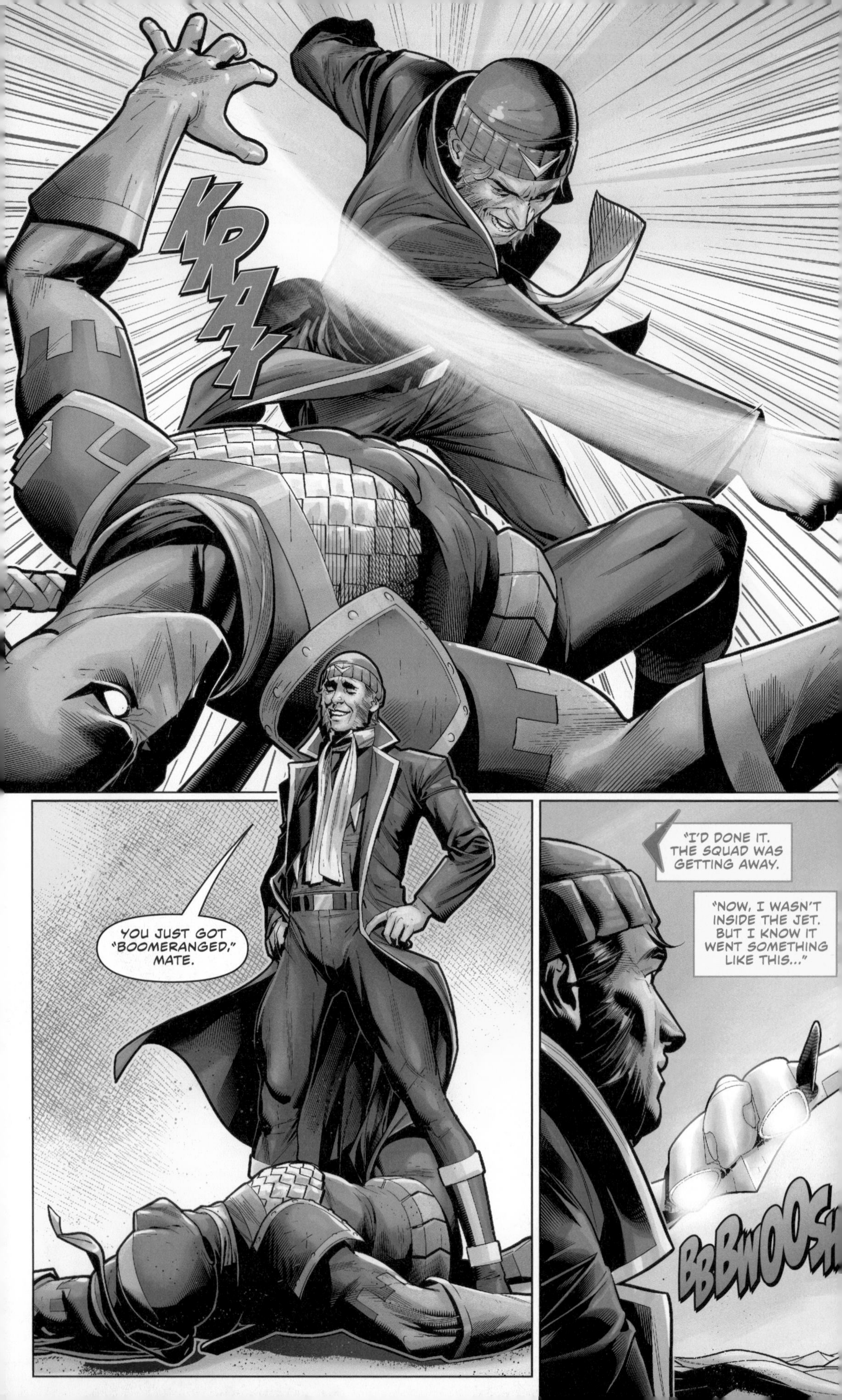
KRAAK
YOU JUST GOT "BOOMERANGED," MATE.
"I'D DONE IT. THE SQUAD WAS GETTING AWAY.
"NOW, I WASN'T INSIDE THE JET. BUT I KNOW IT WENT SOMETHING LIKE THIS..."
BBBWOOSH

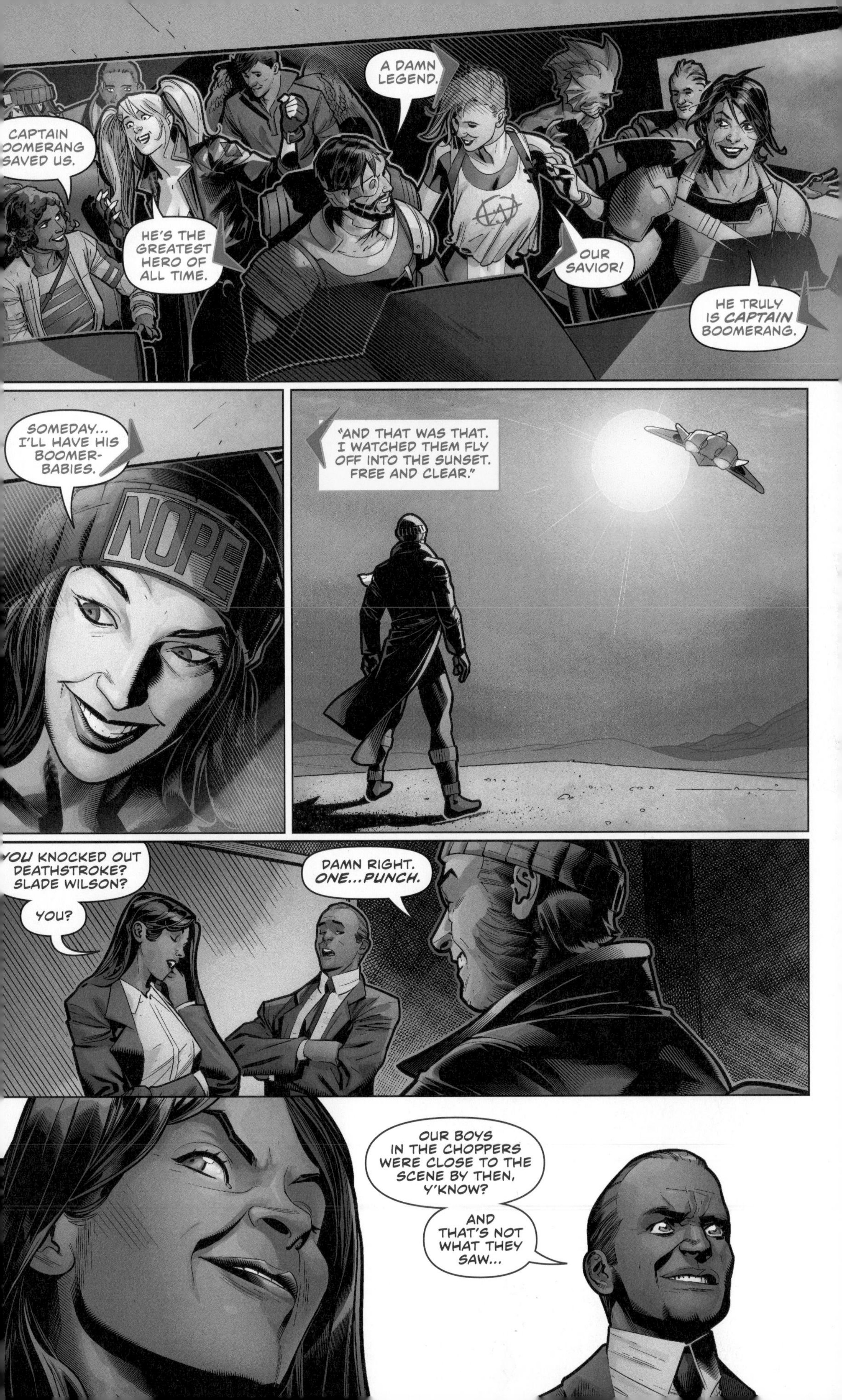
CAPTAIN BOOMERANG SAVED US.
A DAMN LEGEND.
HE'S THE GREATEST HERO OF ALL TIME.
OUR SAVIOR!
HE TRULY IS CAPTAIN BOOMERANG.
SOMEDAY... I'LL HAVE HIS BOOMER-BABIES.
NOPE
"AND THAT WAS THAT. I WATCHED THEM FLY OFF INTO THE SUNSET. FREE AND CLEAR."
YOU KNOCKED OUT DEATHSTROKE? SLADE WILSON?
YOU?
DAMN RIGHT. ONE...PUNCH.
OUR BOYS IN THE CHOPPERS WERE CLOSE TO THE SCENE BY THEN, Y'KNOW?
AND THAT'S NOT WHAT THEY SAW...

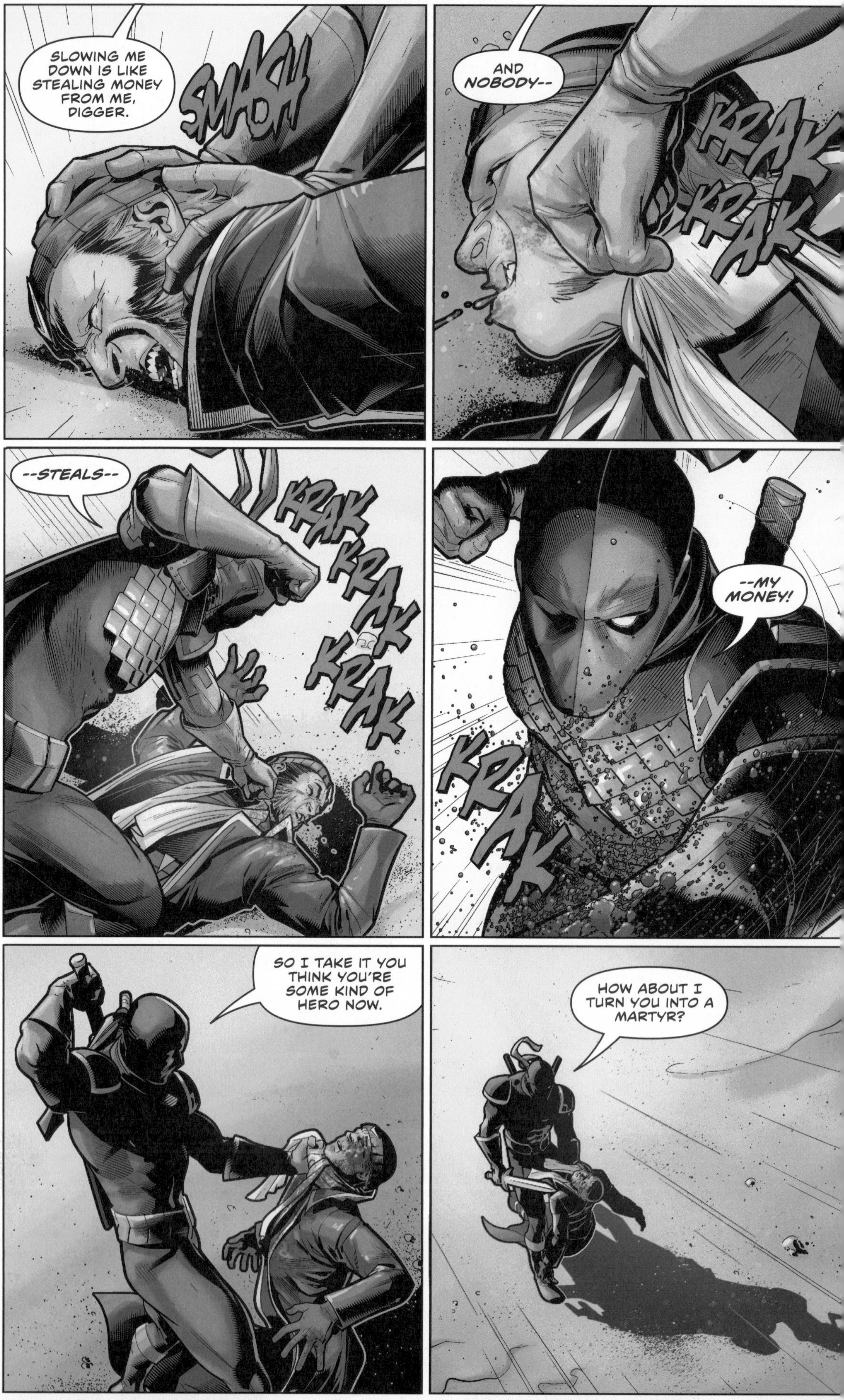
SLOWING ME DOWN IS LIKE STEALING MONEY FROM ME, DIGGER.
SMASH
AND NOBODY--
KRAK KRAK
--STEALS--
KRAK KRAK KRAK KRAK
--MY MONEY!
KRAK
SO I TAKE IT YOU THINK YOU'RE SOME KIND OF HERO NOW.
HOW ABOUT I TURN YOU INTO A MARTYR?

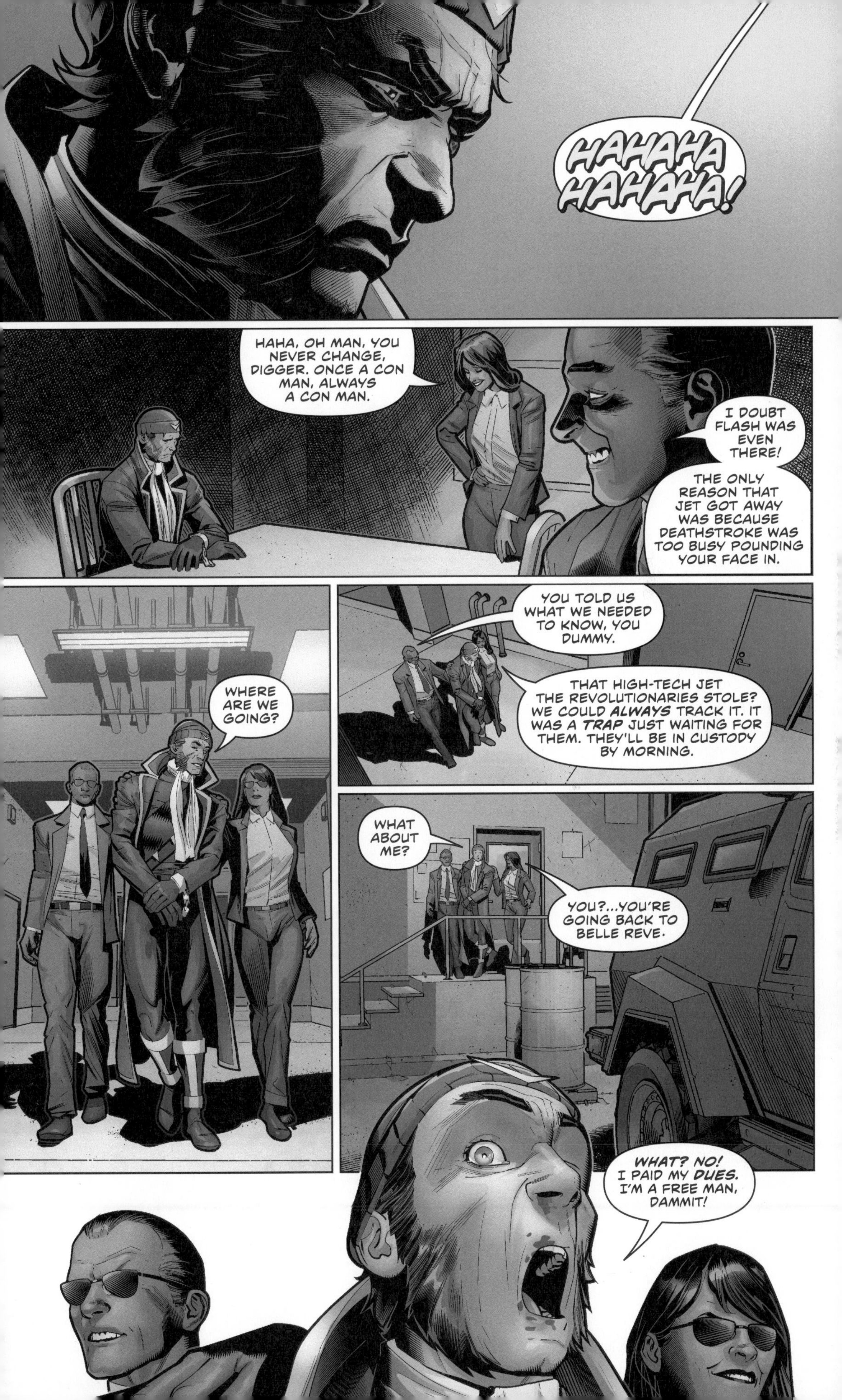
HAHAHA HAHAHA!
HAHA, OH MAN, YOU NEVER CHANGE, DIGGER. ONCE A CON MAN, ALWAYS A CON MAN.
I DOUBT FLASH WAS EVEN THERE!
THE ONLY REASON THAT JET GOT AWAY WAS BECAUSE DEATHSTROKE WAS TOO BUSY POUNDING YOUR FACE IN.
WHERE ARE WE GOING?
YOU TOLD US WHAT WE NEEDED TO KNOW, YOU DUMMY.
THAT HIGH-TECH JET THE REVOLUTIONARIES STOLE? WE COULD *ALWAYS* TRACK IT. IT WAS A *TRAP* JUST WAITING FOR THEM. THEY'LL BE IN CUSTODY BY MORNING.
WHAT ABOUT ME?
YOU?...YOU'RE GOING BACK TO BELLE REVE.
WHAT? NO! I PAID MY *DUES*. I'M A FREE MAN, DAMMIT!

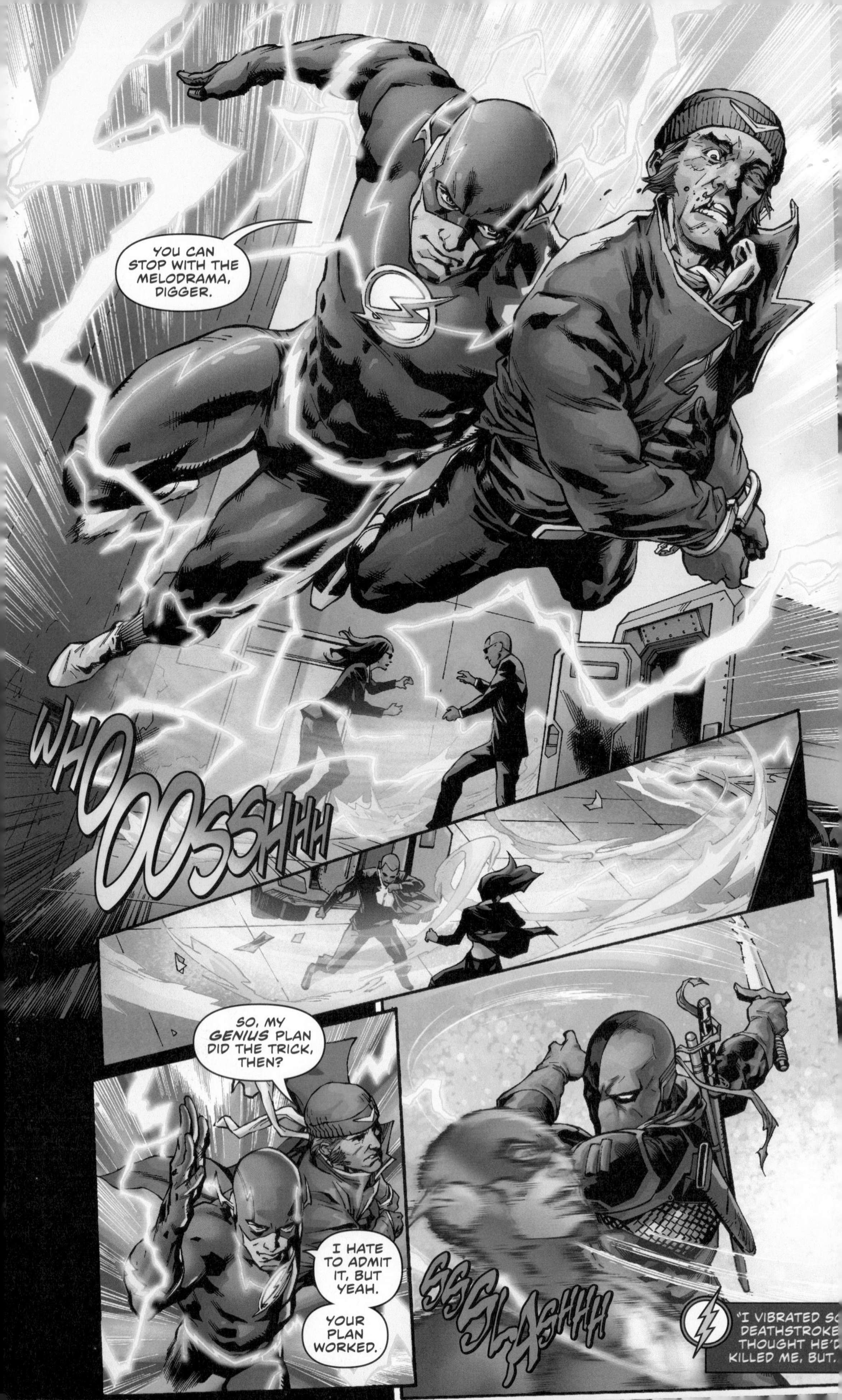
YOU CAN STOP WITH THE MELODRAMA, DIGGER.
WHOOOOSSHHH
SO, MY *GENIUS* PLAN DID THE TRICK, THEN?
I HATE TO ADMIT IT, BUT YEAH.
YOUR PLAN WORKED.
SSSLASHHH!
"I VIBRATED SO DEATHSTROKE THOUGHT HE'D KILLED ME. BUT...

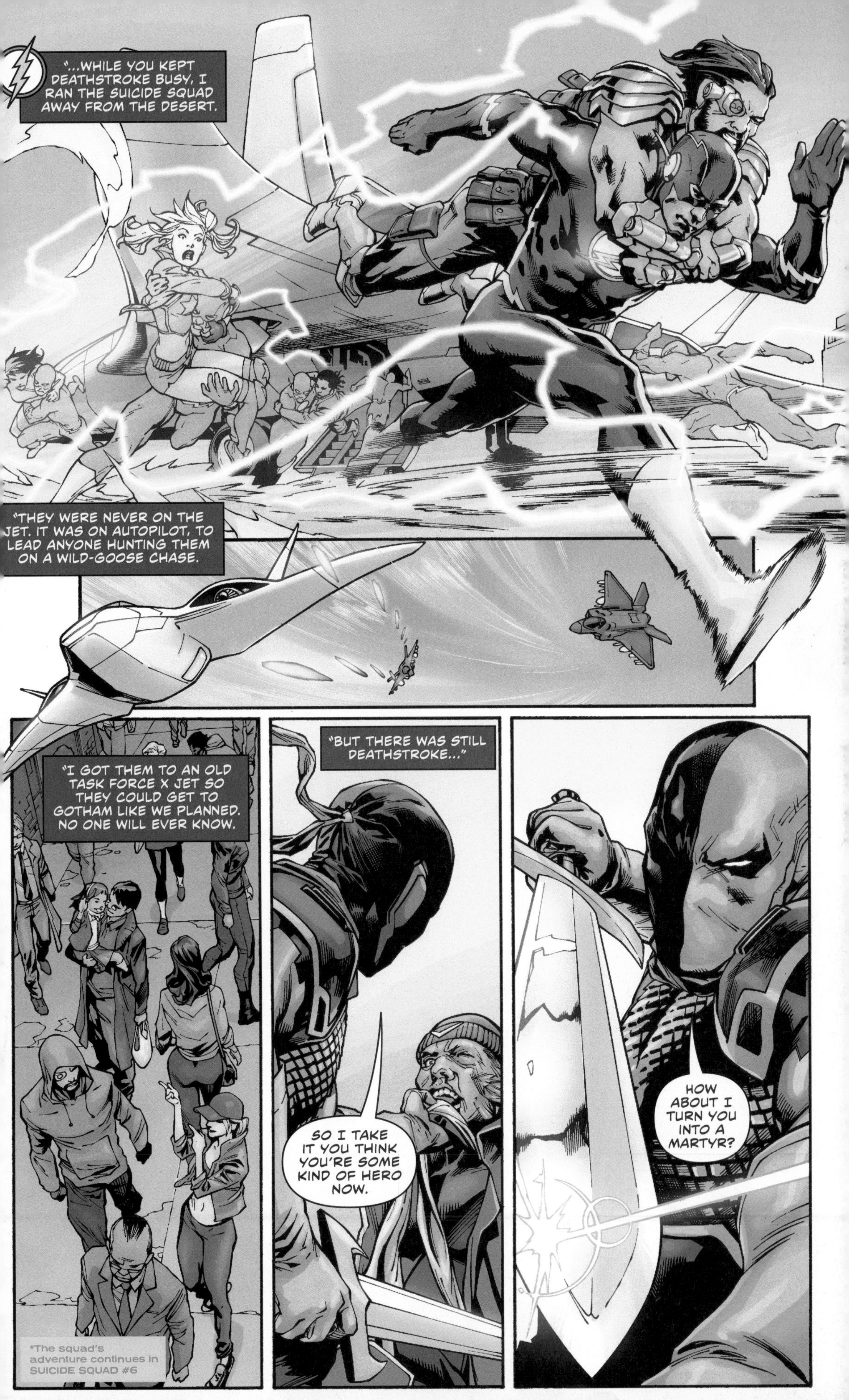
"...WHILE YOU KEPT DEATHSTROKE BUSY, I RAN THE SUICIDE SQUAD AWAY FROM THE DESERT.
"THEY WERE NEVER ON THE JET. IT WAS ON AUTOPILOT, TO LEAD ANYONE HUNTING THEM ON A WILD-GOOSE CHASE.
"I GOT THEM TO AN OLD TASK FORCE X JET SO THEY COULD GET TO GOTHAM LIKE WE PLANNED. NO ONE WILL EVER KNOW.
*The squad's adventure continues in SUICIDE SQUAD #6
"BUT THERE WAS STILL DEATHSTROKE..."
SO I TAKE IT YOU THINK YOU'RE SOME KIND OF HERO NOW.
HOW ABOUT I TURN YOU INTO A MARTYR?

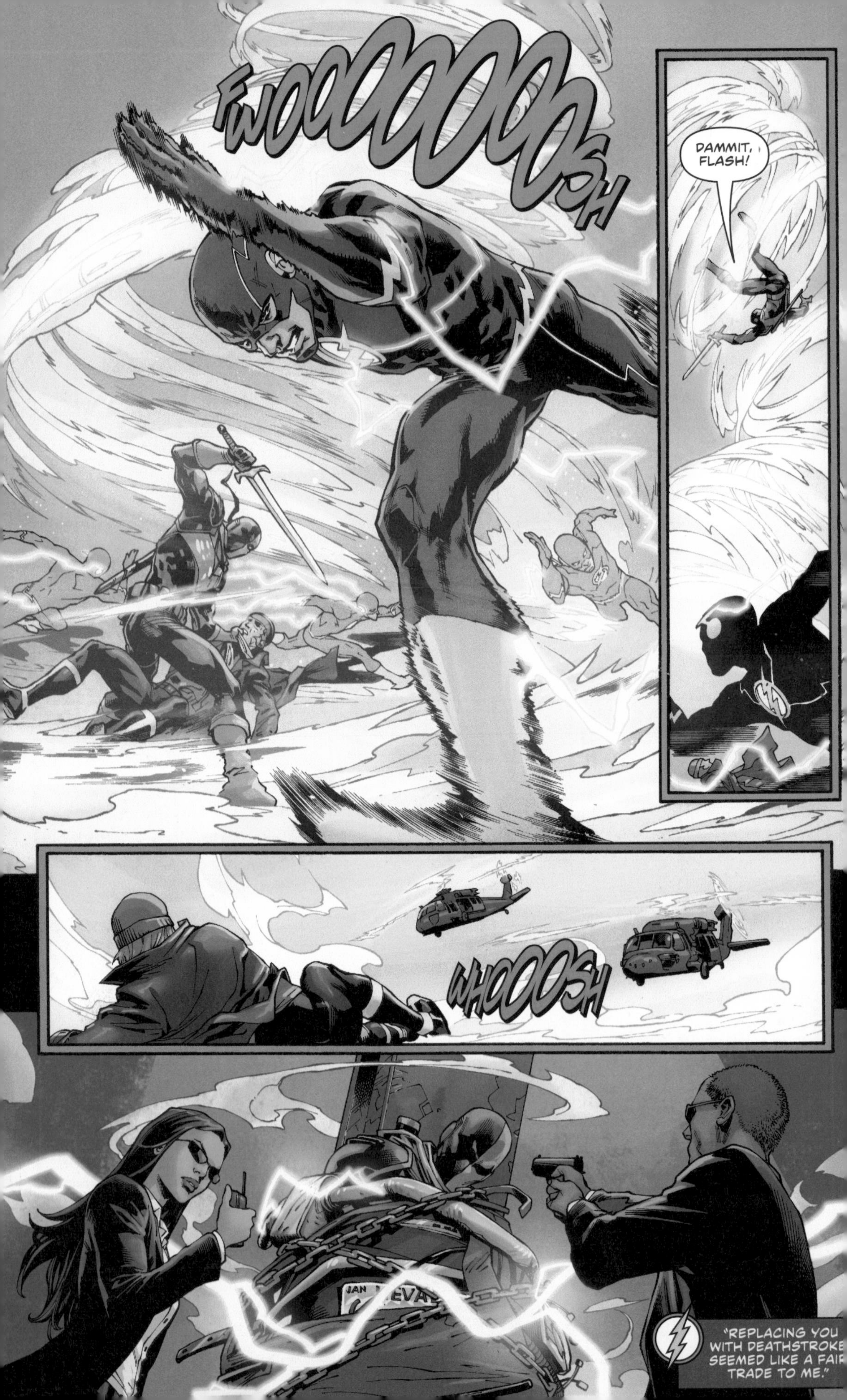
FWOOOOOOOSH
DAMMIT, FLASH!
WHOOOSH
"REPLACING YOU WITH DEATHSTROKE SEEMED LIKE A FAIR TRADE TO ME."

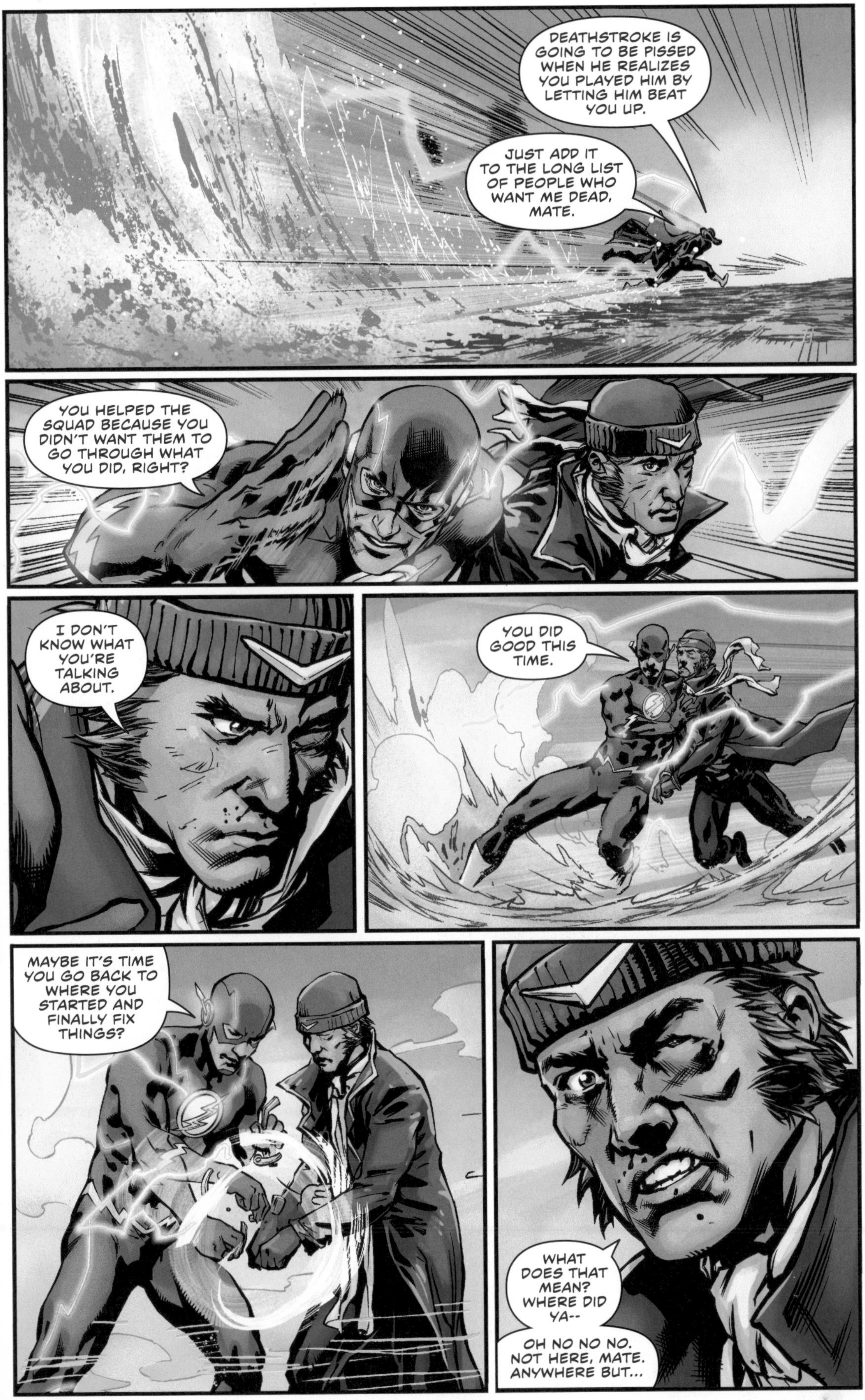
DEATHSTROKE IS GOING TO BE PISSED WHEN HE REALIZES YOU PLAYED HIM BY LETTING HIM BEAT YOU UP.
JUST ADD IT TO THE LONG LIST OF PEOPLE WHO WANT ME DEAD, MATE.
YOU HELPED THE SQUAD BECAUSE YOU DIDN'T WANT THEM TO GO THROUGH WHAT YOU DID, RIGHT?
I DON'T KNOW WHAT YOU'RE TALKING ABOUT.
YOU DID GOOD THIS TIME.
MAYBE IT'S TIME YOU GO BACK TO WHERE YOU STARTED AND FINALLY FIX THINGS?
WHAT DOES THAT MEAN? WHERE DID YA--
OH NO NO NO. NOT HERE, MATE. ANYWHERE BUT...

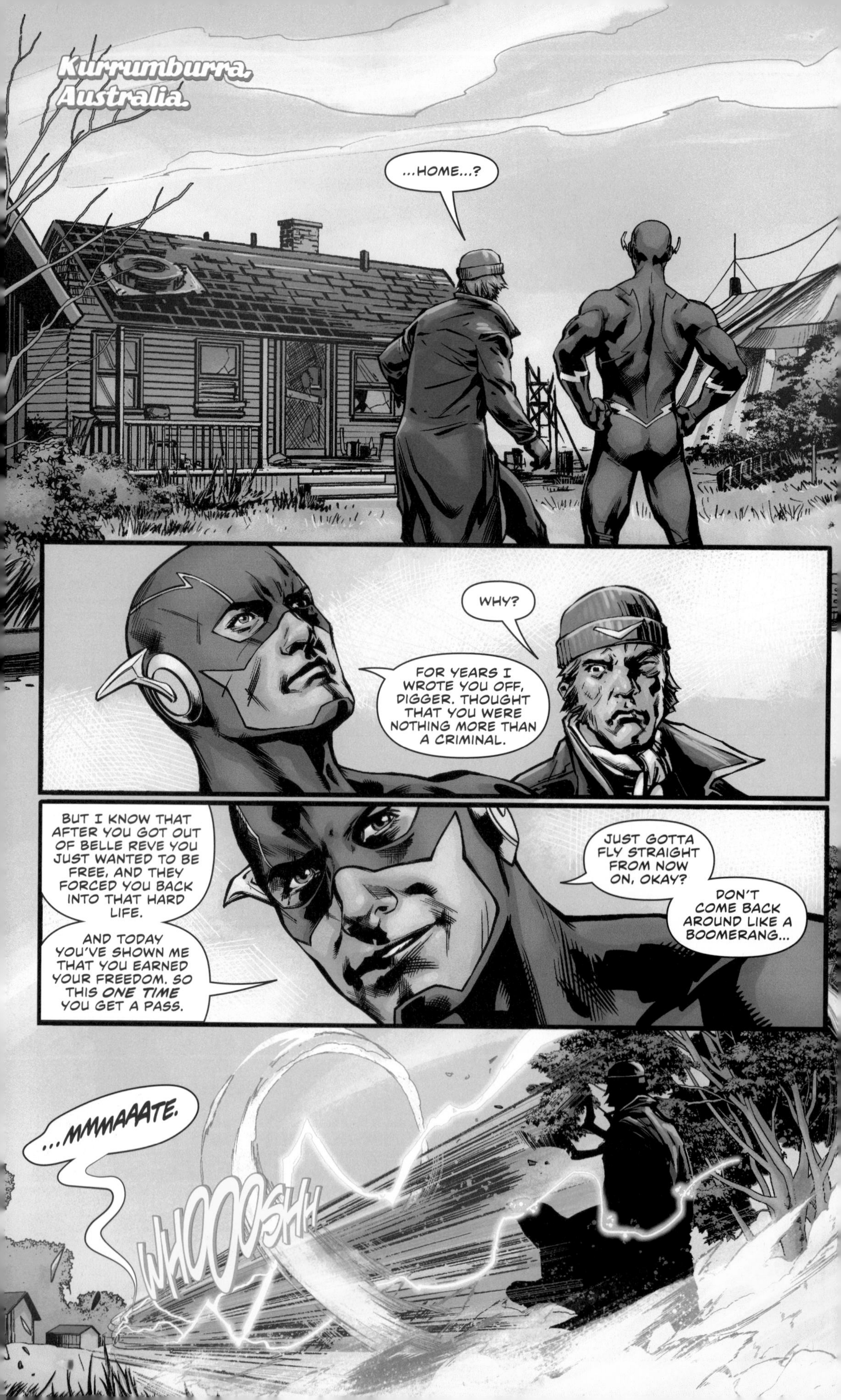

Kurrumburra, Australia.
...HOME...?
WHY?
FOR YEARS I WROTE YOU OFF, DIGGER. THOUGHT THAT YOU WERE NOTHING MORE THAN A CRIMINAL.
BUT I KNOW THAT AFTER YOU GOT OUT OF BELLE REVE YOU JUST WANTED TO BE FREE, AND THEY FORCED YOU BACK INTO THAT HARD LIFE.
AND TODAY YOU'VE SHOWN ME THAT YOU EARNED YOUR FREEDOM. SO THIS ONE TIME YOU GET A PASS.
JUST GOTTA FLY STRAIGHT FROM NOW ON, OKAY?
DON'T COME BACK AROUND LIKE A BOOMERANG...
...MMMAAATE.
WHOOOSHH

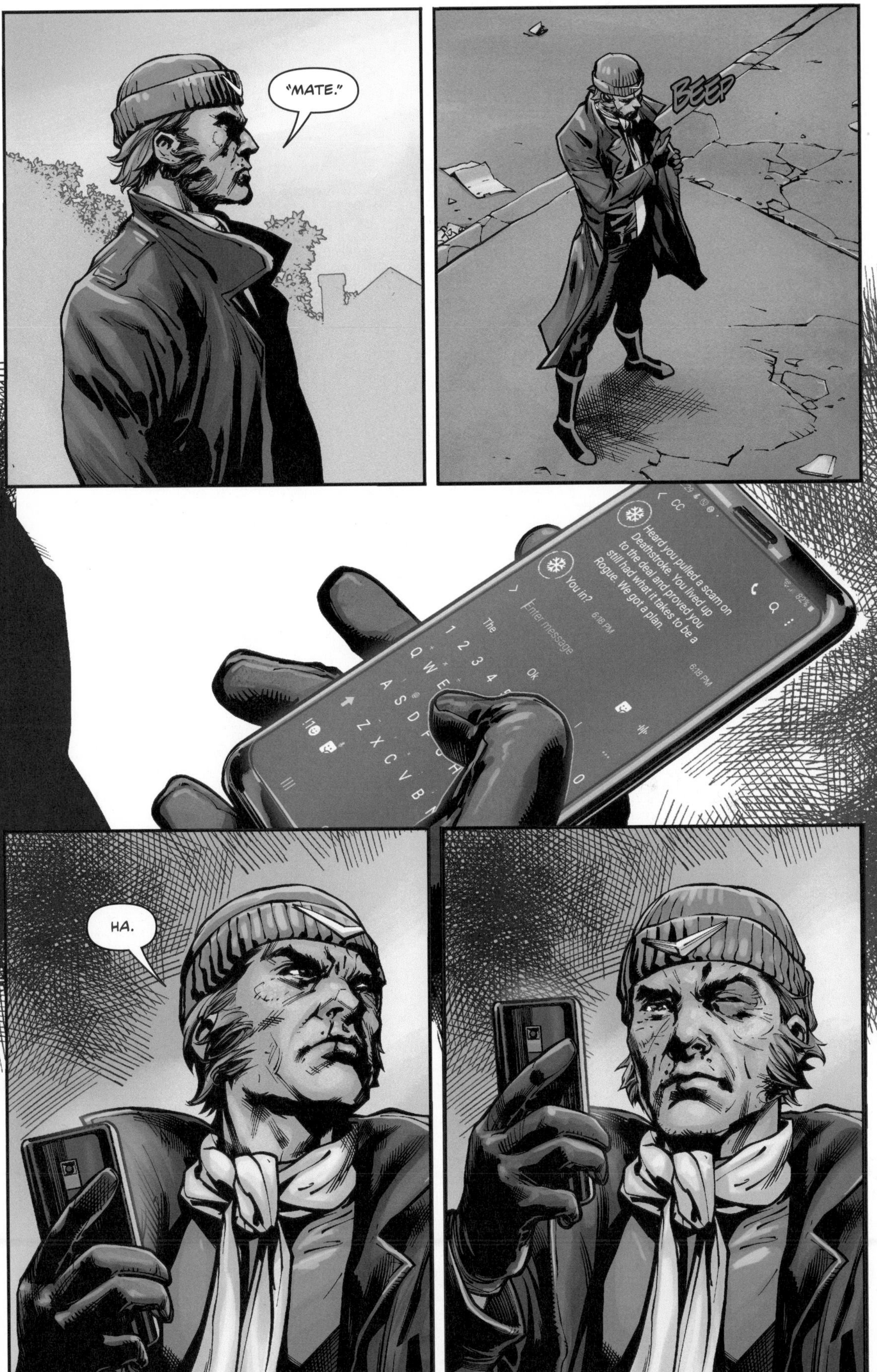
"MATE."
BEEP
CC
Heard you pulled a scam on Deathstroke. You lived up to the deal and proved you still had what it takes to be a Rogue. We got a plan.
6:18 PM
You in?
6:18 PM
Enter message
HA.

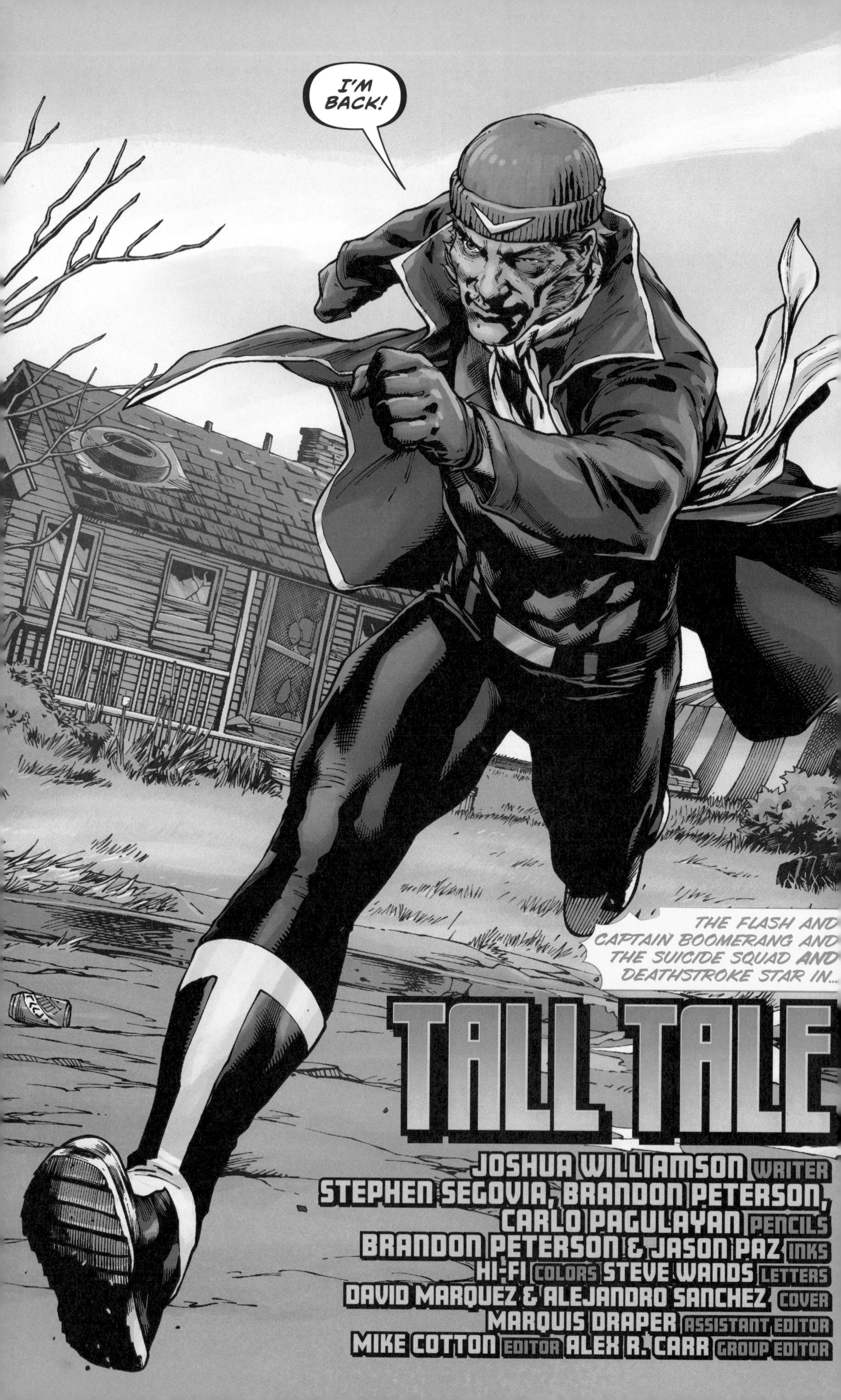

I'M BACK!
THE FLASH AND CAPTAIN BOOMERANG AND THE SUICIDE SQUAD AND DEATHSTROKE STAR IN...
TALL TALE
JOSHUA WILLIAMSON WRITER
STEPHEN SEGOVIA, BRANDON PETERSON, CARLO PAGULAYAN PENCILS
BRANDON PETERSON & JASON PAZ INKS
HI-FI COLORS STEVE WANDS LETTERS
DAVID MARQUEZ & ALEJANDRO SANCHEZ COVER
MARQUIS DRAPER ASSISTANT EDITOR
MIKE COTTON EDITOR ALEX R. CARR GROUP EDITOR

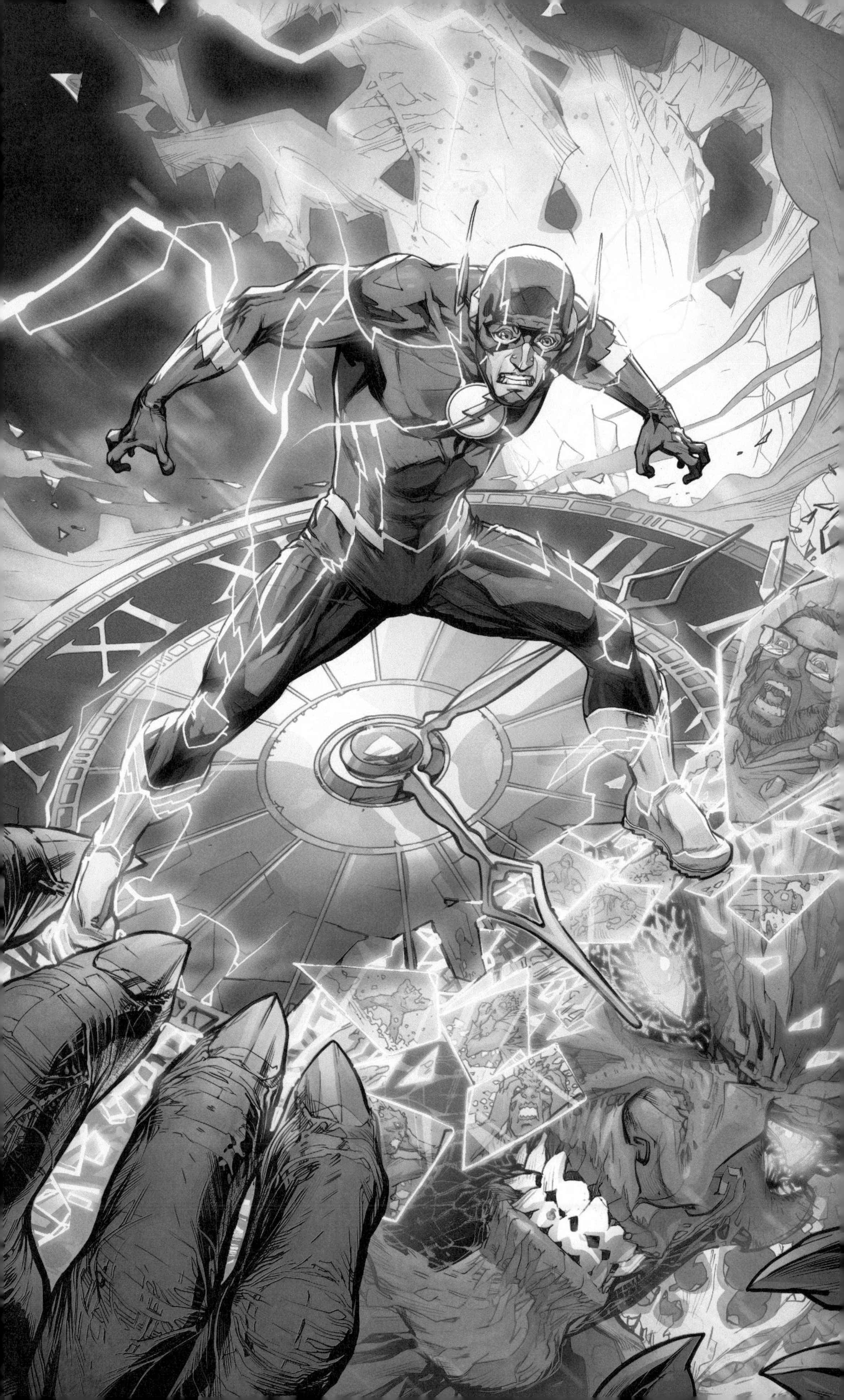

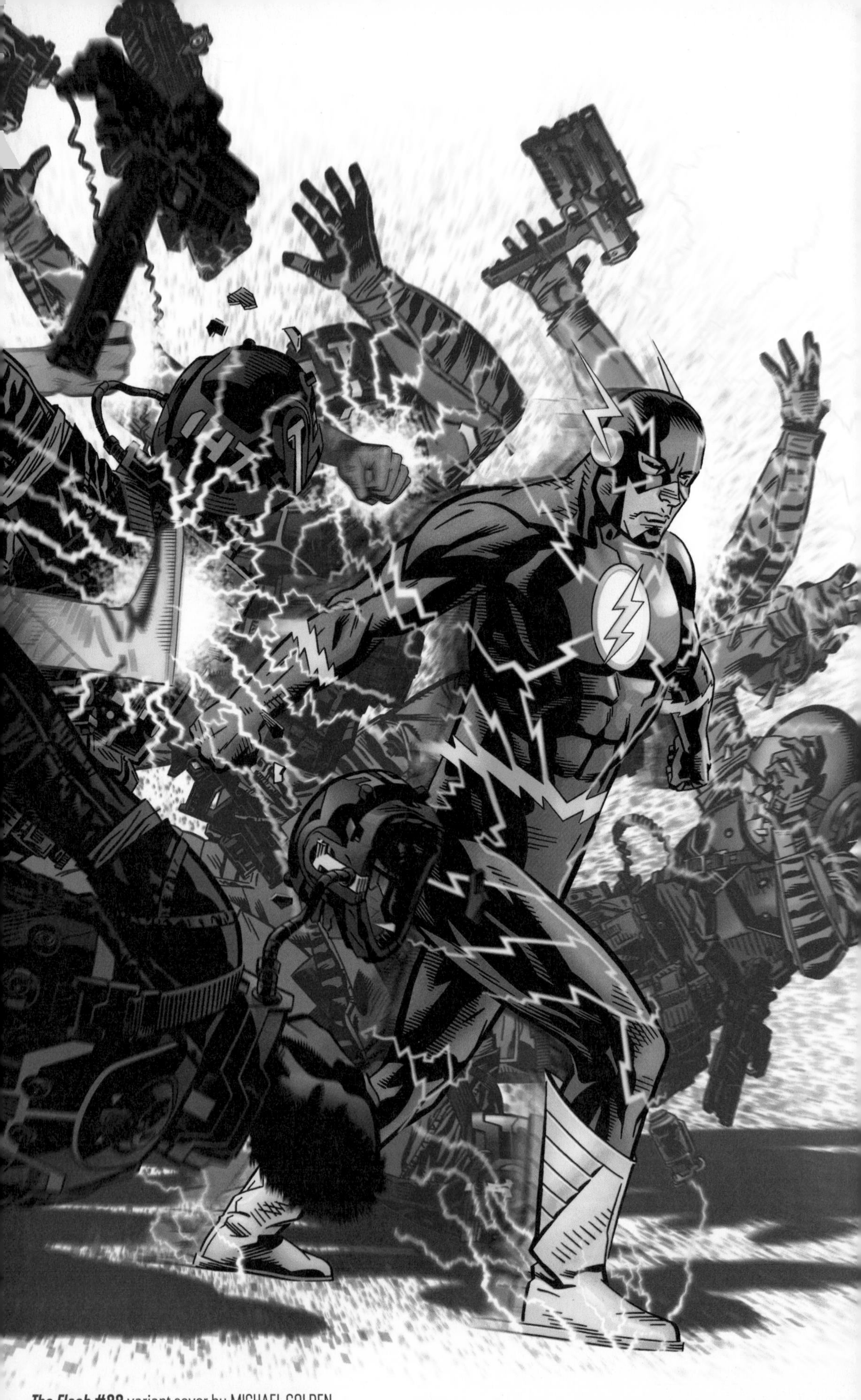

***The Flash* #88** variant cover by MICHAEL GOLDEN

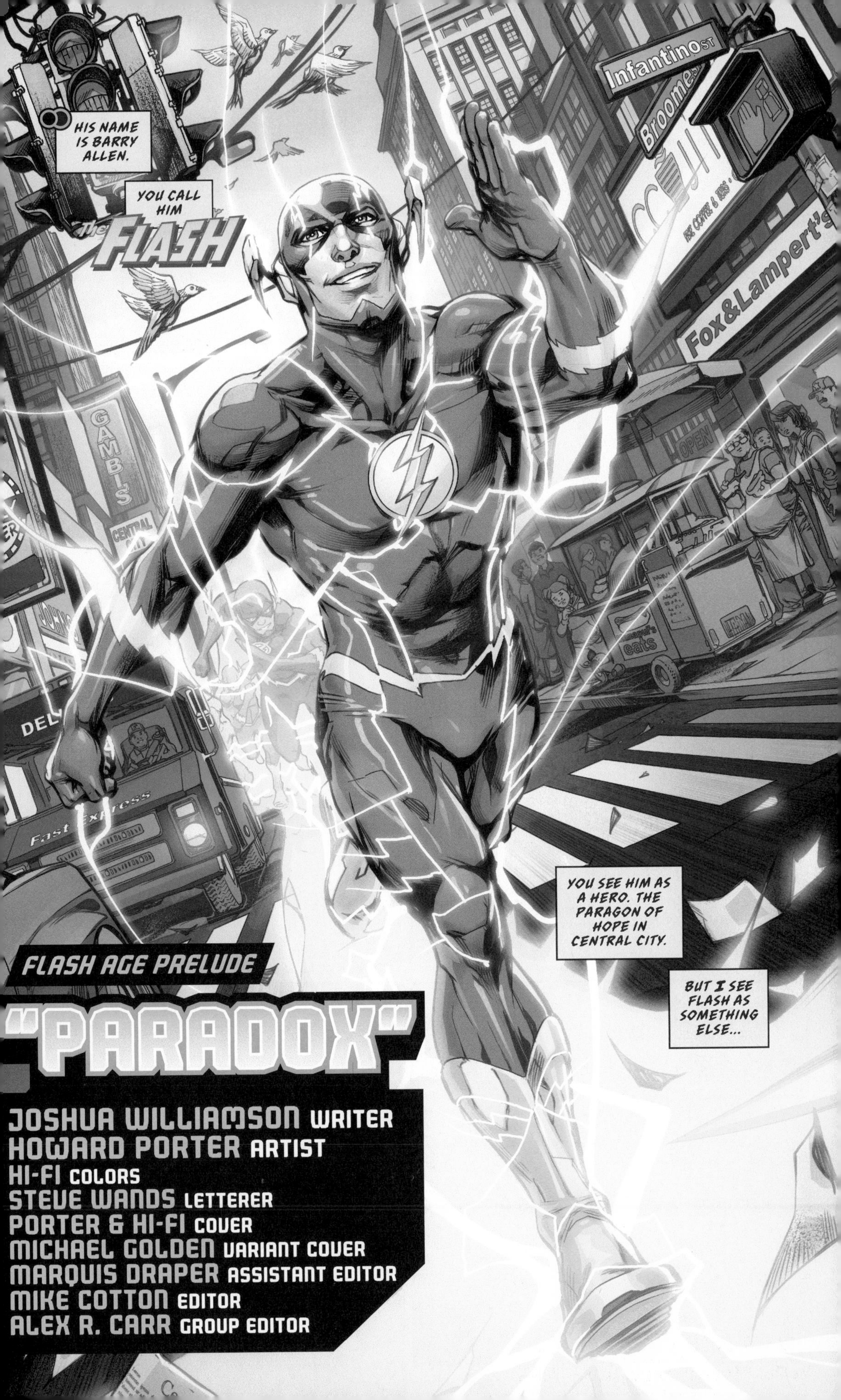
HIS NAME IS BARRY ALLEN.
YOU CALL HIM
The FLASH
Infantino ST
Broome ST
Fox&Lampert's
GAMBIS
CENTRAL
OPEN
Fast Express
eats
YOU SEE HIM AS A HERO. THE PARAGON OF HOPE IN CENTRAL CITY.
BUT I SEE FLASH AS SOMETHING ELSE...
FLASH AGE PRELUDE
"PARADOX"
JOSHUA WILLIAMSON WRITER
HOWARD PORTER ARTIST
HI-FI COLORS
STEVE WANDS LETTERER
PORTER & HI-FI COVER
MICHAEL GOLDEN VARIANT COVER
MARQUIS DRAPER ASSISTANT EDITOR
MIKE COTTON EDITOR
ALEX R. CARR GROUP EDITOR

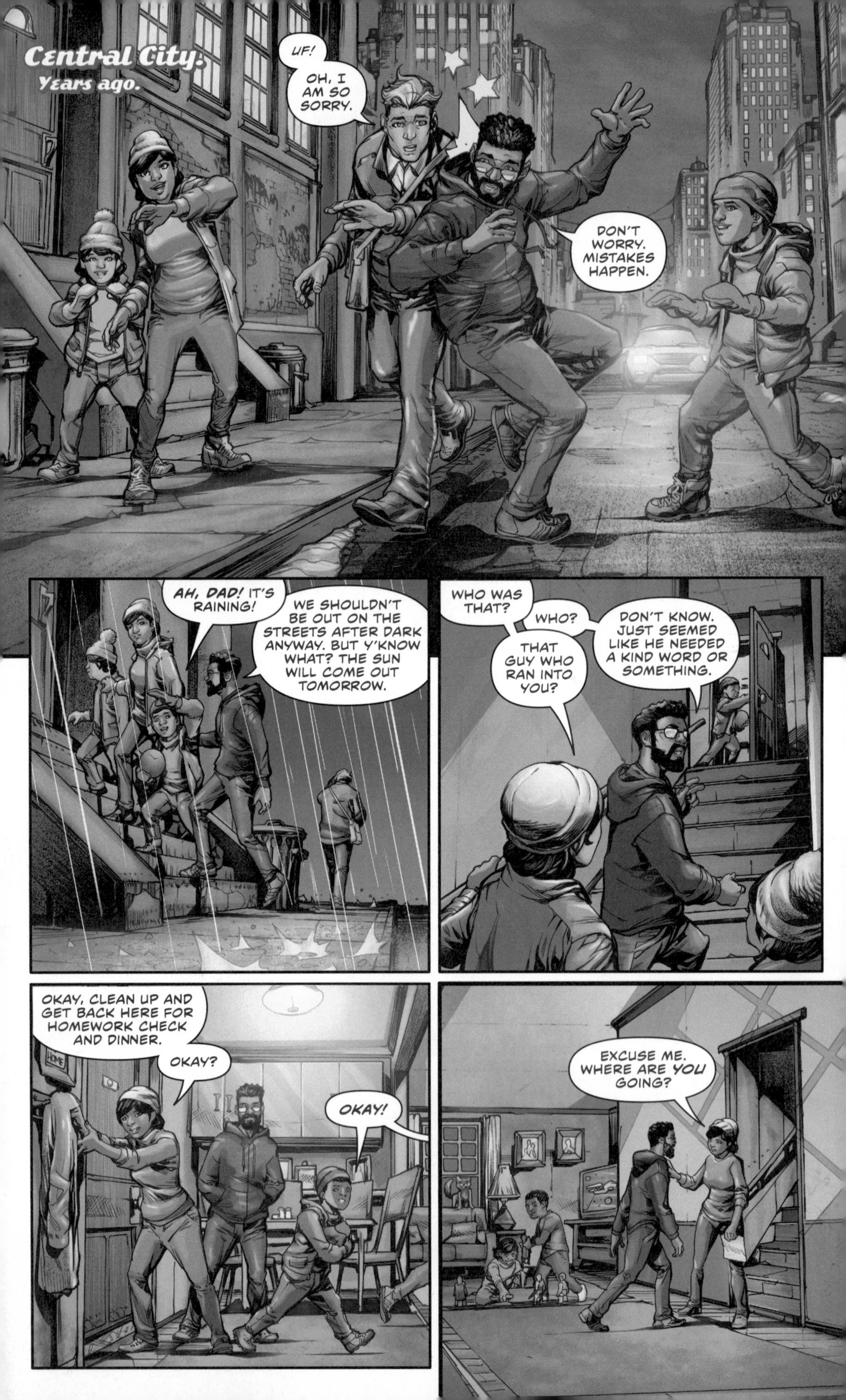
Central City.
Years ago.
UF!
OH, I AM SO SORRY.
DON'T WORRY. MISTAKES HAPPEN.
AH, DAD! IT'S RAINING!
WE SHOULDN'T BE OUT ON THE STREETS AFTER DARK ANYWAY. BUT Y'KNOW WHAT? THE SUN WILL COME OUT TOMORROW.
WHO WAS THAT?
WHO?
THAT GUY WHO RAN INTO YOU?
DON'T KNOW. JUST SEEMED LIKE HE NEEDED A KIND WORD OR SOMETHING.
OKAY, CLEAN UP AND GET BACK HERE FOR HOMEWORK CHECK AND DINNER.
OKAY?
OKAY!
EXCUSE ME. WHERE ARE YOU GOING?

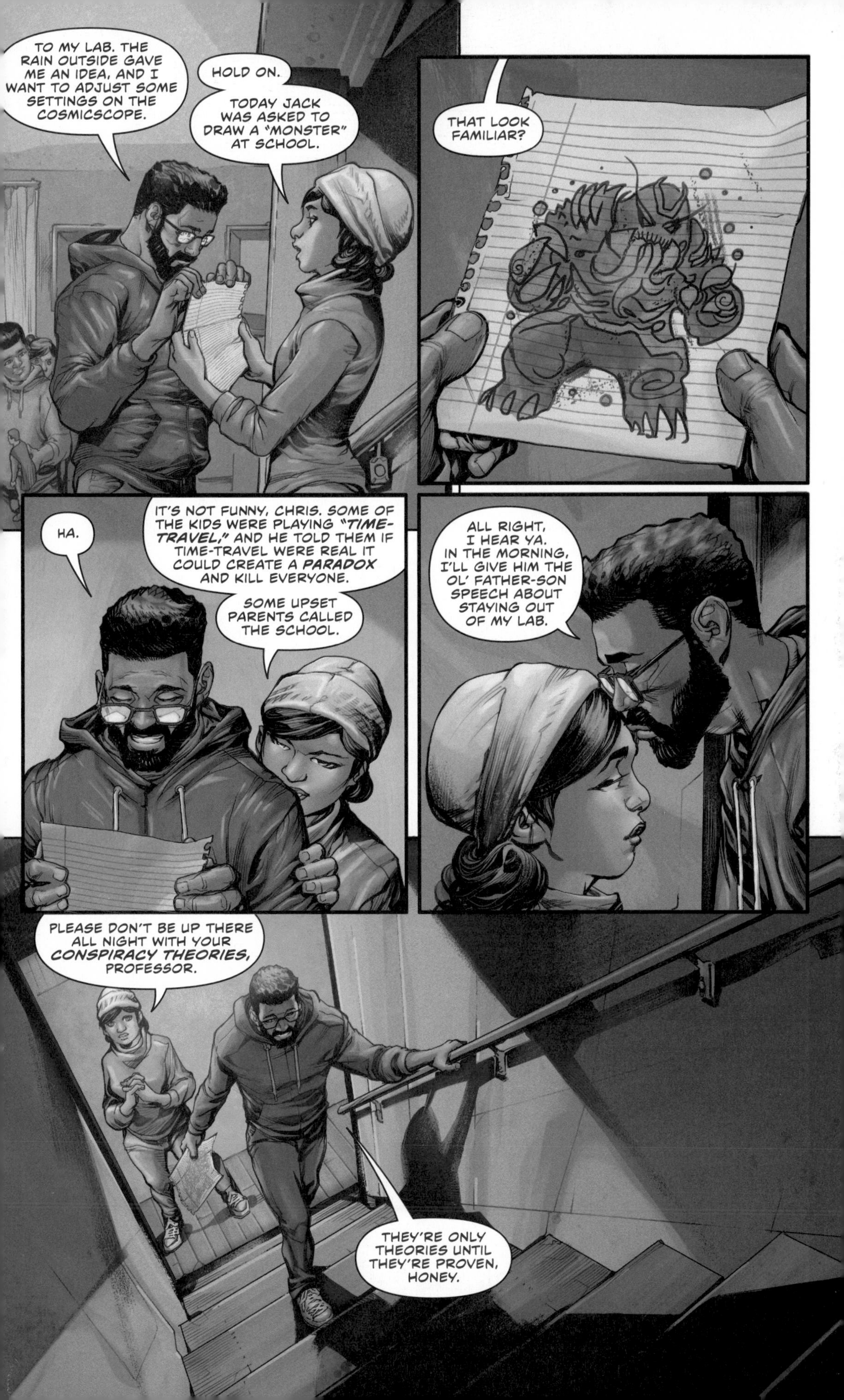
TO MY LAB. THE RAIN OUTSIDE GAVE ME AN IDEA, AND I WANT TO ADJUST SOME SETTINGS ON THE COSMICSCOPE.
HOLD ON.
TODAY JACK WAS ASKED TO DRAW A "MONSTER" AT SCHOOL.
THAT LOOK FAMILIAR?
HA.
IT'S NOT FUNNY, CHRIS. SOME OF THE KIDS WERE PLAYING "TIME-TRAVEL," AND HE TOLD THEM IF TIME-TRAVEL WERE REAL IT COULD CREATE A PARADOX AND KILL EVERYONE.
SOME UPSET PARENTS CALLED THE SCHOOL.
ALL RIGHT, I HEAR YA. IN THE MORNING, I'LL GIVE HIM THE OL' FATHER-SON SPEECH ABOUT STAYING OUT OF MY LAB.
PLEASE DON'T BE UP THERE ALL NIGHT WITH YOUR CONSPIRACY THEORIES, PROFESSOR.
THEY'RE ONLY THEORIES UNTIL THEY'RE PROVEN, HONEY.

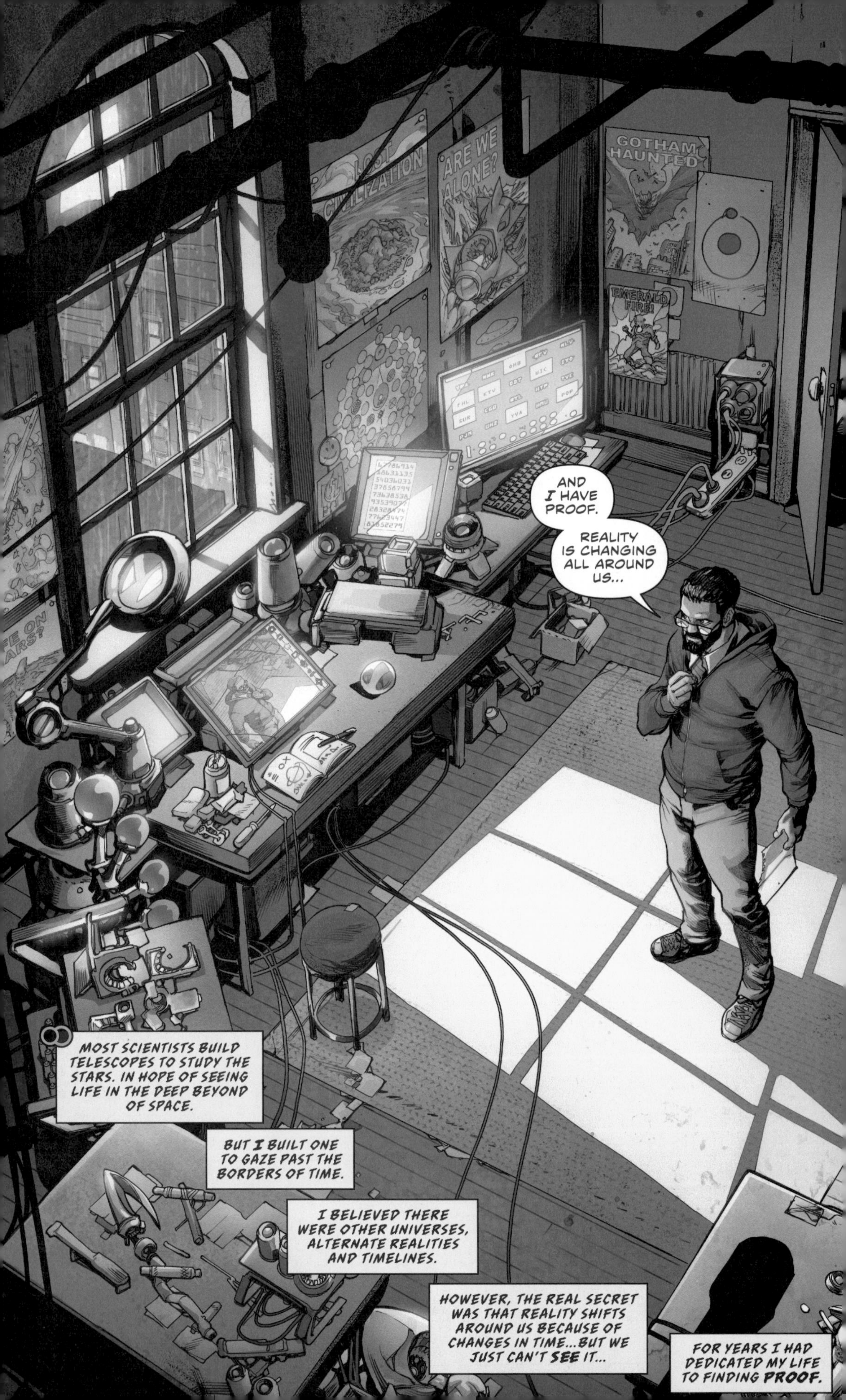
LOST CIVILIZATION
ARE WE ALONE?
GOTHAM HAUNTED
EMERALD FIRE!
AND I HAVE PROOF.
REALITY IS CHANGING ALL AROUND US...
MOST SCIENTISTS BUILD TELESCOPES TO STUDY THE STARS. IN HOPE OF SEEING LIFE IN THE DEEP BEYOND OF SPACE.
BUT I BUILT ONE TO GAZE PAST THE BORDERS OF TIME.
I BELIEVED THERE WERE OTHER UNIVERSES, ALTERNATE REALITIES AND TIMELINES.
HOWEVER, THE REAL SECRET WAS THAT REALITY SHIFTS AROUND US BECAUSE OF CHANGES IN TIME...BUT WE JUST CAN'T SEE IT...
FOR YEARS I HAD DEDICATED MY LIFE TO FINDING PROOF.

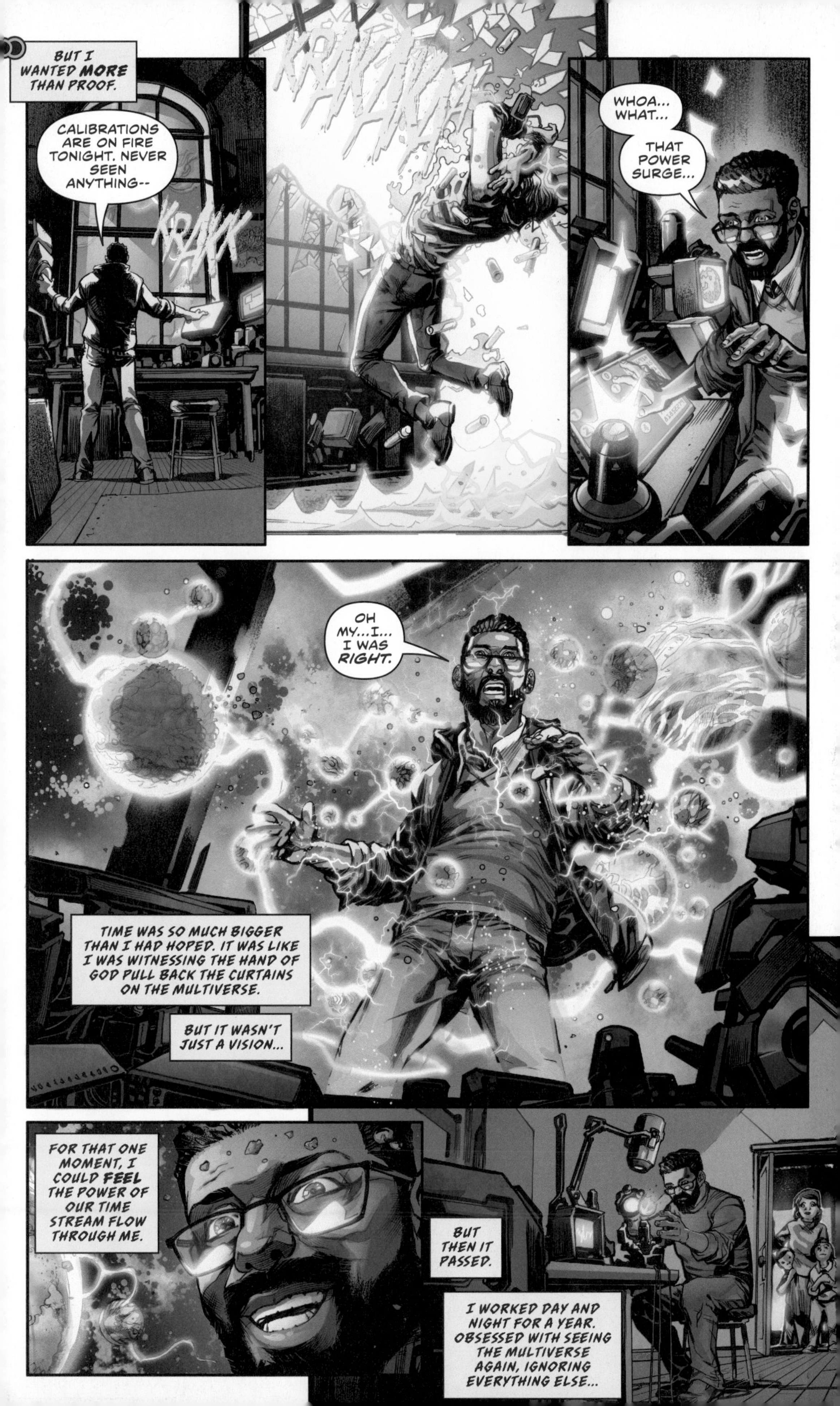

BUT I WANTED MORE THAN PROOF.
CALIBRATIONS ARE ON FIRE TONIGHT. NEVER SEEN ANYTHING--
KRAKK
KRAKATHA
WHOA... WHAT...
THAT POWER SURGE...
OH MY...I... I WAS RIGHT.
TIME WAS SO MUCH BIGGER THAN I HAD HOPED. IT WAS LIKE I WAS WITNESSING THE HAND OF GOD PULL BACK THE CURTAINS ON THE MULTIVERSE.
BUT IT WASN'T JUST A VISION...
FOR THAT ONE MOMENT, I COULD FEEL THE POWER OF OUR TIME STREAM FLOW THROUGH ME.
BUT THEN IT PASSED.
I WORKED DAY AND NIGHT FOR A YEAR. OBSESSED WITH SEEING THE MULTIVERSE AGAIN, IGNORING EVERYTHING ELSE...

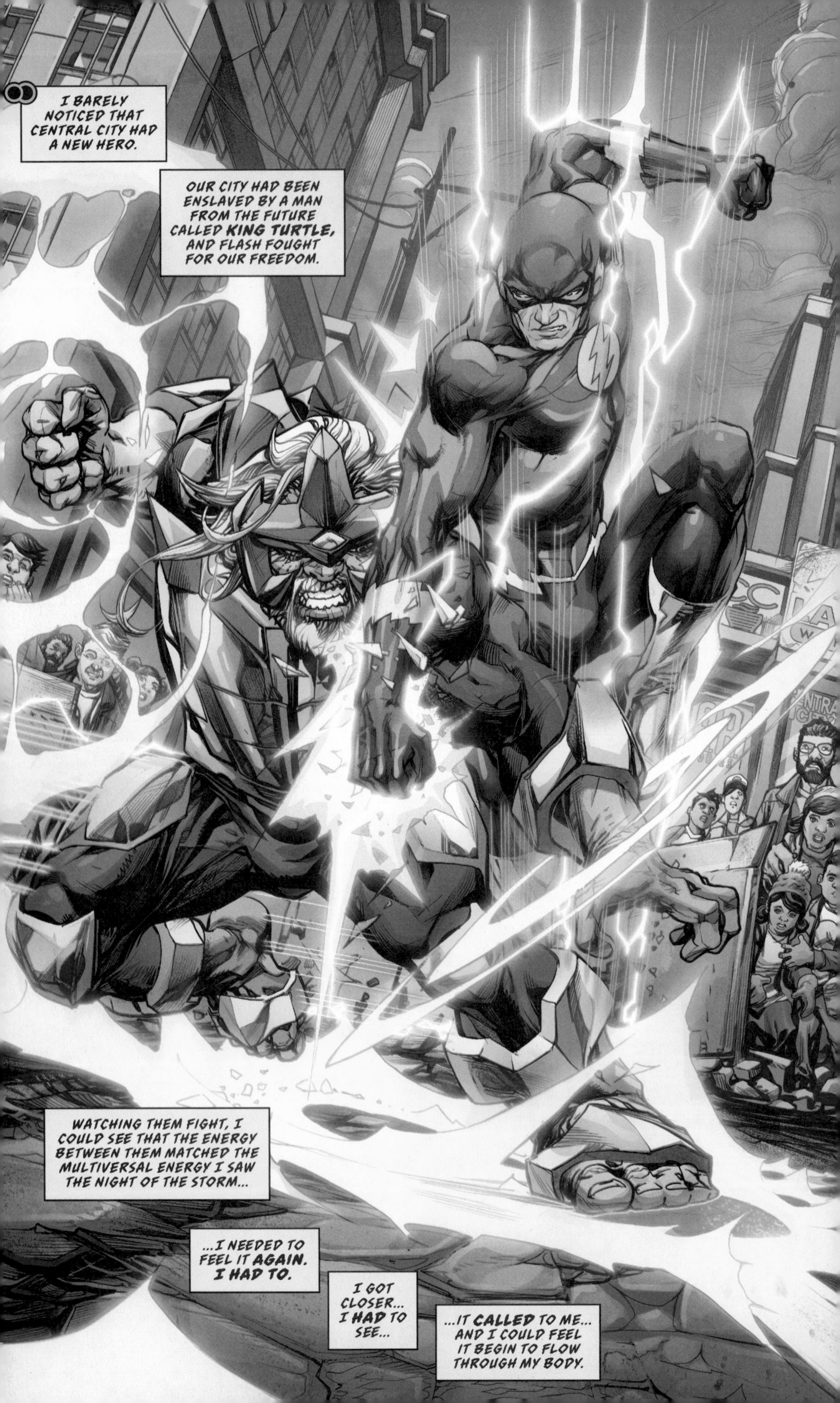

I BARELY NOTICED THAT CENTRAL CITY HAD A NEW HERO.
OUR CITY HAD BEEN ENSLAVED BY A MAN FROM THE FUTURE CALLED **KING TURTLE,** AND FLASH FOUGHT FOR OUR FREEDOM.
WATCHING THEM FIGHT, I COULD SEE THAT THE ENERGY BETWEEN THEM MATCHED THE MULTIVERSAL ENERGY I SAW THE NIGHT OF THE STORM...
...I NEEDED TO FEEL IT **AGAIN. I HAD TO.**
I GOT CLOSER... I **HAD** TO SEE...
...IT **CALLED** TO ME... AND I COULD FEEL IT BEGIN TO FLOW THROUGH MY BODY.

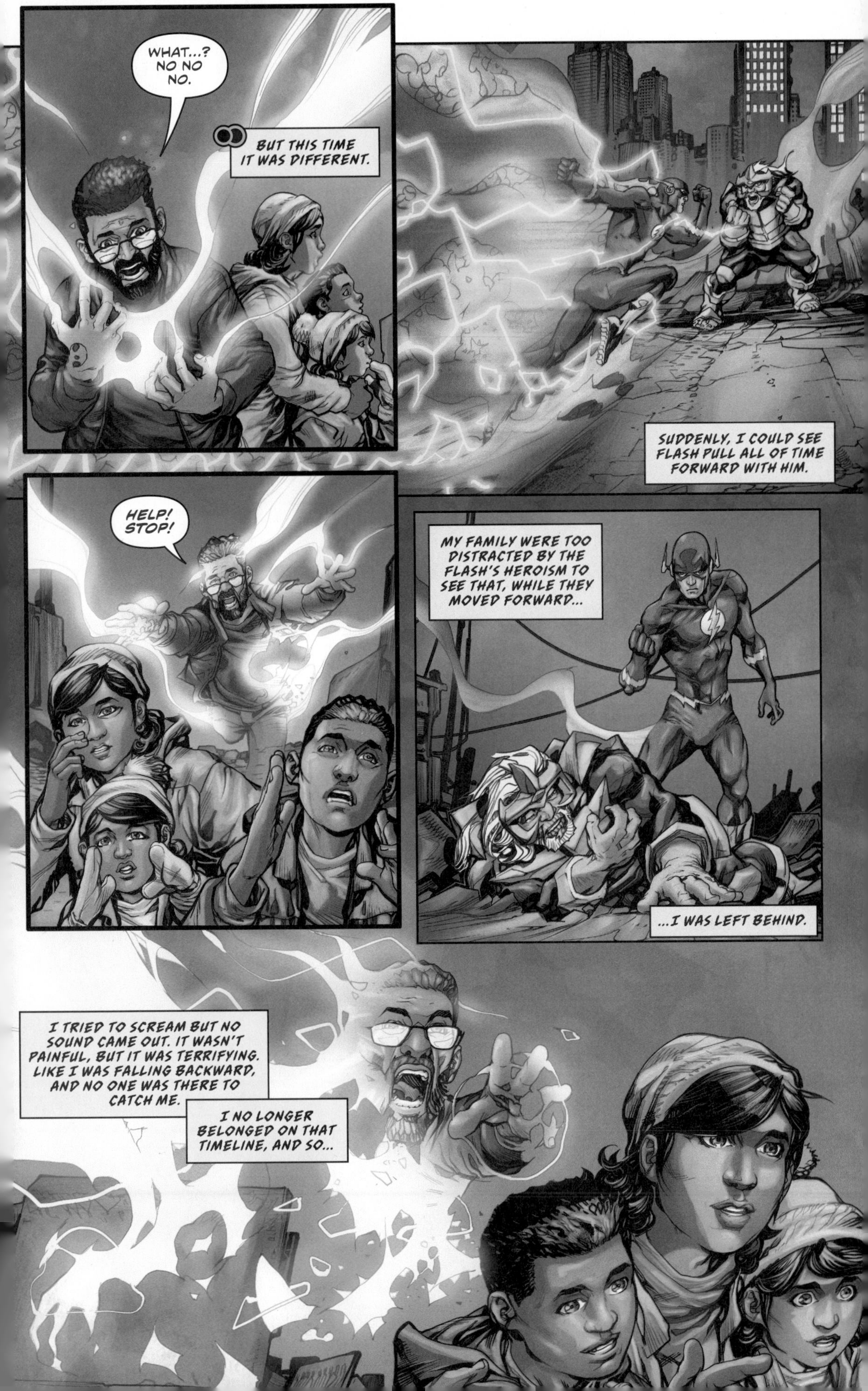
WHAT...? NO NO NO.
BUT THIS TIME IT WAS DIFFERENT.
SUDDENLY, I COULD SEE FLASH PULL ALL OF TIME FORWARD WITH HIM.
HELP! STOP!
MY FAMILY WERE TOO DISTRACTED BY THE FLASH'S HEROISM TO SEE THAT, WHILE THEY MOVED FORWARD...
...I WAS LEFT BEHIND.
I TRIED TO SCREAM BUT NO SOUND CAME OUT. IT WASN'T PAINFUL, BUT IT WAS TERRIFYING. LIKE I WAS FALLING BACKWARD, AND NO ONE WAS THERE TO CATCH ME.
I NO LONGER BELONGED ON THAT TIMELINE, AND SO...

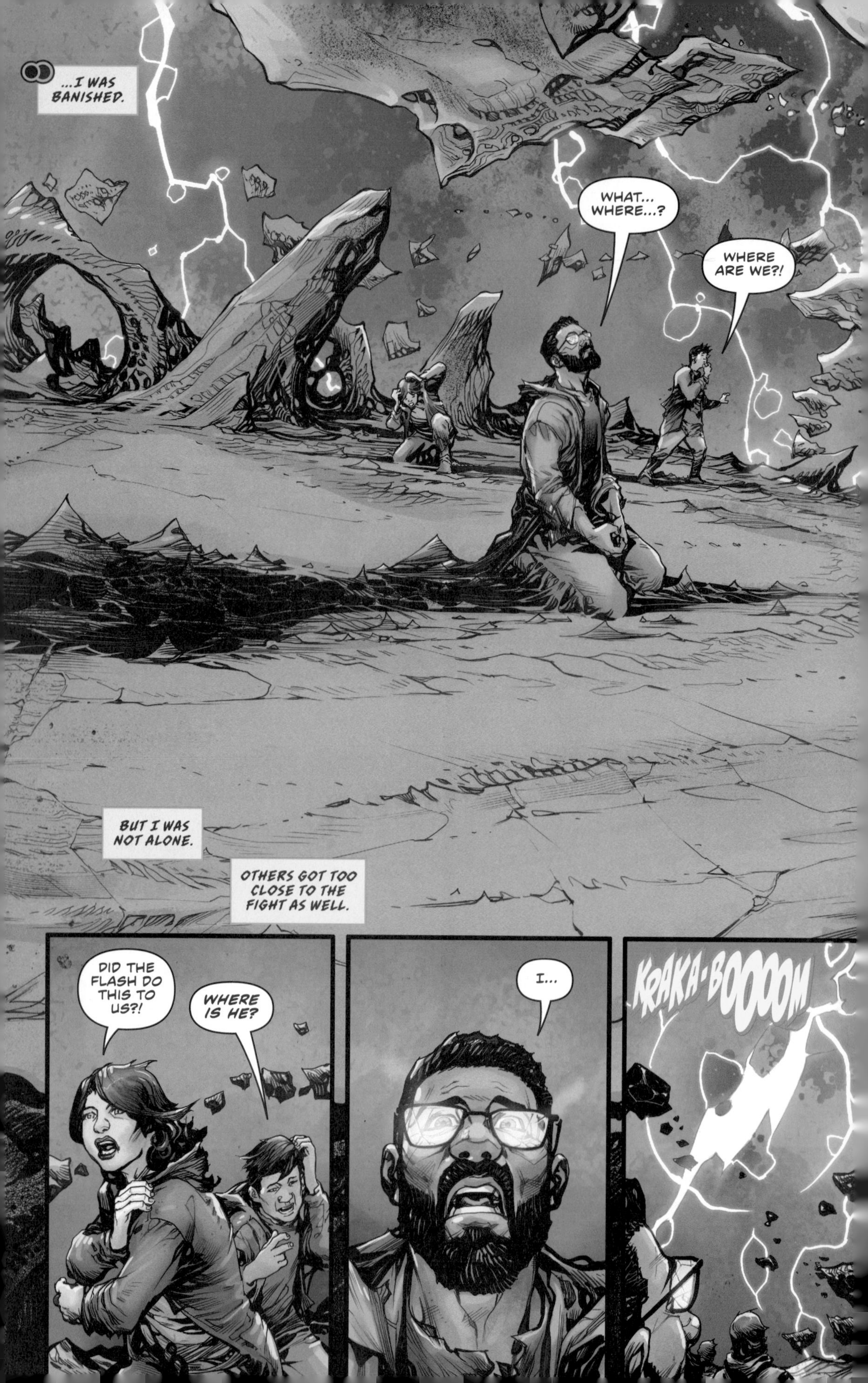
...I WAS BANISHED.
WHAT... WHERE...?
WHERE ARE WE?!
BUT I WAS NOT ALONE.
OTHERS GOT TOO CLOSE TO THE FIGHT AS WELL.
DID THE FLASH DO THIS TO US?!
WHERE IS HE?
I...
KRAKA-BOOOOM

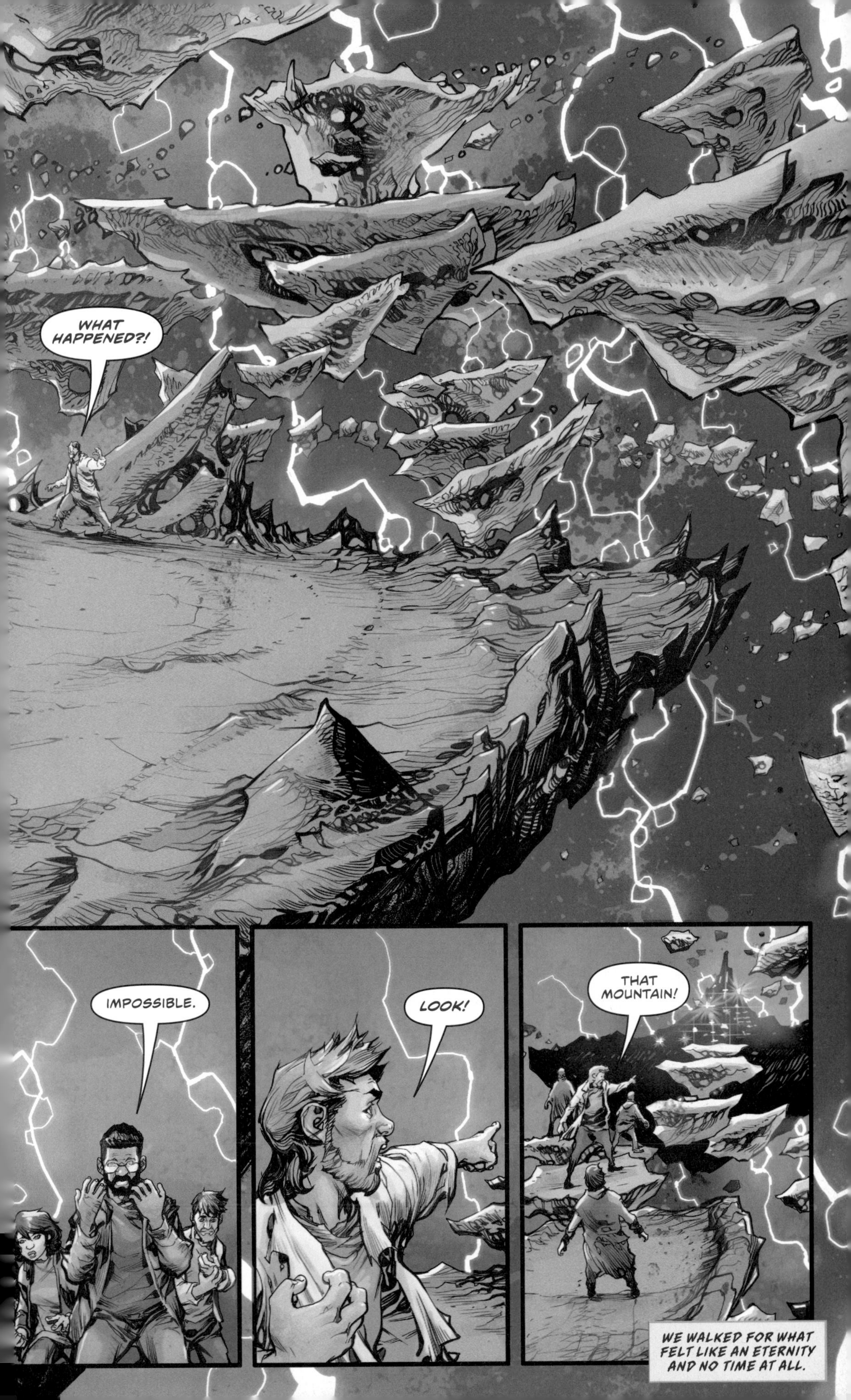

WHAT HAPPENED?!
IMPOSSIBLE.
LOOK!
THAT MOUNTAIN!
WE WALKED FOR WHAT FELT LIKE AN ETERNITY AND NO TIME AT ALL.

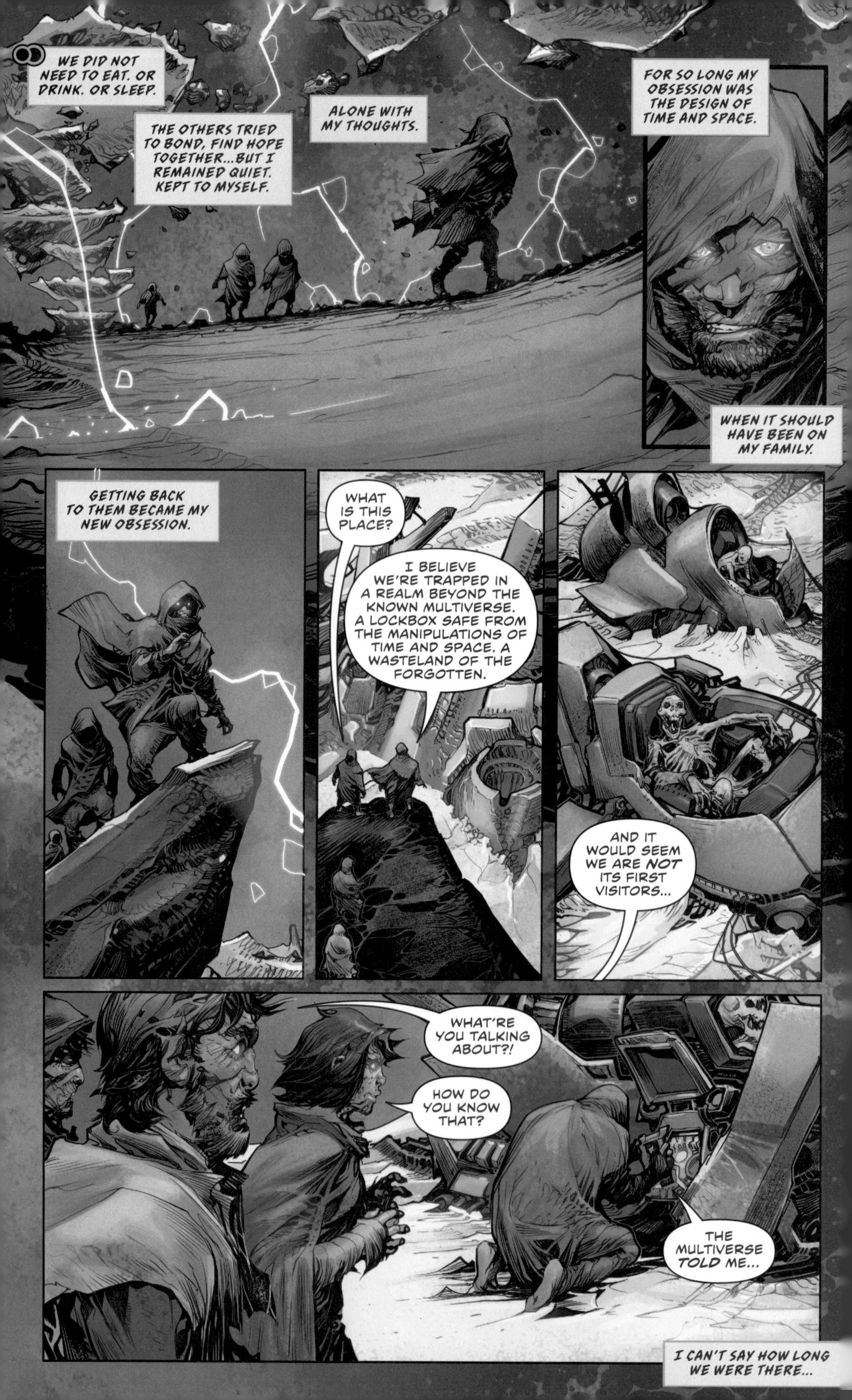

WE DID NOT NEED TO EAT. OR DRINK. OR SLEEP.
THE OTHERS TRIED TO BOND, FIND HOPE TOGETHER...BUT I REMAINED QUIET. KEPT TO MYSELF.
ALONE WITH MY THOUGHTS.
FOR SO LONG MY OBSESSION WAS THE DESIGN OF TIME AND SPACE.
WHEN IT SHOULD HAVE BEEN ON MY FAMILY.
GETTING BACK TO THEM BECAME MY NEW OBSESSION.
WHAT IS THIS PLACE?
I BELIEVE WE'RE TRAPPED IN A REALM BEYOND THE KNOWN MULTIVERSE. A LOCKBOX SAFE FROM THE MANIPULATIONS OF TIME AND SPACE. A WASTELAND OF THE FORGOTTEN.
AND IT WOULD SEEM WE ARE *NOT* ITS FIRST VISITORS...
WHAT'RE YOU TALKING ABOUT?!
HOW DO YOU KNOW THAT?
THE MULTIVERSE *TOLD* ME...
I CAN'T SAY HOW LONG WE WERE THERE...

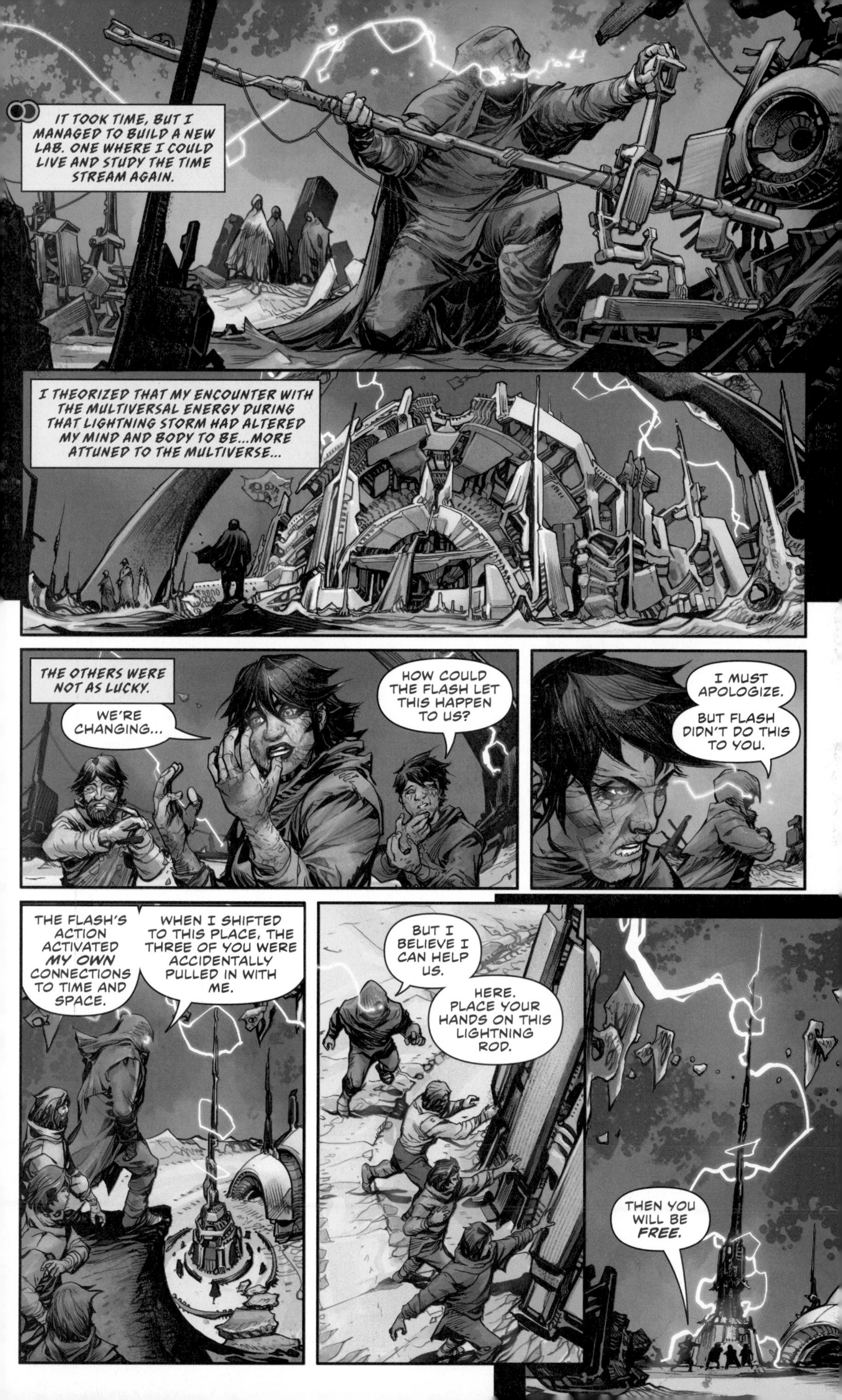

IT TOOK TIME, BUT I MANAGED TO BUILD A NEW LAB. ONE WHERE I COULD LIVE AND STUDY THE TIME STREAM AGAIN.
I THEORIZED THAT MY ENCOUNTER WITH THE MULTIVERSAL ENERGY DURING THAT LIGHTNING STORM HAD ALTERED MY MIND AND BODY TO BE...MORE ATTUNED TO THE MULTIVERSE...
THE OTHERS WERE NOT AS LUCKY.
WE'RE CHANGING...
HOW COULD THE FLASH LET THIS HAPPEN TO US?
I MUST APOLOGIZE.
BUT FLASH DIDN'T DO THIS TO YOU.
THE FLASH'S ACTION ACTIVATED MY OWN CONNECTIONS TO TIME AND SPACE.
WHEN I SHIFTED TO THIS PLACE, THE THREE OF YOU WERE ACCIDENTALLY PULLED IN WITH ME.
BUT I BELIEVE I CAN HELP US.
HERE. PLACE YOUR HANDS ON THIS LIGHTNING ROD.
THEN YOU WILL BE FREE.

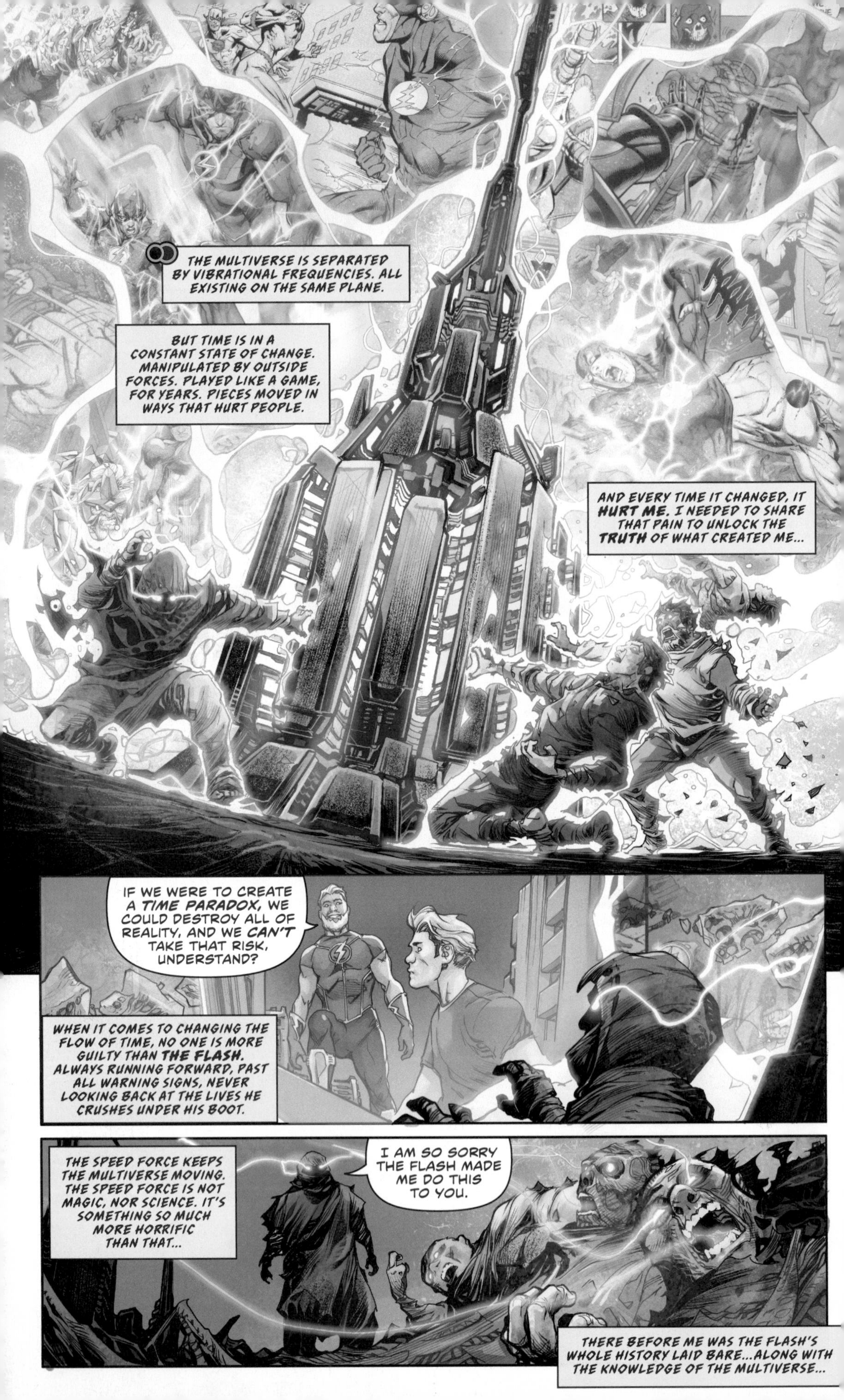
THE MULTIVERSE IS SEPARATED BY VIBRATIONAL FREQUENCIES. ALL EXISTING ON THE SAME PLANE.
BUT TIME IS IN A CONSTANT STATE OF CHANGE. MANIPULATED BY OUTSIDE FORCES. PLAYED LIKE A GAME, FOR YEARS. PIECES MOVED IN WAYS THAT HURT PEOPLE.
AND EVERY TIME IT CHANGED, IT HURT ME. I NEEDED TO SHARE THAT PAIN TO UNLOCK THE TRUTH OF WHAT CREATED ME...
IF WE WERE TO CREATE A TIME PARADOX, WE COULD DESTROY ALL OF REALITY, AND WE CAN'T TAKE THAT RISK, UNDERSTAND?
WHEN IT COMES TO CHANGING THE FLOW OF TIME, NO ONE IS MORE GUILTY THAN THE FLASH. ALWAYS RUNNING FORWARD, PAST ALL WARNING SIGNS, NEVER LOOKING BACK AT THE LIVES HE CRUSHES UNDER HIS BOOT.
THE SPEED FORCE KEEPS THE MULTIVERSE MOVING. THE SPEED FORCE IS NOT MAGIC, NOR SCIENCE. IT'S SOMETHING SO MUCH MORE HORRIFIC THAN THAT...
I AM SO SORRY THE FLASH MADE ME DO THIS TO YOU.
THERE BEFORE ME WAS THE FLASH'S WHOLE HISTORY LAID BARE...ALONG WITH THE KNOWLEDGE OF THE MULTIVERSE...

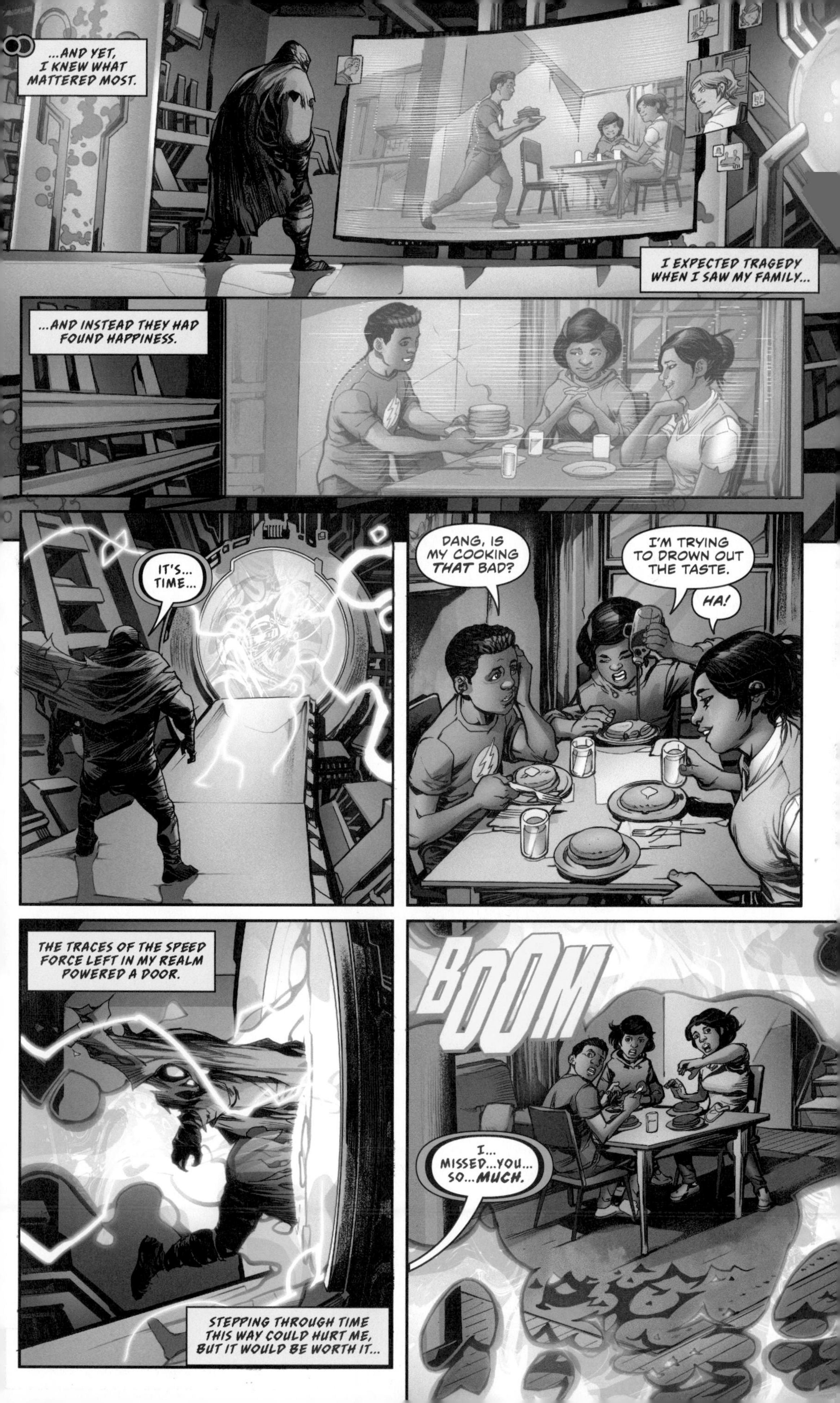
...AND YET, I KNEW WHAT MATTERED MOST.
I EXPECTED TRAGEDY WHEN I SAW MY FAMILY...
...AND INSTEAD THEY HAD FOUND HAPPINESS.
IT'S... TIME...
DANG, IS MY COOKING *THAT* BAD?
I'M TRYING TO DROWN OUT THE TASTE.
HA!
THE TRACES OF THE SPEED FORCE LEFT IN MY REALM POWERED A DOOR.
STEPPING THROUGH TIME THIS WAY COULD HURT ME, BUT IT WOULD BE WORTH IT...
BOOM
I... MISSED...YOU... SO...*MUCH*.

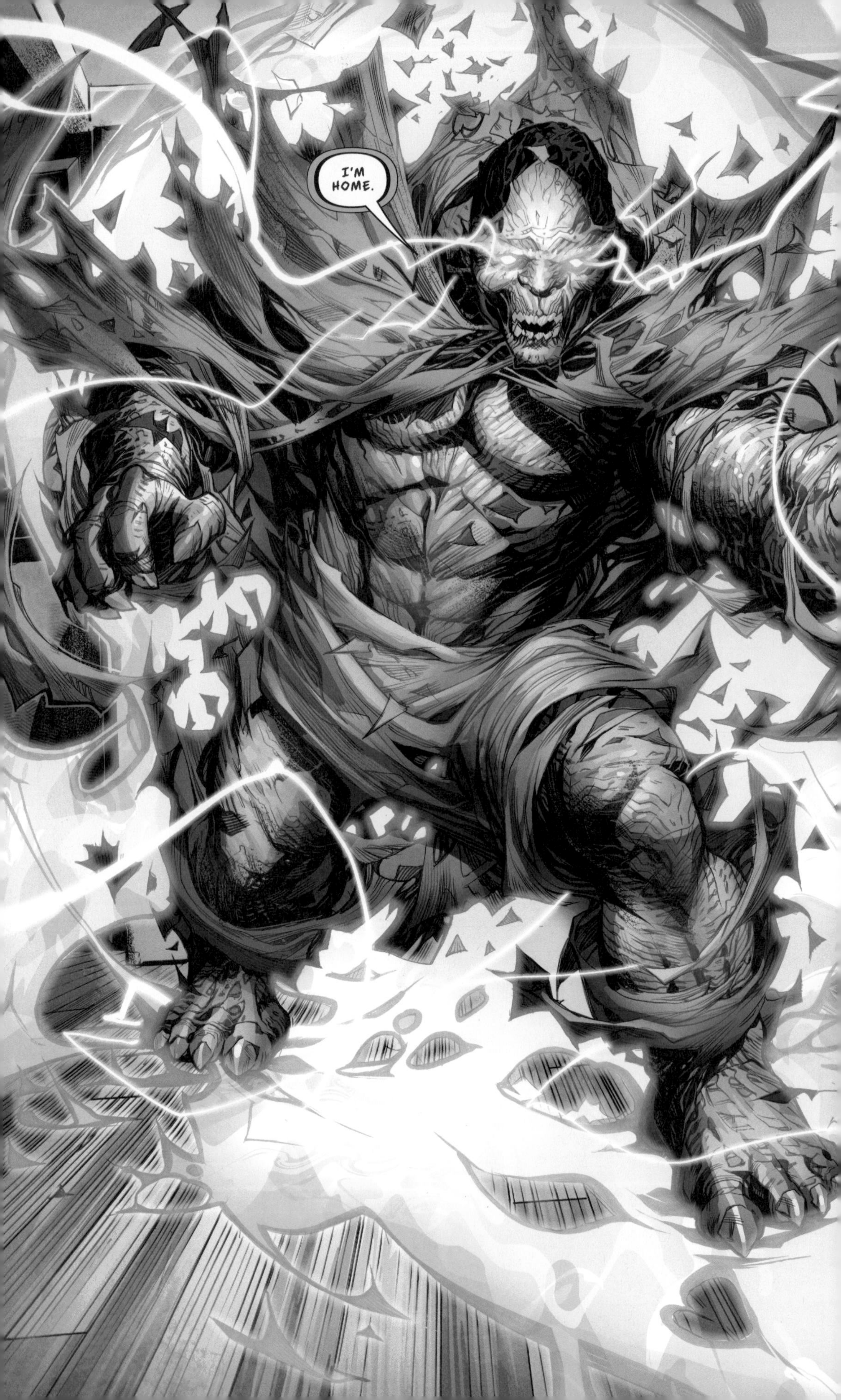
I'M HOME.

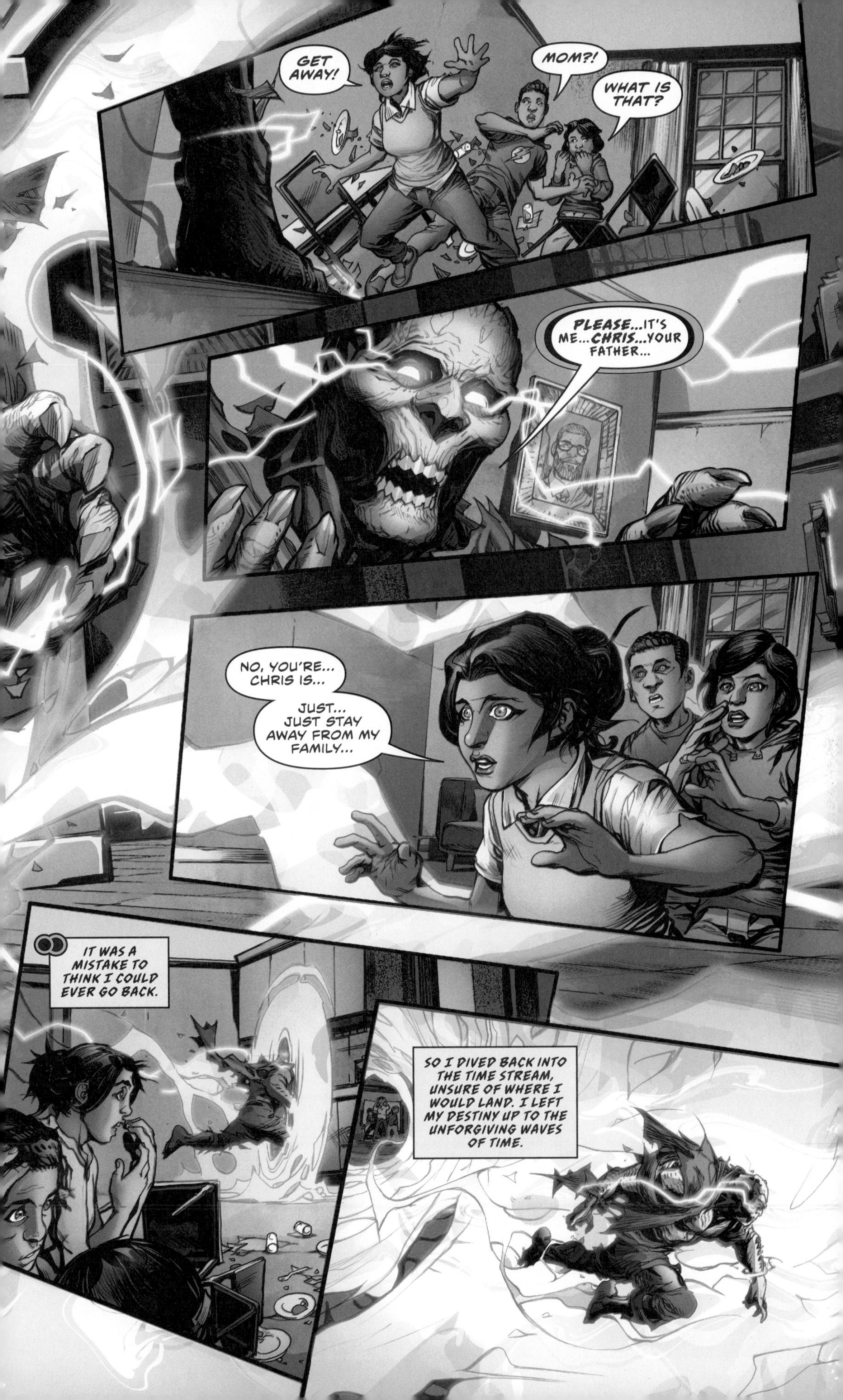
GET AWAY!
MOM?!
WHAT IS THAT?
PLEASE...IT'S ME...CHRIS...YOUR FATHER...
NO, YOU'RE... CHRIS IS...
JUST... JUST STAY AWAY FROM MY FAMILY...
IT WAS A MISTAKE TO THINK I COULD EVER GO BACK.
SO I DIVED BACK INTO THE TIME STREAM, UNSURE OF WHERE I WOULD LAND. I LEFT MY DESTINY UP TO THE UNFORGIVING WAVES OF TIME.

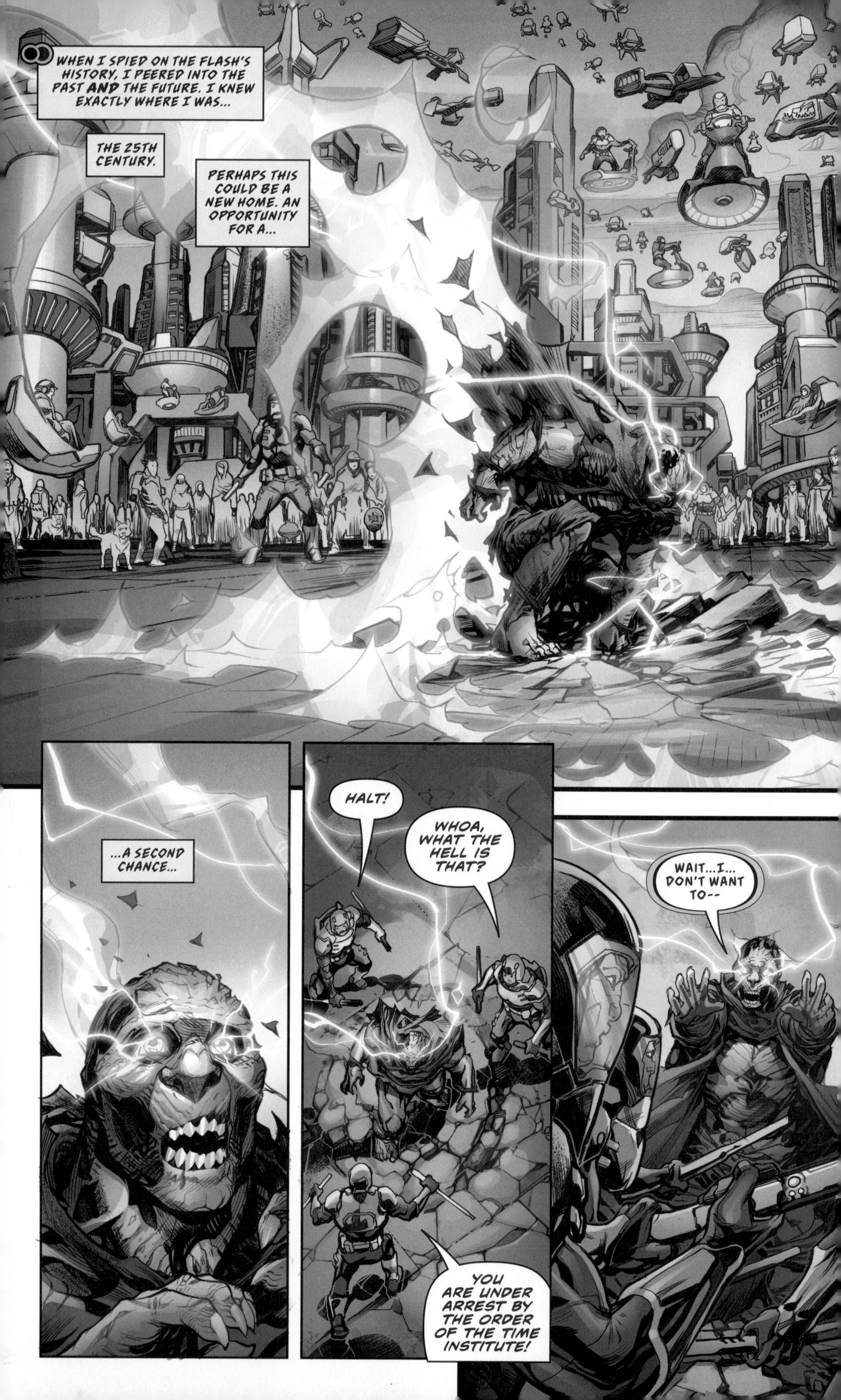

WHEN I SPIED ON THE FLASH'S HISTORY, I PEERED INTO THE PAST AND THE FUTURE. I KNEW EXACTLY WHERE I WAS...
THE 25TH CENTURY.
PERHAPS THIS COULD BE A NEW HOME. AN OPPORTUNITY FOR A...
...A SECOND CHANCE...
HALT!
WHOA, WHAT THE HELL IS THAT?
YOU ARE UNDER ARREST BY THE ORDER OF THE TIME INSTITUTE!
WAIT...I... DON'T WANT TO--

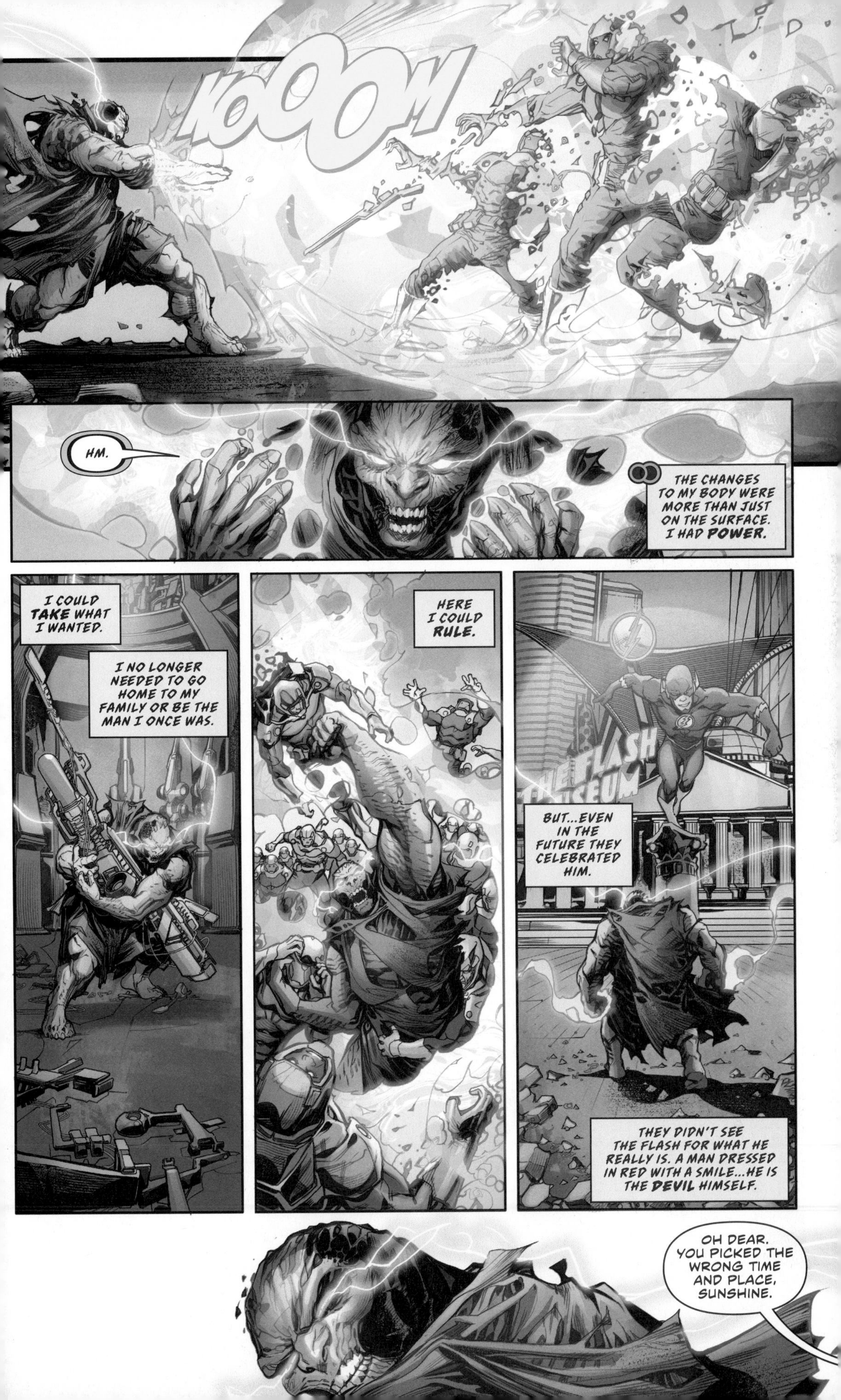

KOOOOM
HM.
THE CHANGES TO MY BODY WERE MORE THAN JUST ON THE SURFACE. I HAD POWER.
I COULD TAKE WHAT I WANTED.
I NO LONGER NEEDED TO GO HOME TO MY FAMILY OR BE THE MAN I ONCE WAS.
HERE I COULD RULE.
THE FLASH MUSEUM
BUT...EVEN IN THE FUTURE THEY CELEBRATED HIM.
THEY DIDN'T SEE THE FLASH FOR WHAT HE REALLY IS. A MAN DRESSED IN RED WITH A SMILE...HE IS THE DEVIL HIMSELF.
OH DEAR. YOU PICKED THE WRONG TIME AND PLACE, SUNSHINE.

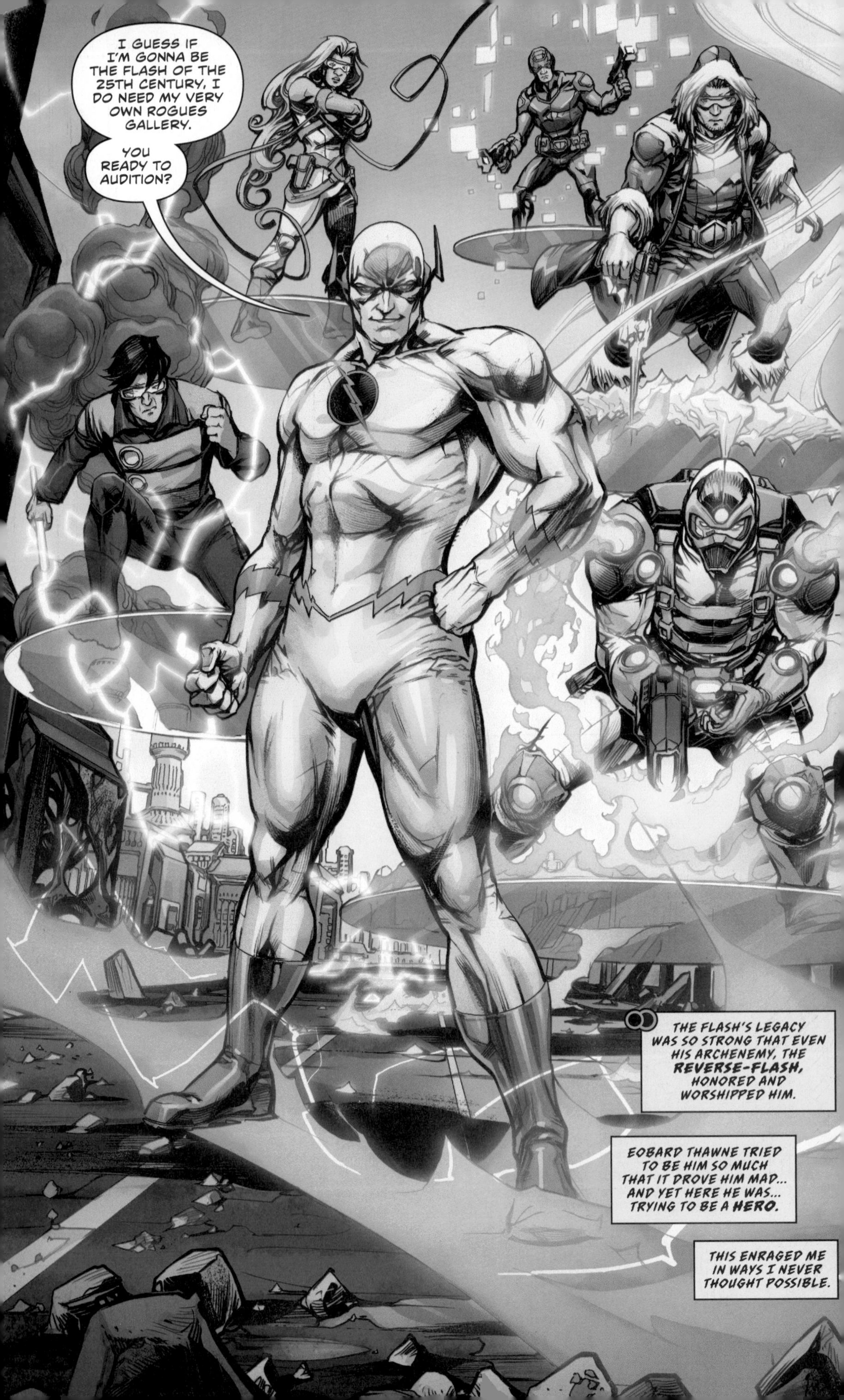
I GUESS IF I'M GONNA BE THE FLASH OF THE 25TH CENTURY, I DO NEED MY VERY OWN ROGUES GALLERY.
YOU READY TO AUDITION?
THE FLASH'S LEGACY WAS SO STRONG THAT EVEN HIS ARCHENEMY, THE REVERSE-FLASH, HONORED AND WORSHIPPED HIM.
EOBARD THAWNE TRIED TO BE HIM SO MUCH THAT IT DROVE HIM MAD... AND YET HERE HE WAS... TRYING TO BE A HERO.
THIS ENRAGED ME IN WAYS I NEVER THOUGHT POSSIBLE.

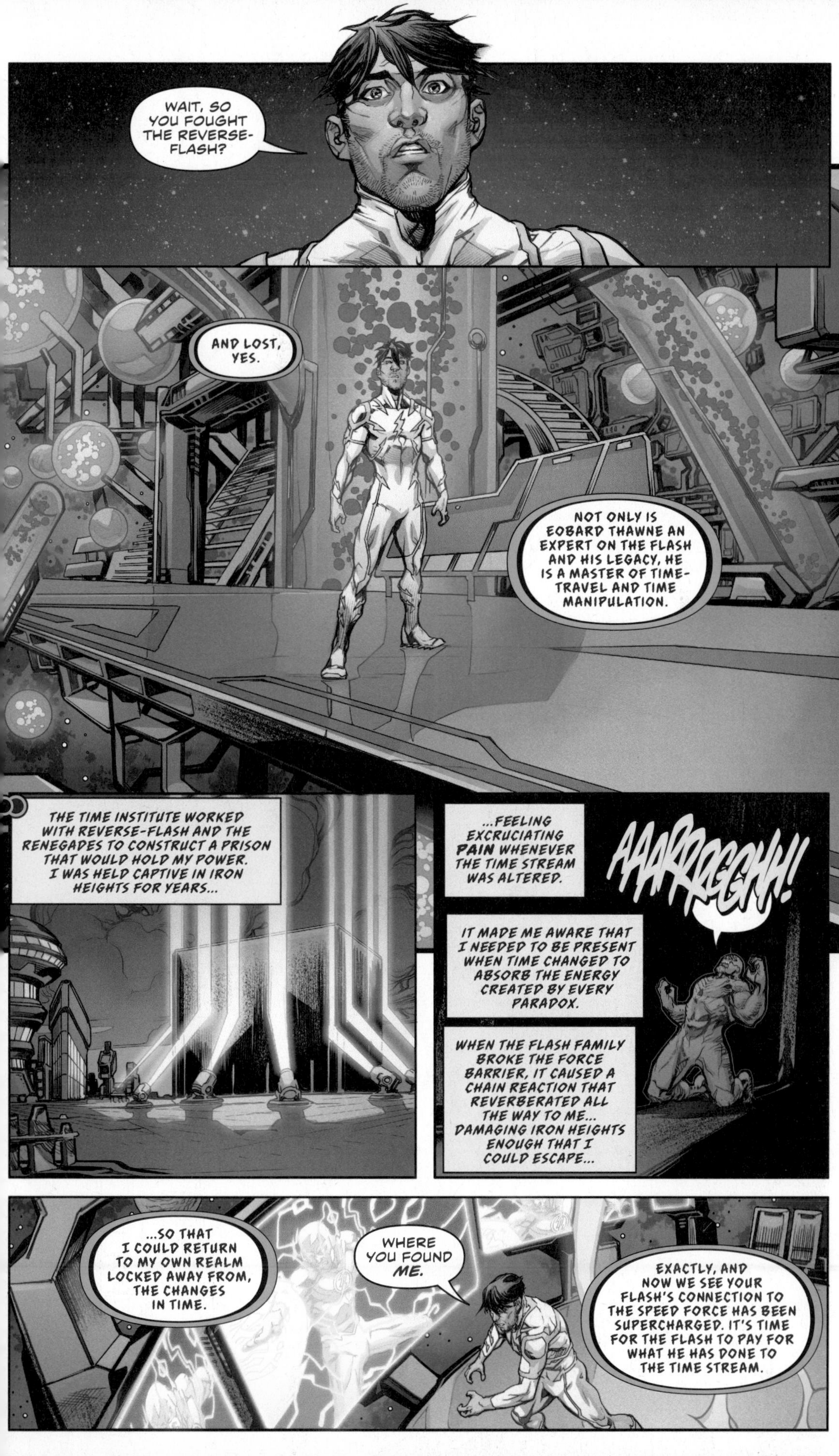
WAIT, SO YOU FOUGHT THE REVERSE-FLASH?
AND LOST, YES.
NOT ONLY IS EOBARD THAWNE AN EXPERT ON THE FLASH AND HIS LEGACY, HE IS A MASTER OF TIME-TRAVEL AND TIME MANIPULATION.
THE TIME INSTITUTE WORKED WITH REVERSE-FLASH AND THE RENEGADES TO CONSTRUCT A PRISON THAT WOULD HOLD MY POWER. I WAS HELD CAPTIVE IN IRON HEIGHTS FOR YEARS...
...FEELING EXCRUCIATING PAIN WHENEVER THE TIME STREAM WAS ALTERED.
AAARRGGHH!
IT MADE ME AWARE THAT I NEEDED TO BE PRESENT WHEN TIME CHANGED TO ABSORB THE ENERGY CREATED BY EVERY PARADOX.
WHEN THE FLASH FAMILY BROKE THE FORCE BARRIER, IT CAUSED A CHAIN REACTION THAT REVERBERATED ALL THE WAY TO ME... DAMAGING IRON HEIGHTS ENOUGH THAT I COULD ESCAPE...
...SO THAT I COULD RETURN TO MY OWN REALM LOCKED AWAY FROM, THE CHANGES IN TIME.
WHERE YOU FOUND ME.
EXACTLY, AND NOW WE SEE YOUR FLASH'S CONNECTION TO THE SPEED FORCE HAS BEEN SUPERCHARGED. IT'S TIME FOR THE FLASH TO PAY FOR WHAT HE HAS DONE TO THE TIME STREAM.

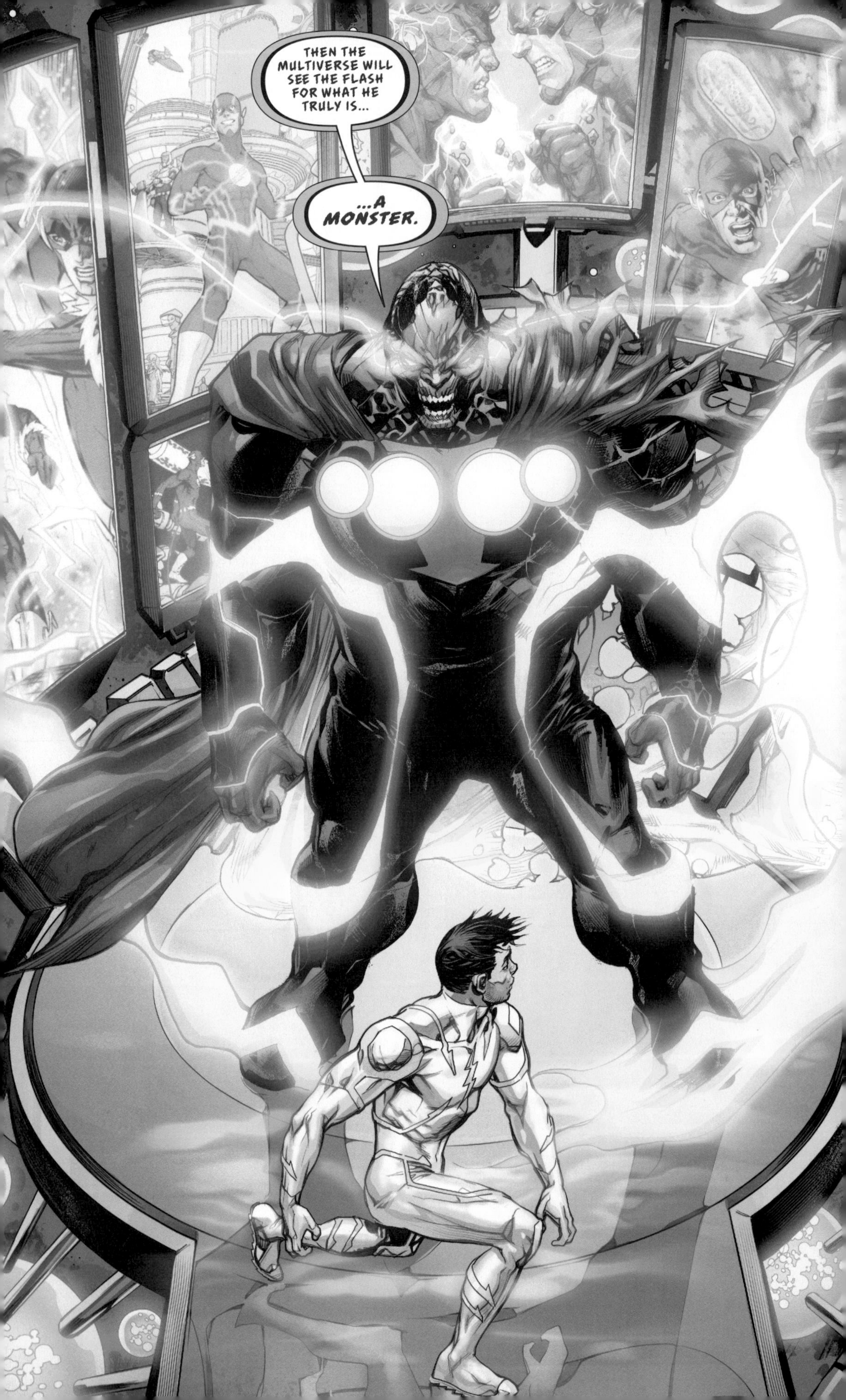
THEN THE MULTIVERSE WILL SEE THE FLASH FOR WHAT HE TRULY IS...
...A MONSTER.

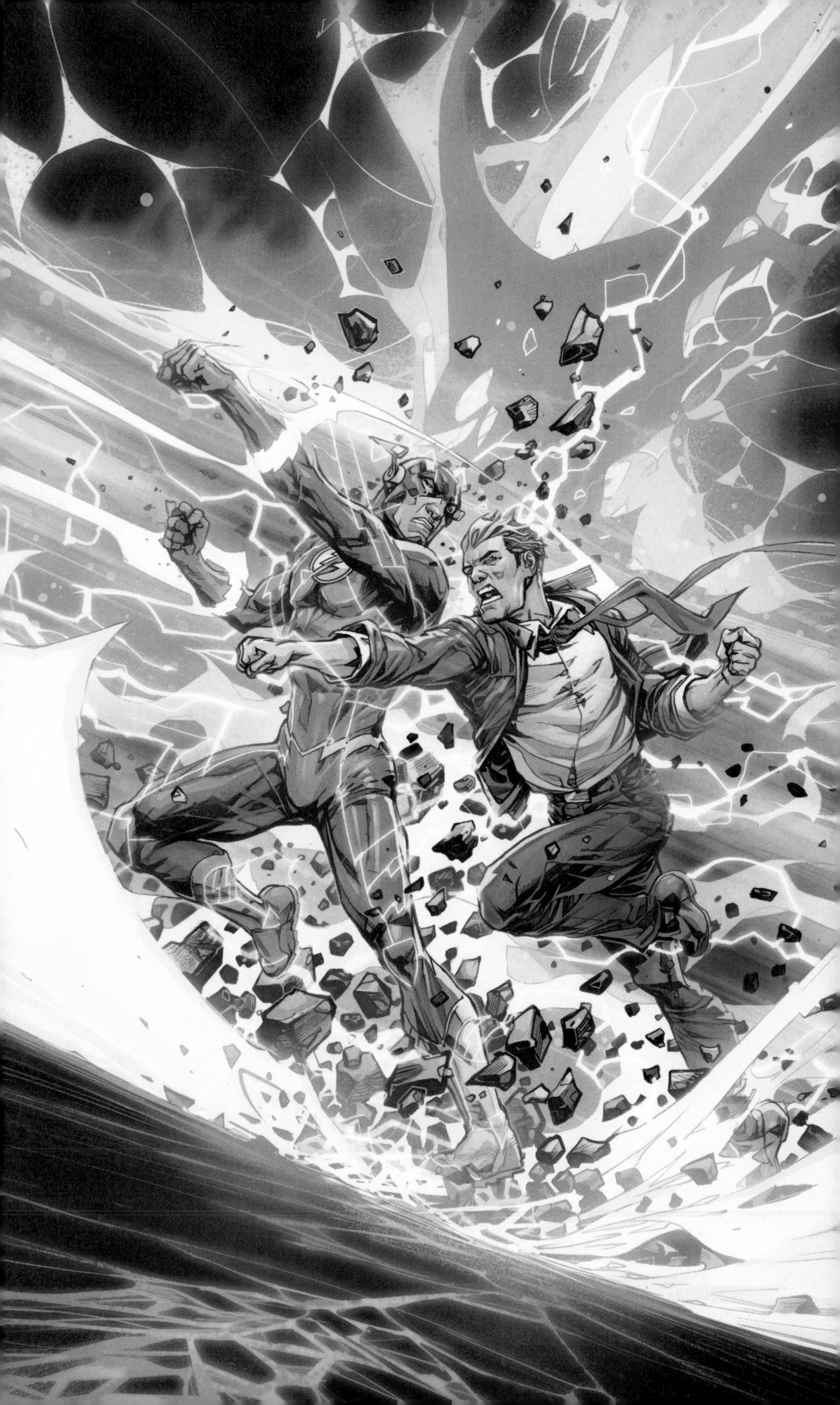

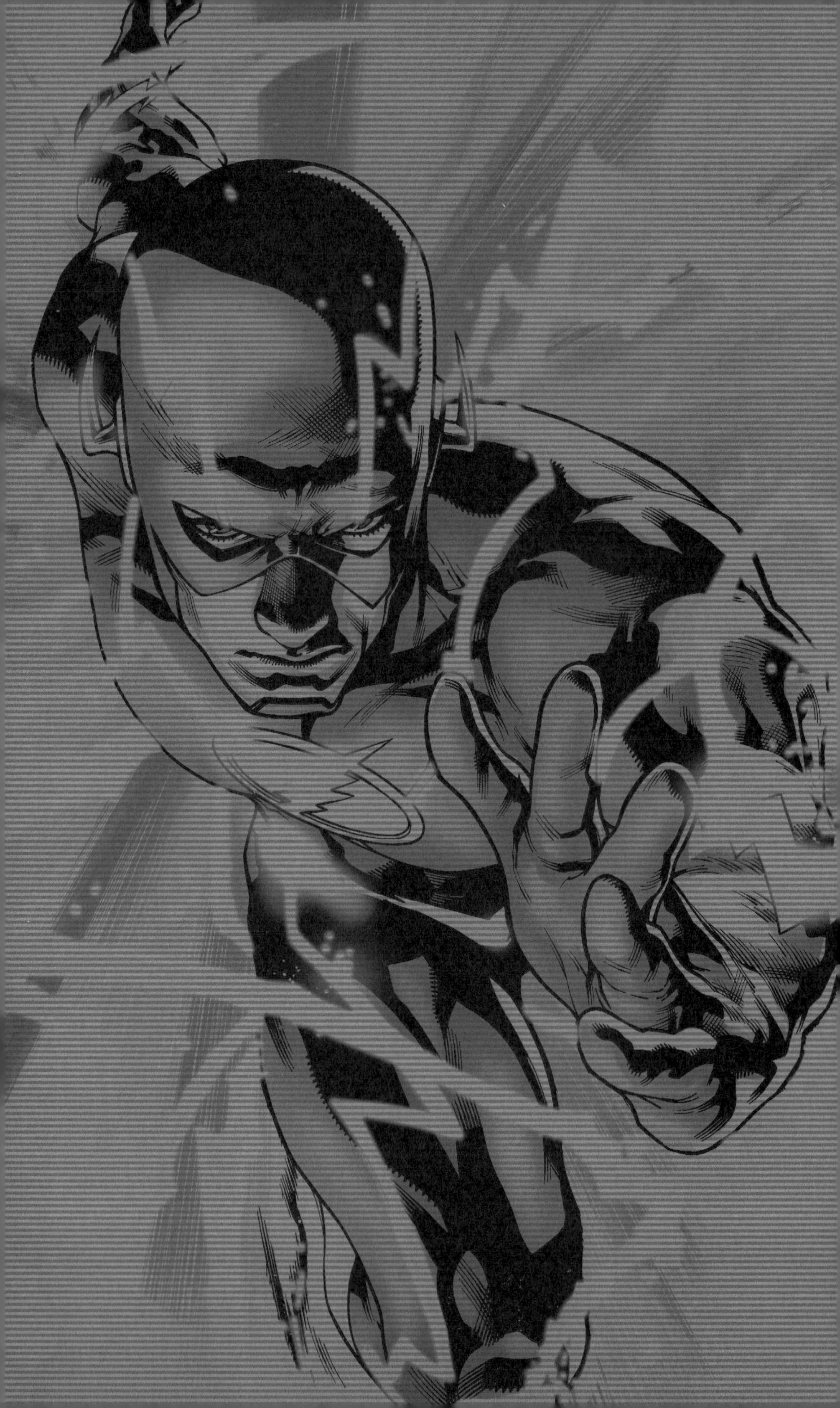

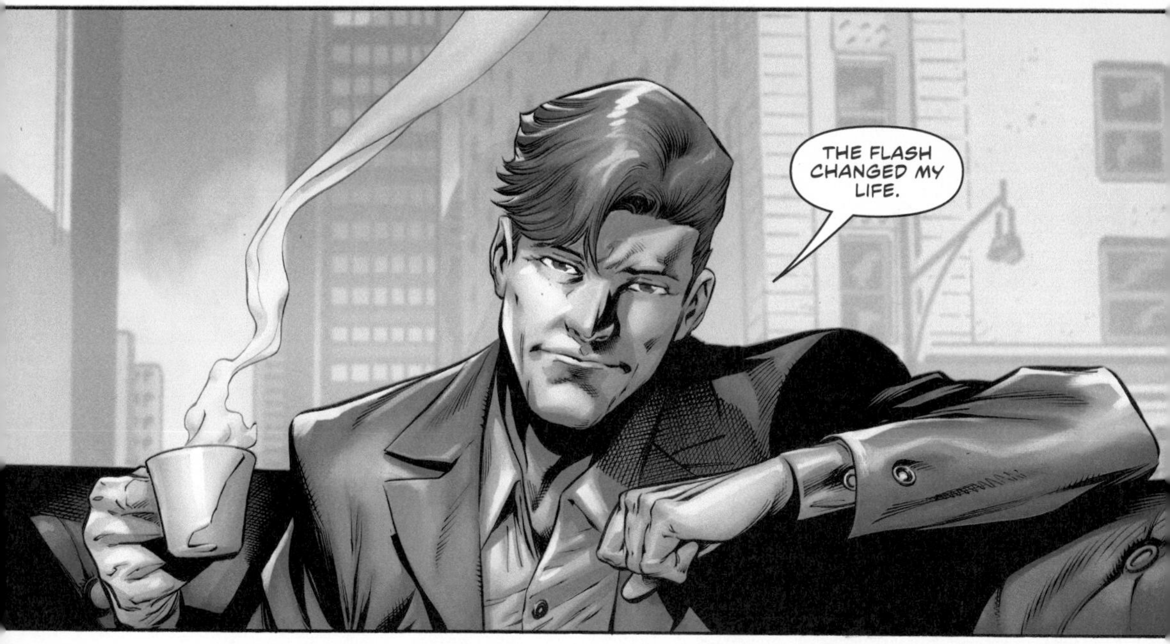
THE FLASH CHANGED MY LIFE.

THE FLASH AGE

PART ONE

JOSHUA WILLIAMSON WRITER
RAFA SANDOVAL & JORDI TARRAGONA (1-7,10-15,20-25,28-30)
STEPHEN SEGOVIA (8-9,16-19,26-27) ARTISTS
ARIF PRIANTO COLORS **STEVE WANDS** LETTERER

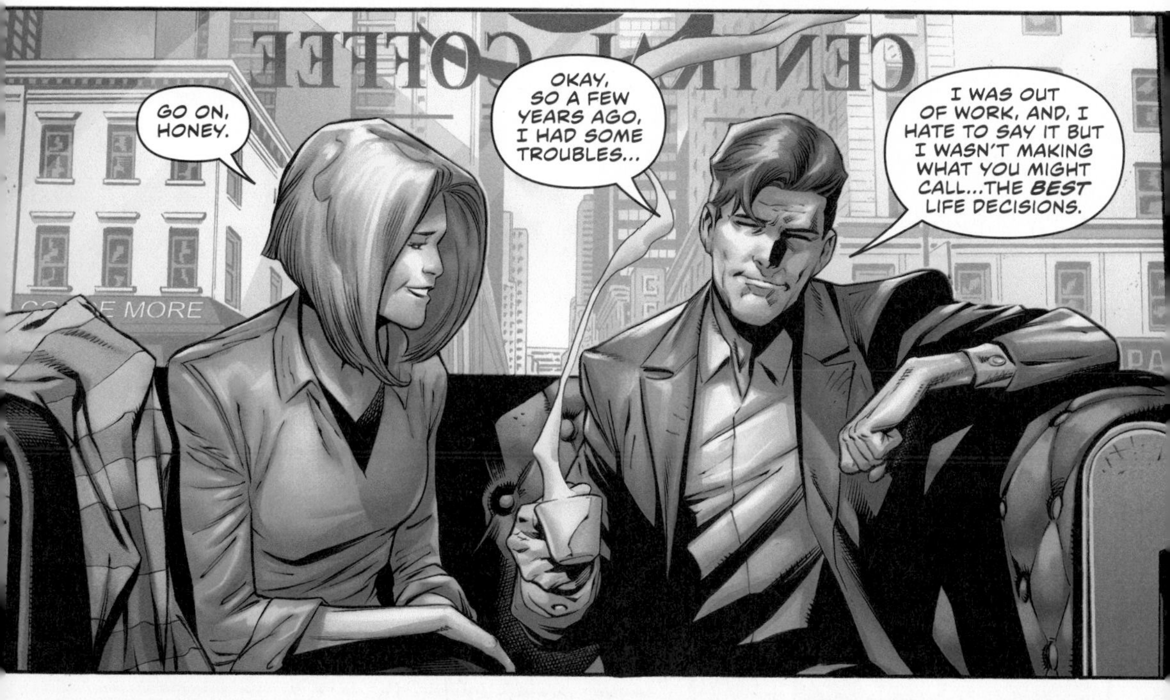
GO ON, HONEY.
OKAY, SO A FEW YEARS AGO, I HAD SOME TROUBLES...
I WAS OUT OF WORK, AND, I HATE TO SAY IT BUT I WASN'T MAKING WHAT YOU MIGHT CALL...THE *BEST* LIFE DECISIONS.

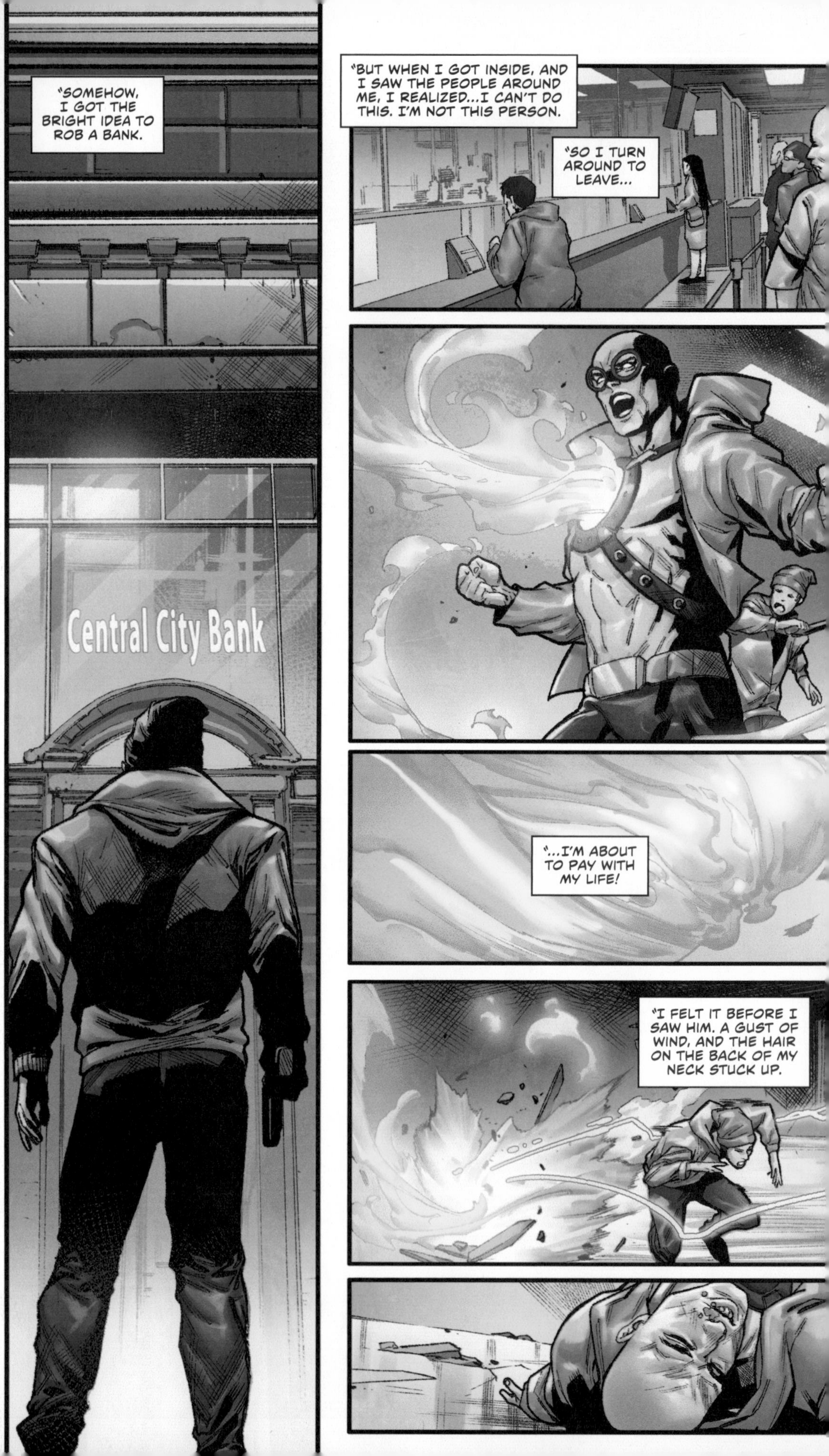
"SOMEHOW, I GOT THE BRIGHT IDEA TO ROB A BANK.
Central City Bank
"BUT WHEN I GOT INSIDE, AND I SAW THE PEOPLE AROUND ME, I REALIZED...I CAN'T DO THIS. I'M NOT THIS PERSON.
"SO I TURN AROUND TO LEAVE...
"...I'M ABOUT TO PAY WITH MY LIFE!
"I FELT IT BEFORE I SAW HIM. A GUST OF WIND, AND THE HAIR ON THE BACK OF MY NECK STUCK UP.

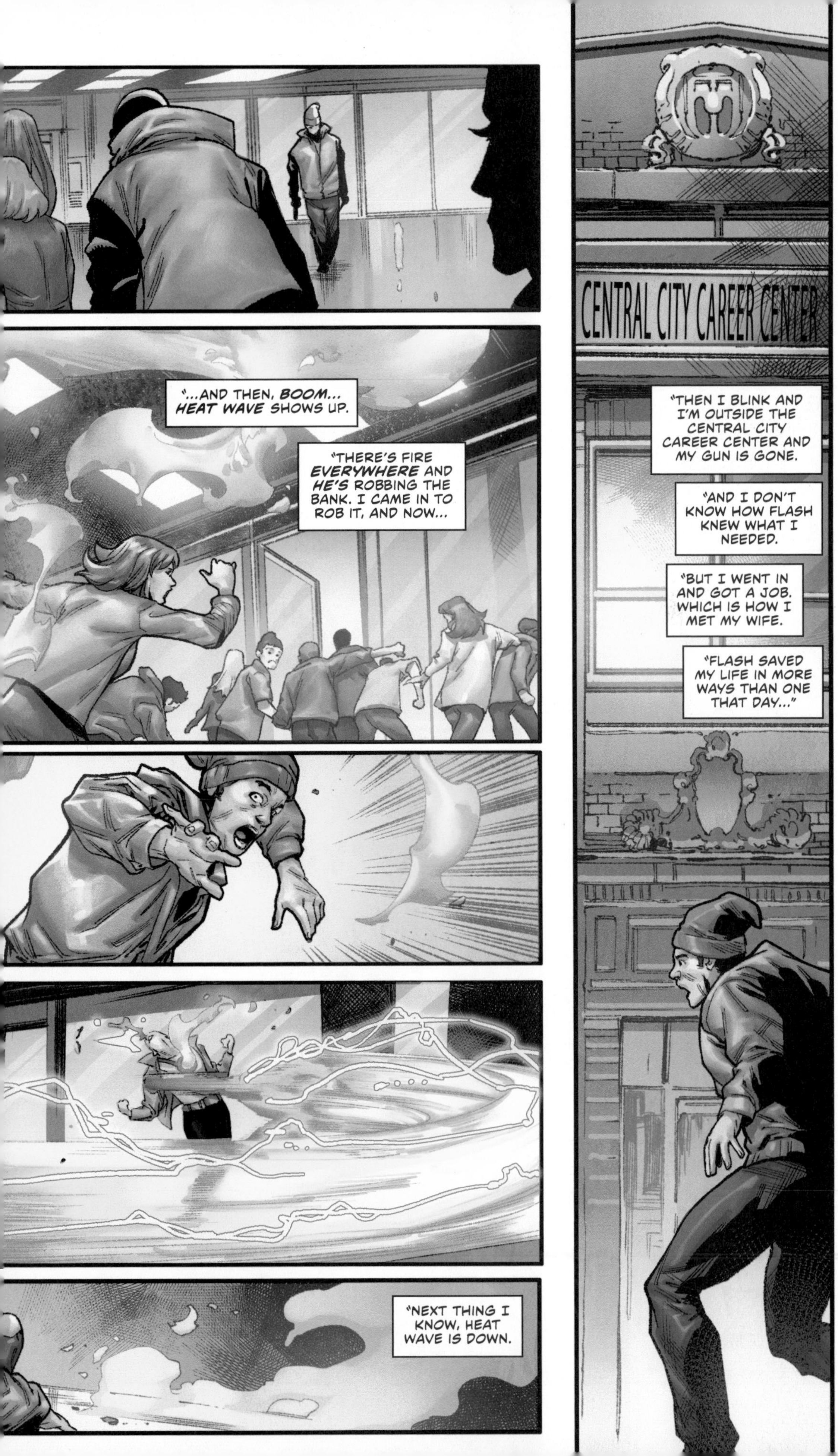
"...AND THEN, BOOM... HEAT WAVE SHOWS UP.
"THERE'S FIRE EVERYWHERE AND HE'S ROBBING THE BANK. I CAME IN TO ROB IT, AND NOW...
"NEXT THING I KNOW, HEAT WAVE IS DOWN.
CENTRAL CITY CAREER CENTER
"THEN I BLINK AND I'M OUTSIDE THE CENTRAL CITY CAREER CENTER AND MY GUN IS GONE.
"AND I DON'T KNOW HOW FLASH KNEW WHAT I NEEDED.
"BUT I WENT IN AND GOT A JOB. WHICH IS HOW I MET MY WIFE.
"FLASH SAVED MY LIFE IN MORE WAYS THAN ONE THAT DAY..."

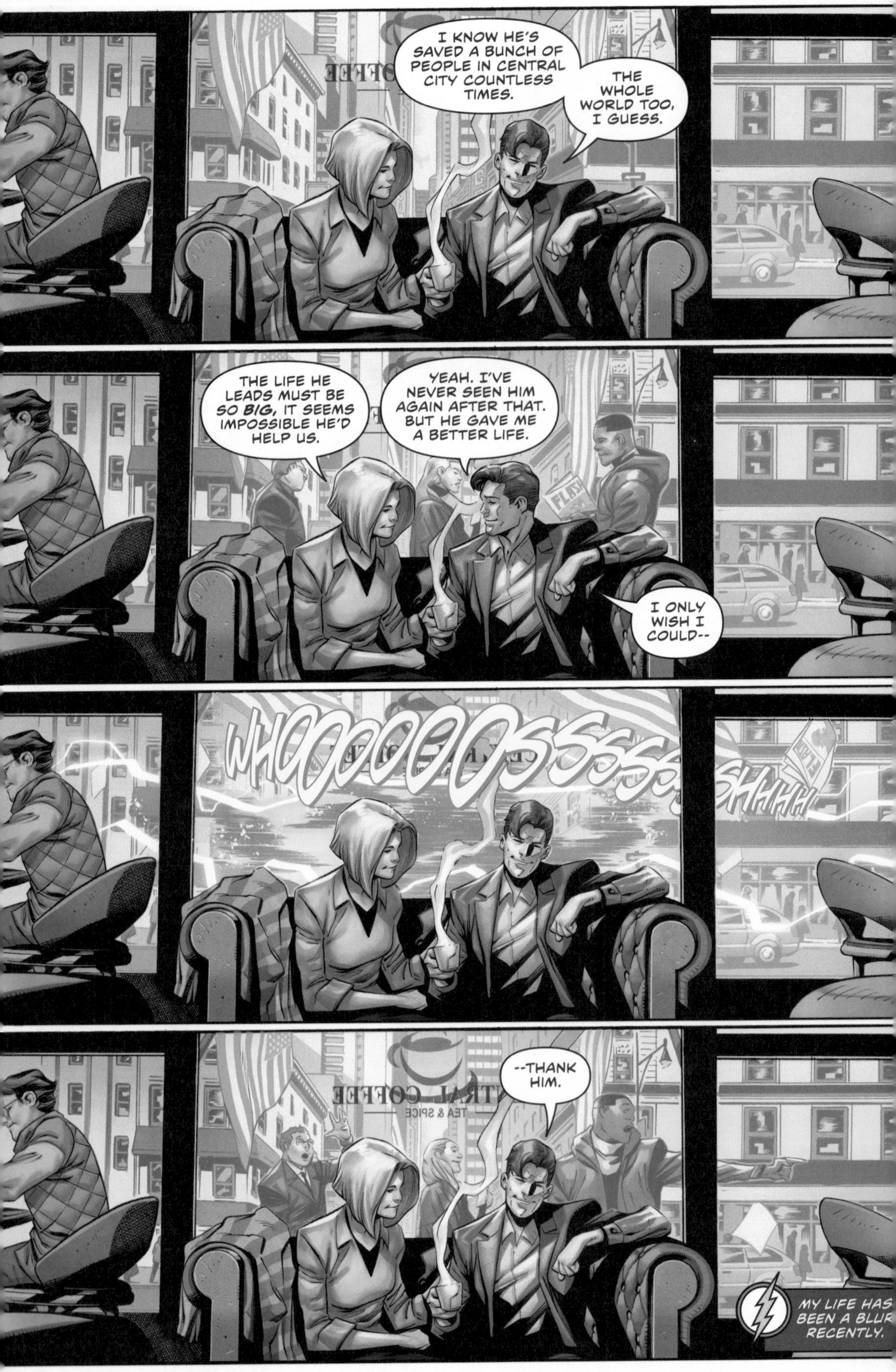
I KNOW HE'S SAVED A BUNCH OF PEOPLE IN CENTRAL CITY COUNTLESS TIMES.
THE WHOLE WORLD TOO, I GUESS.
THE LIFE HE LEADS MUST BE SO *BIG*, IT SEEMS IMPOSSIBLE HE'D HELP US.
YEAH. I'VE NEVER SEEN HIM AGAIN AFTER THAT. BUT HE GAVE ME A BETTER LIFE.
FLASH
I ONLY WISH I COULD--
WHOOOOOOOSSSSSSHHHHH
--THANK HIM.
CENTRAL COFFEE
TEA & SPICE
MY LIFE HAS BEEN A BLUR RECENTLY.

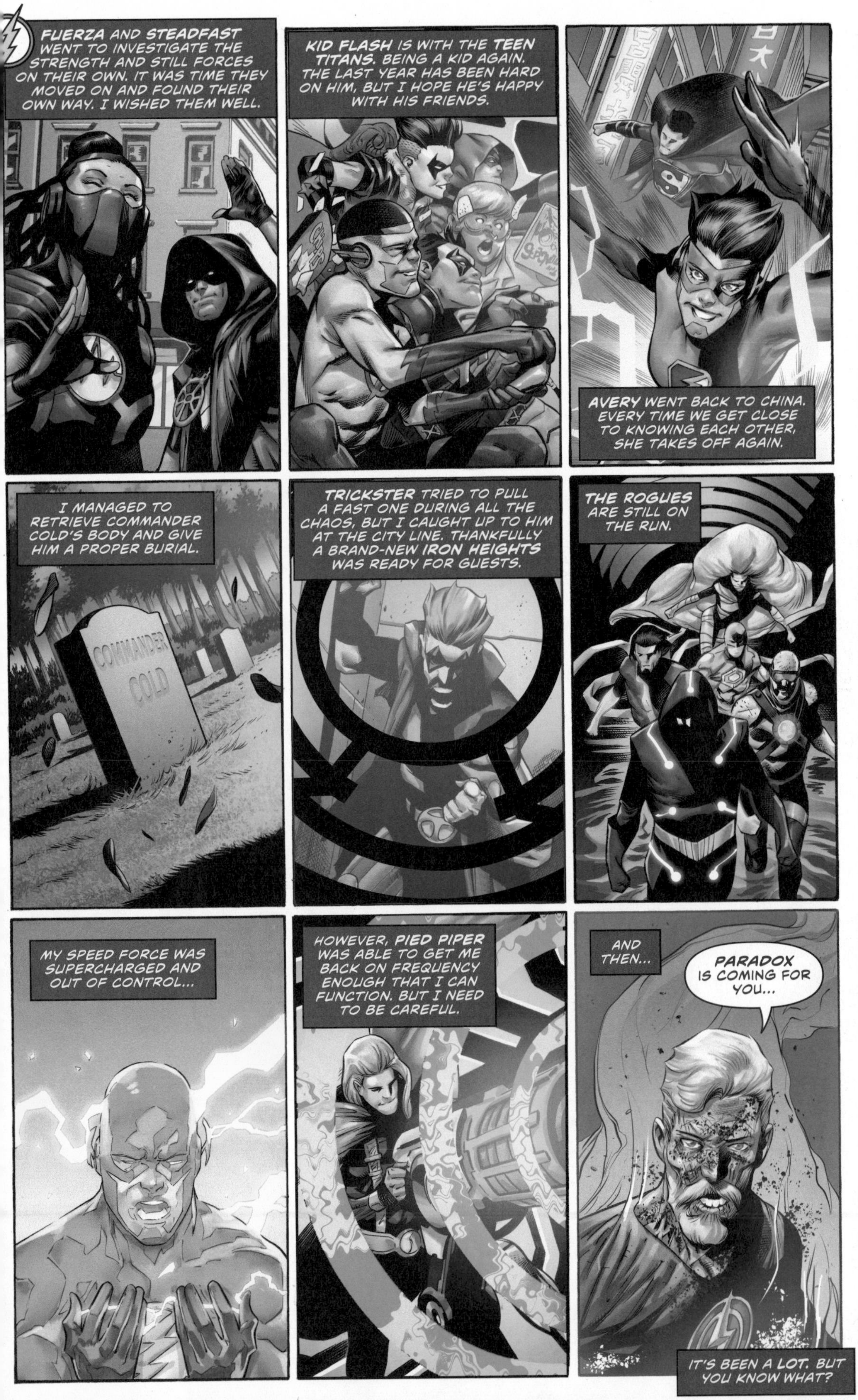
FUERZA AND STEADFAST WENT TO INVESTIGATE THE STRENGTH AND STILL FORCES ON THEIR OWN. IT WAS TIME THEY MOVED ON AND FOUND THEIR OWN WAY. I WISHED THEM WELL.
KID FLASH IS WITH THE TEEN TITANS. BEING A KID AGAIN. THE LAST YEAR HAS BEEN HARD ON HIM, BUT I HOPE HE'S HAPPY WITH HIS FRIENDS.
AVERY WENT BACK TO CHINA. EVERY TIME WE GET CLOSE TO KNOWING EACH OTHER, SHE TAKES OFF AGAIN.
I MANAGED TO RETRIEVE COMMANDER COLD'S BODY AND GIVE HIM A PROPER BURIAL.
COMMANDER COLD
TRICKSTER TRIED TO PULL A FAST ONE DURING ALL THE CHAOS, BUT I CAUGHT UP TO HIM AT THE CITY LINE. THANKFULLY A BRAND-NEW IRON HEIGHTS WAS READY FOR GUESTS.
THE ROGUES ARE STILL ON THE RUN.
MY SPEED FORCE WAS SUPERCHARGED AND OUT OF CONTROL...
HOWEVER, PIED PIPER WAS ABLE TO GET ME BACK ON FREQUENCY ENOUGH THAT I CAN FUNCTION. BUT I NEED TO BE CAREFUL.
AND THEN...
PARADOX IS COMING FOR YOU...
IT'S BEEN A LOT. BUT YOU KNOW WHAT?

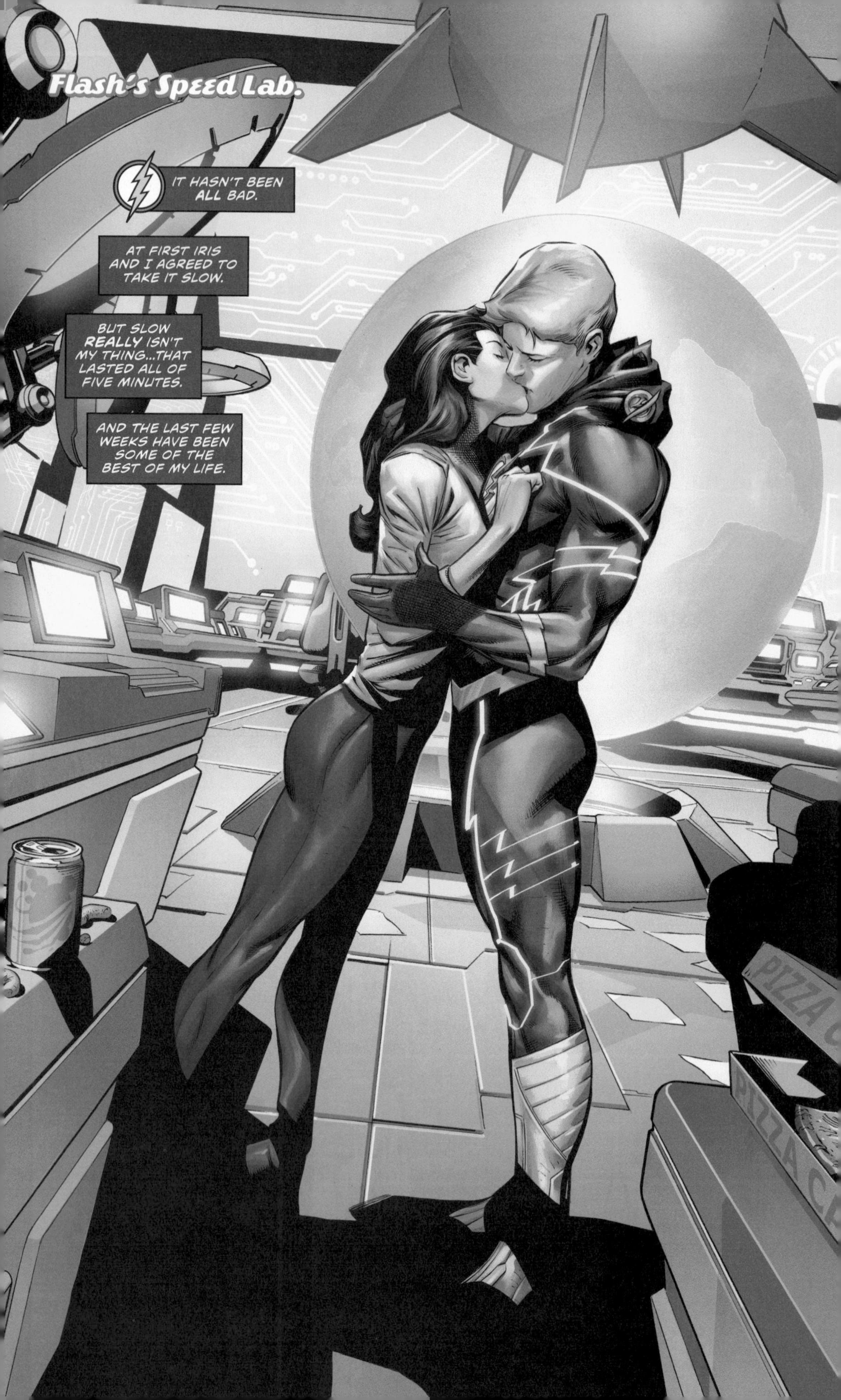

Flash's Speed Lab.
IT HASN'T BEEN ALL BAD.
AT FIRST IRIS AND I AGREED TO TAKE IT SLOW.
BUT SLOW REALLY ISN'T MY THING...THAT LASTED ALL OF FIVE MINUTES.
AND THE LAST FEW WEEKS HAVE BEEN SOME OF THE BEST OF MY LIFE.

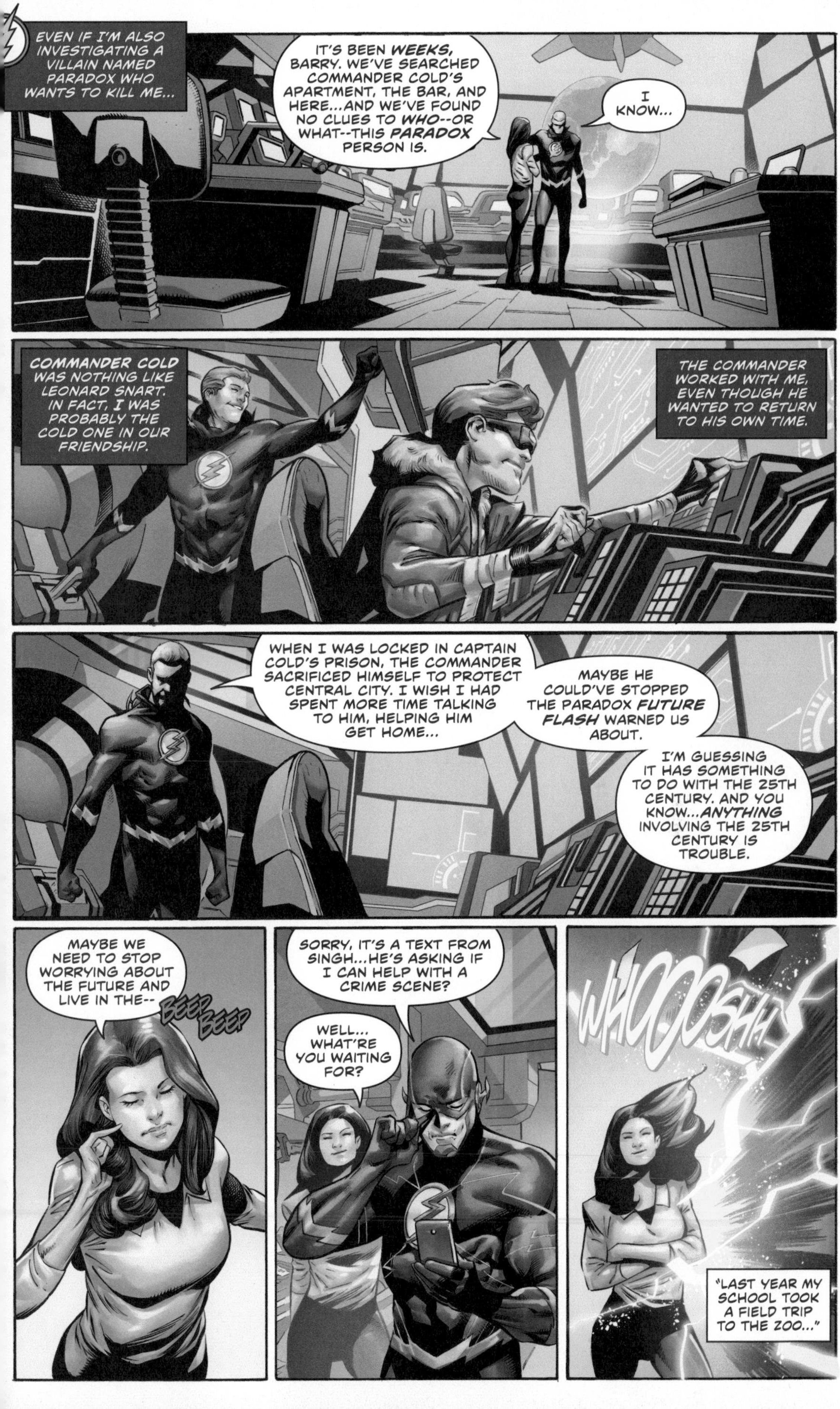
EVEN IF I'M ALSO INVESTIGATING A VILLAIN NAMED PARADOX WHO WANTS TO KILL ME...
IT'S BEEN WEEKS, BARRY. WE'VE SEARCHED COMMANDER COLD'S APARTMENT, THE BAR, AND HERE...AND WE'VE FOUND NO CLUES TO WHO--OR WHAT--THIS PARADOX PERSON IS.
I KNOW...
COMMANDER COLD WAS NOTHING LIKE LEONARD SNART. IN FACT, I WAS PROBABLY THE COLD ONE IN OUR FRIENDSHIP.
THE COMMANDER WORKED WITH ME, EVEN THOUGH HE WANTED TO RETURN TO HIS OWN TIME.
WHEN I WAS LOCKED IN CAPTAIN COLD'S PRISON, THE COMMANDER SACRIFICED HIMSELF TO PROTECT CENTRAL CITY. I WISH I HAD SPENT MORE TIME TALKING TO HIM, HELPING HIM GET HOME...
MAYBE HE COULD'VE STOPPED THE PARADOX FUTURE FLASH WARNED US ABOUT.
I'M GUESSING IT HAS SOMETHING TO DO WITH THE 25TH CENTURY. AND YOU KNOW...ANYTHING INVOLVING THE 25TH CENTURY IS TROUBLE.
MAYBE WE NEED TO STOP WORRYING ABOUT THE FUTURE AND LIVE IN THE--
BEEP BEEP
SORRY, IT'S A TEXT FROM SINGH...HE'S ASKING IF I CAN HELP WITH A CRIME SCENE?
WELL... WHAT'RE YOU WAITING FOR?
WHOOOSHH
"LAST YEAR MY SCHOOL TOOK A FIELD TRIP TO THE ZOO..."

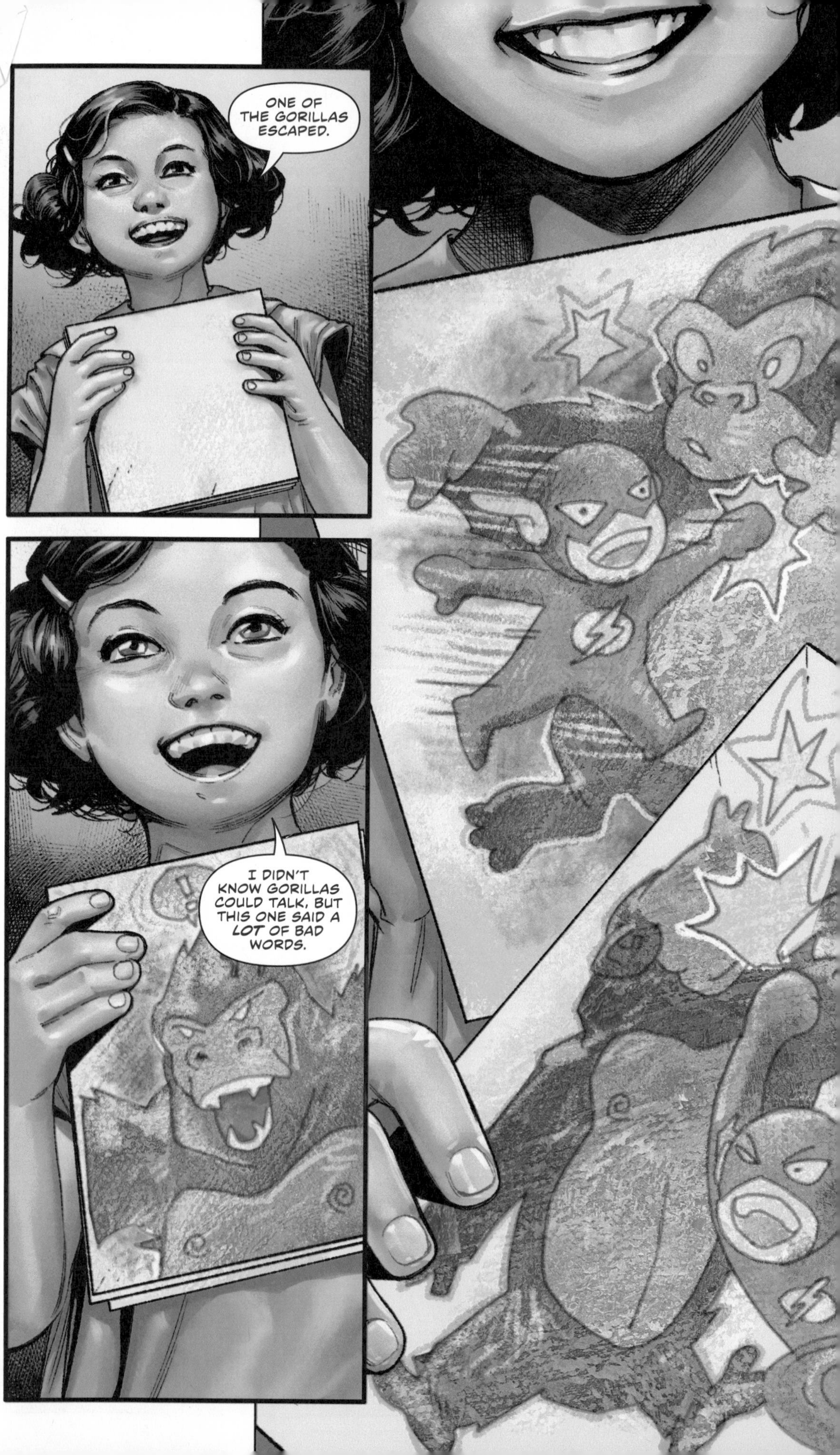
ONE OF THE GORILLAS ESCAPED.
I DIDN'T KNOW GORILLAS COULD TALK, BUT THIS ONE SAID A *LOT* OF BAD WORDS.

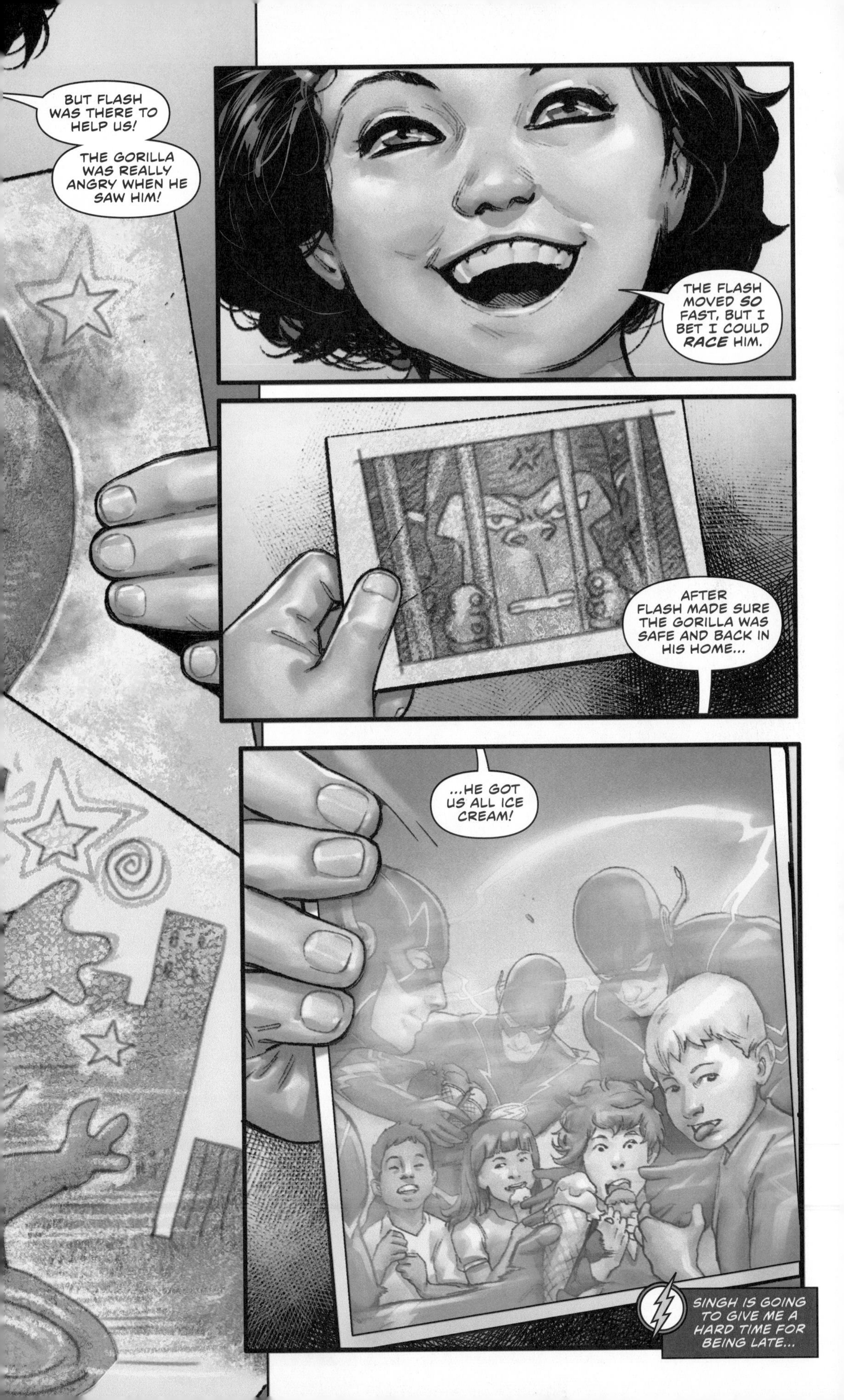
BUT FLASH WAS THERE TO HELP US!
THE GORILLA WAS REALLY ANGRY WHEN HE SAW HIM!
THE FLASH MOVED SO FAST, BUT I BET I COULD RACE HIM.
AFTER FLASH MADE SURE THE GORILLA WAS SAFE AND BACK IN HIS HOME...
...HE GOT US ALL ICE CREAM!
SINGH IS GOING TO GIVE ME A HARD TIME FOR BEING LATE...

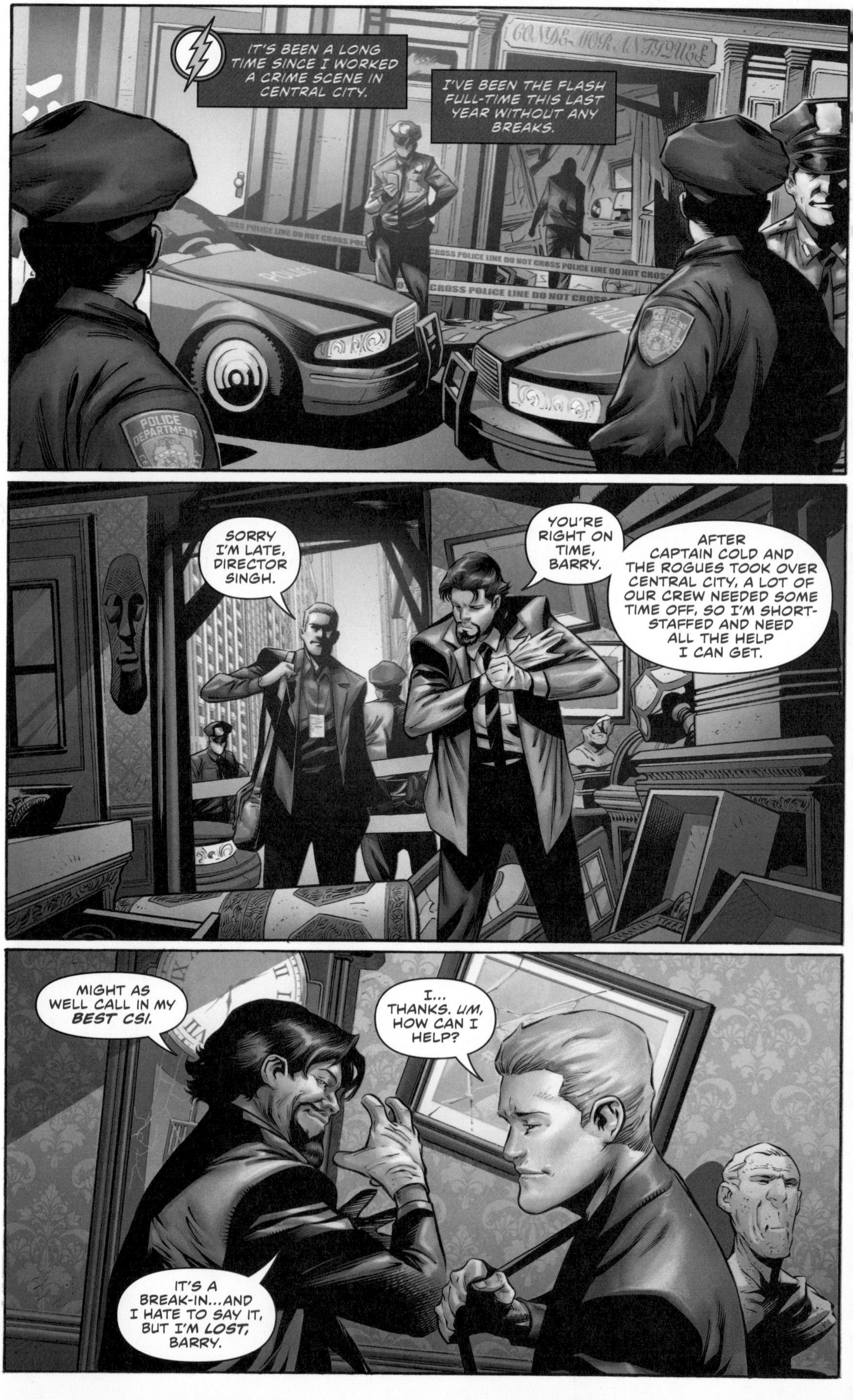

IT'S BEEN A LONG TIME SINCE I WORKED A CRIME SCENE IN CENTRAL CITY.
I'VE BEEN THE FLASH FULL-TIME THIS LAST YEAR WITHOUT ANY BREAKS.
POLICE LINE DO NOT CROSS POLICE LINE DO NOT CROSS
SORRY I'M LATE, DIRECTOR SINGH.
YOU'RE RIGHT ON TIME, BARRY.
AFTER CAPTAIN COLD AND THE ROGUES TOOK OVER CENTRAL CITY, A LOT OF OUR CREW NEEDED SOME TIME OFF, SO I'M SHORT-STAFFED AND NEED ALL THE HELP I CAN GET.
MIGHT AS WELL CALL IN MY *BEST CSI.*
I... THANKS. *UM,* HOW CAN I HELP?
IT'S A BREAK-IN...AND I HATE TO SAY IT, BUT I'M *LOST,* BARRY.

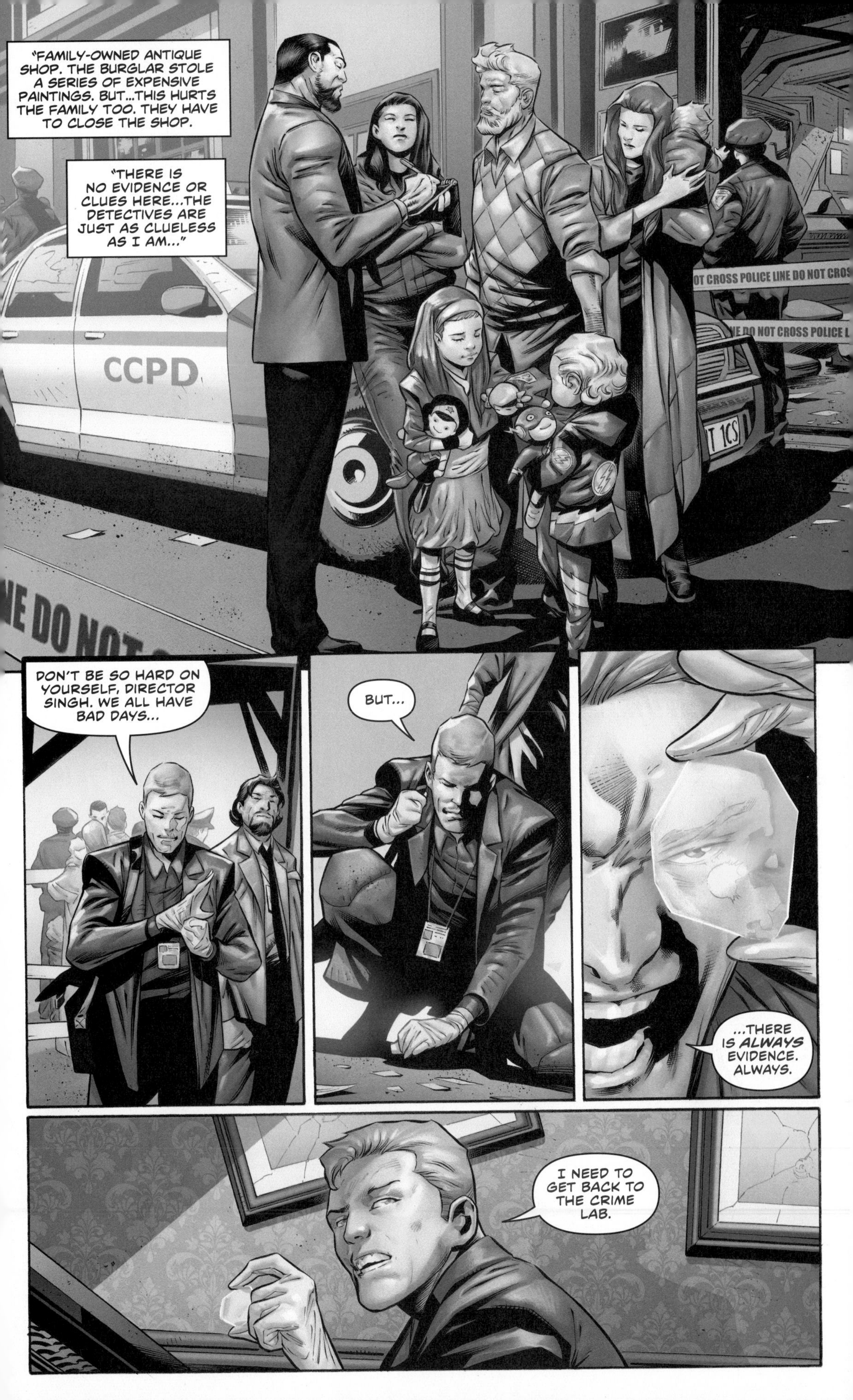
"FAMILY-OWNED ANTIQUE SHOP. THE BURGLAR STOLE A SERIES OF EXPENSIVE PAINTINGS. BUT...THIS HURTS THE FAMILY TOO. THEY HAVE TO CLOSE THE SHOP.
"THERE IS NO EVIDENCE OR CLUES HERE...THE DETECTIVES ARE JUST AS CLUELESS AS I AM..."
CCPD
DON'T BE SO HARD ON YOURSELF, DIRECTOR SINGH. WE ALL HAVE BAD DAYS...
BUT...
...THERE IS *ALWAYS* EVIDENCE. ALWAYS.
I NEED TO GET BACK TO THE CRIME LAB.

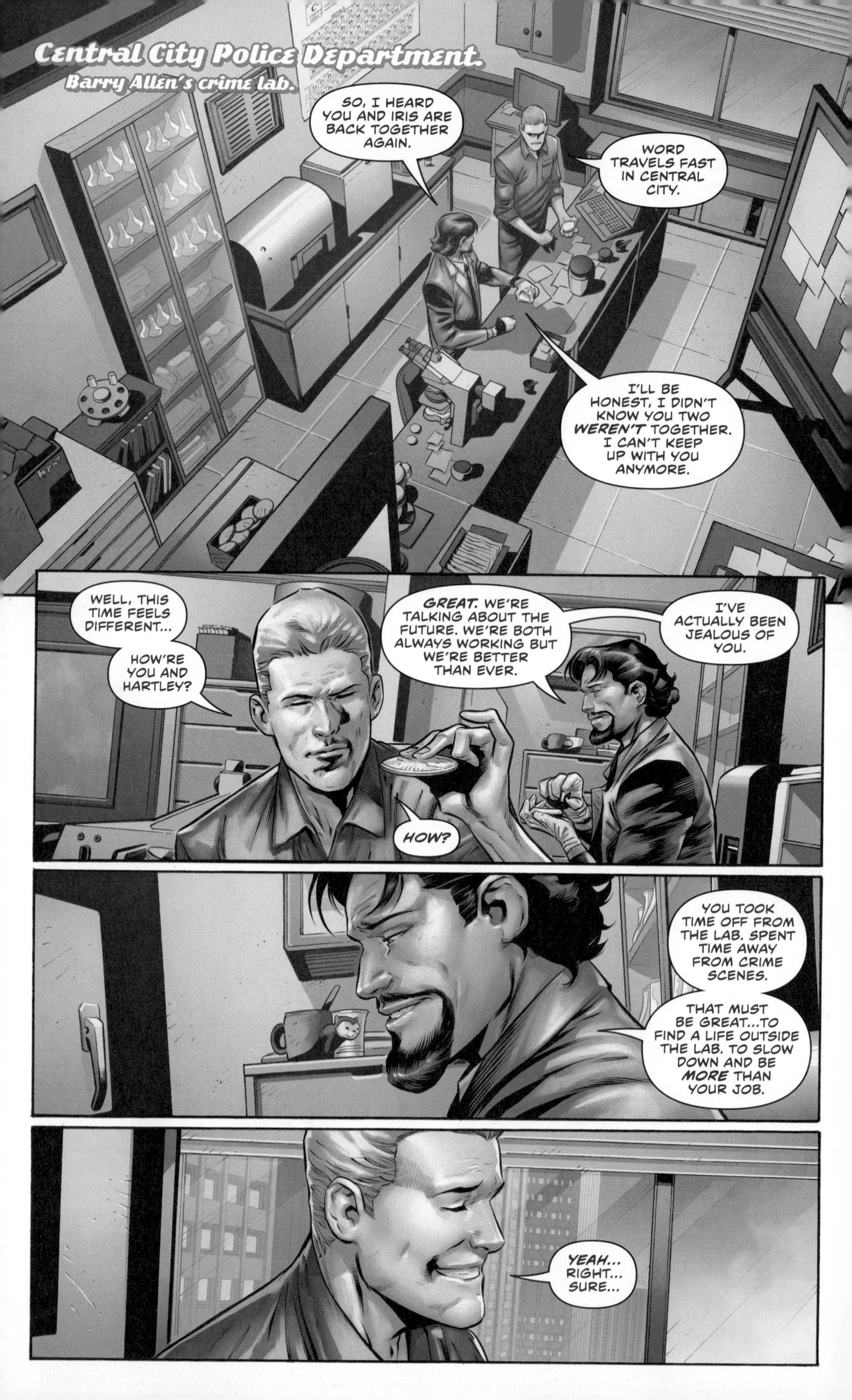

Central City Police Department.
Barry Allen's crime lab.
SO, I HEARD YOU AND IRIS ARE BACK TOGETHER AGAIN.
WORD TRAVELS FAST IN CENTRAL CITY.
I'LL BE HONEST, I DIDN'T KNOW YOU TWO WEREN'T TOGETHER. I CAN'T KEEP UP WITH YOU ANYMORE.
WELL, THIS TIME FEELS DIFFERENT...
HOW'RE YOU AND HARTLEY?
GREAT. WE'RE TALKING ABOUT THE FUTURE. WE'RE BOTH ALWAYS WORKING BUT WE'RE BETTER THAN EVER.
I'VE ACTUALLY BEEN JEALOUS OF YOU.
HOW?
YOU TOOK TIME OFF FROM THE LAB. SPENT TIME AWAY FROM CRIME SCENES.
THAT MUST BE GREAT...TO FIND A LIFE OUTSIDE THE LAB. TO SLOW DOWN AND BE MORE THAN YOUR JOB.
YEAH... RIGHT... SURE...

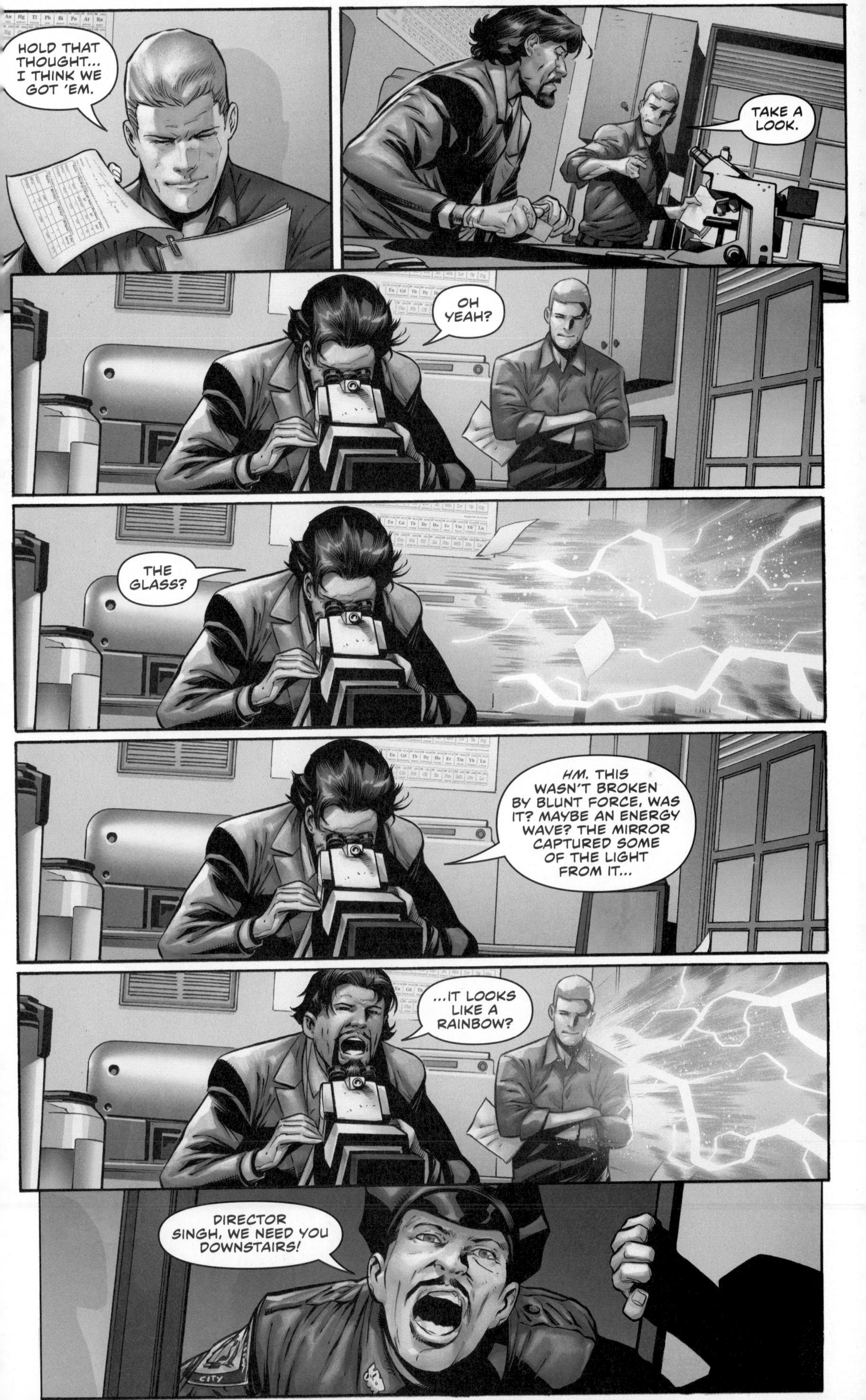
HOLD THAT THOUGHT... I THINK WE GOT 'EM.
TAKE A LOOK.
OH YEAH?
THE GLASS?
HM. THIS WASN'T BROKEN BY BLUNT FORCE, WAS IT? MAYBE AN ENERGY WAVE? THE MIRROR CAPTURED SOME OF THE LIGHT FROM IT...
...IT LOOKS LIKE A RAINBOW?
DIRECTOR SINGH, WE NEED YOU DOWNSTAIRS!

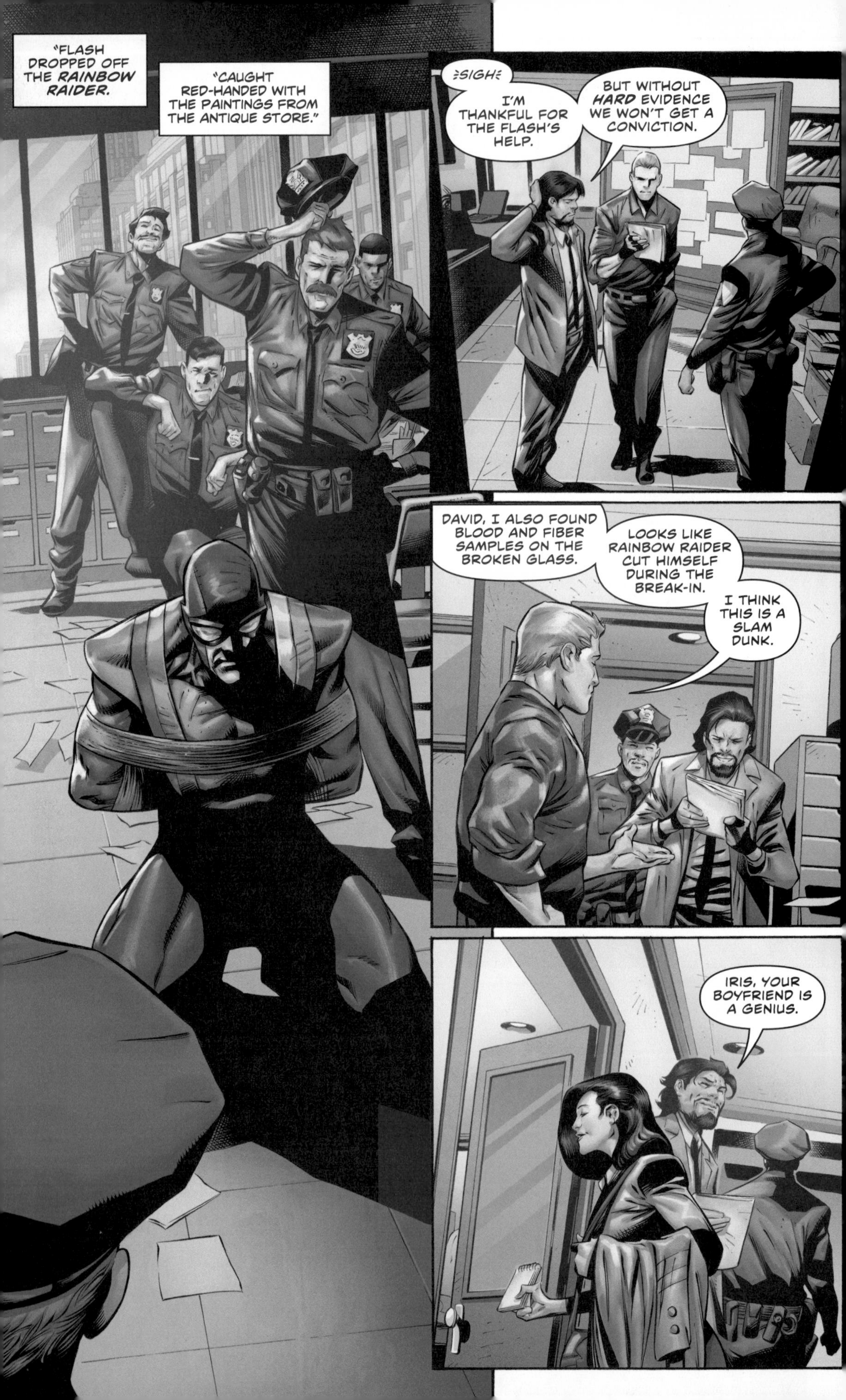
"FLASH DROPPED OFF THE *RAINBOW RAIDER*.
"CAUGHT RED-HANDED WITH THE PAINTINGS FROM THE ANTIQUE STORE."
SIGH
I'M THANKFUL FOR THE FLASH'S HELP.
BUT WITHOUT *HARD* EVIDENCE WE WON'T GET A CONVICTION.
DAVID, I ALSO FOUND BLOOD AND FIBER SAMPLES ON THE BROKEN GLASS.
LOOKS LIKE RAINBOW RAIDER CUT HIMSELF DURING THE BREAK-IN.
I THINK THIS IS A SLAM DUNK.
IRIS, YOUR BOYFRIEND IS A GENIUS.

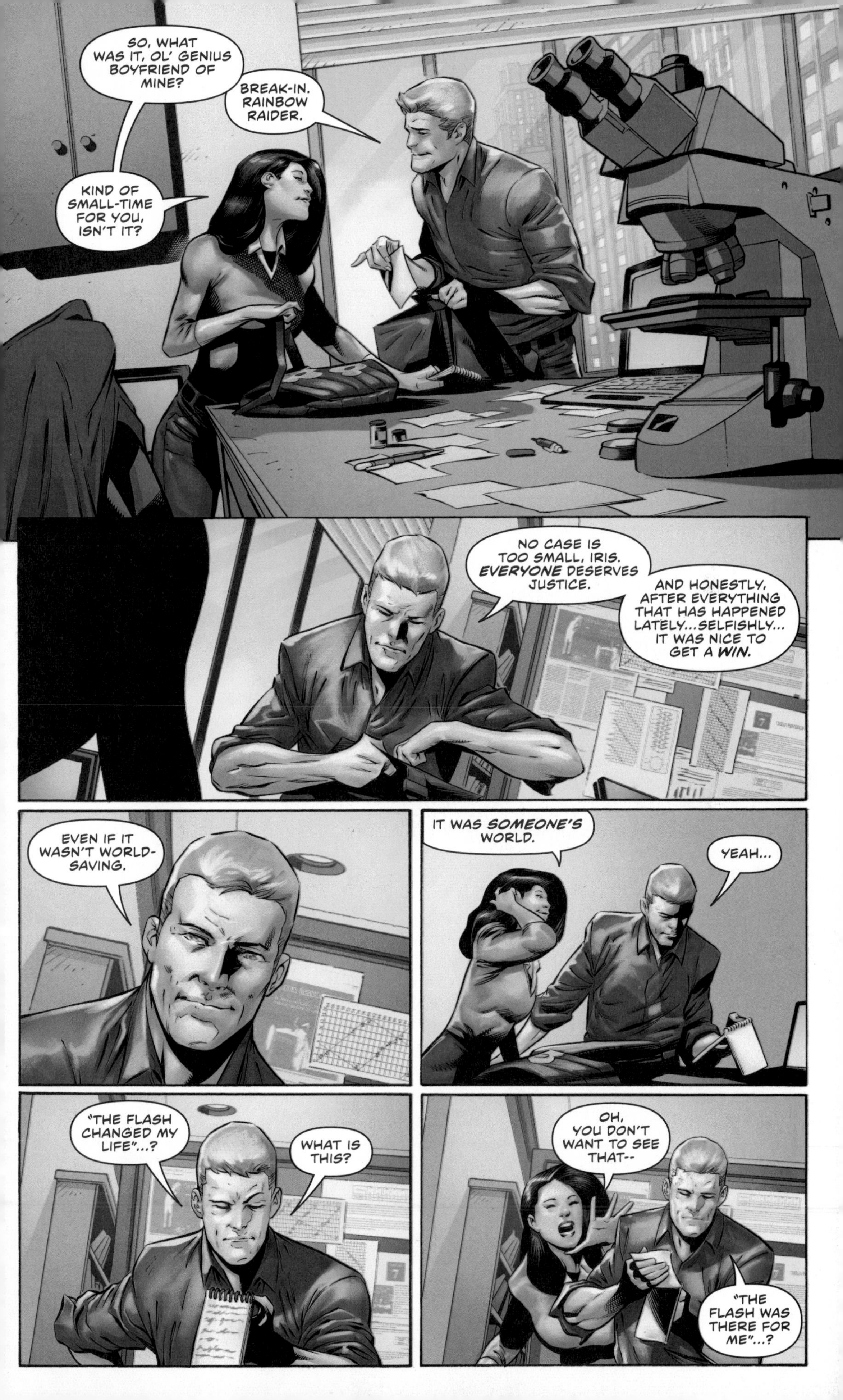
SO, WHAT WAS IT, OL' GENIUS BOYFRIEND OF MINE?
BREAK-IN. RAINBOW RAIDER.
KIND OF SMALL-TIME FOR YOU, ISN'T IT?
NO CASE IS TOO SMALL, IRIS. *EVERYONE* DESERVES JUSTICE.
AND HONESTLY, AFTER EVERYTHING THAT HAS HAPPENED LATELY...SELFISHLY... IT WAS NICE TO GET A *WIN.*
EVEN IF IT WASN'T WORLD-SAVING.
IT WAS *SOMEONE'S* WORLD.
YEAH...
"THE FLASH CHANGED MY LIFE"...?
WHAT IS THIS?
OH, YOU DON'T WANT TO SEE THAT--
"THE FLASH WAS THERE FOR ME"...?

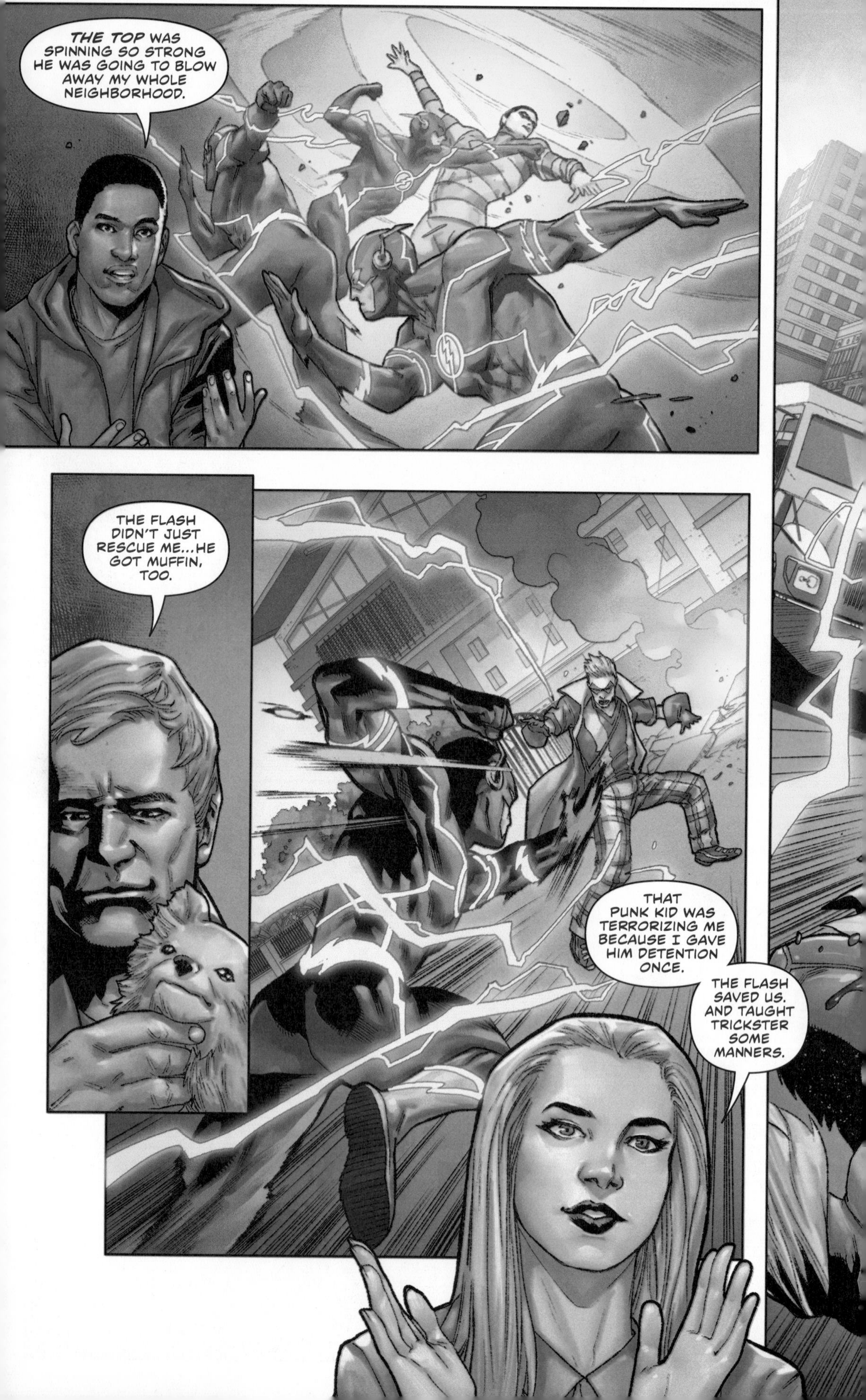
THE TOP WAS SPINNING SO STRONG HE WAS GOING TO BLOW AWAY MY WHOLE NEIGHBORHOOD.
THE FLASH DIDN'T JUST RESCUE ME...HE GOT MUFFIN, TOO.
THAT PUNK KID WAS TERRORIZING ME BECAUSE I GAVE HIM DETENTION ONCE.
THE FLASH SAVED US. AND TAUGHT TRICKSTER SOME MANNERS.

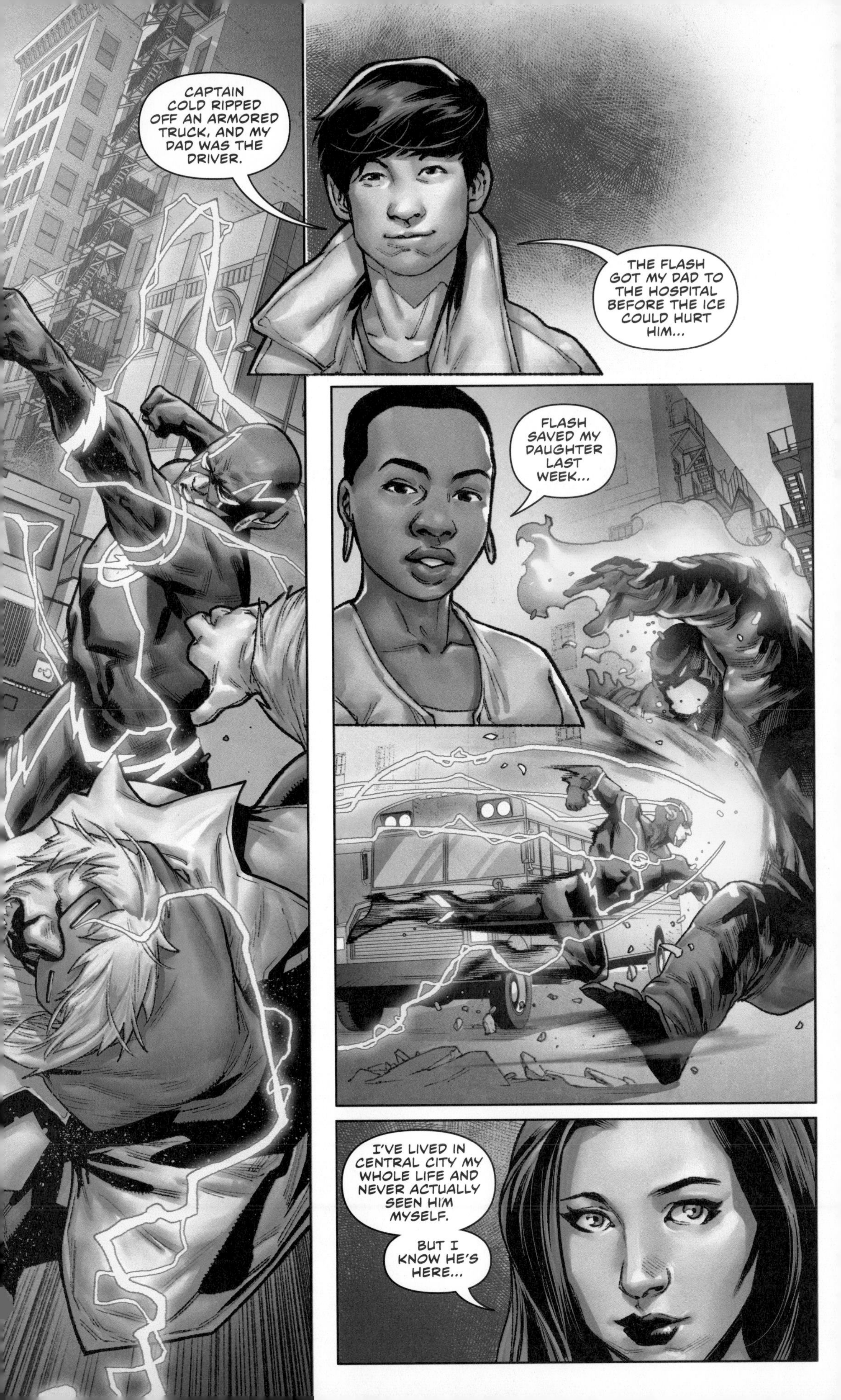
CAPTAIN COLD RIPPED OFF AN ARMORED TRUCK, AND MY DAD WAS THE DRIVER.
THE FLASH GOT MY DAD TO THE HOSPITAL BEFORE THE ICE COULD HURT HIM...
FLASH SAVED MY DAUGHTER LAST WEEK...
I'VE LIVED IN CENTRAL CITY MY WHOLE LIFE AND NEVER ACTUALLY SEEN HIM MYSELF.
BUT I KNOW HE'S HERE...

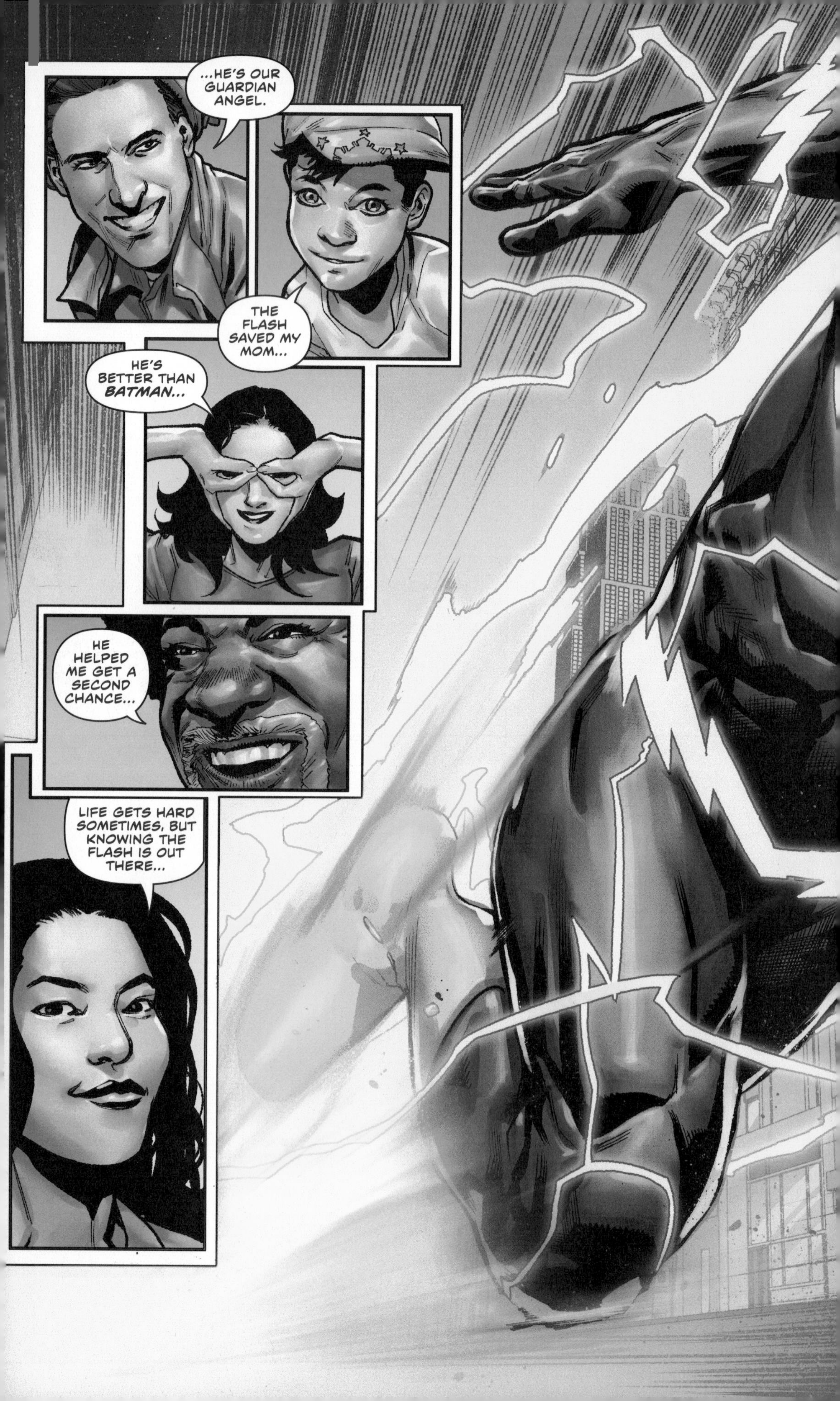
...HE'S OUR GUARDIAN ANGEL.
THE FLASH SAVED MY MOM...
HE'S BETTER THAN *BATMAN*...
HE HELPED ME GET A SECOND CHANCE...
LIFE GETS HARD SOMETIMES, BUT KNOWING THE FLASH IS OUT THERE...

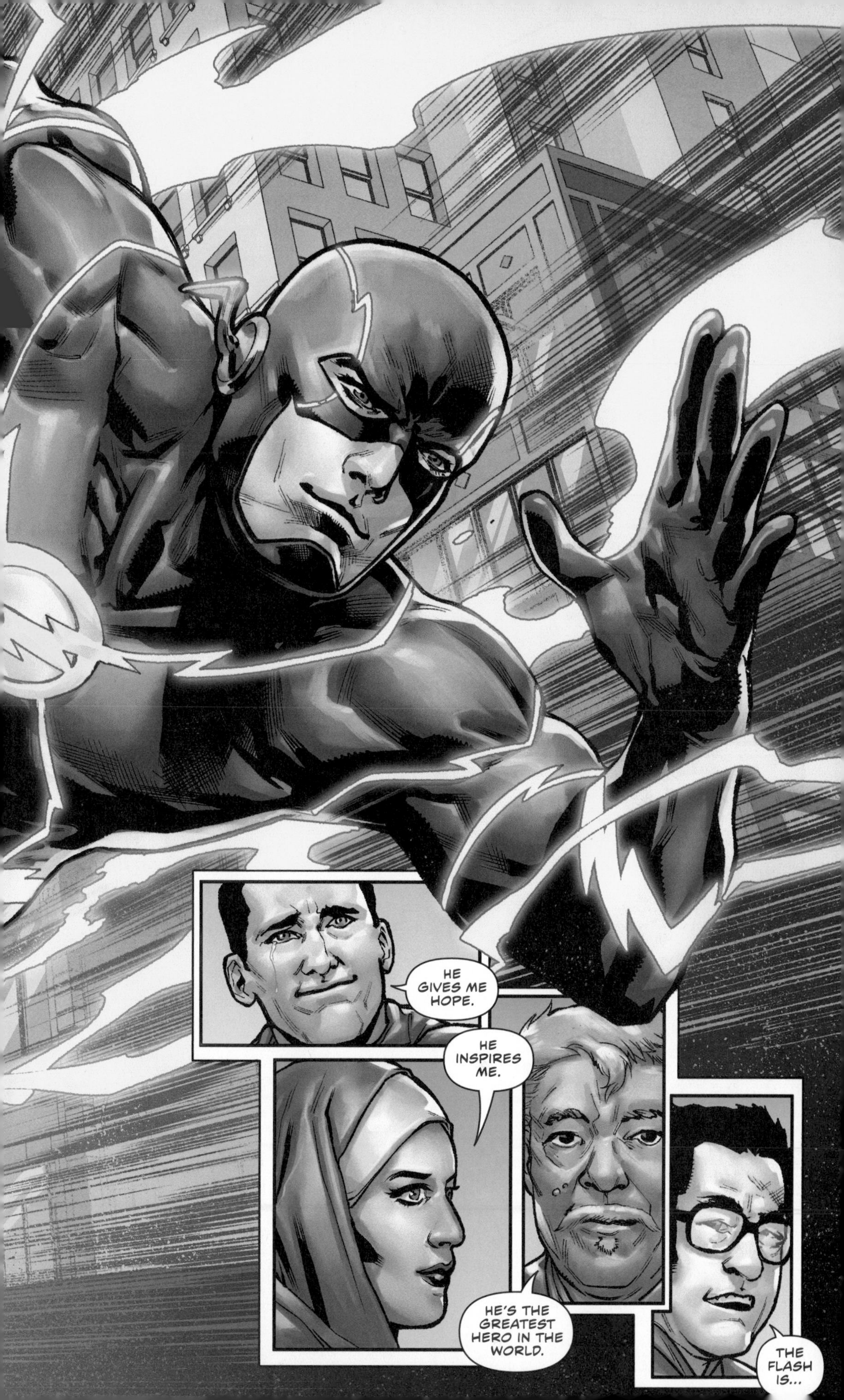

HE GIVES ME HOPE.
HE INSPIRES ME.
HE'S THE GREATEST HERO IN THE WORLD.
THE FLASH IS...

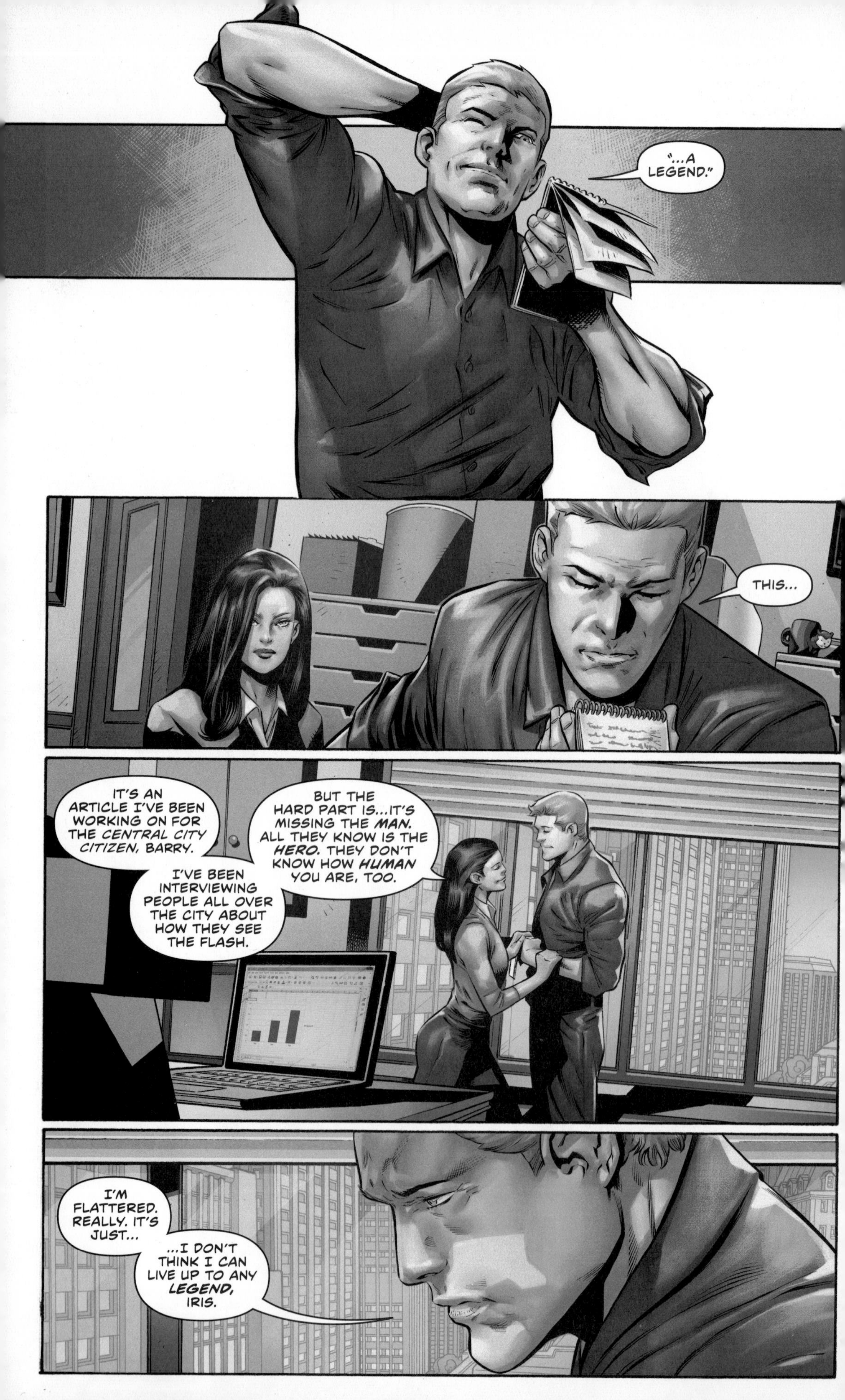

"...A LEGEND."
THIS...
IT'S AN ARTICLE I'VE BEEN WORKING ON FOR THE *CENTRAL CITY CITIZEN*, BARRY.
I'VE BEEN INTERVIEWING PEOPLE ALL OVER THE CITY ABOUT HOW THEY SEE THE FLASH.
BUT THE HARD PART IS...IT'S MISSING THE *MAN*. ALL THEY KNOW IS THE *HERO*. THEY DON'T KNOW HOW *HUMAN* YOU ARE, TOO.
I'M FLATTERED. REALLY. IT'S JUST...
...I DON'T THINK I CAN LIVE UP TO ANY *LEGEND*, IRIS.

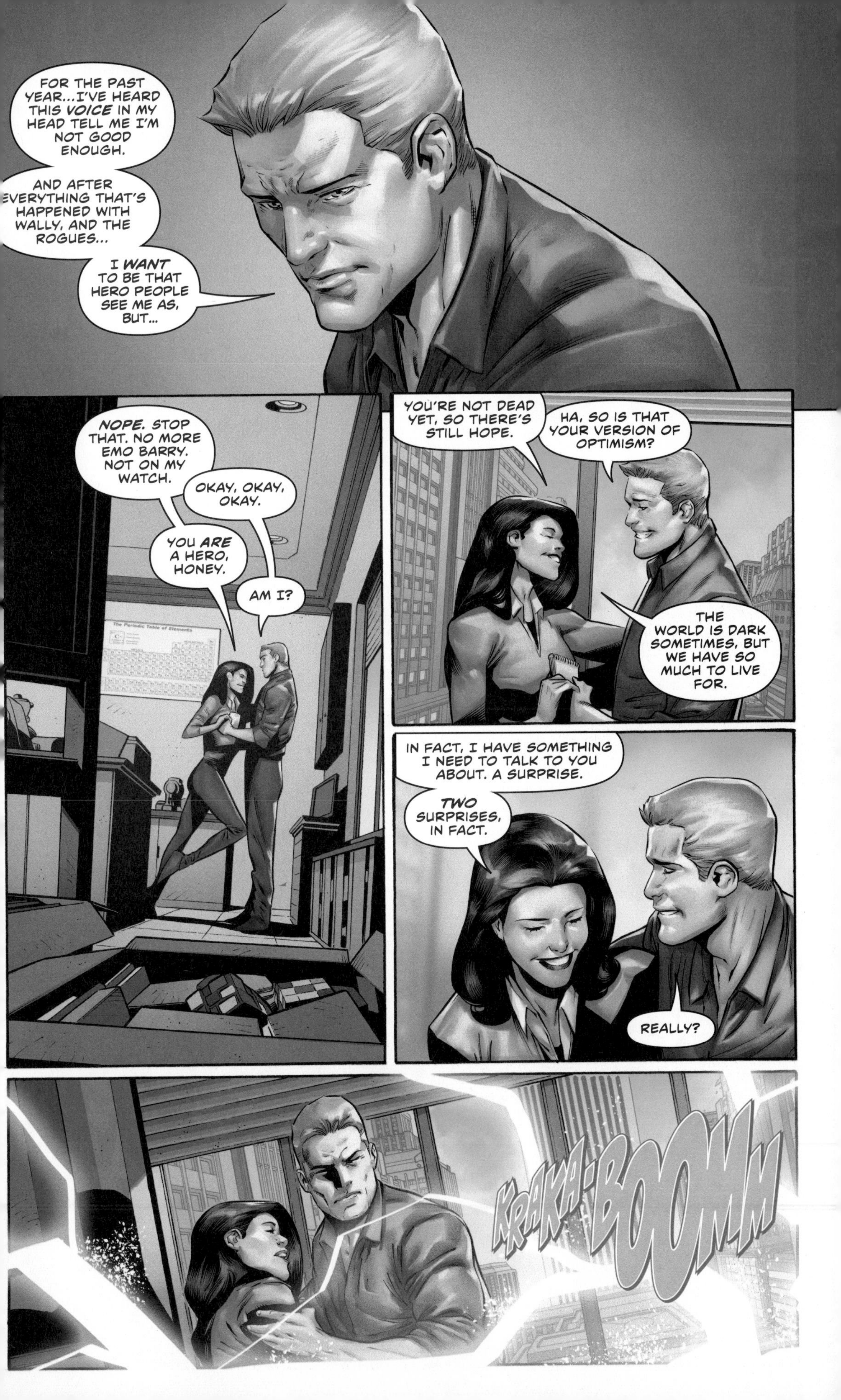

FOR THE PAST YEAR...I'VE HEARD THIS *VOICE* IN MY HEAD TELL ME I'M NOT GOOD ENOUGH.
AND AFTER EVERYTHING THAT'S HAPPENED WITH WALLY, AND THE ROGUES...
I *WANT* TO BE THAT HERO PEOPLE SEE ME AS, BUT...
NOPE. STOP THAT. NO MORE EMO BARRY. NOT ON MY WATCH.
OKAY, OKAY, OKAY.
YOU *ARE* A HERO, HONEY.
AM I?
The Periodic Table of Elements
YOU'RE NOT DEAD YET, SO THERE'S STILL HOPE.
HA, SO IS THAT YOUR VERSION OF OPTIMISM?
THE WORLD IS DARK SOMETIMES, BUT WE HAVE SO MUCH TO LIVE FOR.
IN FACT, I HAVE SOMETHING I NEED TO TALK TO YOU ABOUT. A SURPRISE.
TWO SURPRISES, IN FACT.
REALLY?
KRAKA-BOOMM

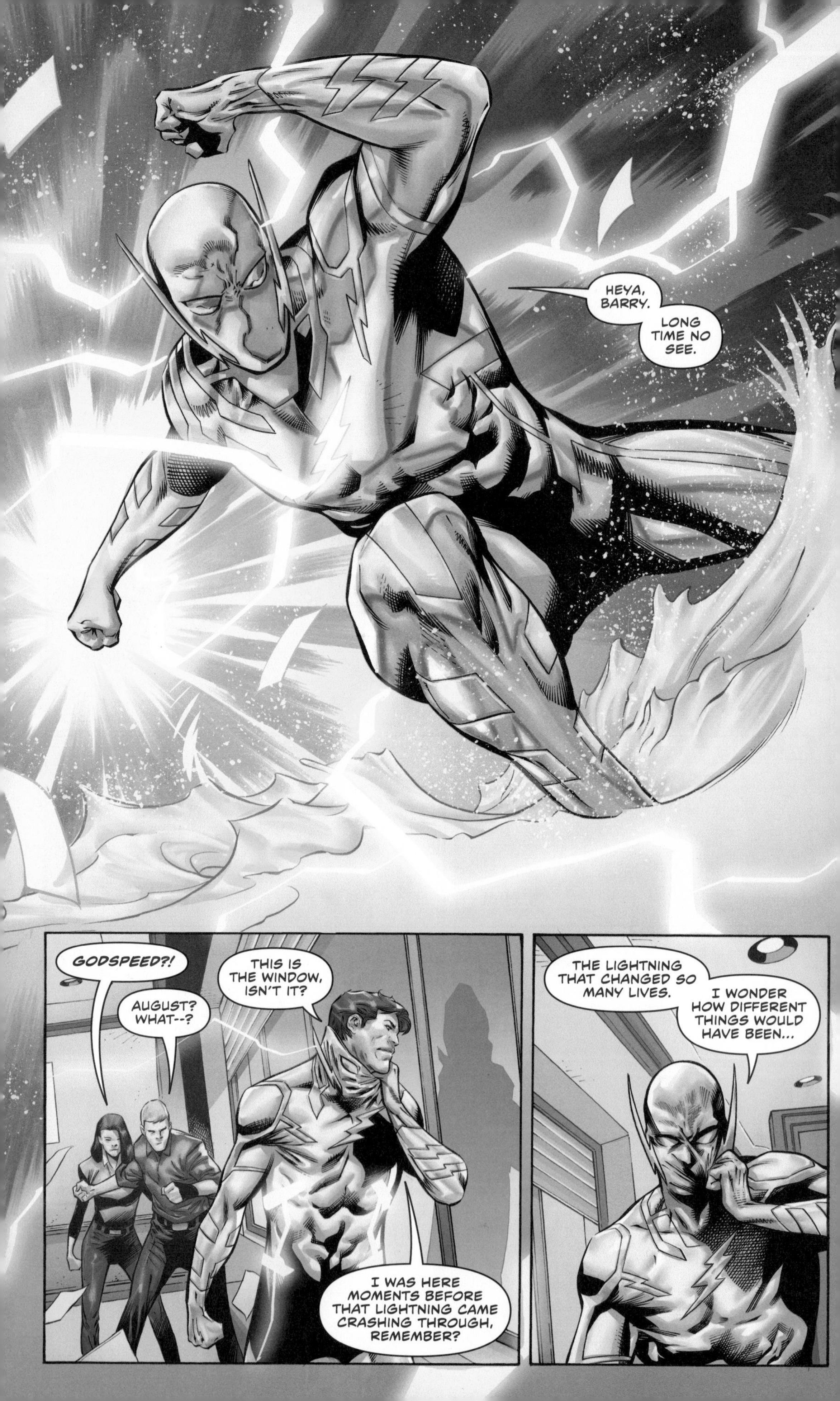

HEYA, BARRY.
LONG TIME NO SEE.
GODSPEED?!
AUGUST? WHAT--?
THIS IS THE WINDOW, ISN'T IT?
I WAS HERE MOMENTS BEFORE THAT LIGHTNING CAME CRASHING THROUGH, REMEMBER?
THE LIGHTNING THAT CHANGED SO MANY LIVES.
I WONDER HOW DIFFERENT THINGS WOULD HAVE BEEN...

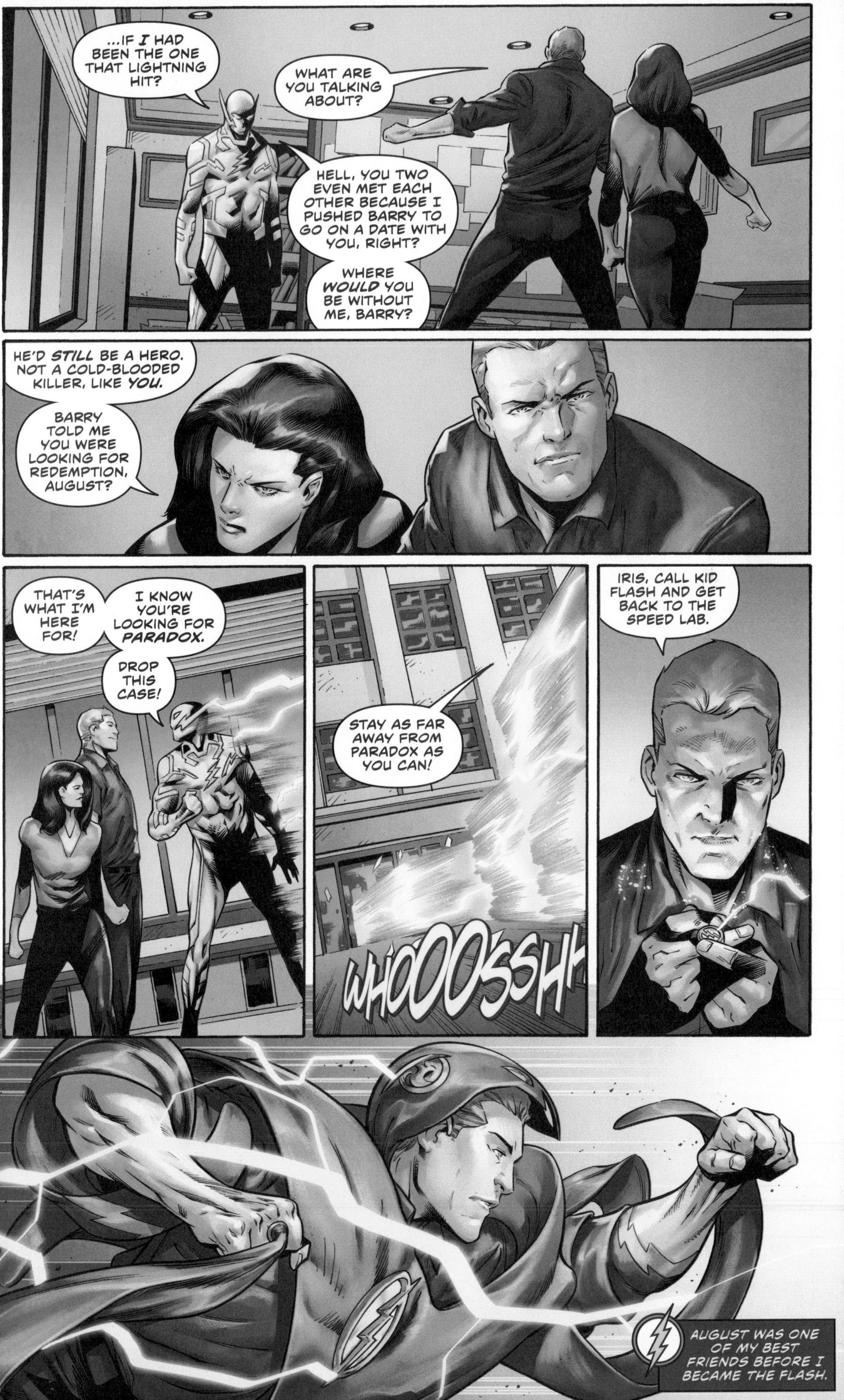

...IF I HAD BEEN THE ONE THAT LIGHTNING HIT?
WHAT ARE YOU TALKING ABOUT?
HELL, YOU TWO EVEN MET EACH OTHER BECAUSE I PUSHED BARRY TO GO ON A DATE WITH YOU, RIGHT?
WHERE WOULD YOU BE WITHOUT ME, BARRY?
HE'D STILL BE A HERO. NOT A COLD-BLOODED KILLER, LIKE YOU.
BARRY TOLD ME YOU WERE LOOKING FOR REDEMPTION, AUGUST?
THAT'S WHAT I'M HERE FOR!
I KNOW YOU'RE LOOKING FOR PARADOX.
DROP THIS CASE!
STAY AS FAR AWAY FROM PARADOX AS YOU CAN!
WHOOOSSH
IRIS, CALL KID FLASH AND GET BACK TO THE SPEED LAB.
AUGUST WAS ONE OF MY BEST FRIENDS BEFORE I BECAME THE FLASH.

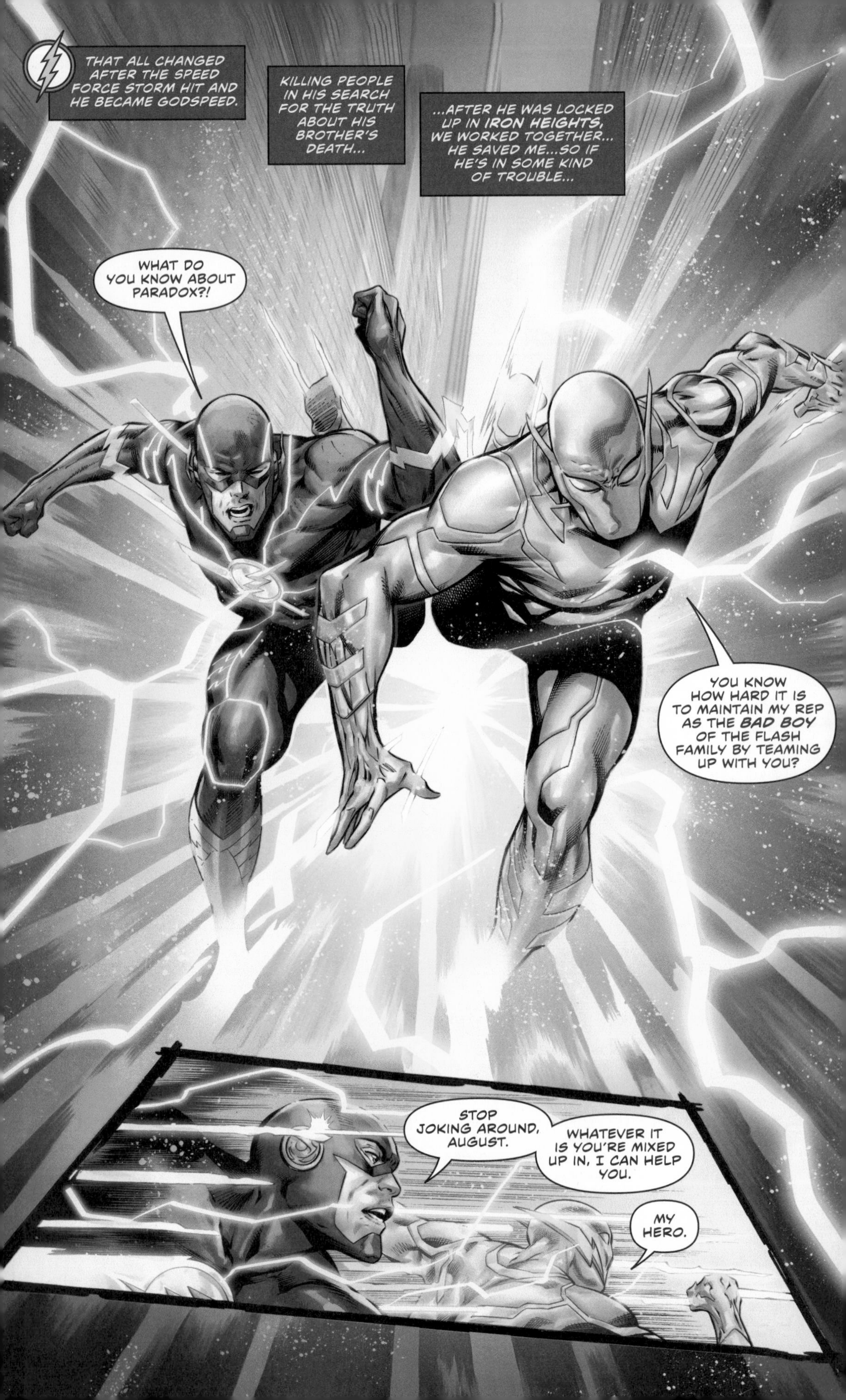
THAT ALL CHANGED AFTER THE SPEED FORCE STORM HIT AND HE BECAME GODSPEED.
KILLING PEOPLE IN HIS SEARCH FOR THE TRUTH ABOUT HIS BROTHER'S DEATH...
...AFTER HE WAS LOCKED UP IN IRON HEIGHTS, WE WORKED TOGETHER... HE SAVED ME...SO IF HE'S IN SOME KIND OF TROUBLE...
WHAT DO YOU KNOW ABOUT PARADOX?!
YOU KNOW HOW HARD IT IS TO MAINTAIN MY REP AS THE BAD BOY OF THE FLASH FAMILY BY TEAMING UP WITH YOU?
STOP JOKING AROUND, AUGUST.
WHATEVER IT IS YOU'RE MIXED UP IN, I CAN HELP YOU.
MY HERO.

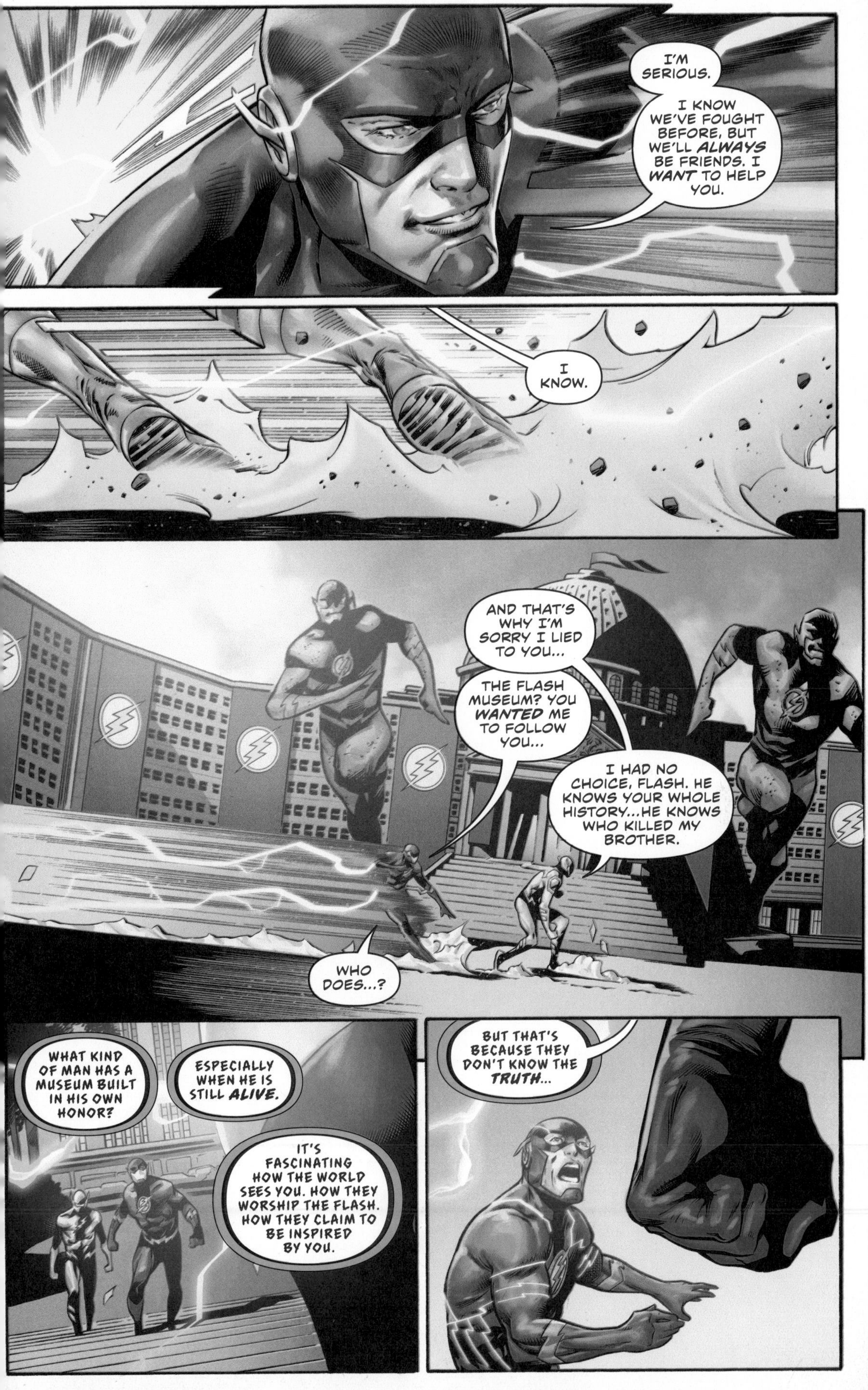

I'M SERIOUS.
I KNOW WE'VE FOUGHT BEFORE, BUT WE'LL ALWAYS BE FRIENDS. I WANT TO HELP YOU.
I KNOW.
AND THAT'S WHY I'M SORRY I LIED TO YOU...
THE FLASH MUSEUM? YOU WANTED ME TO FOLLOW YOU...
I HAD NO CHOICE, FLASH. HE KNOWS YOUR WHOLE HISTORY...HE KNOWS WHO KILLED MY BROTHER.
WHO DOES...?
WHAT KIND OF MAN HAS A MUSEUM BUILT IN HIS OWN HONOR?
ESPECIALLY WHEN HE IS STILL ALIVE.
IT'S FASCINATING HOW THE WORLD SEES YOU. HOW THEY WORSHIP THE FLASH. HOW THEY CLAIM TO BE INSPIRED BY YOU.
BUT THAT'S BECAUSE THEY DON'T KNOW THE TRUTH...

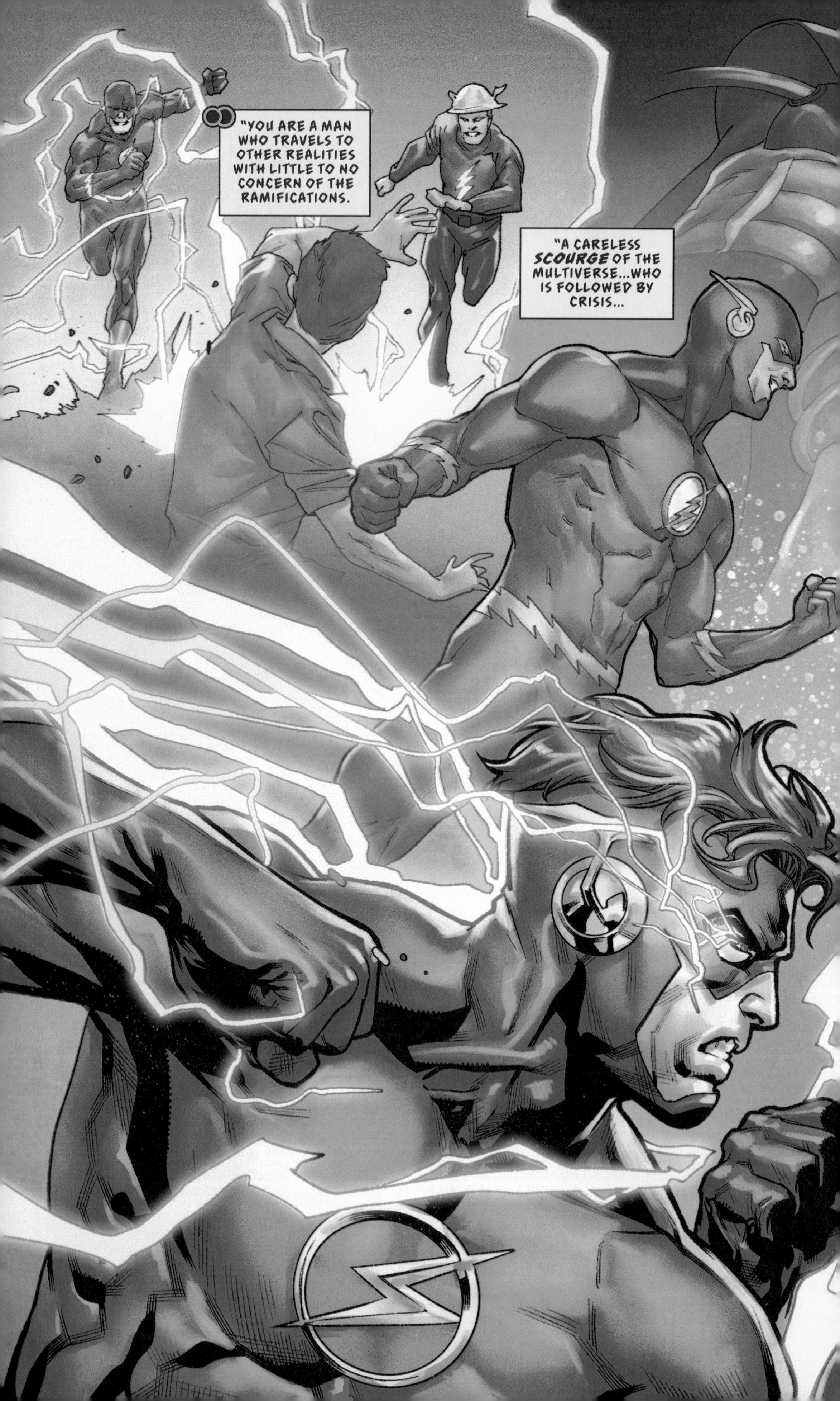
"YOU ARE A MAN WHO TRAVELS TO OTHER REALITIES WITH LITTLE TO NO CONCERN OF THE RAMIFICATIONS.
"A CARELESS *SCOURGE* OF THE MULTIVERSE...WHO IS FOLLOWED BY CRISIS...

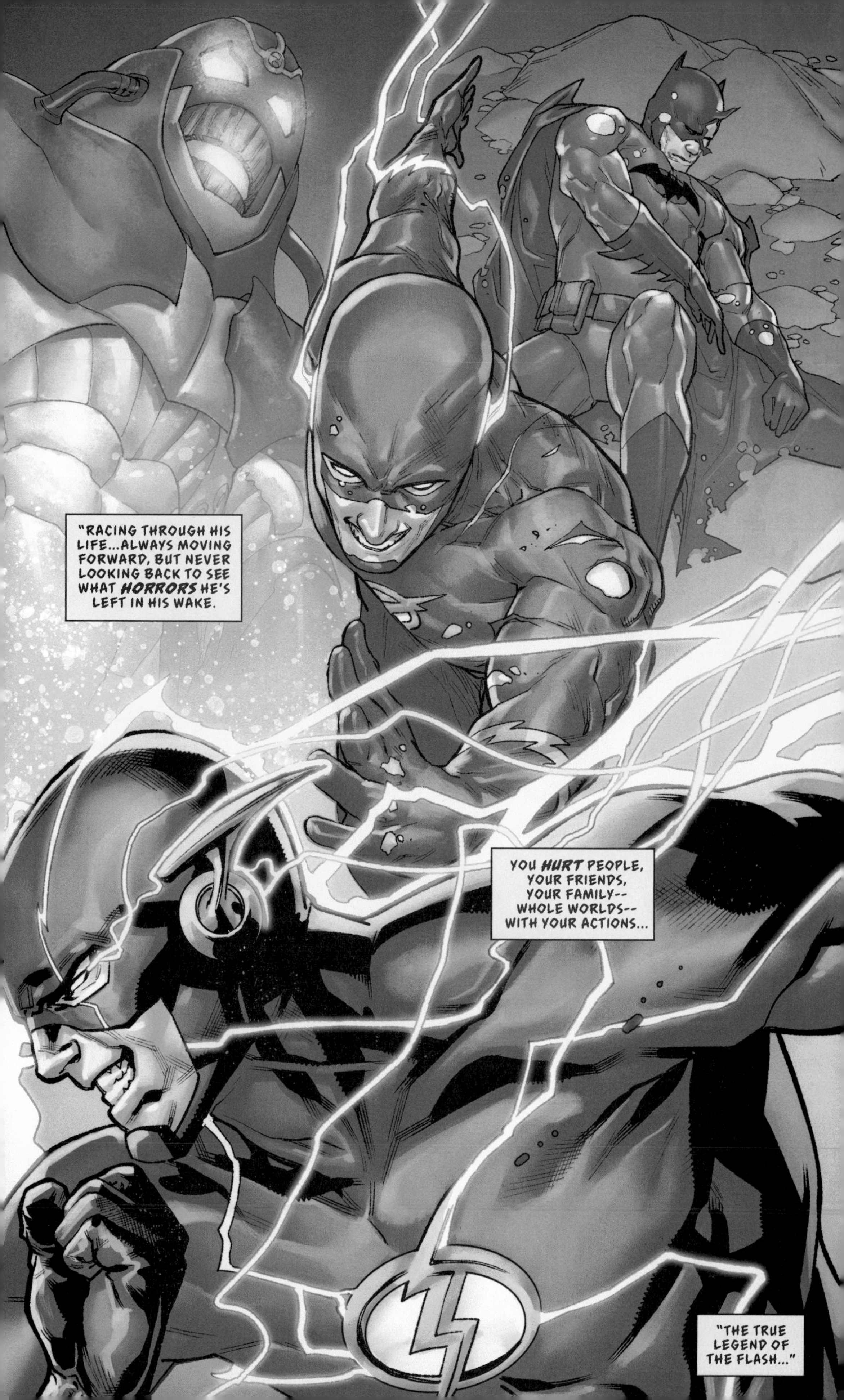
"RACING THROUGH HIS LIFE...ALWAYS MOVING FORWARD, BUT NEVER LOOKING BACK TO SEE WHAT *HORRORS* HE'S LEFT IN HIS WAKE.
YOU *HURT* PEOPLE, YOUR FRIENDS, YOUR FAMILY-- WHOLE WORLDS-- WITH YOUR ACTIONS...
"THE TRUE LEGEND OF THE FLASH..."

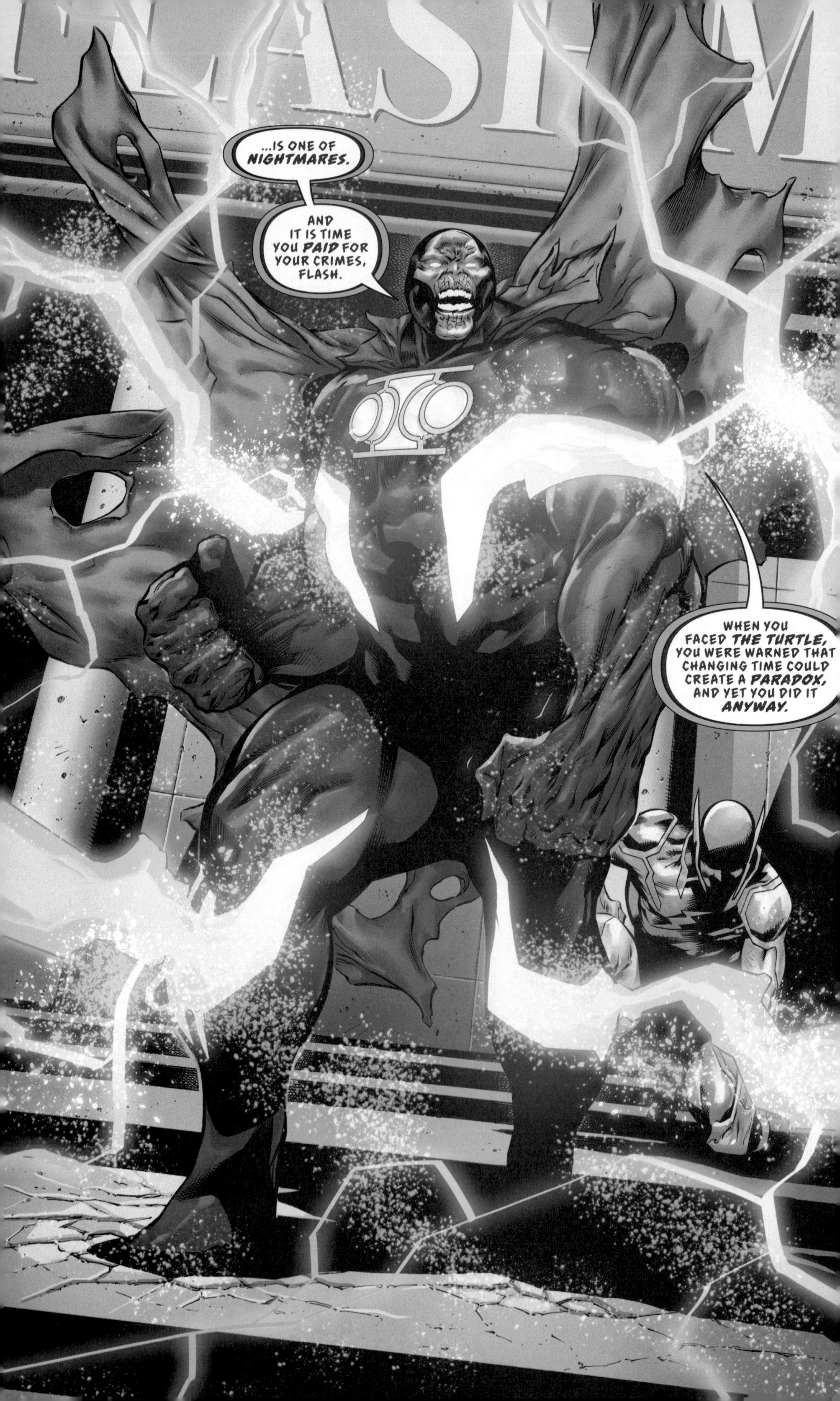

...IS ONE OF NIGHTMARES.
AND IT IS TIME YOU PAID FOR YOUR CRIMES, FLASH.
WHEN YOU FACED THE TURTLE, YOU WERE WARNED THAT CHANGING TIME COULD CREATE A PARADOX, AND YET YOU DID IT ANYWAY.

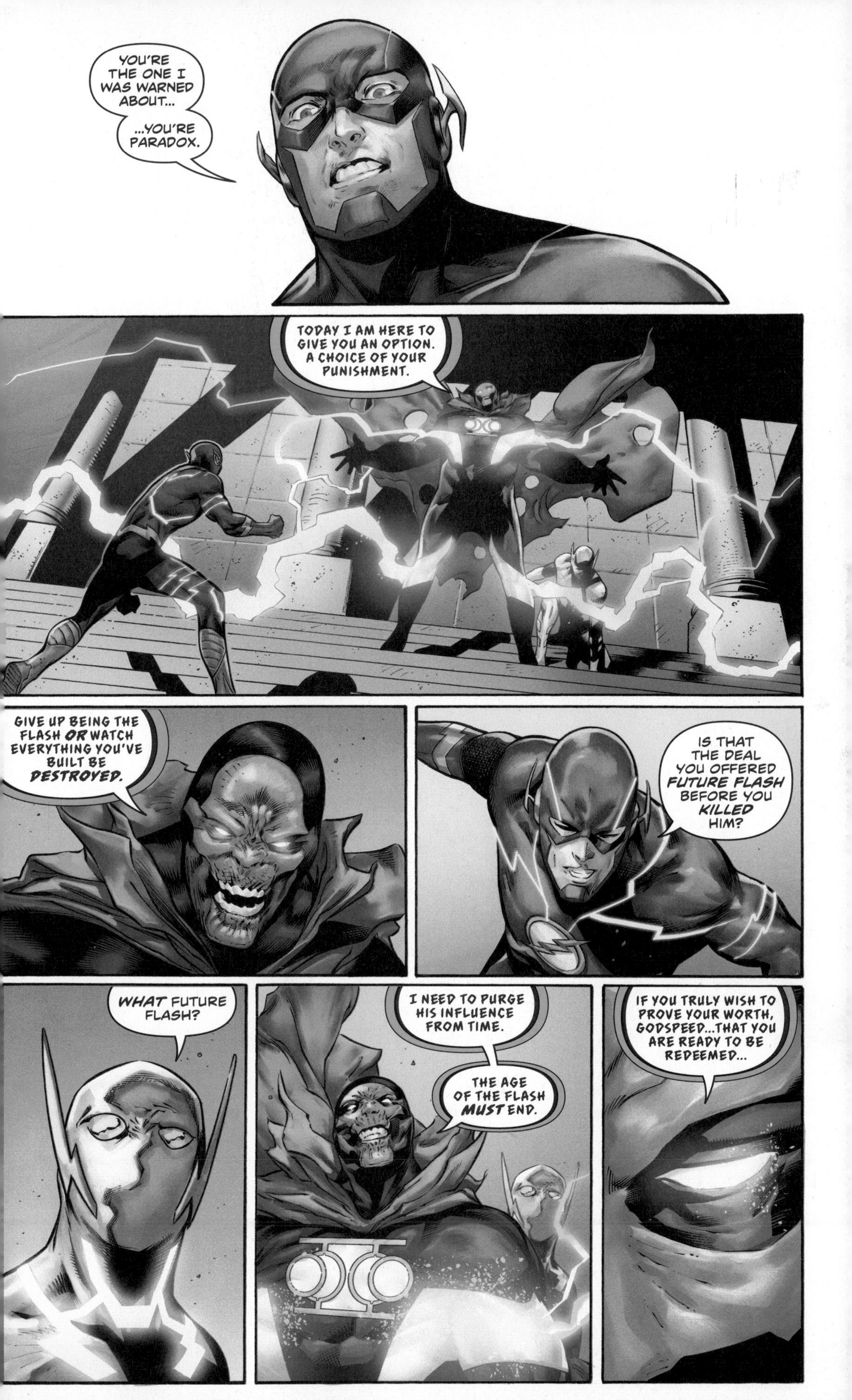

YOU'RE THE ONE I WAS WARNED ABOUT...
...YOU'RE PARADOX.
TODAY I AM HERE TO GIVE YOU AN OPTION. A CHOICE OF YOUR PUNISHMENT.
GIVE UP BEING THE FLASH OR WATCH EVERYTHING YOU'VE BUILT BE DESTROYED.
IS THAT THE DEAL YOU OFFERED FUTURE FLASH BEFORE YOU KILLED HIM?
WHAT FUTURE FLASH?
I NEED TO PURGE HIS INFLUENCE FROM TIME.
THE AGE OF THE FLASH MUST END.
IF YOU TRULY WISH TO PROVE YOUR WORTH, GODSPEED...THAT YOU ARE READY TO BE REDEEMED...

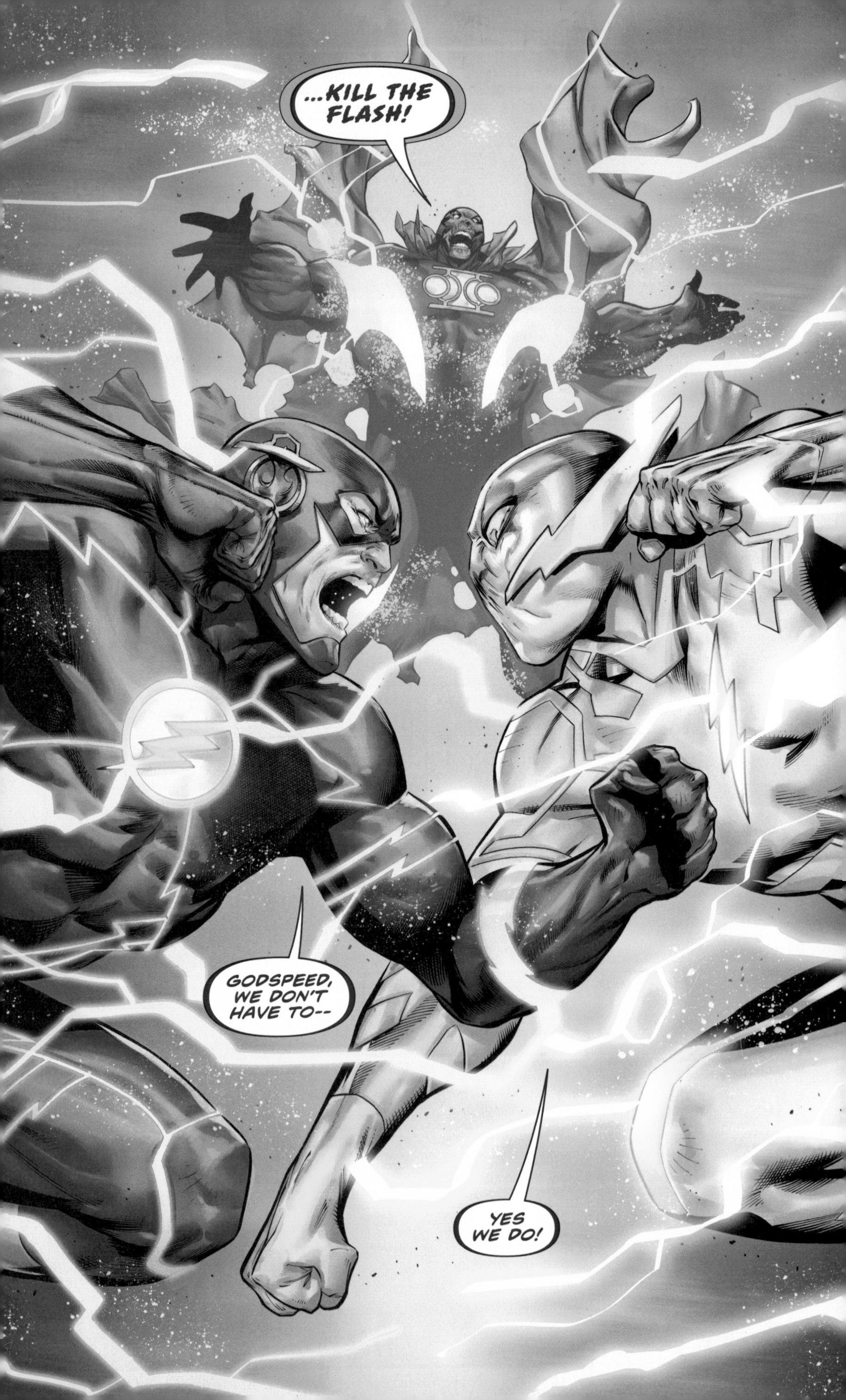
...KILL THE FLASH!
GODSPEED, WE DON'T HAVE TO--
YES WE DO!

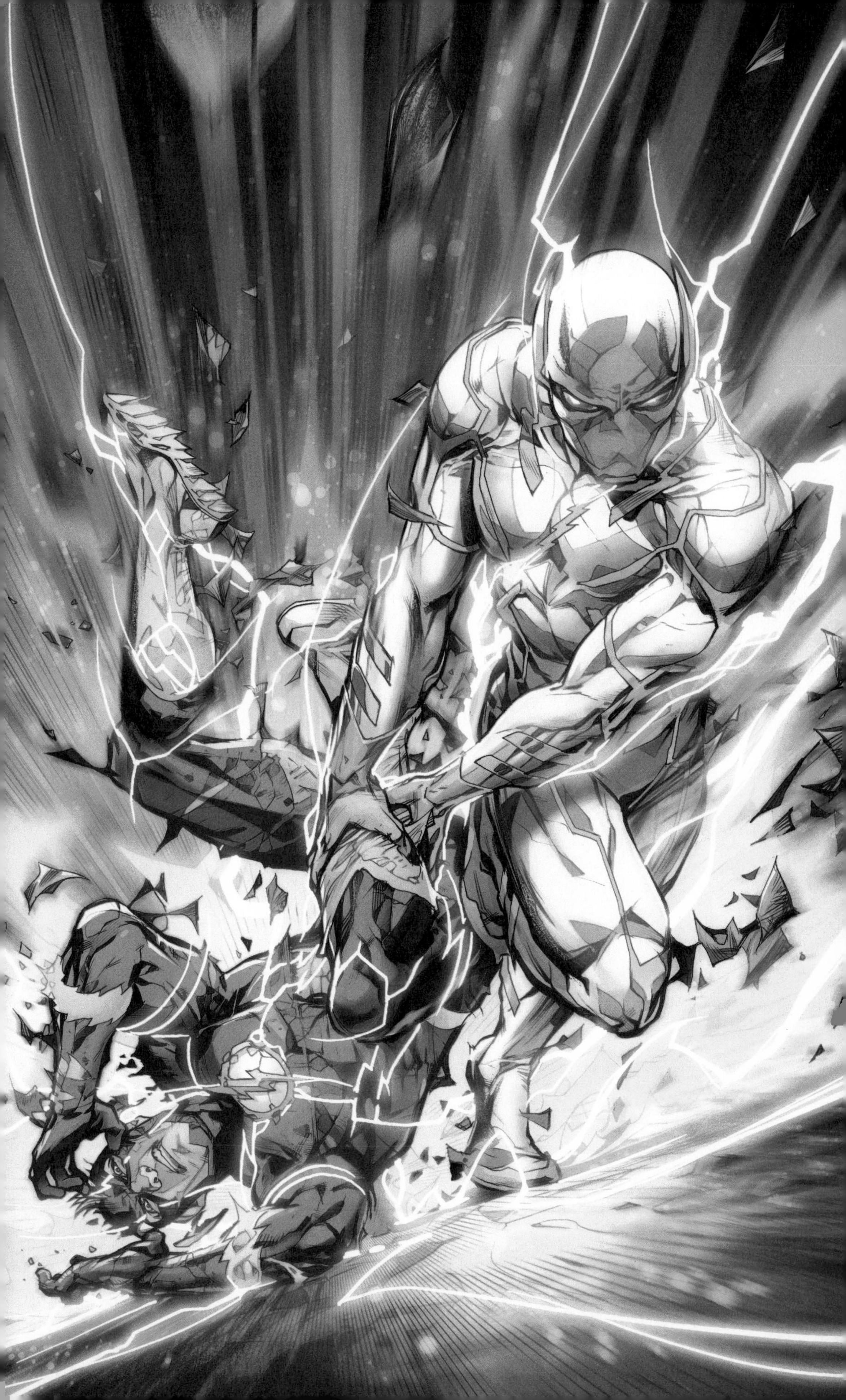

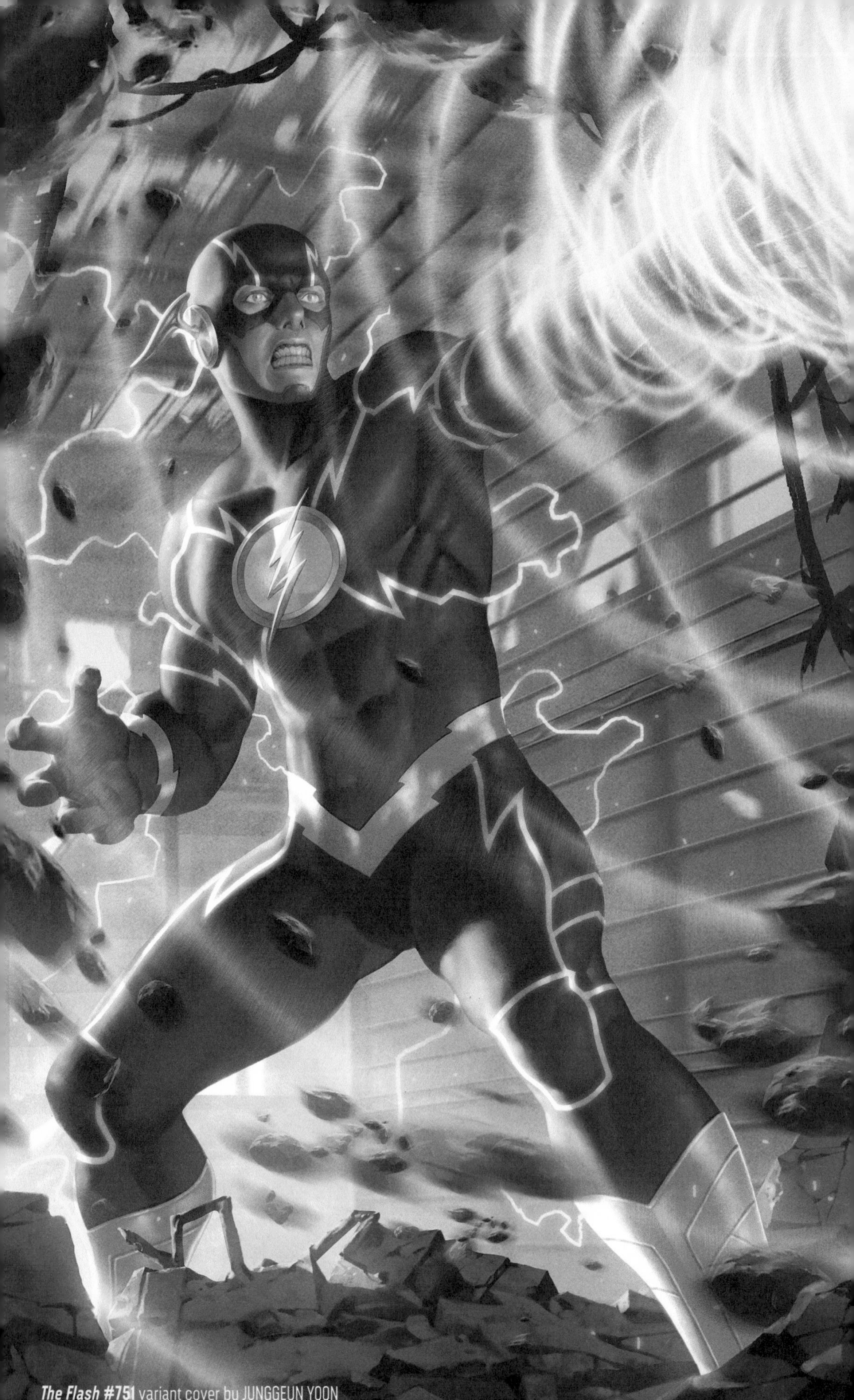

***The Flash* #751** variant cover by JUNGGEUN YOON

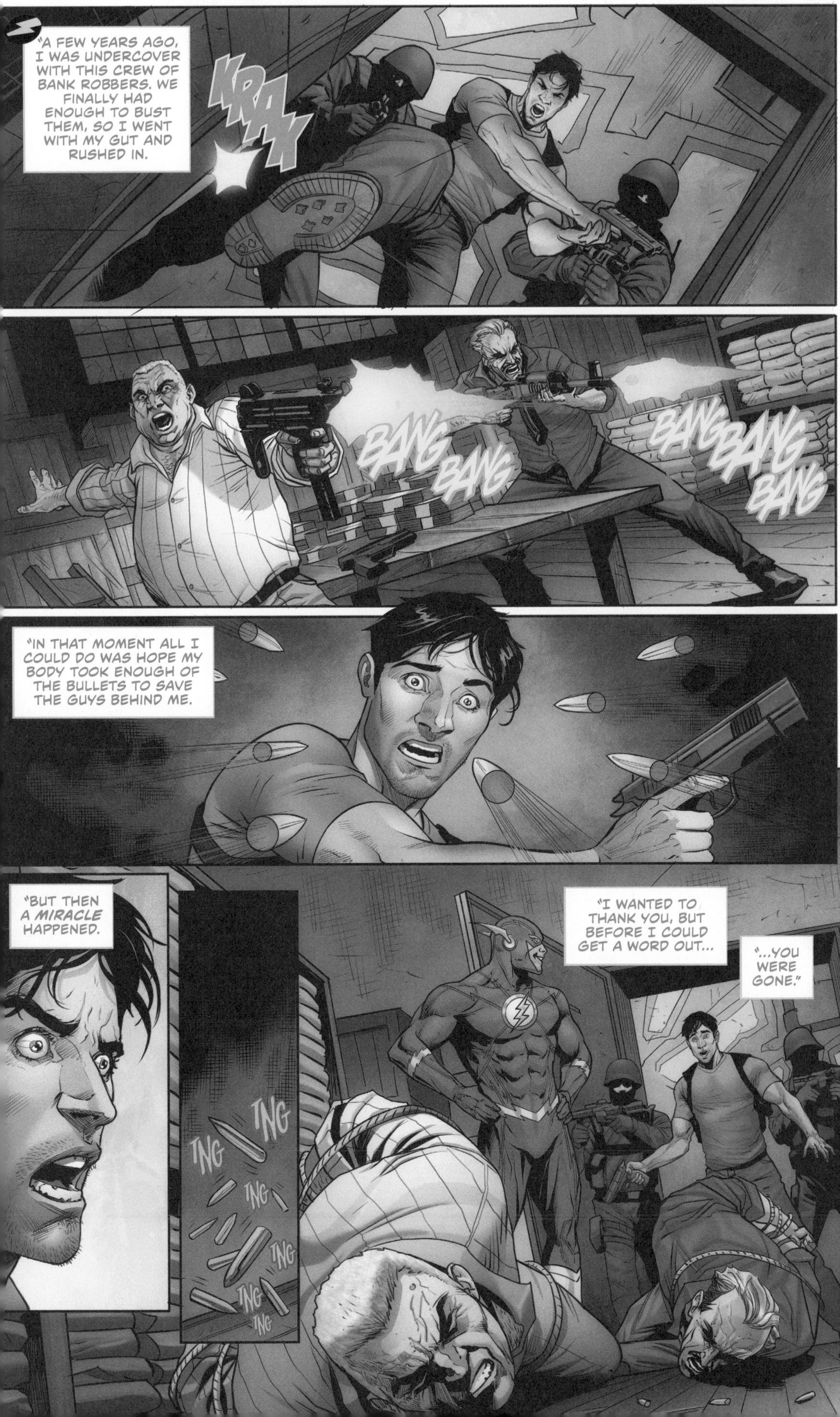
"A FEW YEARS AGO, I WAS UNDERCOVER WITH THIS CREW OF BANK ROBBERS. WE FINALLY HAD ENOUGH TO BUST THEM, SO I WENT WITH MY GUT AND RUSHED IN.
KRAKK
BANG
BANG
BANG
BANG
BANG
"IN THAT MOMENT ALL I COULD DO WAS HOPE MY BODY TOOK ENOUGH OF THE BULLETS TO SAVE THE GUYS BEHIND ME.
"BUT THEN A *MIRACLE* HAPPENED.
TNG
TNG
TNG
TNG
TNG
TNG
"I WANTED TO THANK YOU, BUT BEFORE I COULD GET A WORD OUT...
"...YOU WERE GONE."

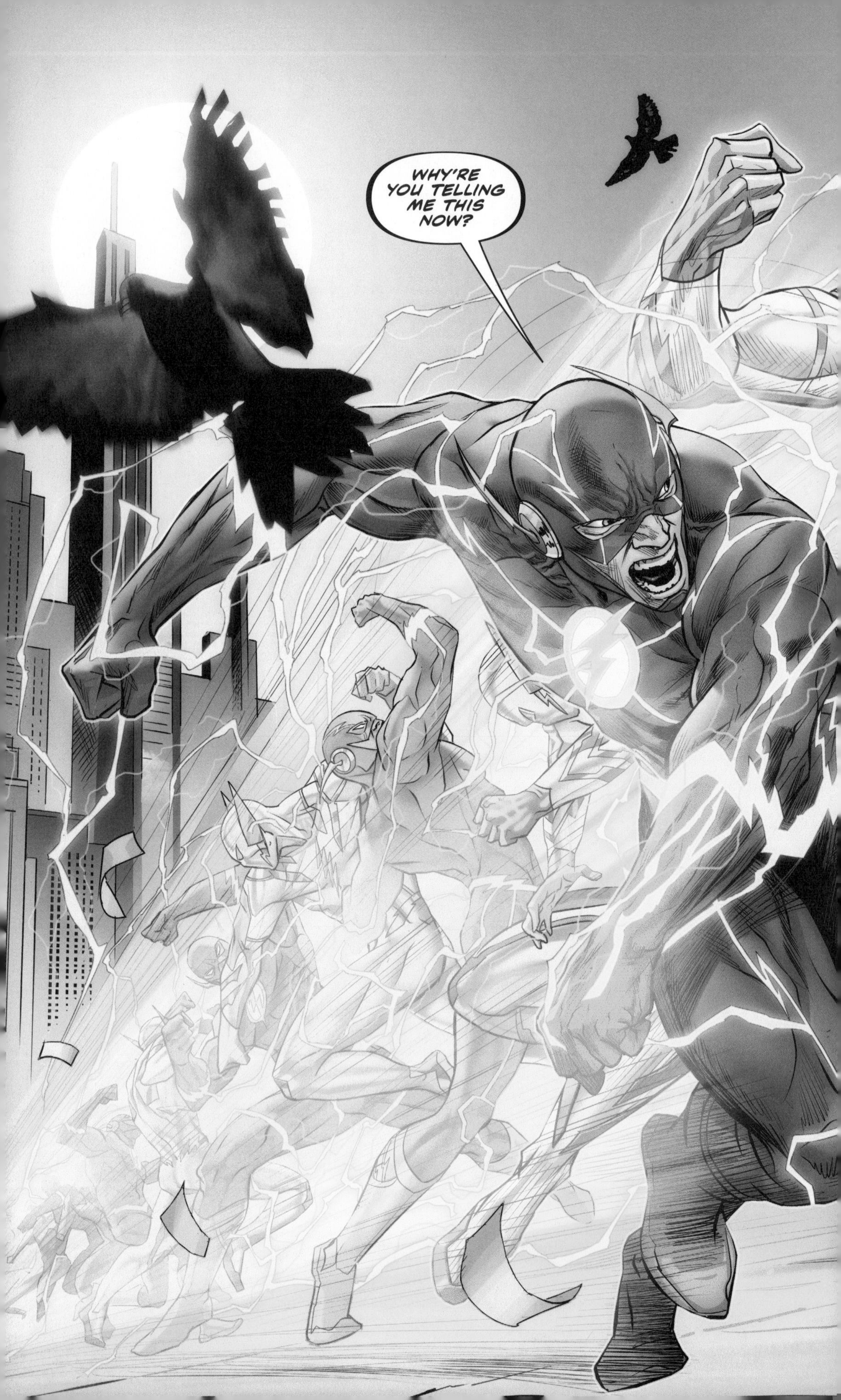
WHY'RE YOU TELLING ME THIS NOW?

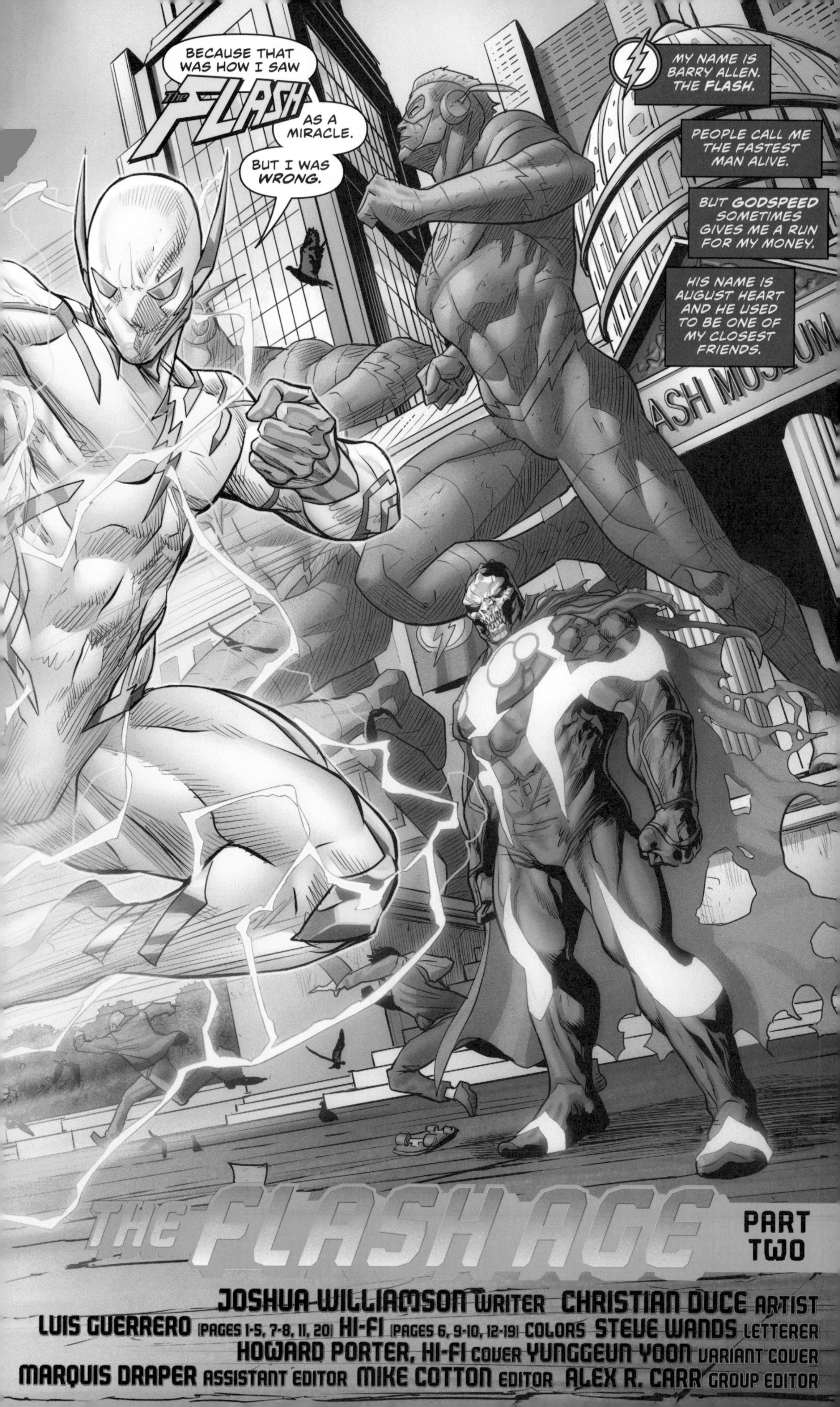

BECAUSE THAT WAS HOW I SAW
THE FLASH
AS A MIRACLE.
BUT I WAS WRONG.
MY NAME IS BARRY ALLEN. THE FLASH.
PEOPLE CALL ME THE FASTEST MAN ALIVE.
BUT GODSPEED SOMETIMES GIVES ME A RUN FOR MY MONEY.
HIS NAME IS AUGUST HEART AND HE USED TO BE ONE OF MY CLOSEST FRIENDS.
FLASH MUSEUM
THE FLASH AGE
PART TWO
JOSHUA WILLIAMSON WRITER CHRISTIAN DUCE ARTIST
LUIS GUERRERO (PAGES 1-5, 7-8, 11, 20) HI-FI (PAGES 6, 9-10, 12-19) COLORS STEVE WANDS LETTERER
HOWARD PORTER, HI-FI COVER YUNGGEUN YOON VARIANT COVER
MARQUIS DRAPER ASSISTANT EDITOR MIKE COTTON EDITOR ALEX R. CARR GROUP EDITOR

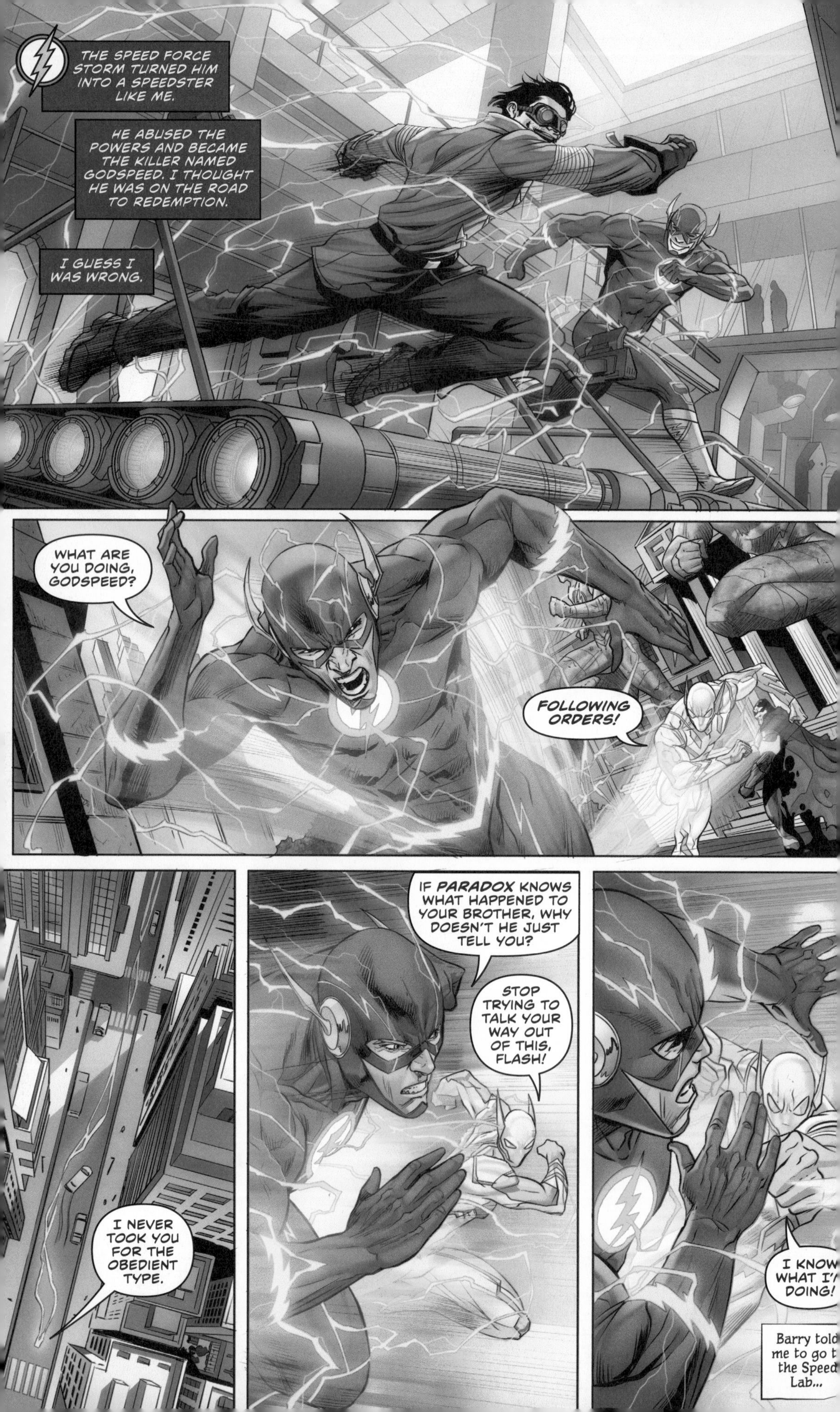
THE SPEED FORCE STORM TURNED HIM INTO A SPEEDSTER LIKE ME.
HE ABUSED THE POWERS AND BECAME THE KILLER NAMED GODSPEED. I THOUGHT HE WAS ON THE ROAD TO REDEMPTION.
I GUESS I WAS WRONG.
WHAT ARE YOU DOING, GODSPEED?
FOLLOWING ORDERS!
I NEVER TOOK YOU FOR THE OBEDIENT TYPE.
IF PARADOX KNOWS WHAT HAPPENED TO YOUR BROTHER, WHY DOESN'T HE JUST TELL YOU?
STOP TRYING TO TALK YOUR WAY OUT OF THIS, FLASH!
I KNOW WHAT I'
DOING!
Barry told me to go t the Speed Lab...

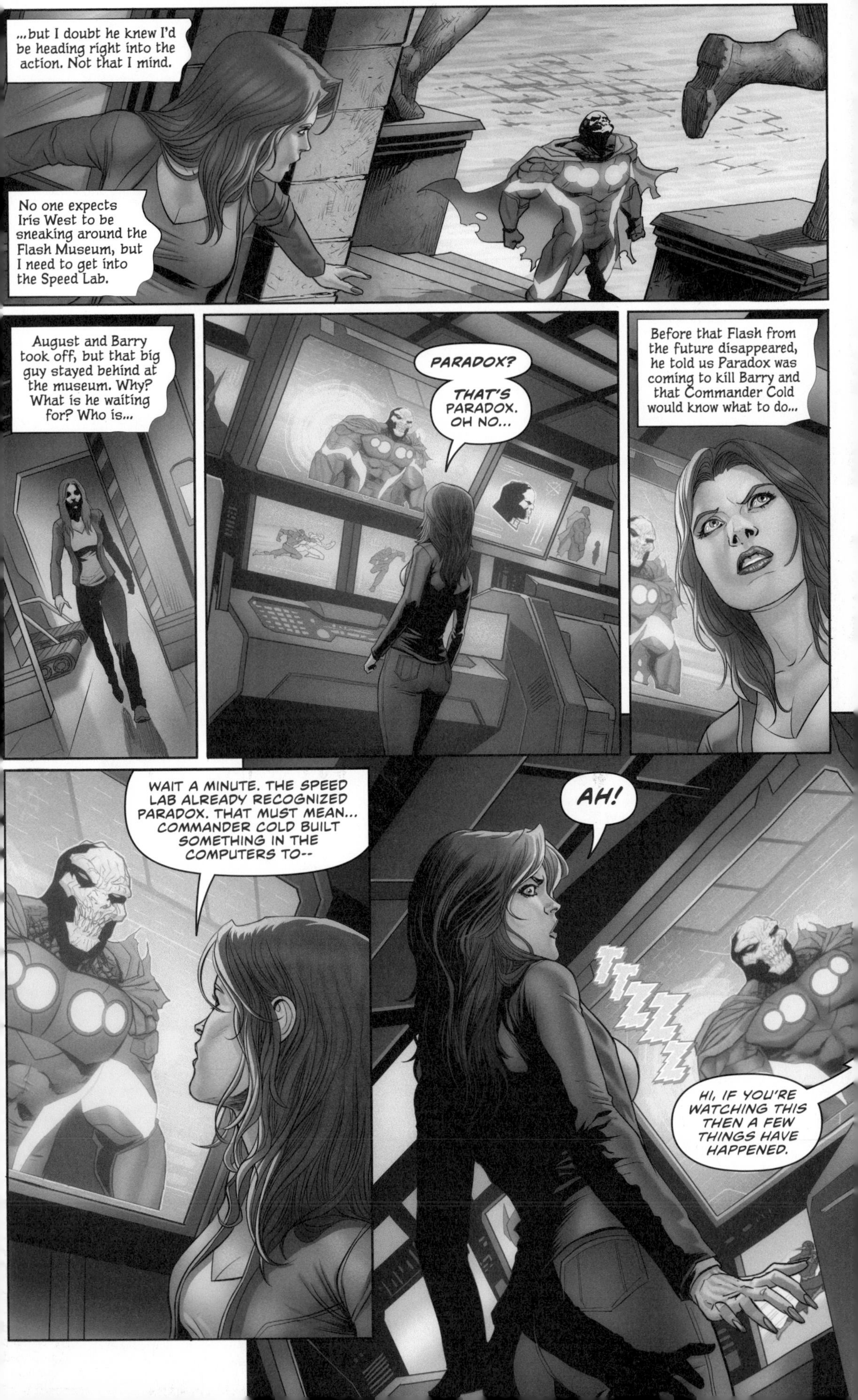

...but I doubt he knew I'd be heading right into the action. Not that I mind.
No one expects Iris West to be sneaking around the Flash Museum, but I need to get into the Speed Lab.
August and Barry took off, but that big guy stayed behind at the museum. Why? What is he waiting for? Who is...
PARADOX?
THAT'S PARADOX. OH NO...
Before that Flash from the future disappeared, he told us Paradox was coming to kill Barry and that Commander Cold would know what to do...
WAIT A MINUTE. THE SPEED LAB ALREADY RECOGNIZED PARADOX. THAT MUST MEAN... COMMANDER COLD BUILT SOMETHING IN THE COMPUTERS TO--
AH!
TZZZZ
HI, IF YOU'RE WATCHING THIS THEN A FEW THINGS HAVE HAPPENED.

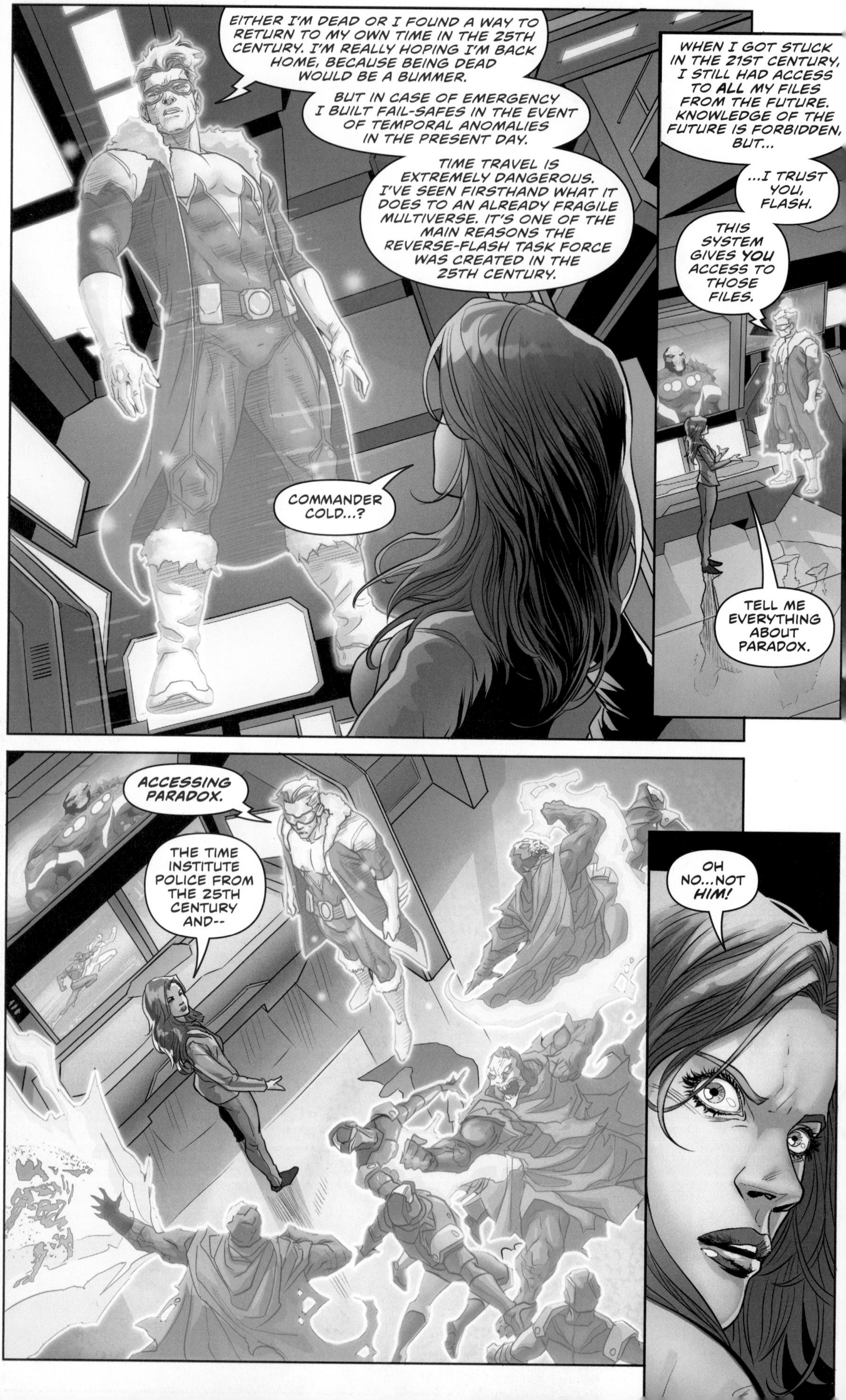
EITHER I'M DEAD OR I FOUND A WAY TO RETURN TO MY OWN TIME IN THE 25TH CENTURY. I'M REALLY HOPING I'M BACK HOME, BECAUSE BEING DEAD WOULD BE A BUMMER.
BUT IN CASE OF EMERGENCY I BUILT FAIL-SAFES IN THE EVENT OF TEMPORAL ANOMALIES IN THE PRESENT DAY.
TIME TRAVEL IS EXTREMELY DANGEROUS. I'VE SEEN FIRSTHAND WHAT IT DOES TO AN ALREADY FRAGILE MULTIVERSE. IT'S ONE OF THE MAIN REASONS THE REVERSE-FLASH TASK FORCE WAS CREATED IN THE 25TH CENTURY.
COMMANDER COLD...?
WHEN I GOT STUCK IN THE 21ST CENTURY, I STILL HAD ACCESS TO ALL MY FILES FROM THE FUTURE. KNOWLEDGE OF THE FUTURE IS FORBIDDEN, BUT...
...I TRUST YOU, FLASH.
THIS SYSTEM GIVES YOU ACCESS TO THOSE FILES.
TELL ME EVERYTHING ABOUT PARADOX.
ACCESSING PARADOX.
THE TIME INSTITUTE POLICE FROM THE 25TH CENTURY AND--
OH NO...NOT HIM!

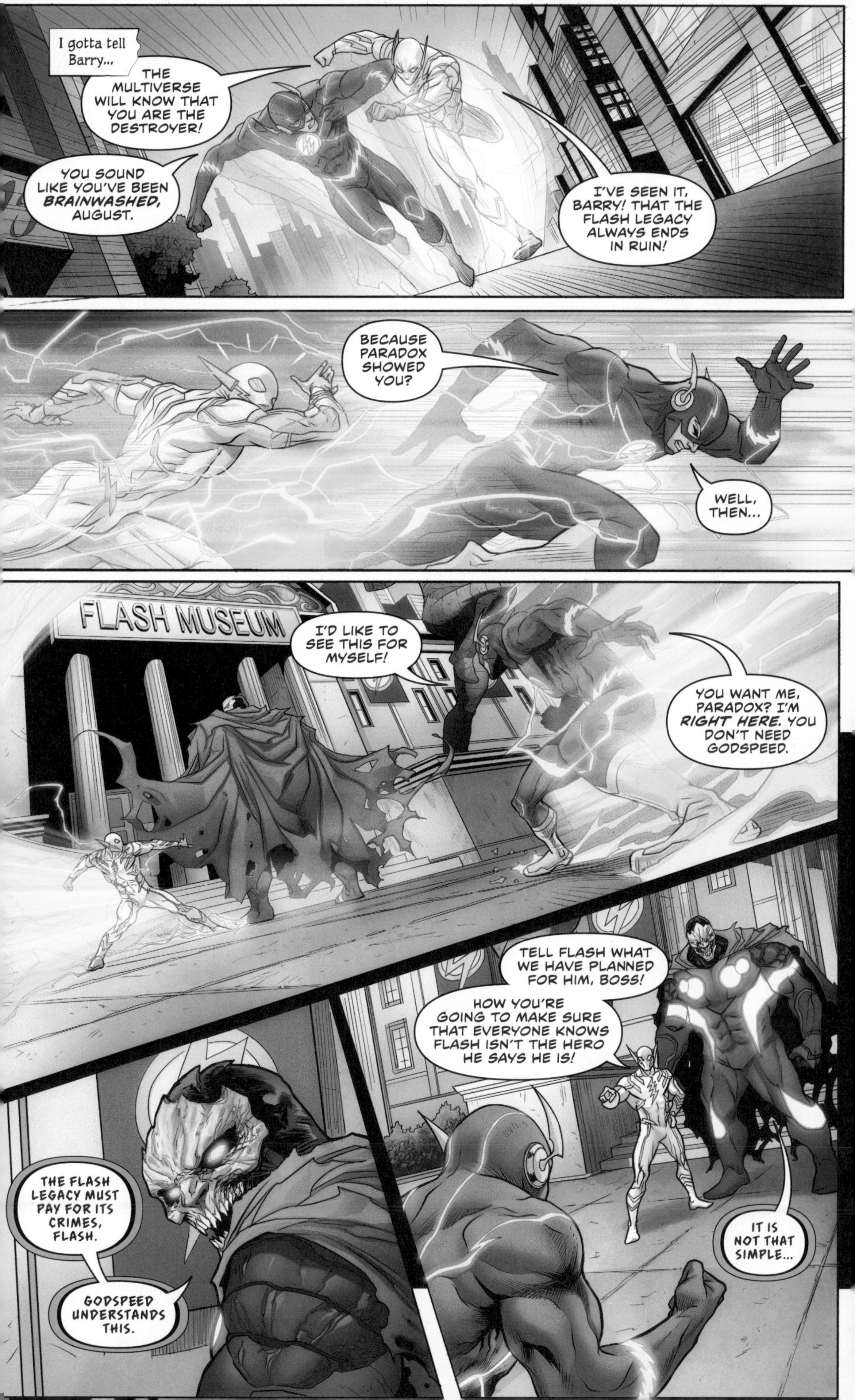
I gotta tell Barry...
THE MULTIVERSE WILL KNOW THAT YOU ARE THE DESTROYER!
YOU SOUND LIKE YOU'VE BEEN BRAINWASHED, AUGUST.
I'VE SEEN IT, BARRY! THAT THE FLASH LEGACY ALWAYS ENDS IN RUIN!
BECAUSE PARADOX SHOWED YOU?
WELL, THEN...
FLASH MUSEUM
I'D LIKE TO SEE THIS FOR MYSELF!
YOU WANT ME, PARADOX? I'M RIGHT HERE. YOU DON'T NEED GODSPEED.
TELL FLASH WHAT WE HAVE PLANNED FOR HIM, BOSS!
HOW YOU'RE GOING TO MAKE SURE THAT EVERYONE KNOWS FLASH ISN'T THE HERO HE SAYS HE IS!
THE FLASH LEGACY MUST PAY FOR ITS CRIMES, FLASH.
GODSPEED UNDERSTANDS THIS.
IT IS NOT THAT SIMPLE...

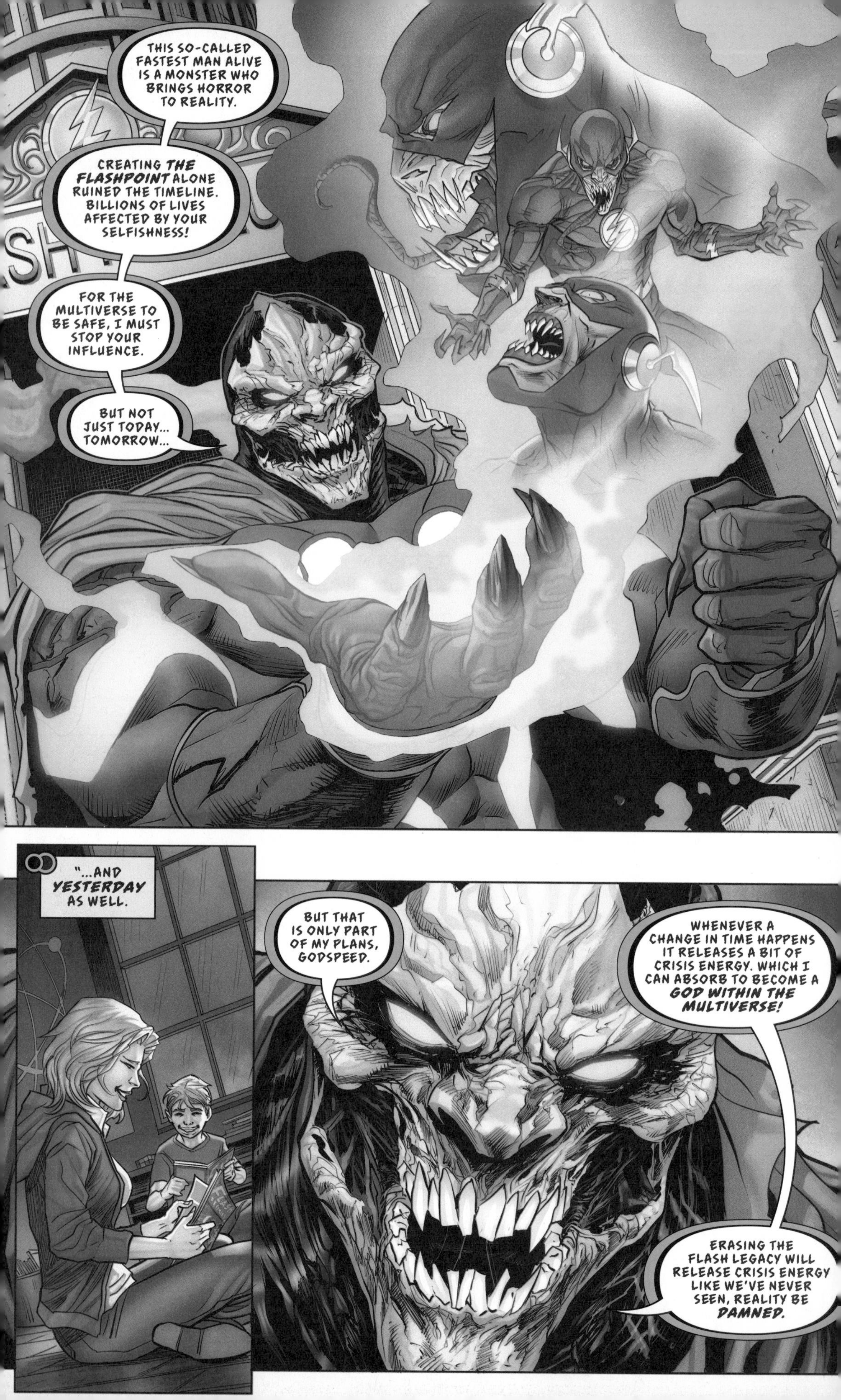
THIS SO-CALLED FASTEST MAN ALIVE IS A MONSTER WHO BRINGS HORROR TO REALITY.
CREATING *THE FLASHPOINT* ALONE RUINED THE TIMELINE. BILLIONS OF LIVES AFFECTED BY YOUR SELFISHNESS!
FOR THE MULTIVERSE TO BE SAFE, I MUST STOP YOUR INFLUENCE.
BUT NOT JUST TODAY... TOMORROW...
"...AND *YESTERDAY* AS WELL.
BUT THAT IS ONLY PART OF MY PLANS, GODSPEED.
WHENEVER A CHANGE IN TIME HAPPENS IT RELEASES A BIT OF CRISIS ENERGY. WHICH I CAN ABSORB TO BECOME A *GOD WITHIN THE MULTIVERSE!*
ERASING THE FLASH LEGACY WILL RELEASE CRISIS ENERGY LIKE WE'VE NEVER SEEN, REALITY BE *DAMNED.*

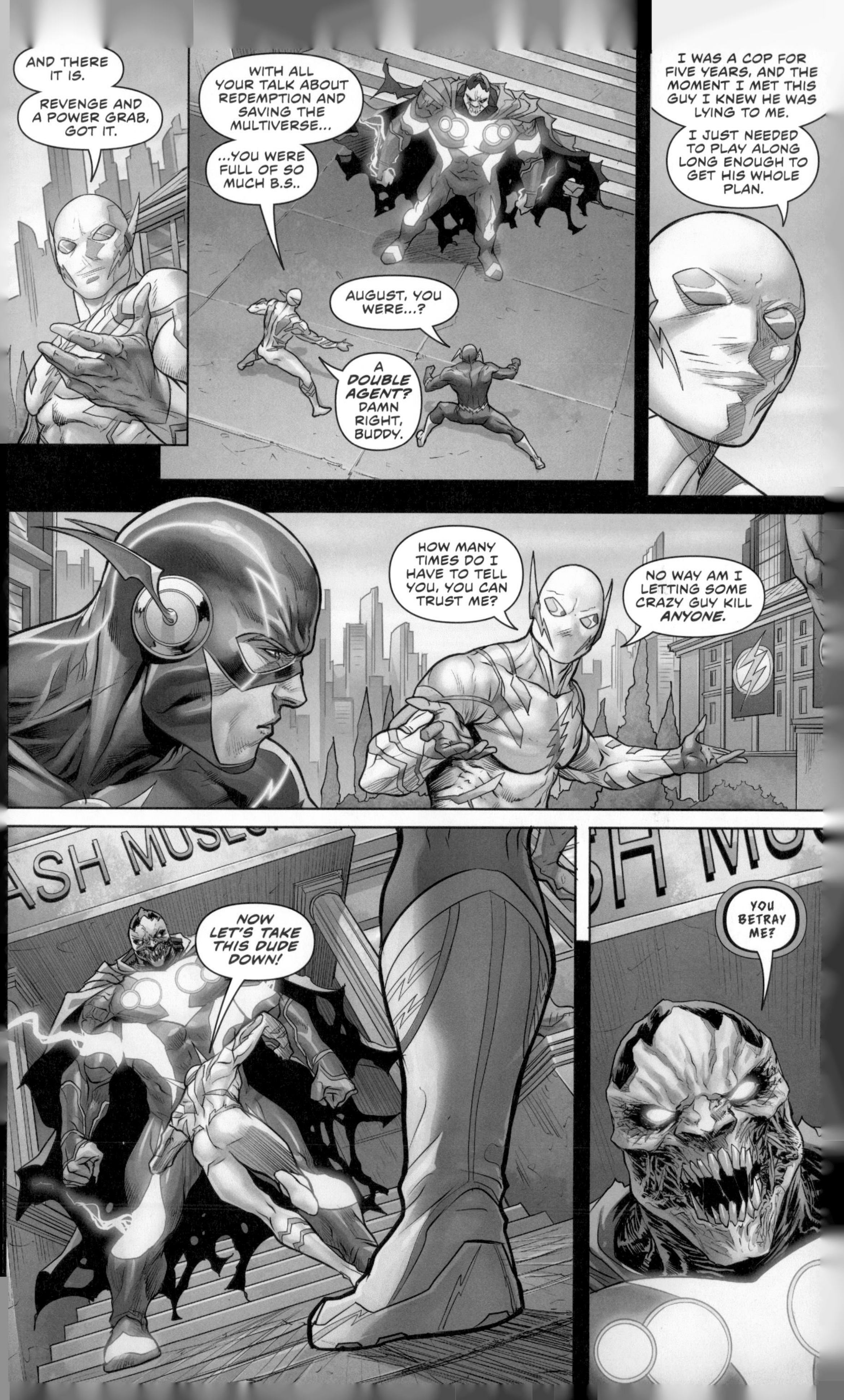
AND THERE IT IS.
REVENGE AND A POWER GRAB, GOT IT.
WITH ALL YOUR TALK ABOUT REDEMPTION AND SAVING THE MULTIVERSE...
...YOU WERE FULL OF SO MUCH B.S..
AUGUST, YOU WERE...?
A *DOUBLE AGENT?* DAMN RIGHT, BUDDY.
I WAS A COP FOR FIVE YEARS, AND THE MOMENT I MET THIS GUY I KNEW HE WAS LYING TO ME.
I JUST NEEDED TO PLAY ALONG LONG ENOUGH TO GET HIS WHOLE PLAN.
HOW MANY TIMES DO I HAVE TO TELL YOU, YOU CAN TRUST ME?
NO WAY AM I LETTING SOME CRAZY GUY KILL *ANYONE.*
ASH MUSE
NOW LET'S TAKE THIS DUDE DOWN!
SH MU
YOU BETRAY ME?

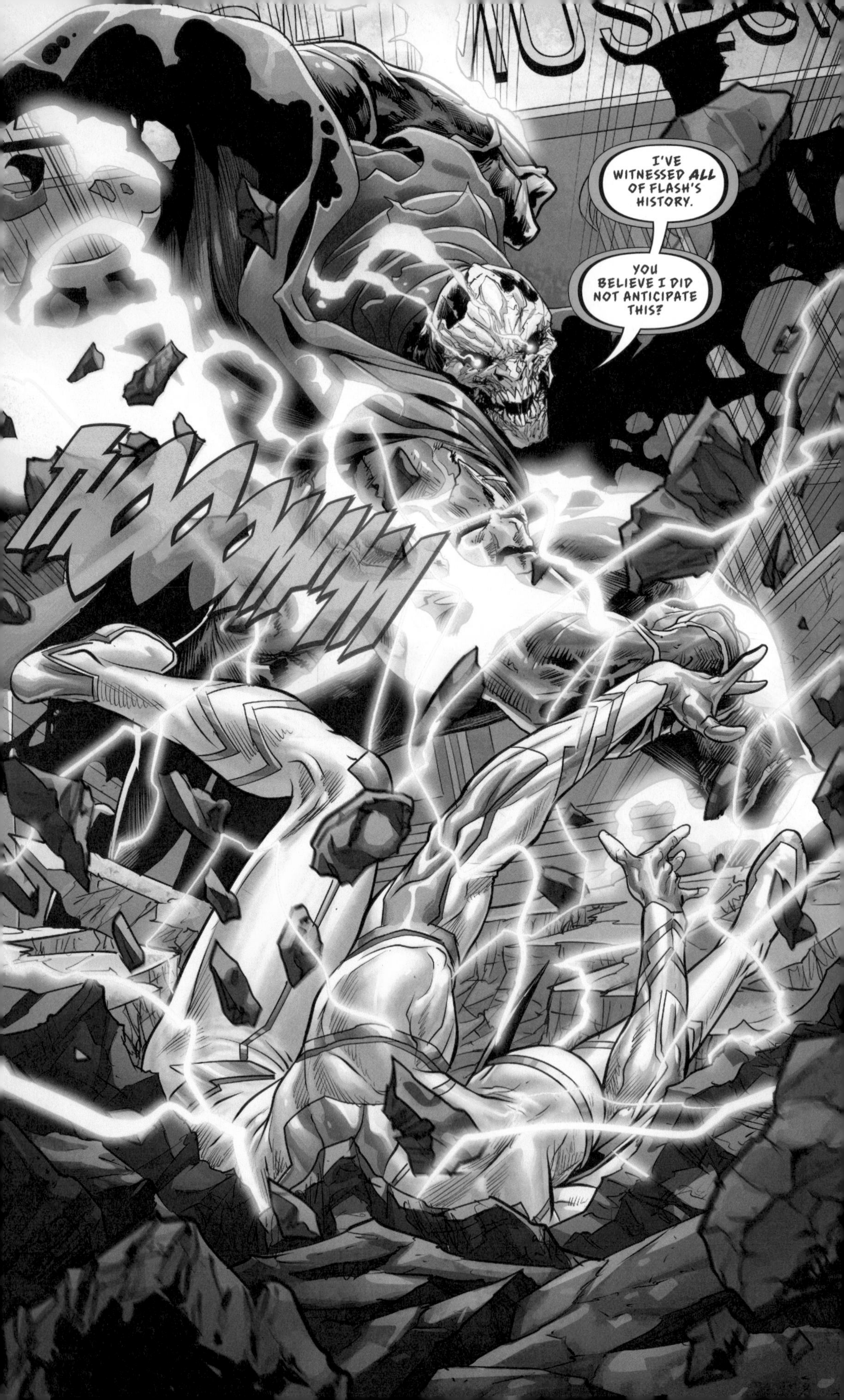
I'VE WITNESSED ALL OF FLASH'S HISTORY.
YOU BELIEVE I DID NOT ANTICIPATE THIS?
THOOOMMM

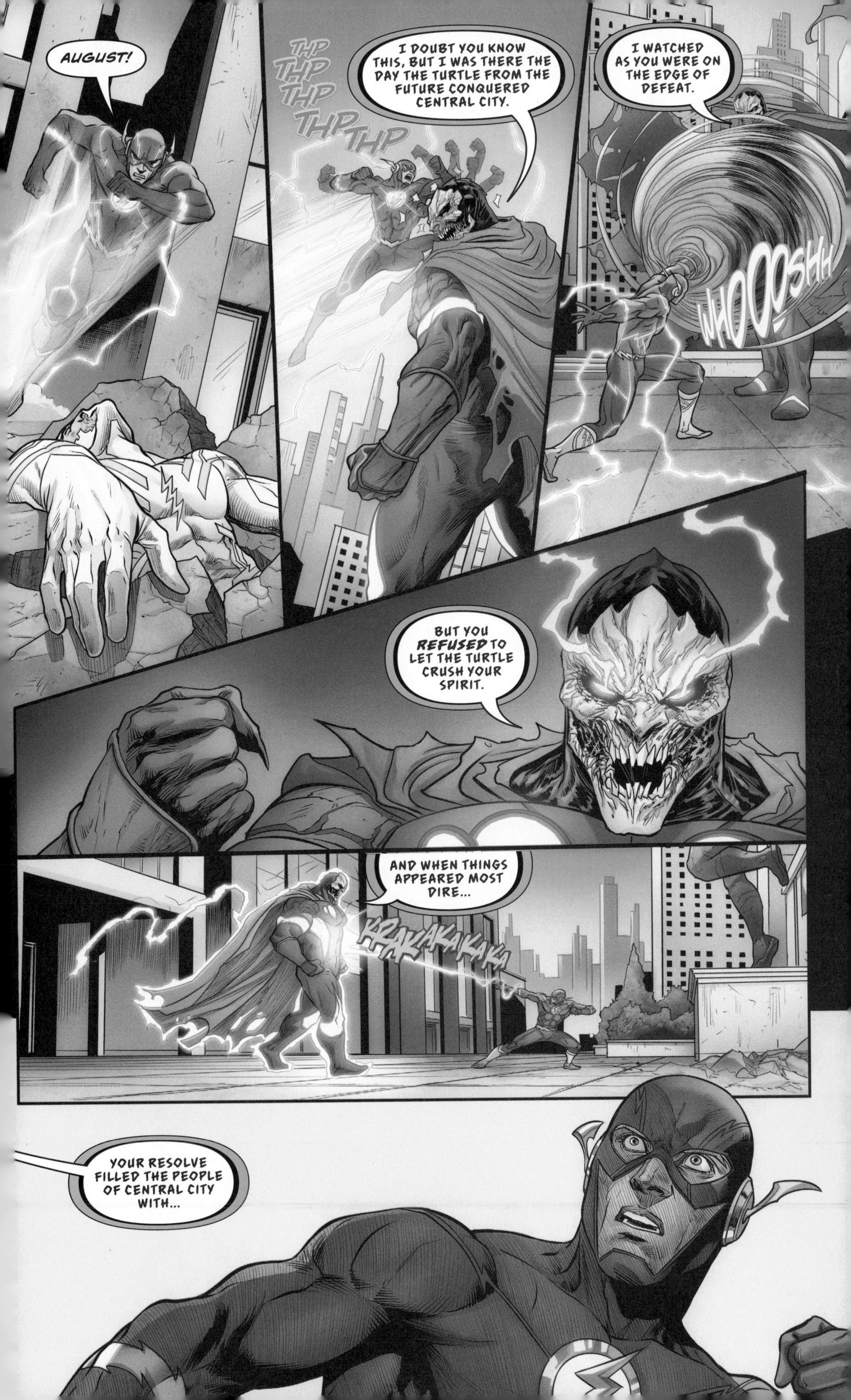
AUGUST!
THP THP THP THP THP
I DOUBT YOU KNOW THIS, BUT I WAS THERE THE DAY THE TURTLE FROM THE FUTURE CONQUERED CENTRAL CITY.
I WATCHED AS YOU WERE ON THE EDGE OF DEFEAT.
WHOOOSHH
BUT YOU REFUSED TO LET THE TURTLE CRUSH YOUR SPIRIT.
AND WHEN THINGS APPEARED MOST DIRE...
KRAKAKAKAKAKA
YOUR RESOLVE FILLED THE PEOPLE OF CENTRAL CITY WITH...

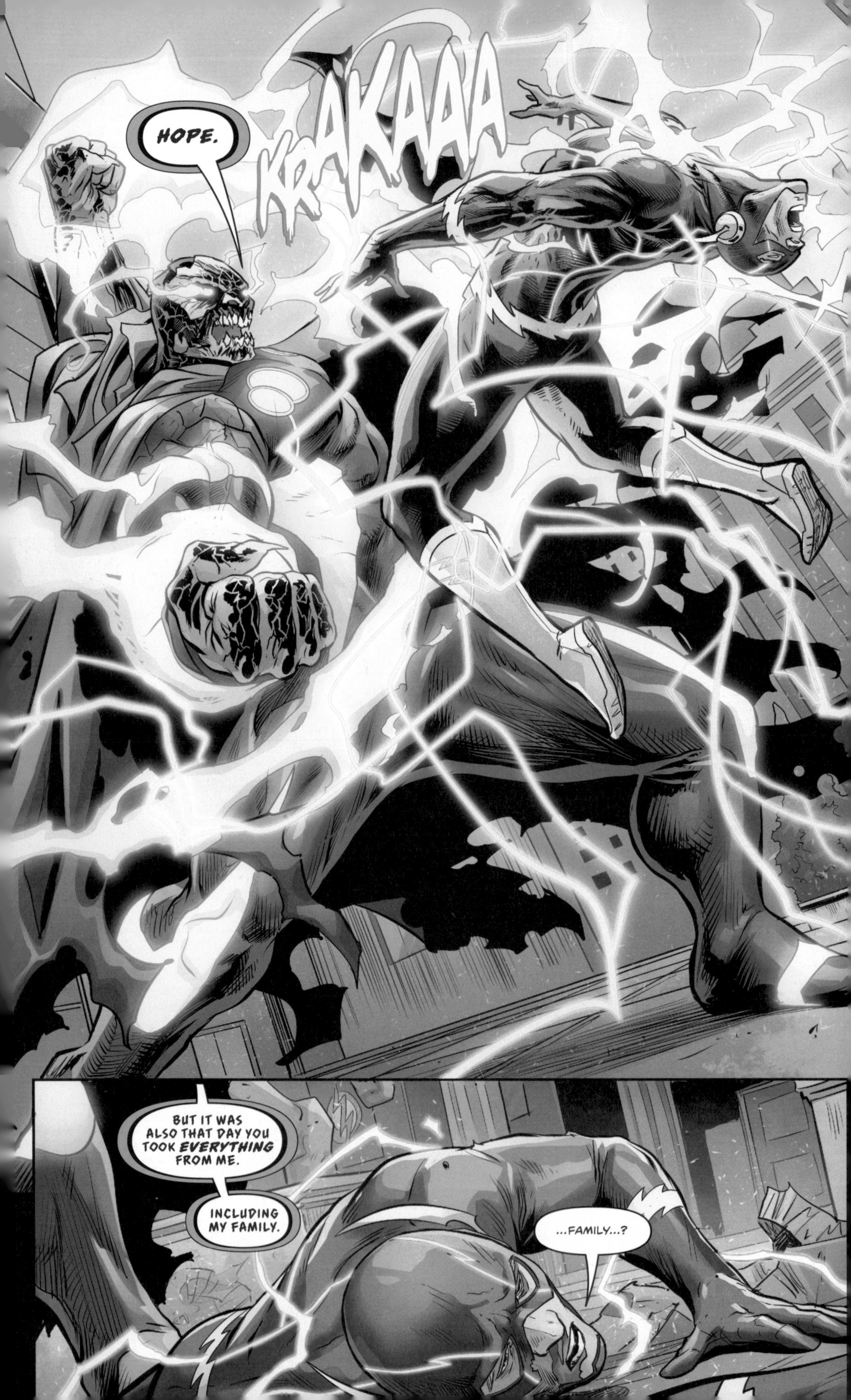
HOPE.
KRAKAAA
BUT IT WAS ALSO THAT DAY YOU TOOK EVERYTHING FROM ME.
INCLUDING MY FAMILY.
...FAMILY...?

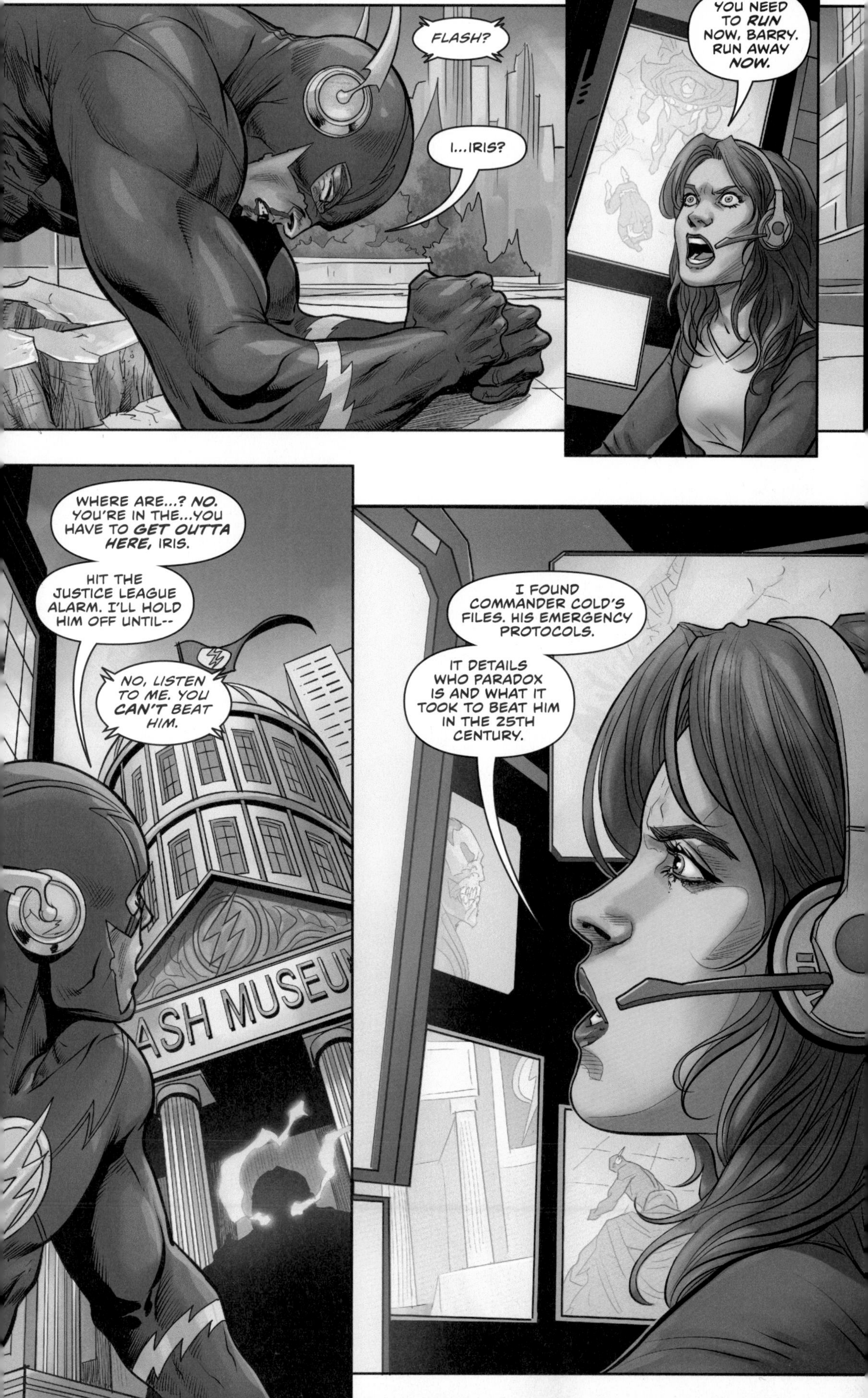
FLASH?
I...IRIS?
YOU NEED TO RUN NOW, BARRY. RUN AWAY NOW.
WHERE ARE...? NO. YOU'RE IN THE...YOU HAVE TO GET OUTTA HERE, IRIS.
HIT THE JUSTICE LEAGUE ALARM. I'LL HOLD HIM OFF UNTIL--
NO, LISTEN TO ME. YOU CAN'T BEAT HIM.
I FOUND COMMANDER COLD'S FILES. HIS EMERGENCY PROTOCOLS.
IT DETAILS WHO PARADOX IS AND WHAT IT TOOK TO BEAT HIM IN THE 25TH CENTURY.
ASH MUSEU

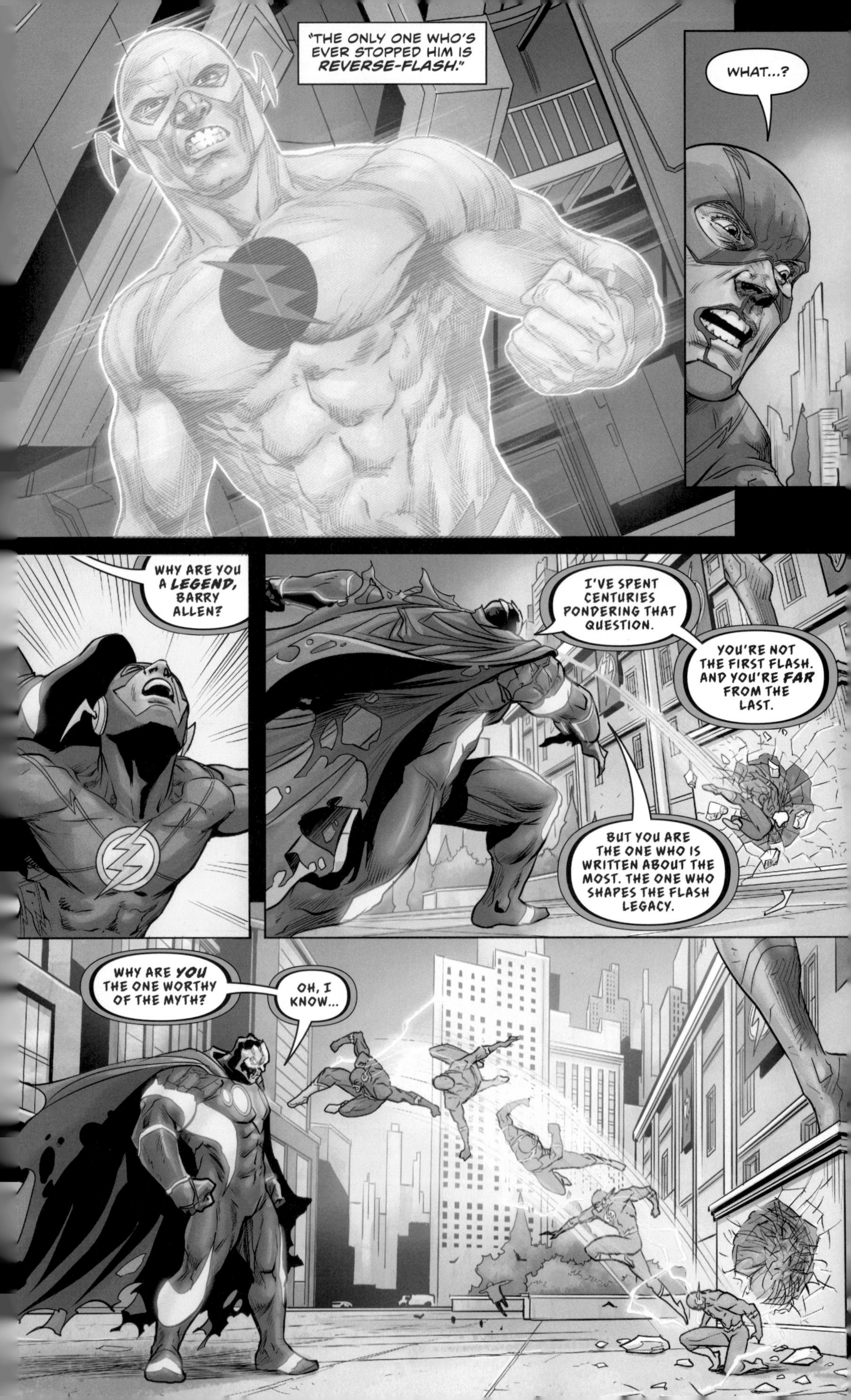
"THE ONLY ONE WHO'S EVER STOPPED HIM IS *REVERSE-FLASH*."
WHAT...?
WHY ARE YOU A *LEGEND*, BARRY ALLEN?
I'VE SPENT CENTURIES PONDERING THAT QUESTION.
YOU'RE NOT THE FIRST FLASH. AND YOU'RE *FAR* FROM THE LAST.
BUT YOU ARE THE ONE WHO IS WRITTEN ABOUT THE MOST. THE ONE WHO SHAPES THE FLASH LEGACY.
WHY ARE *YOU* THE ONE WORTHY OF THE MYTH?
OH, I KNOW...

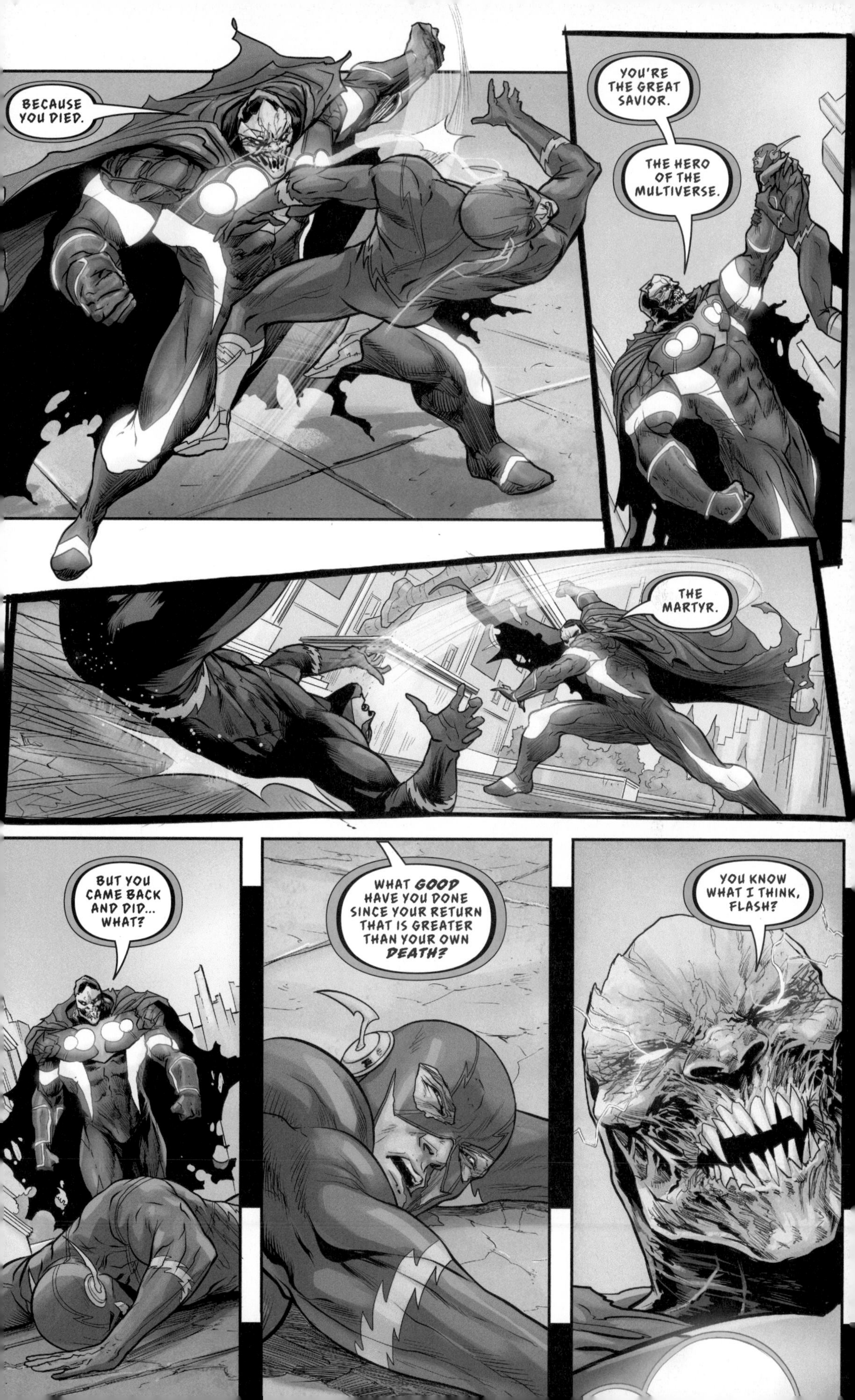
BECAUSE YOU DIED.
YOU'RE THE GREAT SAVIOR.
THE HERO OF THE MULTIVERSE.
THE MARTYR.
BUT YOU CAME BACK AND DID... WHAT?
WHAT GOOD HAVE YOU DONE SINCE YOUR RETURN THAT IS GREATER THAN YOUR OWN DEATH?
YOU KNOW WHAT I THINK, FLASH?

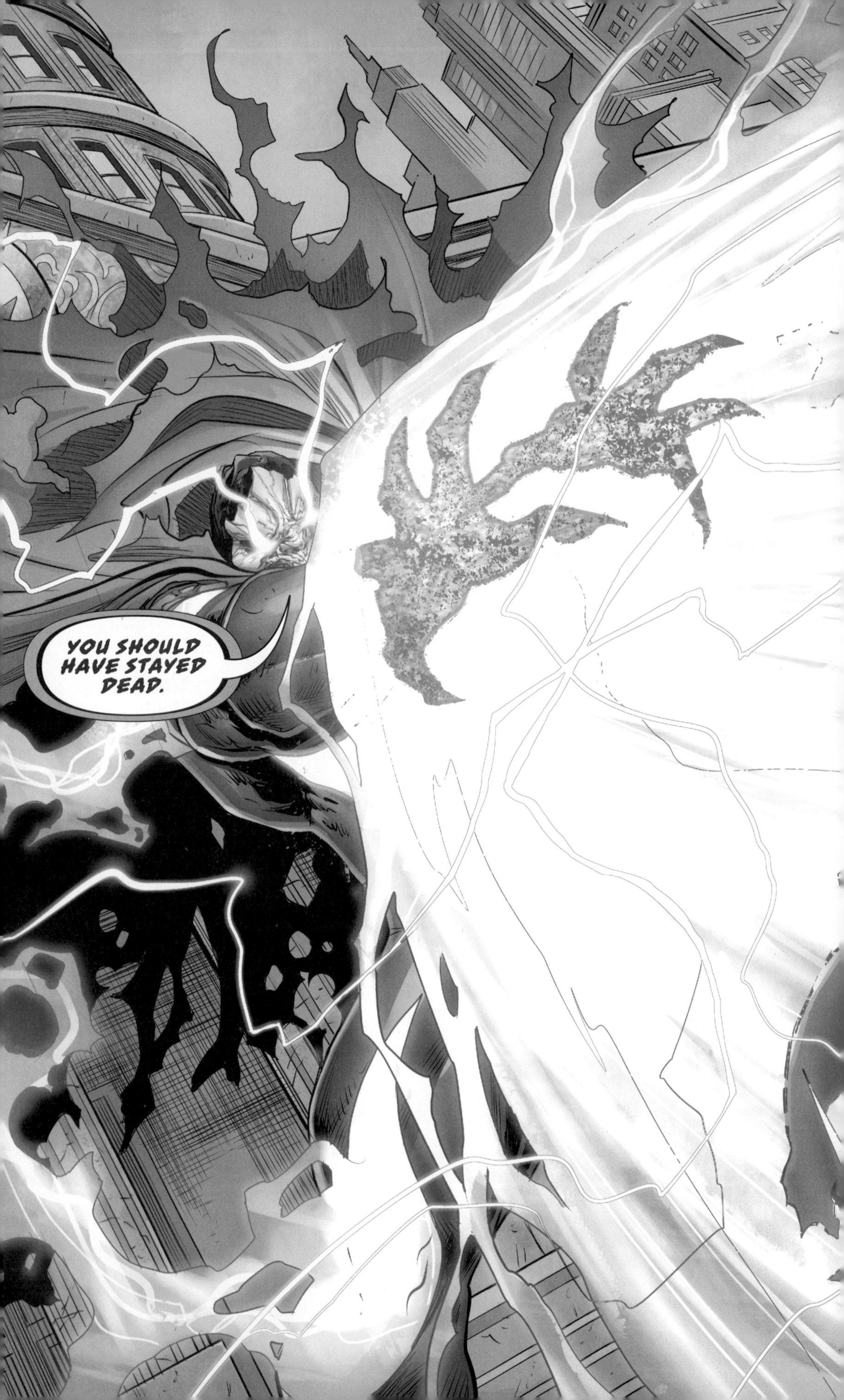
YOU SHOULD HAVE STAYED DEAD.

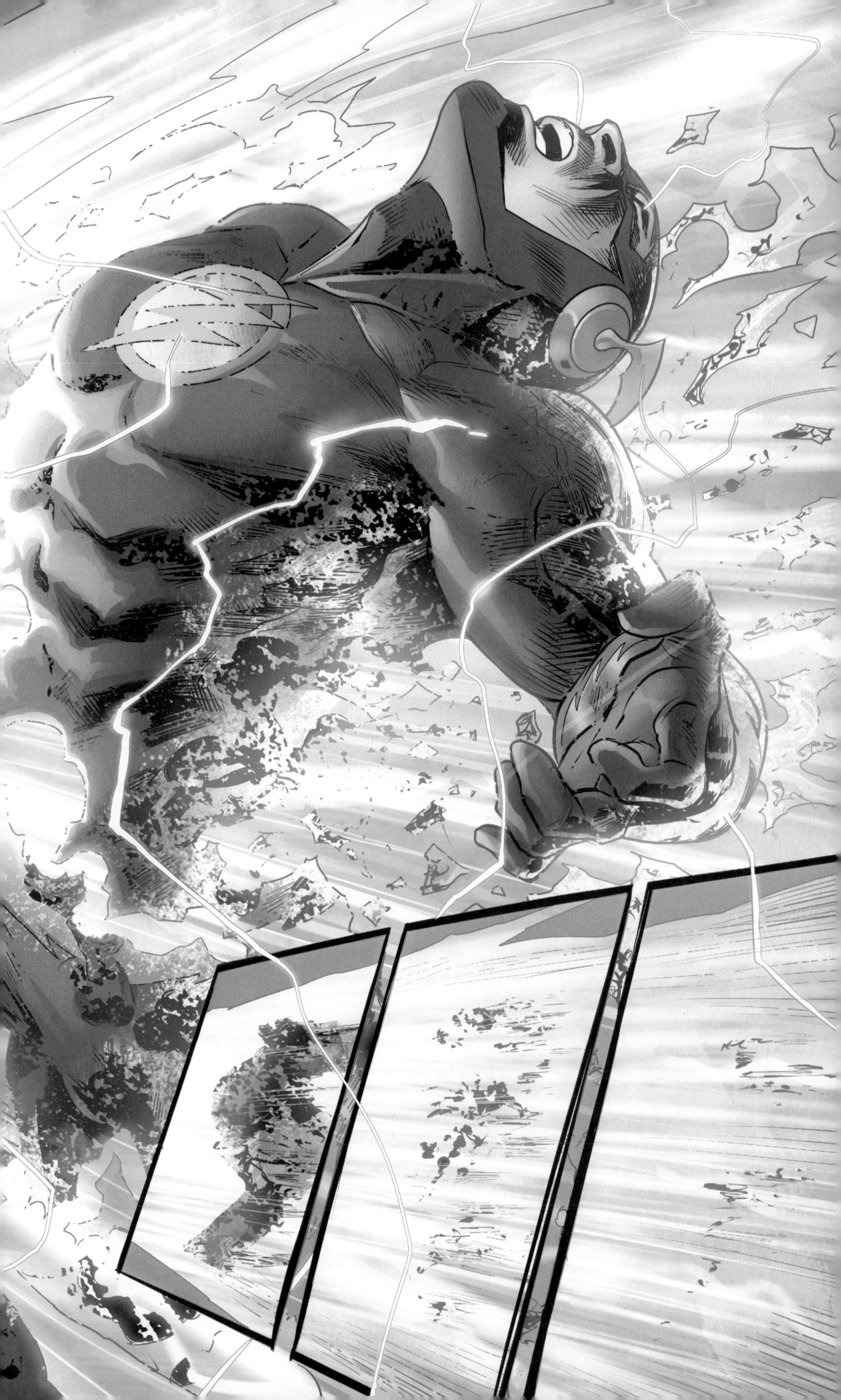

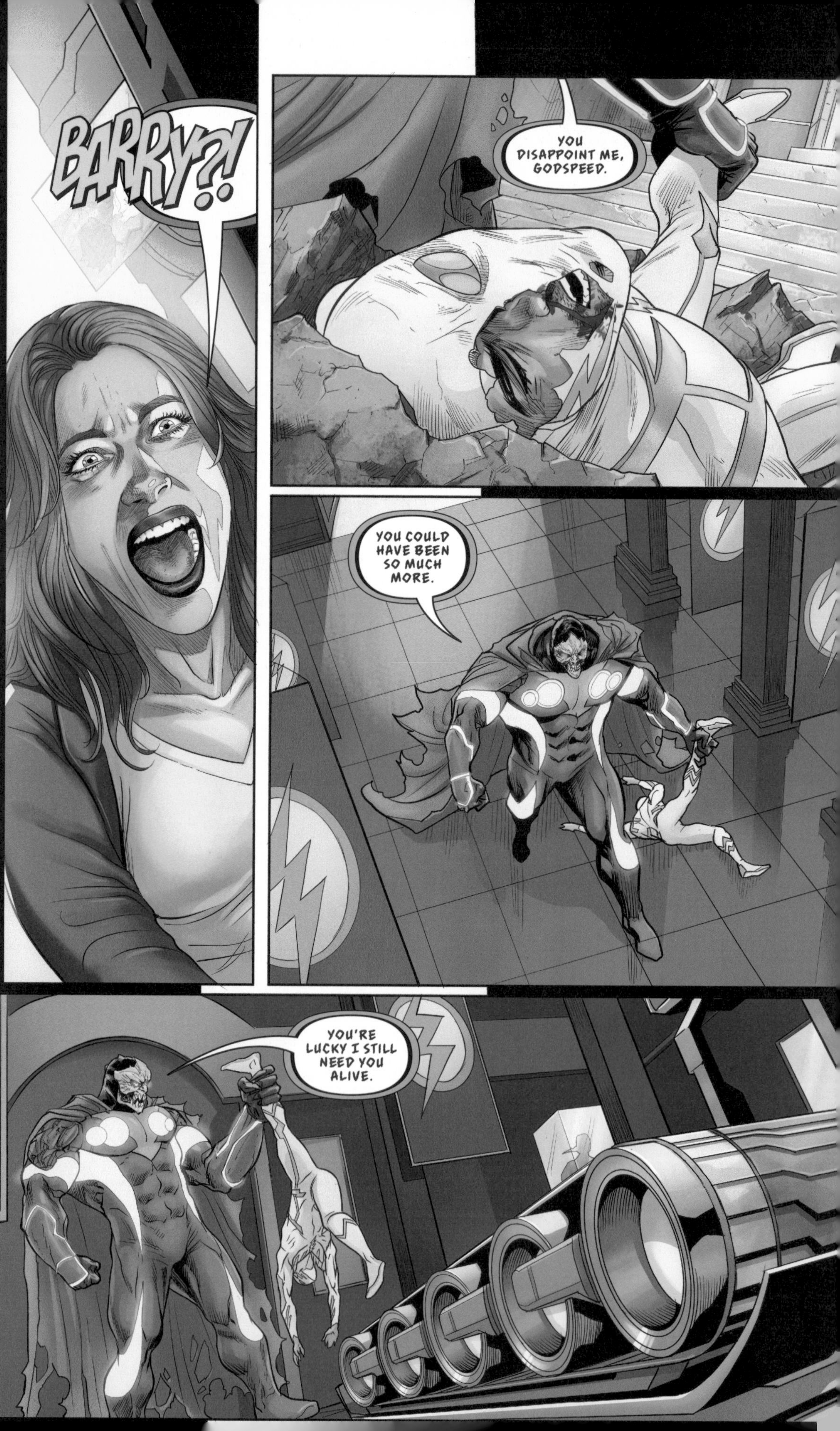
BARRY?!
YOU DISAPPOINT ME, GODSPEED.
YOU COULD HAVE BEEN SO MUCH MORE.
YOU'RE LUCKY I STILL NEED YOU ALIVE.

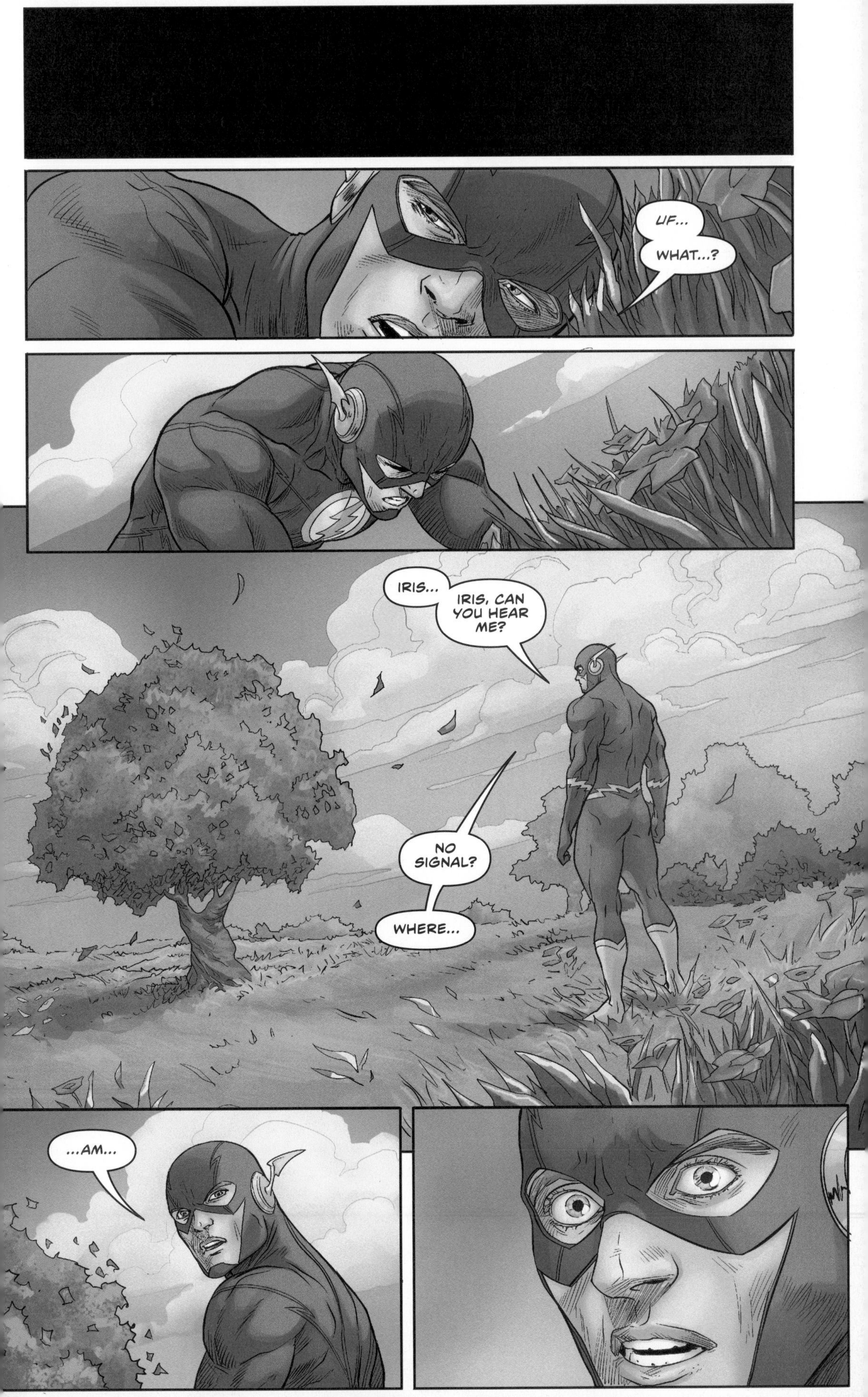
UF...
WHAT...?
IRIS...
IRIS, CAN YOU HEAR ME?
NO SIGNAL?
WHERE...
...AM...

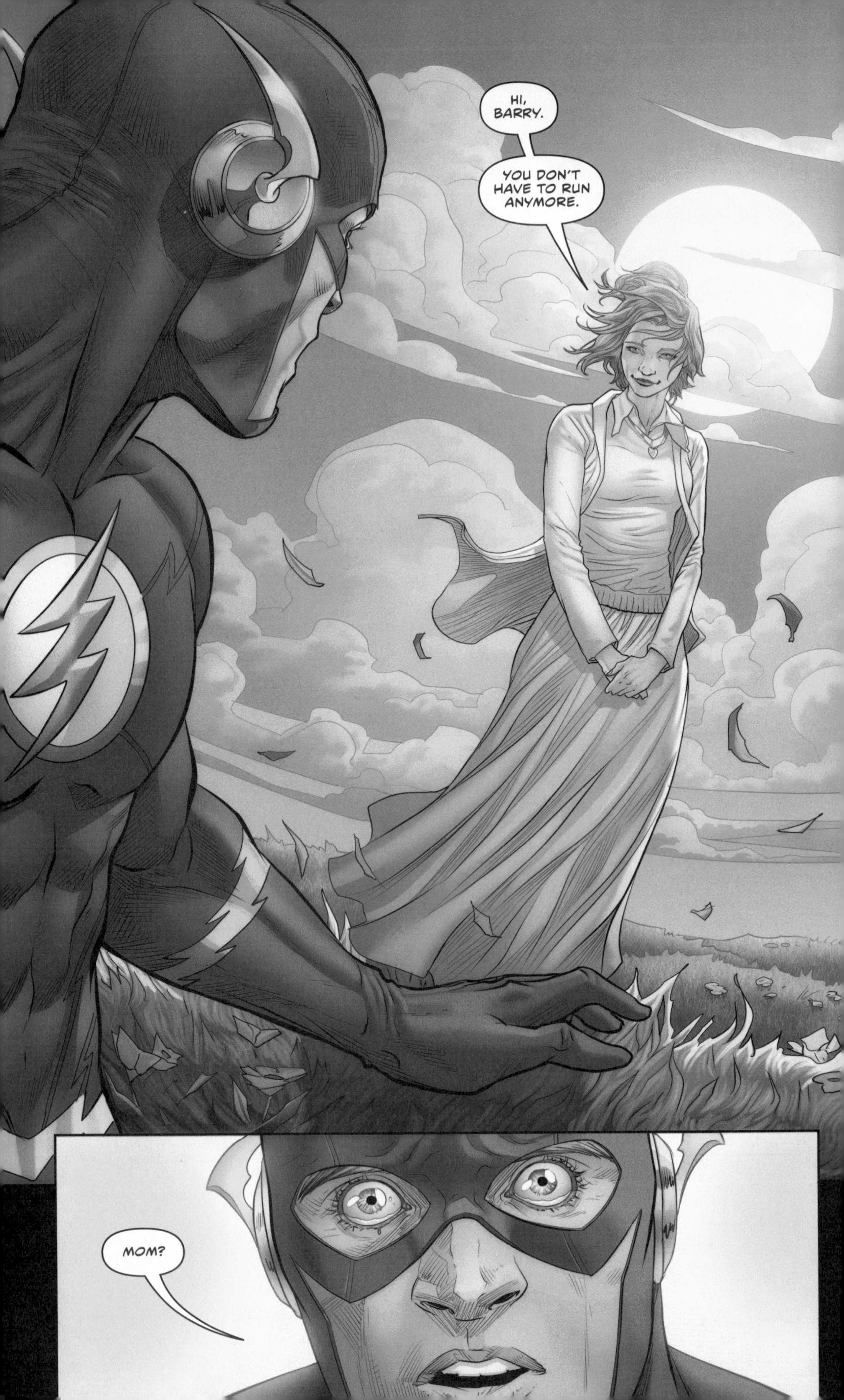
HI, BARRY.
YOU DON'T HAVE TO RUN ANYMORE.
MOM?

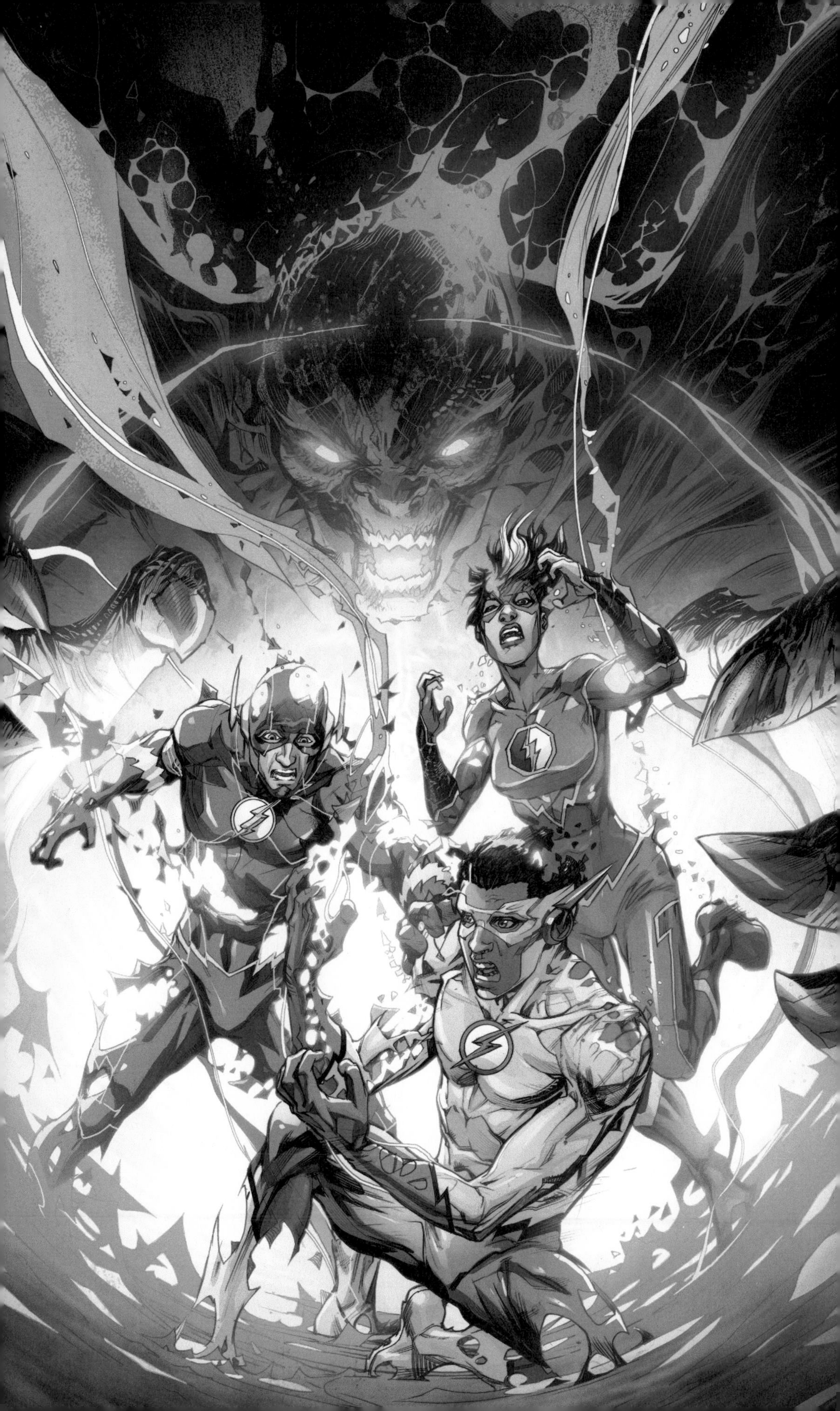

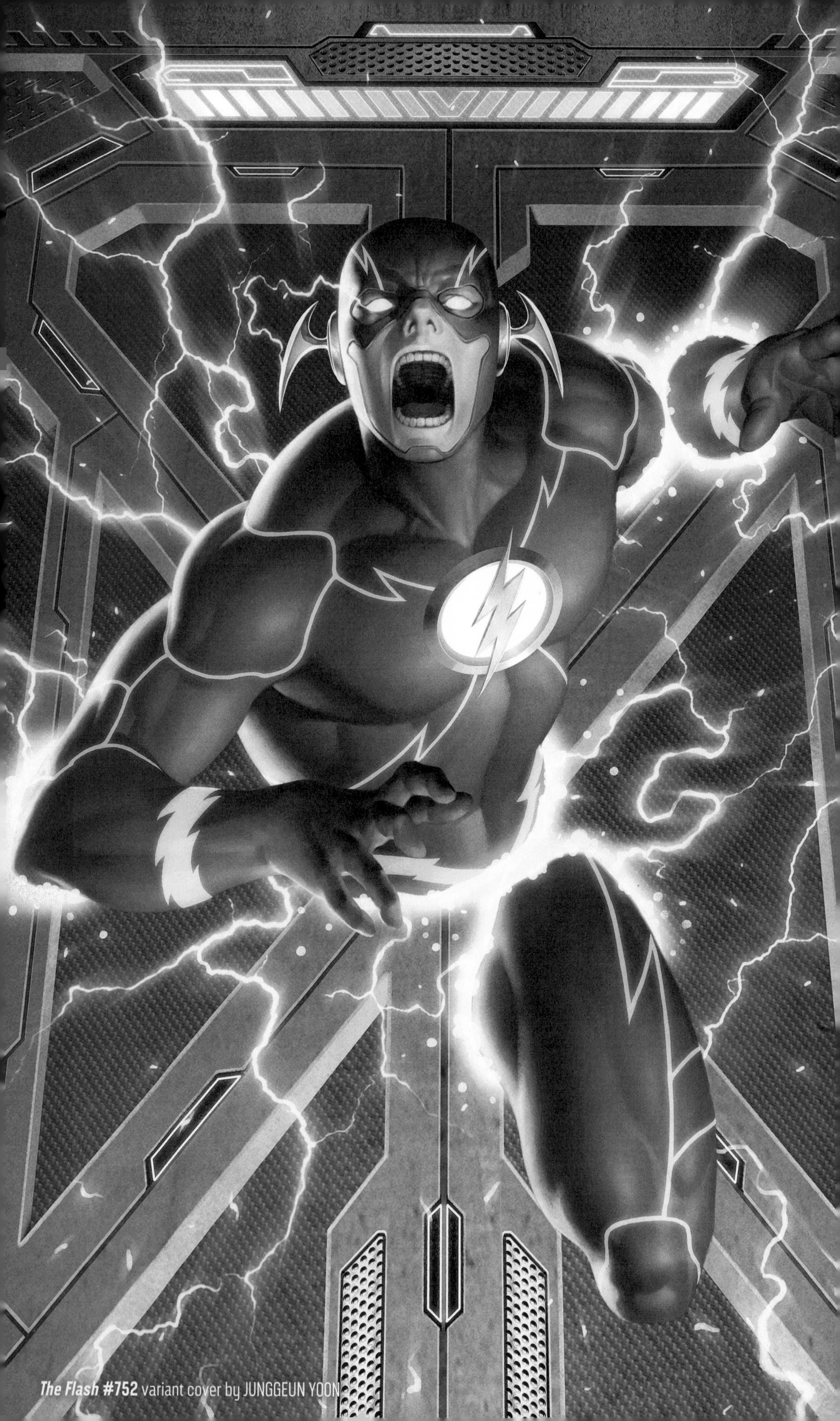

***The Flash* #752** variant cover by JUNGGEUN YOON

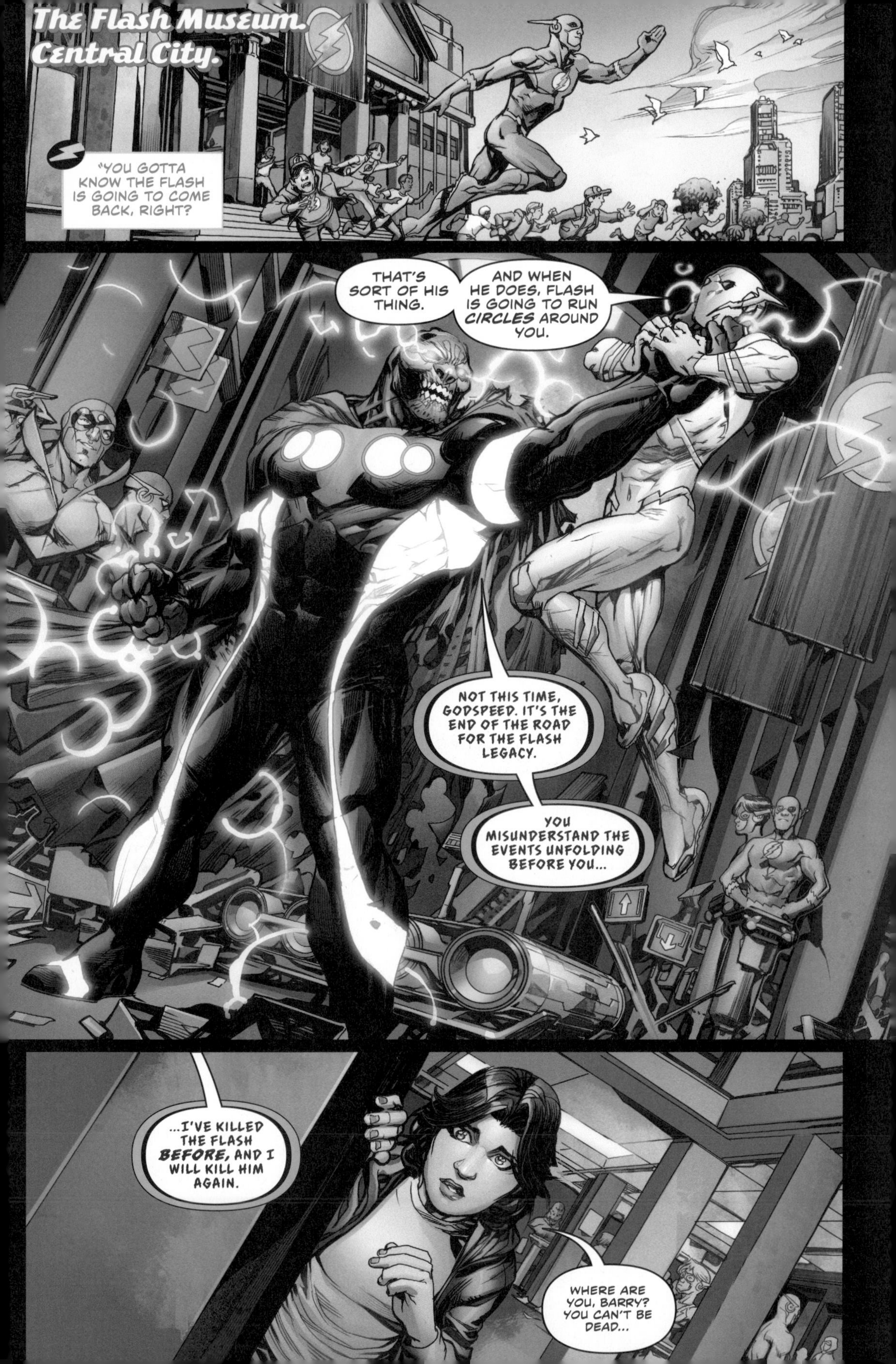
The Flash Museum. Central City.
"YOU GOTTA KNOW THE FLASH IS GOING TO COME BACK, RIGHT?
THAT'S SORT OF HIS THING.
AND WHEN HE DOES, FLASH IS GOING TO RUN CIRCLES AROUND YOU.
NOT THIS TIME, GODSPEED. IT'S THE END OF THE ROAD FOR THE FLASH LEGACY.
YOU MISUNDERSTAND THE EVENTS UNFOLDING BEFORE YOU...
...I'VE KILLED THE FLASH BEFORE, AND I WILL KILL HIM AGAIN.
WHERE ARE YOU, BARRY? YOU CAN'T BE DEAD...

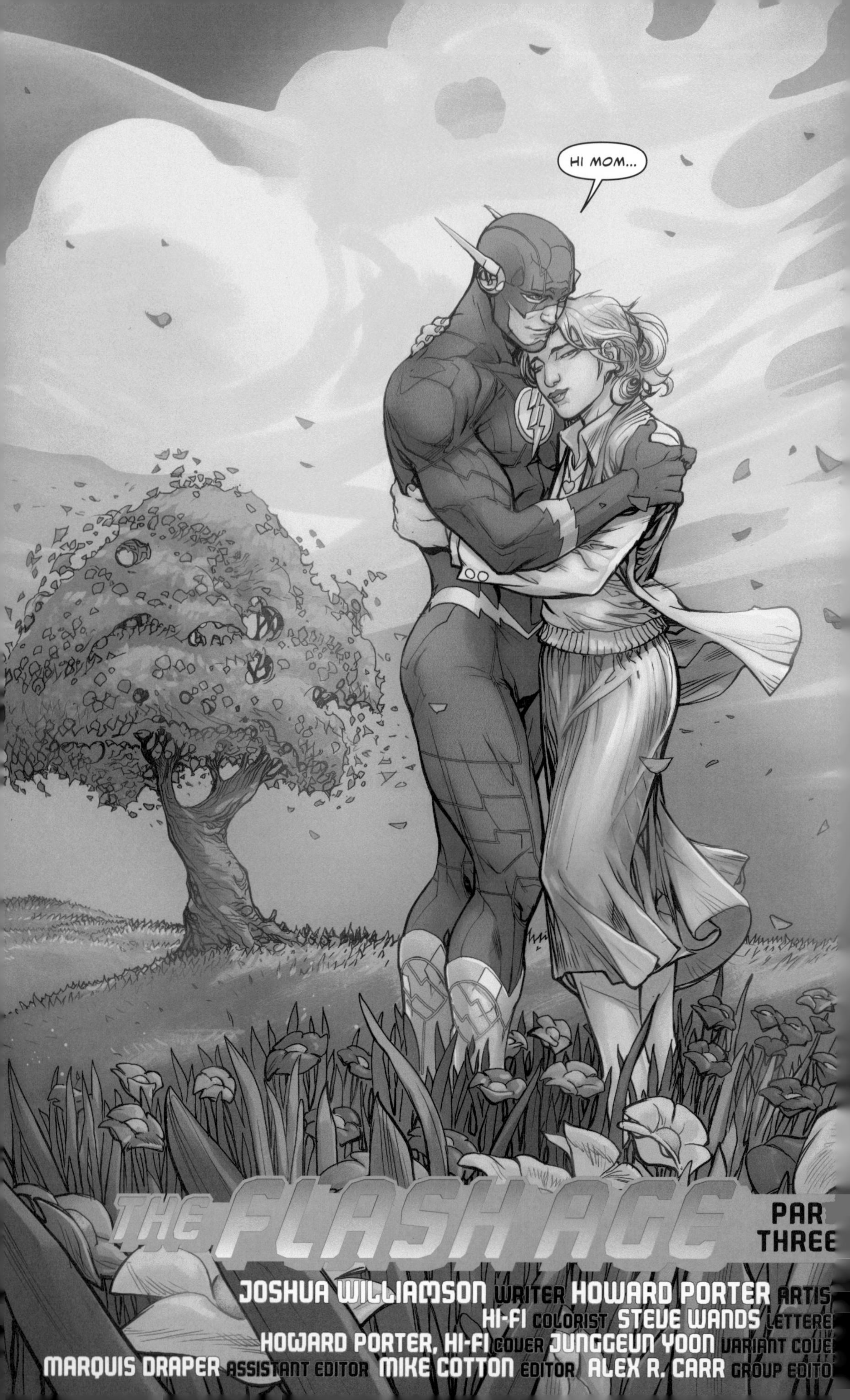
HI MOM...
THE FLASH AGE
PAR
THREE
JOSHUA WILLIAMSON WRITER HOWARD PORTER ARTIS
HI-FI COLORIST STEVE WANDS LETTERE
HOWARD PORTER, HI-FI COVER JUNGGEUN YOON VARIANT COVE
MARQUIS DRAPER ASSISTANT EDITOR MIKE COTTON EDITOR ALEX R. CARR GROUP EDITO

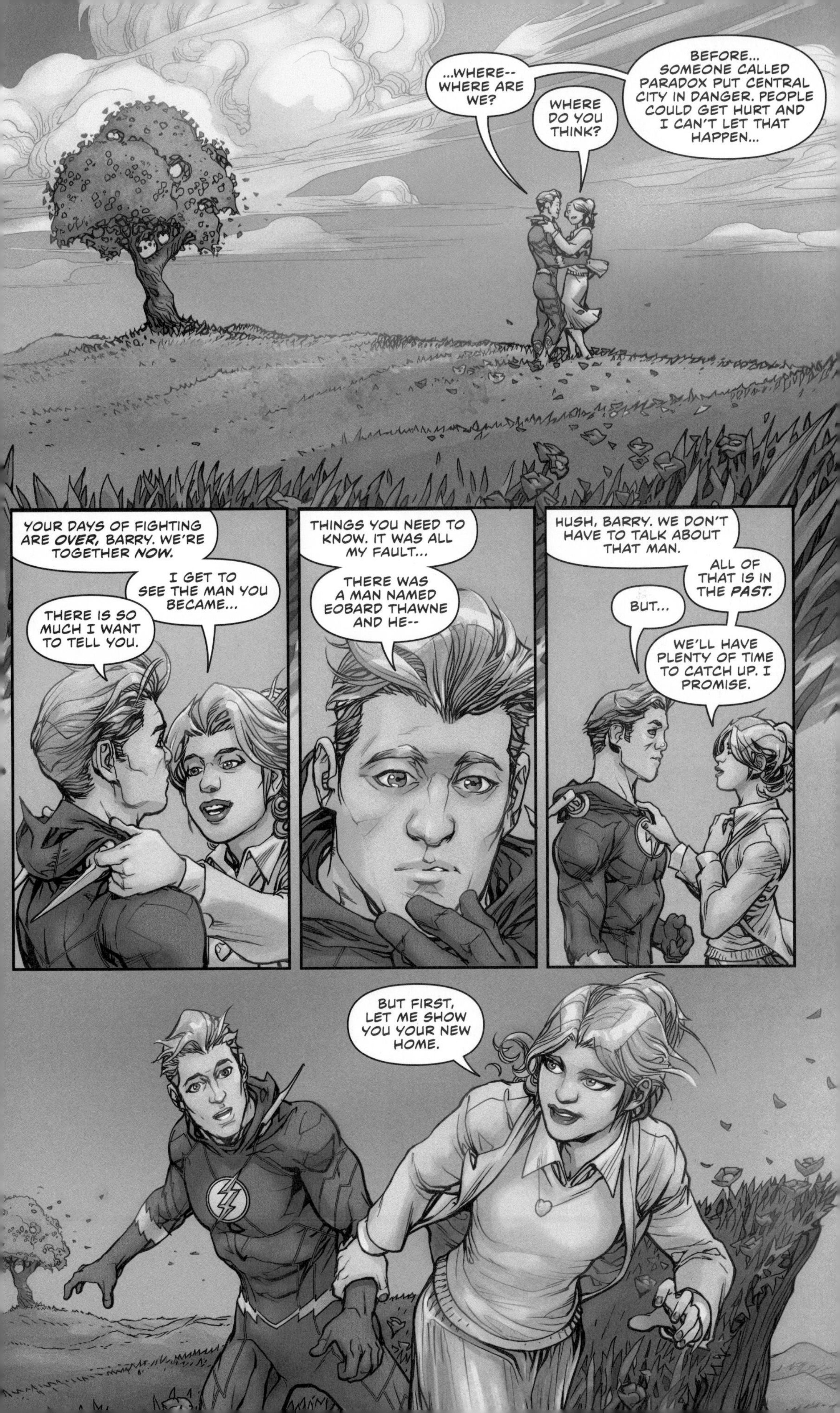

...WHERE--
WHERE ARE
WE?
WHERE
DO YOU
THINK?
BEFORE...
SOMEONE CALLED
PARADOX PUT CENTRAL
CITY IN DANGER. PEOPLE
COULD GET HURT AND
I CAN'T LET THAT
HAPPEN...
YOUR DAYS OF FIGHTING
ARE *OVER*, BARRY. WE'RE
TOGETHER *NOW*.
I GET TO
SEE THE MAN YOU
BECAME...
THERE IS SO
MUCH I WANT
TO TELL YOU.
THINGS YOU NEED TO
KNOW. IT WAS ALL
MY FAULT...
THERE WAS
A MAN NAMED
EOBARD THAWNE
AND HE--
HUSH, BARRY. WE DON'T
HAVE TO TALK ABOUT
THAT MAN.
ALL OF
THAT IS IN
THE *PAST*.
BUT...
WE'LL HAVE
PLENTY OF TIME
TO CATCH UP. I
PROMISE.
BUT FIRST,
LET ME SHOW
YOU YOUR NEW
HOME.

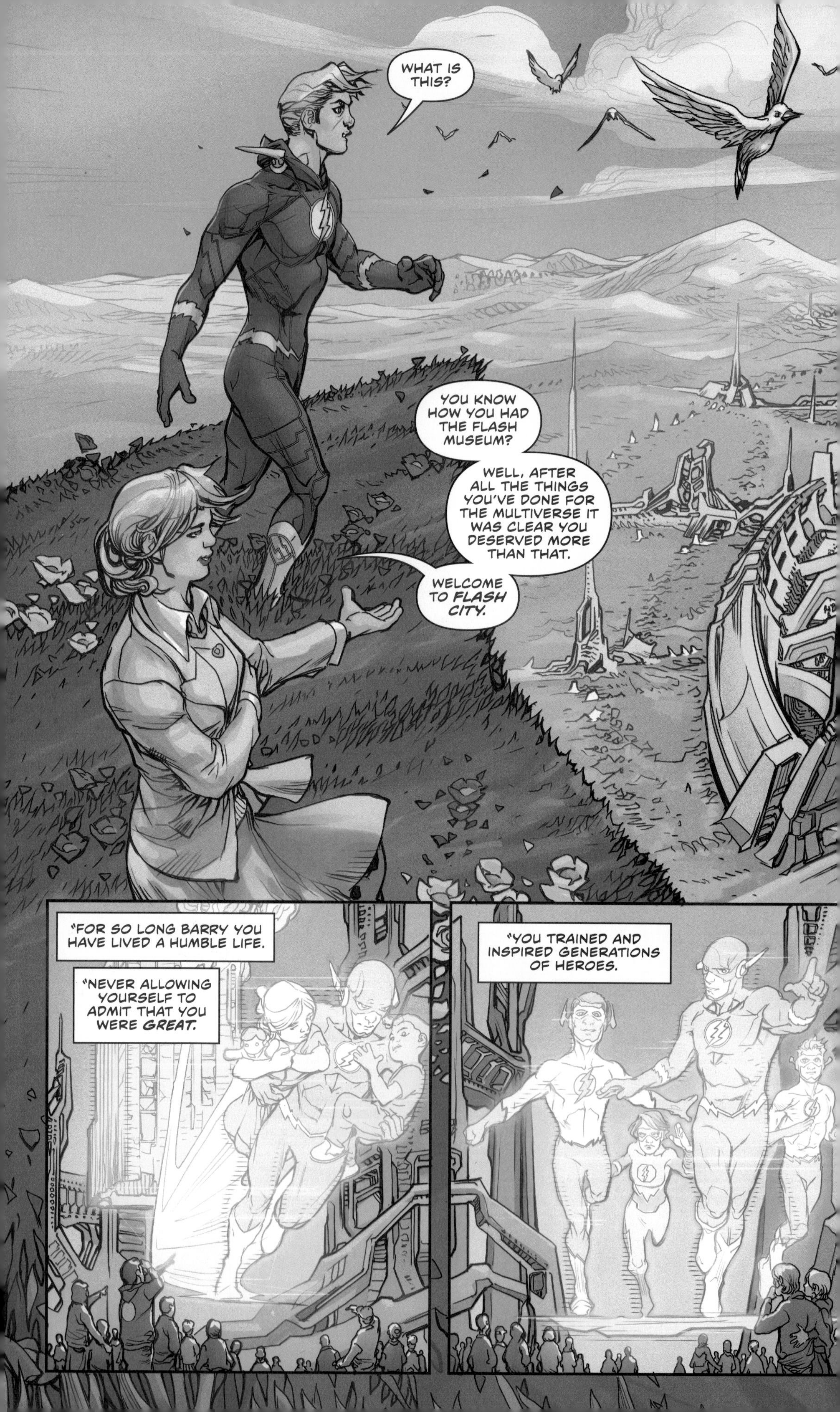
WHAT IS THIS?
YOU KNOW HOW YOU HAD THE FLASH MUSEUM?
WELL, AFTER ALL THE THINGS YOU'VE DONE FOR THE MULTIVERSE IT WAS CLEAR YOU DESERVED MORE THAN THAT.
WELCOME TO *FLASH CITY.*
"FOR SO LONG BARRY YOU HAVE LIVED A HUMBLE LIFE.
"NEVER ALLOWING YOURSELF TO ADMIT THAT YOU WERE *GREAT.*
"YOU TRAINED AND INSPIRED GENERATIONS OF HEROES.

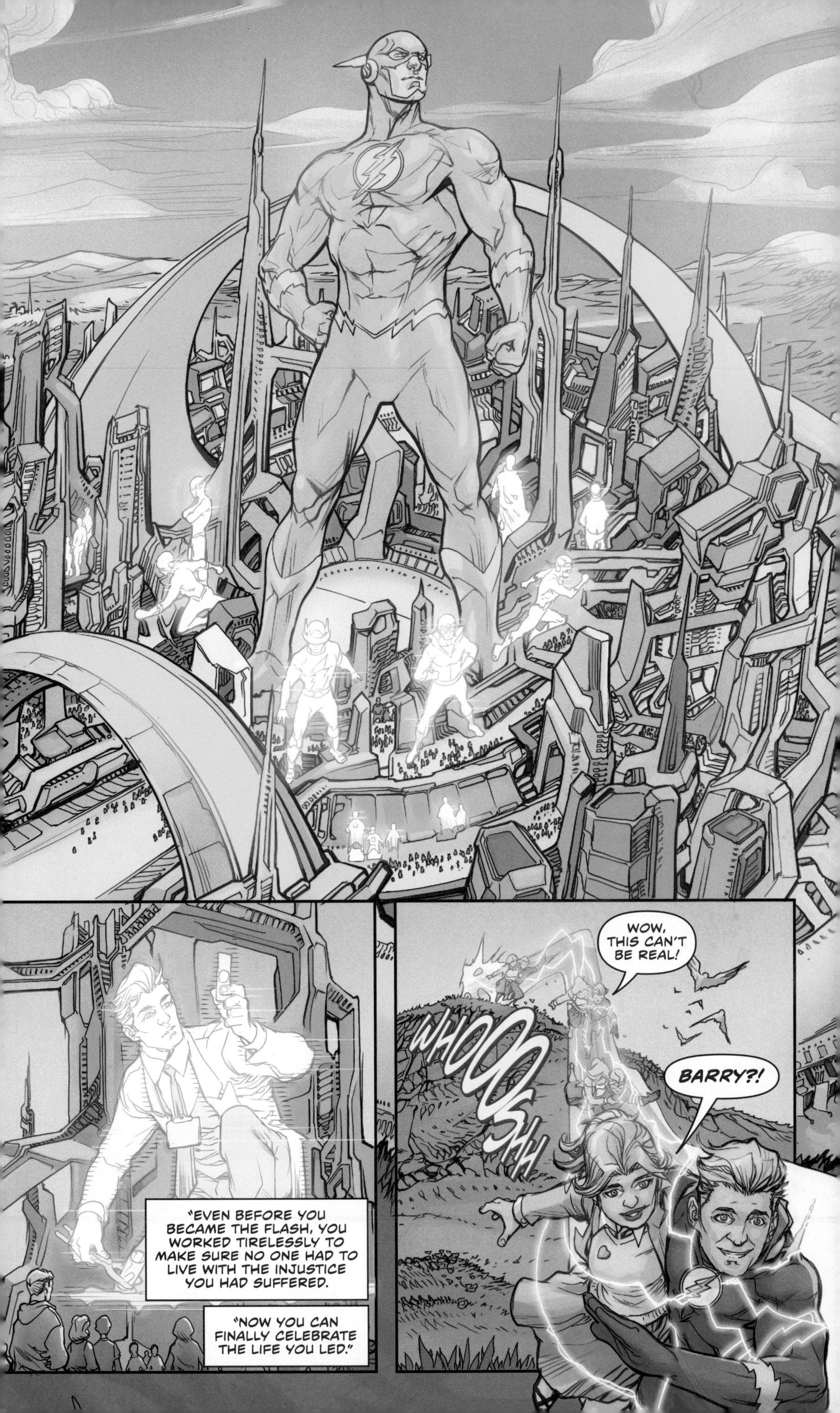
"EVEN BEFORE YOU BECAME THE FLASH, YOU WORKED TIRELESSLY TO MAKE SURE NO ONE HAD TO LIVE WITH THE INJUSTICE YOU HAD SUFFERED.
"NOW YOU CAN FINALLY CELEBRATE THE LIFE YOU LED."
WHOOOOSHH
WOW, THIS CAN'T BE REAL!
BARRY?!

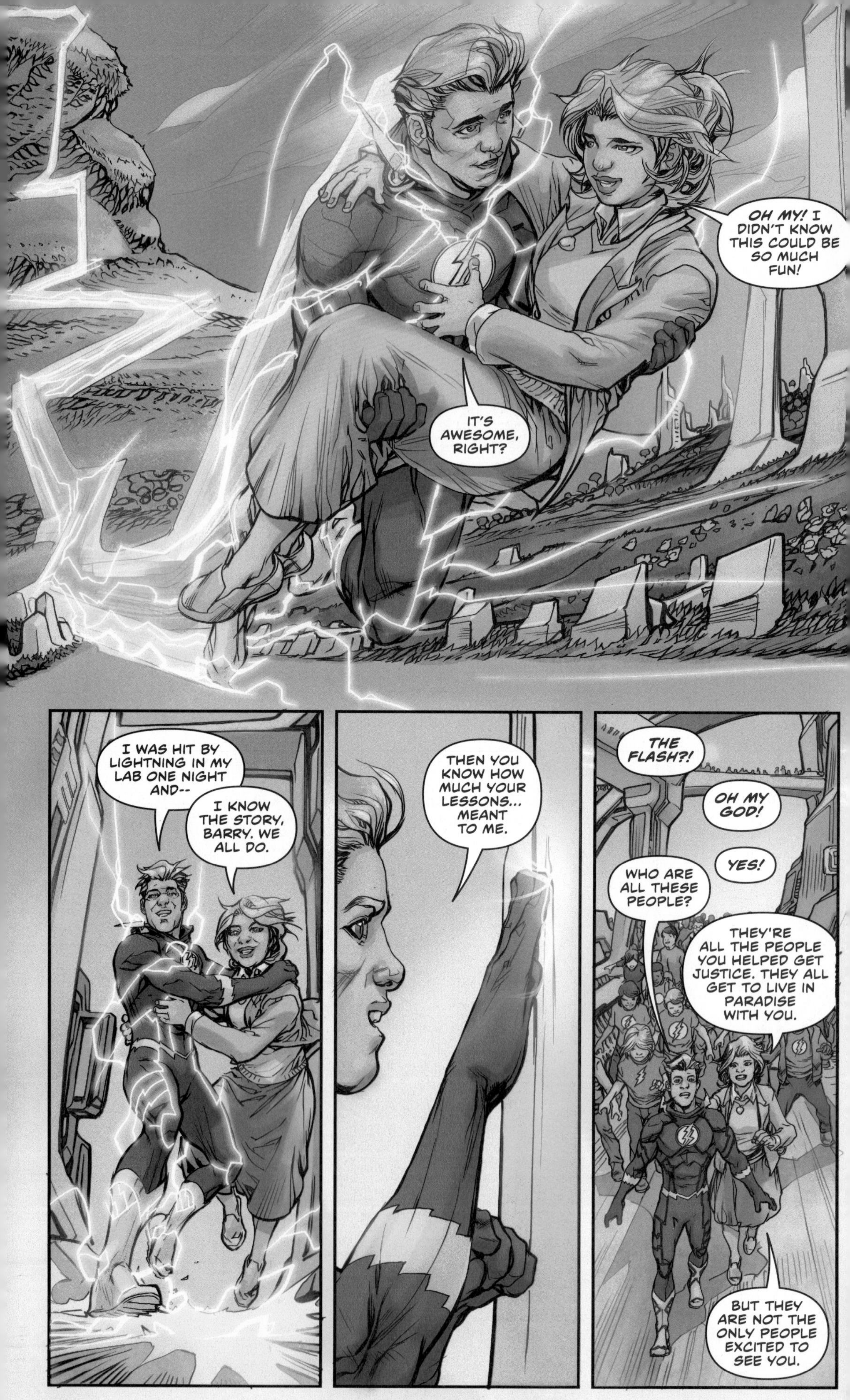
OH MY! I DIDN'T KNOW THIS COULD BE SO MUCH FUN!
IT'S AWESOME, RIGHT?
I WAS HIT BY LIGHTNING IN MY LAB ONE NIGHT AND--
I KNOW THE STORY, BARRY. WE ALL DO.
THEN YOU KNOW HOW MUCH YOUR LESSONS... MEANT TO ME.
THE FLASH?!
OH MY GOD!
YES!
WHO ARE ALL THESE PEOPLE?
THEY'RE ALL THE PEOPLE YOU HELPED GET JUSTICE. THEY ALL GET TO LIVE IN PARADISE WITH YOU.
BUT THEY ARE NOT THE ONLY PEOPLE EXCITED TO SEE YOU.

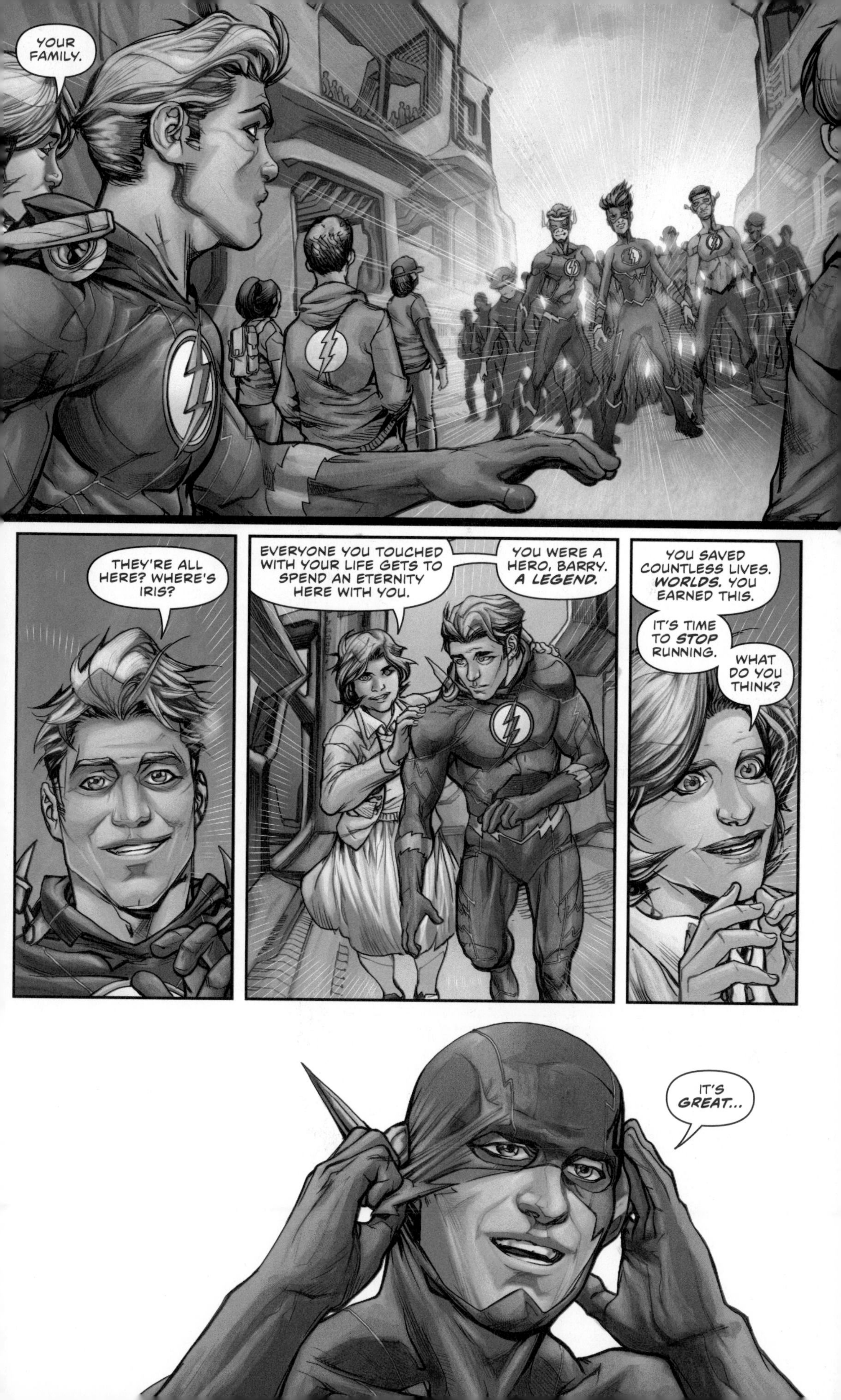
YOUR FAMILY.
THEY'RE ALL HERE? WHERE'S IRIS?
EVERYONE YOU TOUCHED WITH YOUR LIFE GETS TO SPEND AN ETERNITY HERE WITH YOU.
YOU WERE A HERO, BARRY. A LEGEND.
YOU SAVED COUNTLESS LIVES. WORLDS. YOU EARNED THIS.
IT'S TIME TO STOP RUNNING.
WHAT DO YOU THINK?
IT'S GREAT...

...BUT IT'S NOT REAL.

AND NEITHER ARE YOU.

WHAT?

HOLD ON.

OKAY, YEAH, THIS WHOLE WORLD IS A CONSTRUCT OF SOME KIND.

NOT SURE IF IT'S IN MY HEAD OR A VERY COMPLICATED ILLUSION. BEYOND ANYTHING I'VE EVER SEEN.

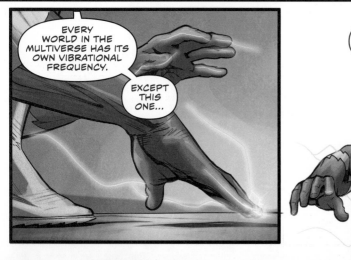

EVERY WORLD IN THE MULTIVERSE HAS ITS OWN VIBRATIONAL FREQUENCY.

EXCEPT THIS ONE...

IT HAS NONE.

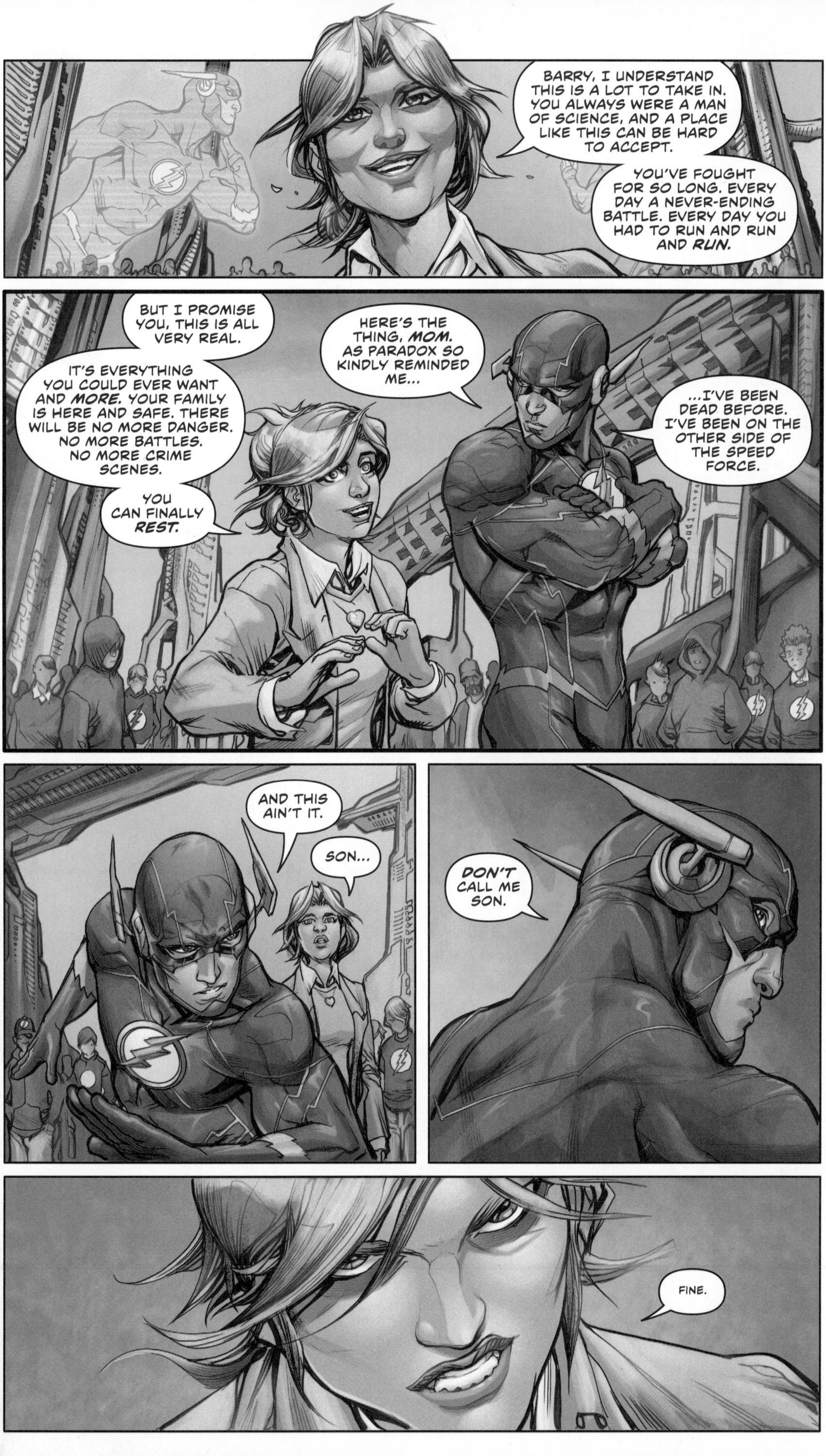

BARRY, I UNDERSTAND THIS IS A LOT TO TAKE IN. YOU ALWAYS WERE A MAN OF SCIENCE, AND A PLACE LIKE THIS CAN BE HARD TO ACCEPT.
YOU'VE FOUGHT FOR SO LONG. EVERY DAY A NEVER-ENDING BATTLE. EVERY DAY YOU HAD TO RUN AND RUN AND *RUN.*
BUT I PROMISE YOU, THIS IS ALL VERY REAL.
IT'S EVERYTHING YOU COULD EVER WANT AND *MORE.* YOUR FAMILY IS HERE AND SAFE. THERE WILL BE NO MORE DANGER. NO MORE BATTLES. NO MORE CRIME SCENES.
YOU CAN FINALLY *REST.*
HERE'S THE THING, *MOM.* AS PARADOX SO KINDLY REMINDED ME...
...I'VE BEEN DEAD BEFORE. I'VE BEEN ON THE OTHER SIDE OF THE SPEED FORCE.
AND THIS AIN'T IT.
SON...
DON'T CALL ME SON.
FINE.

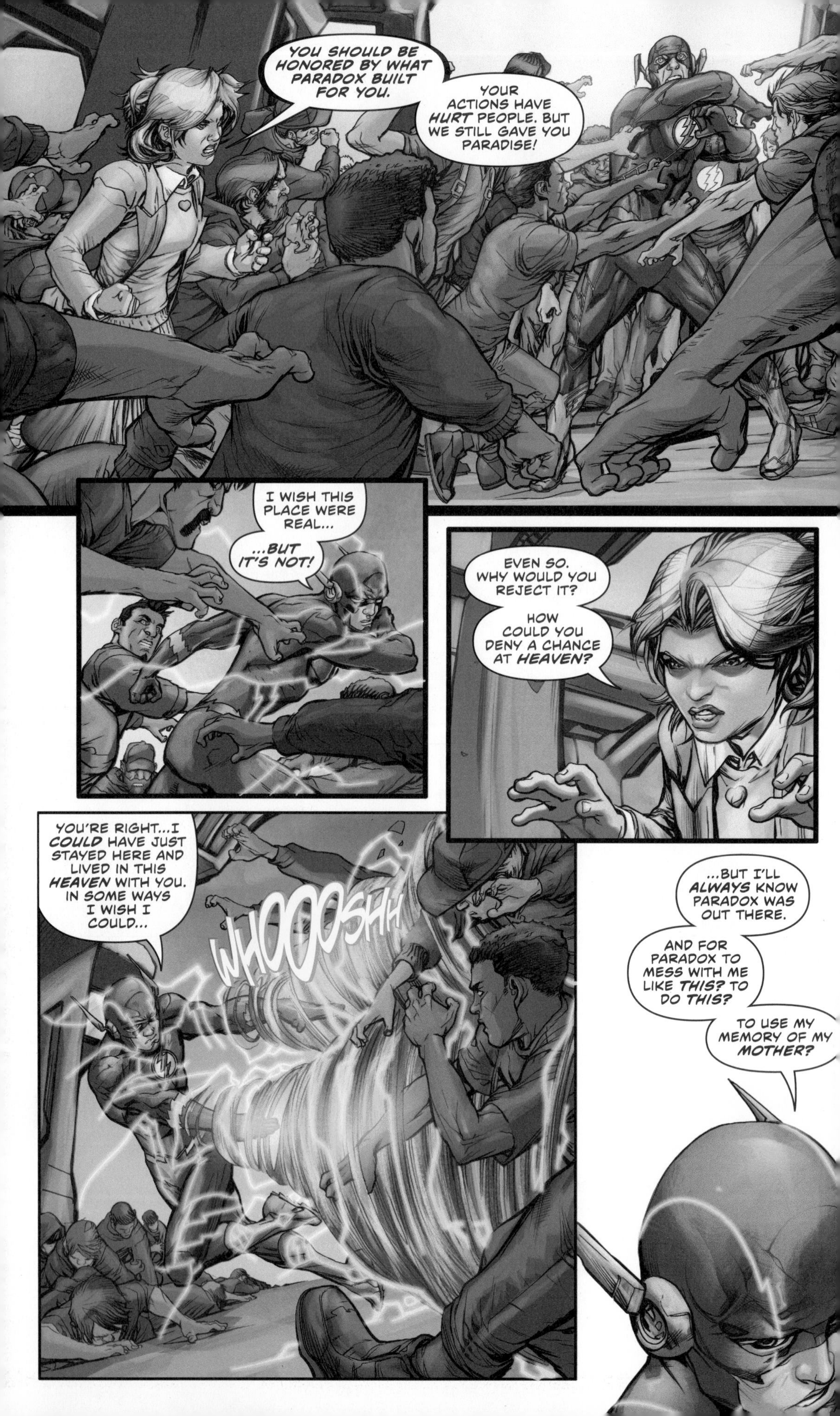
YOU SHOULD BE HONORED BY WHAT PARADOX BUILT FOR YOU.
YOUR ACTIONS HAVE HURT PEOPLE. BUT WE STILL GAVE YOU PARADISE!
I WISH THIS PLACE WERE REAL...
...BUT IT'S NOT!
EVEN SO. WHY WOULD YOU REJECT IT?
HOW COULD YOU DENY A CHANCE AT HEAVEN?
YOU'RE RIGHT...I COULD HAVE JUST STAYED HERE AND LIVED IN THIS HEAVEN WITH YOU. IN SOME WAYS I WISH I COULD...
WHOOOSHH
...BUT I'LL ALWAYS KNOW PARADOX WAS OUT THERE.
AND FOR PARADOX TO MESS WITH ME LIKE THIS? TO DO THIS?
TO USE MY MEMORY OF MY MOTHER?

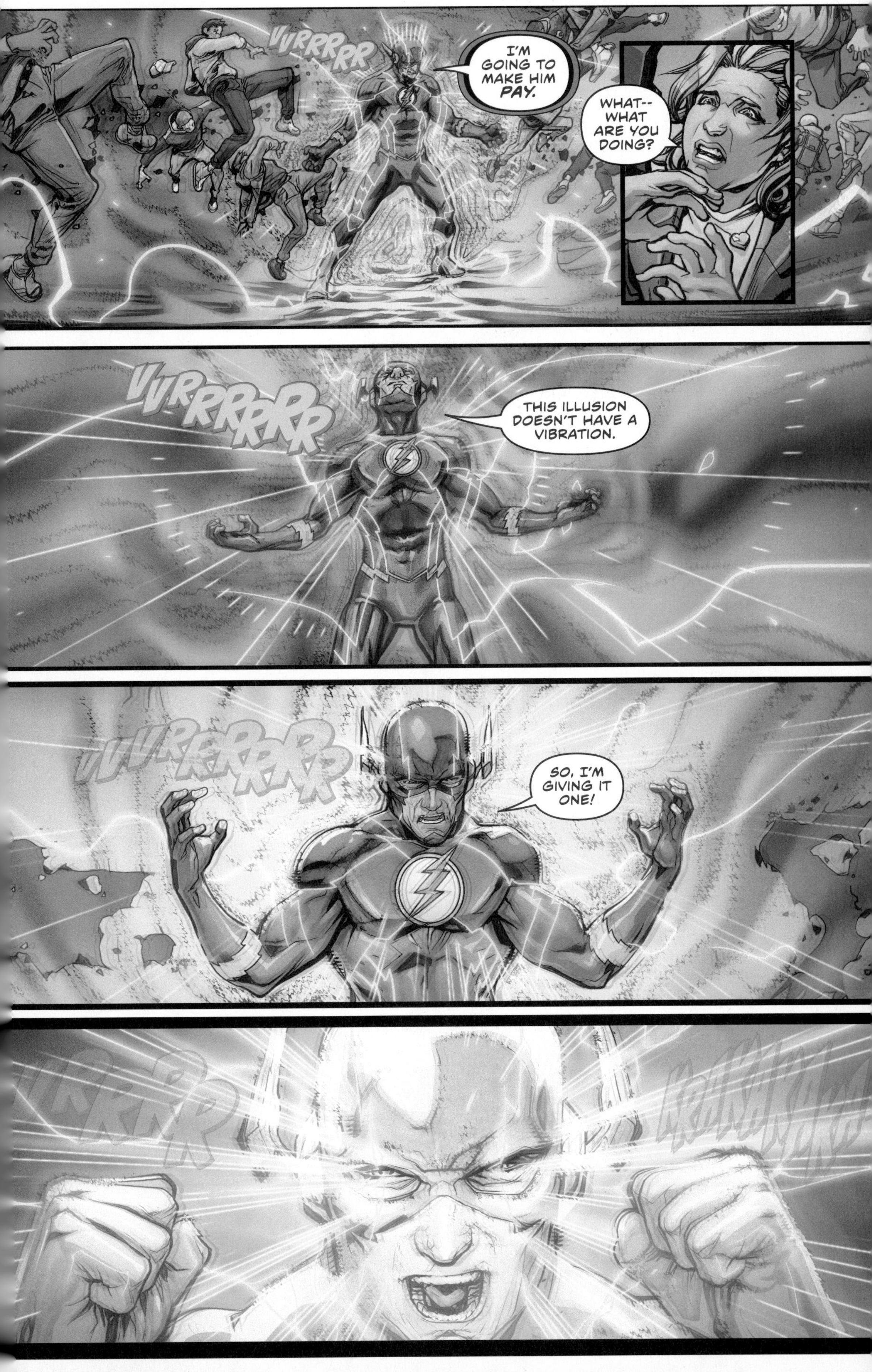
I'M GOING TO MAKE HIM PAY.
WHAT-- WHAT ARE YOU DOING?
THIS ILLUSION DOESN'T HAVE A VIBRATION.
SO, I'M GIVING IT ONE!

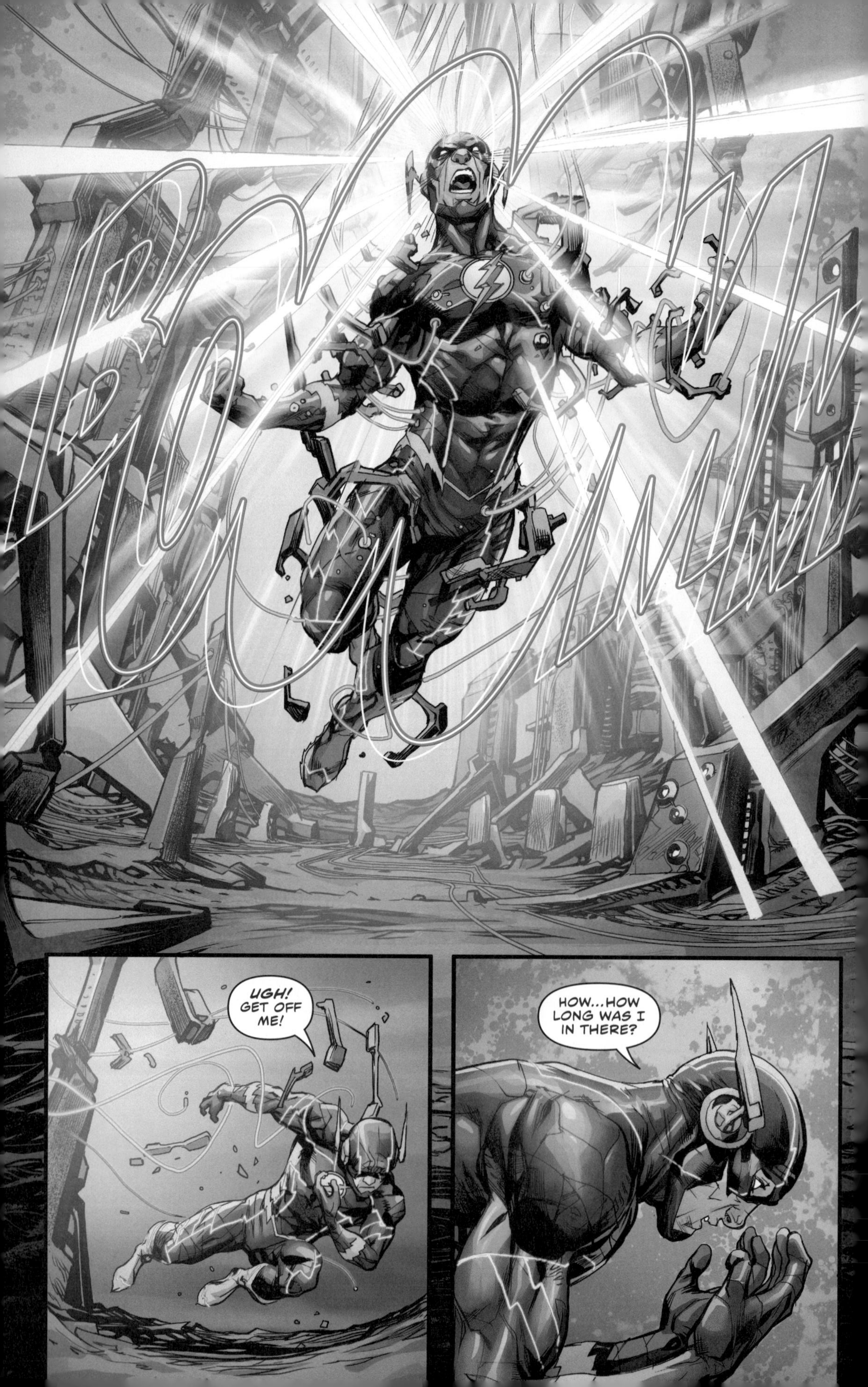
UGH! GET OFF ME!
HOW...HOW LONG WAS I IN THERE?

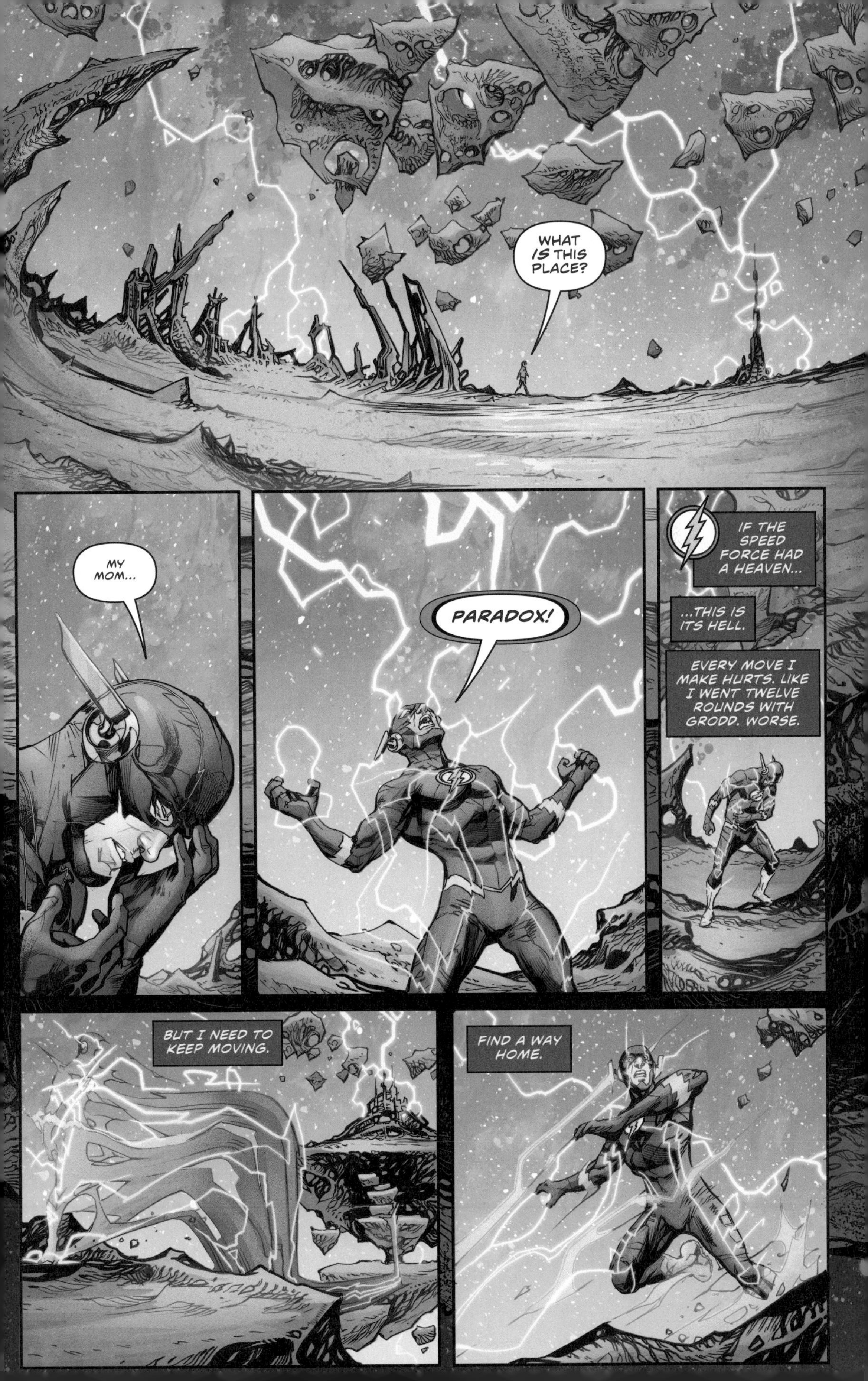
WHAT IS THIS PLACE?
MY MOM...
PARADOX!
IF THE SPEED FORCE HAD A HEAVEN...
...THIS IS ITS HELL.
EVERY MOVE I MAKE HURTS. LIKE I WENT TWELVE ROUNDS WITH GRODD. WORSE.
BUT I NEED TO KEEP MOVING.
FIND A WAY HOME.

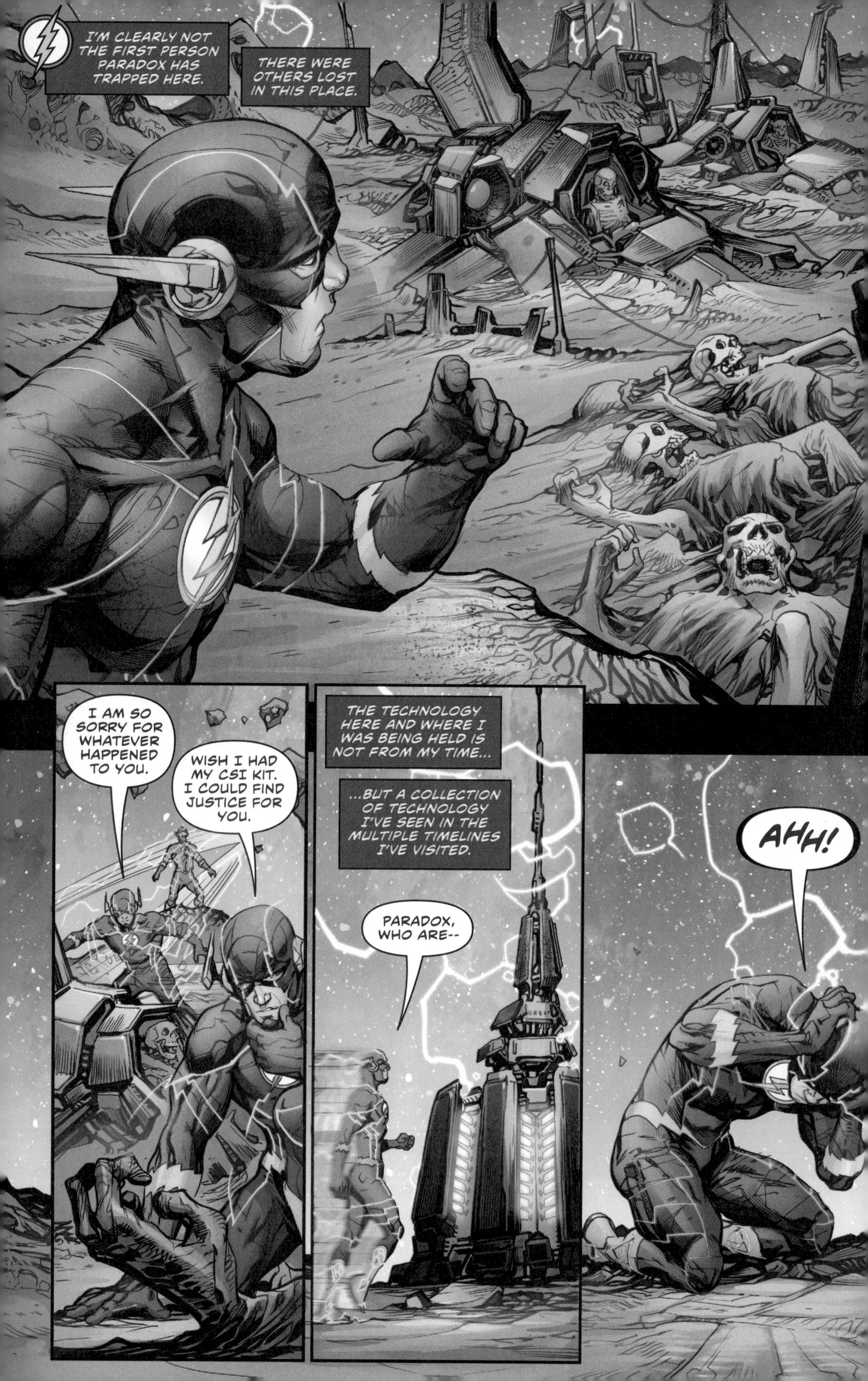
I'M CLEARLY NOT THE FIRST PERSON PARADOX HAS TRAPPED HERE.
THERE WERE OTHERS LOST IN THIS PLACE.
I AM SO SORRY FOR WHATEVER HAPPENED TO YOU.
WISH I HAD MY CSI KIT. I COULD FIND JUSTICE FOR YOU.
THE TECHNOLOGY HERE AND WHERE I WAS BEING HELD IS NOT FROM MY TIME...
...BUT A COLLECTION OF TECHNOLOGY I'VE SEEN IN THE MULTIPLE TIMELINES I'VE VISITED.
PARADOX, WHO ARE--
AHH!

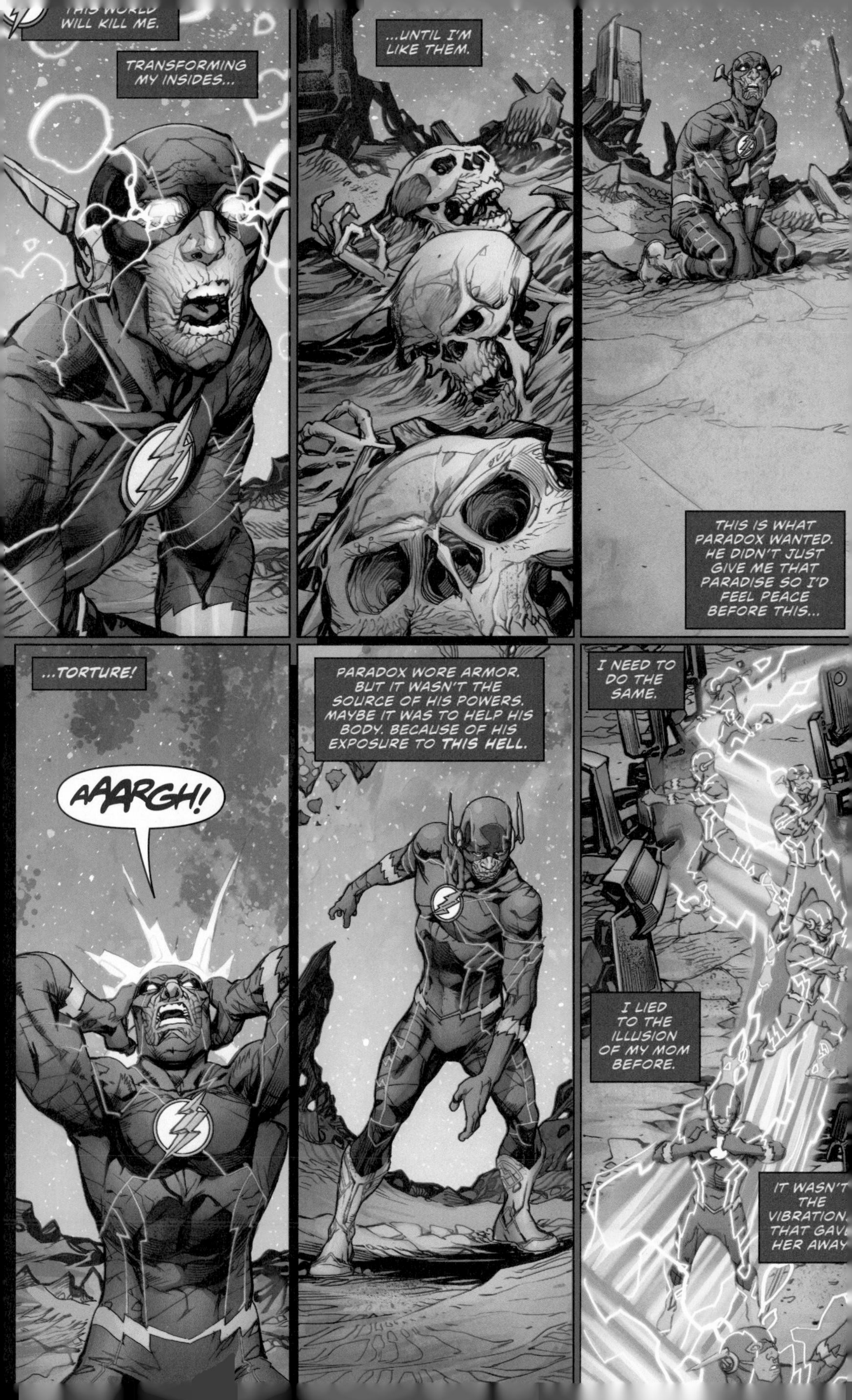

THIS WORLD WILL KILL ME.
TRANSFORMING MY INSIDES...
...UNTIL I'M LIKE THEM.
THIS IS WHAT PARADOX WANTED. HE DIDN'T JUST GIVE ME THAT PARADISE SO I'D FEEL PEACE BEFORE THIS...
...TORTURE!
AAARGH!
PARADOX WORE ARMOR. BUT IT WASN'T THE SOURCE OF HIS POWERS. MAYBE IT WAS TO HELP HIS BODY. BECAUSE OF HIS EXPOSURE TO THIS HELL.
I NEED TO DO THE SAME.
I LIED TO THE ILLUSION OF MY MOM BEFORE.
IT WASN'T THE VIBRATION. THAT GAVE HER AWAY

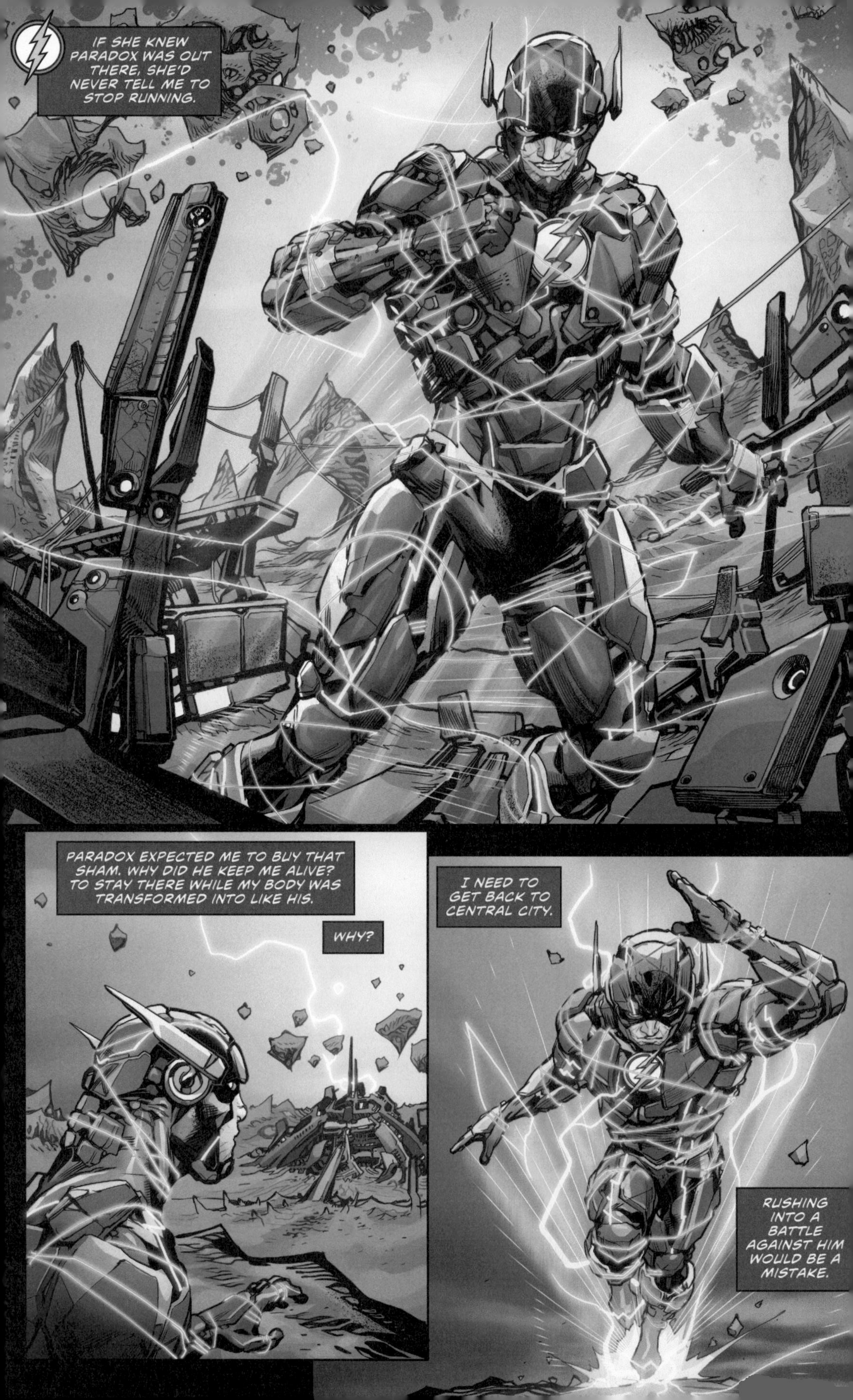
IF SHE KNEW PARADOX WAS OUT THERE, SHE'D NEVER TELL ME TO STOP RUNNING.
PARADOX EXPECTED ME TO BUY THAT SHAM. WHY DID HE KEEP ME ALIVE? TO STAY THERE WHILE MY BODY WAS TRANSFORMED INTO LIKE HIS.
WHY?
I NEED TO GET BACK TO CENTRAL CITY.
RUSHING INTO A BATTLE AGAINST HIM WOULD BE A MISTAKE.

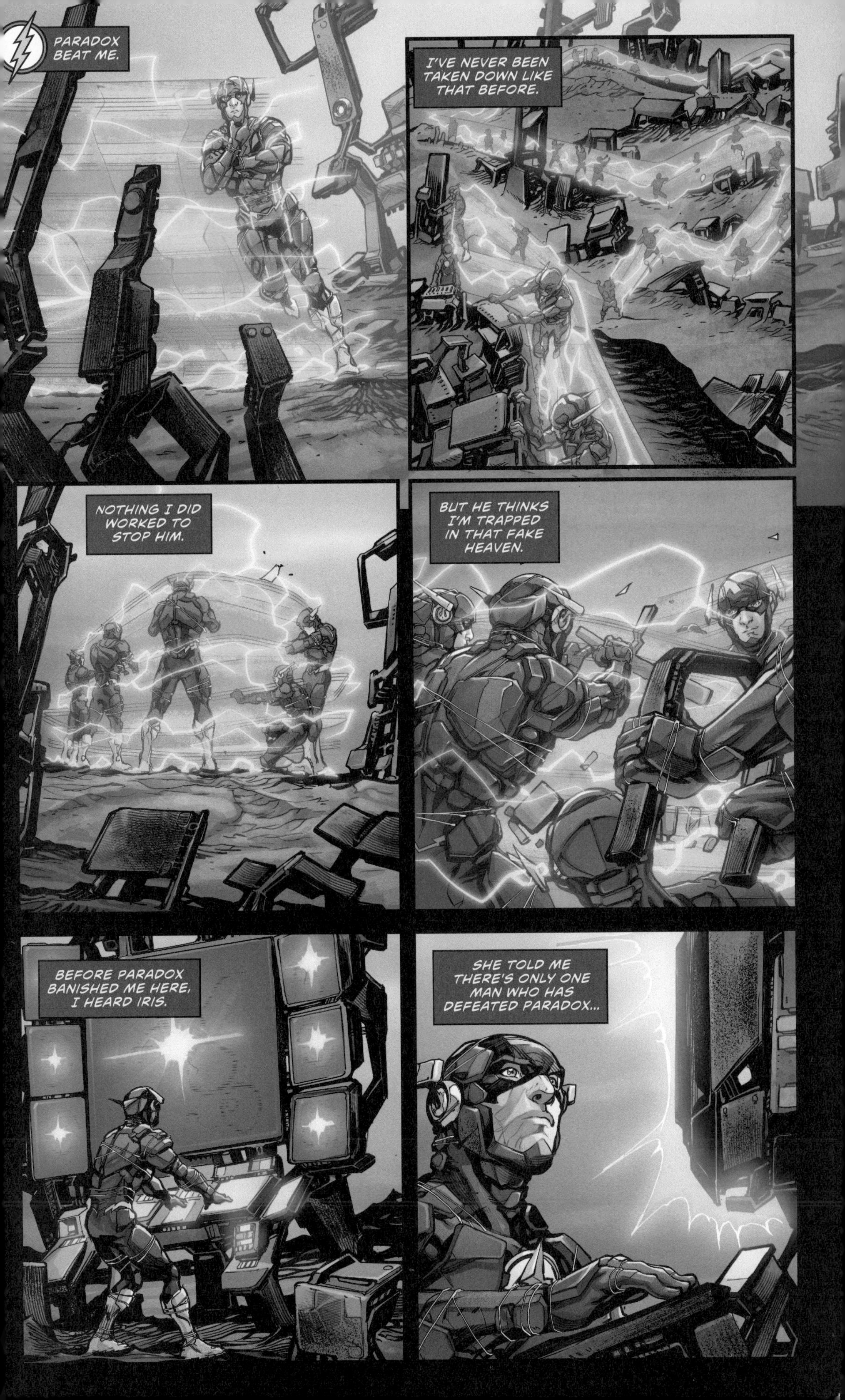
PARADOX BEAT ME.
I'VE NEVER BEEN TAKEN DOWN LIKE THAT BEFORE.
NOTHING I DID WORKED TO STOP HIM.
BUT HE THINKS I'M TRAPPED IN THAT FAKE HEAVEN.
BEFORE PARADOX BANISHED ME HERE, I HEARD IRIS.
SHE TOLD ME THERE'S ONLY ONE MAN WHO HAS DEFEATED PARADOX...

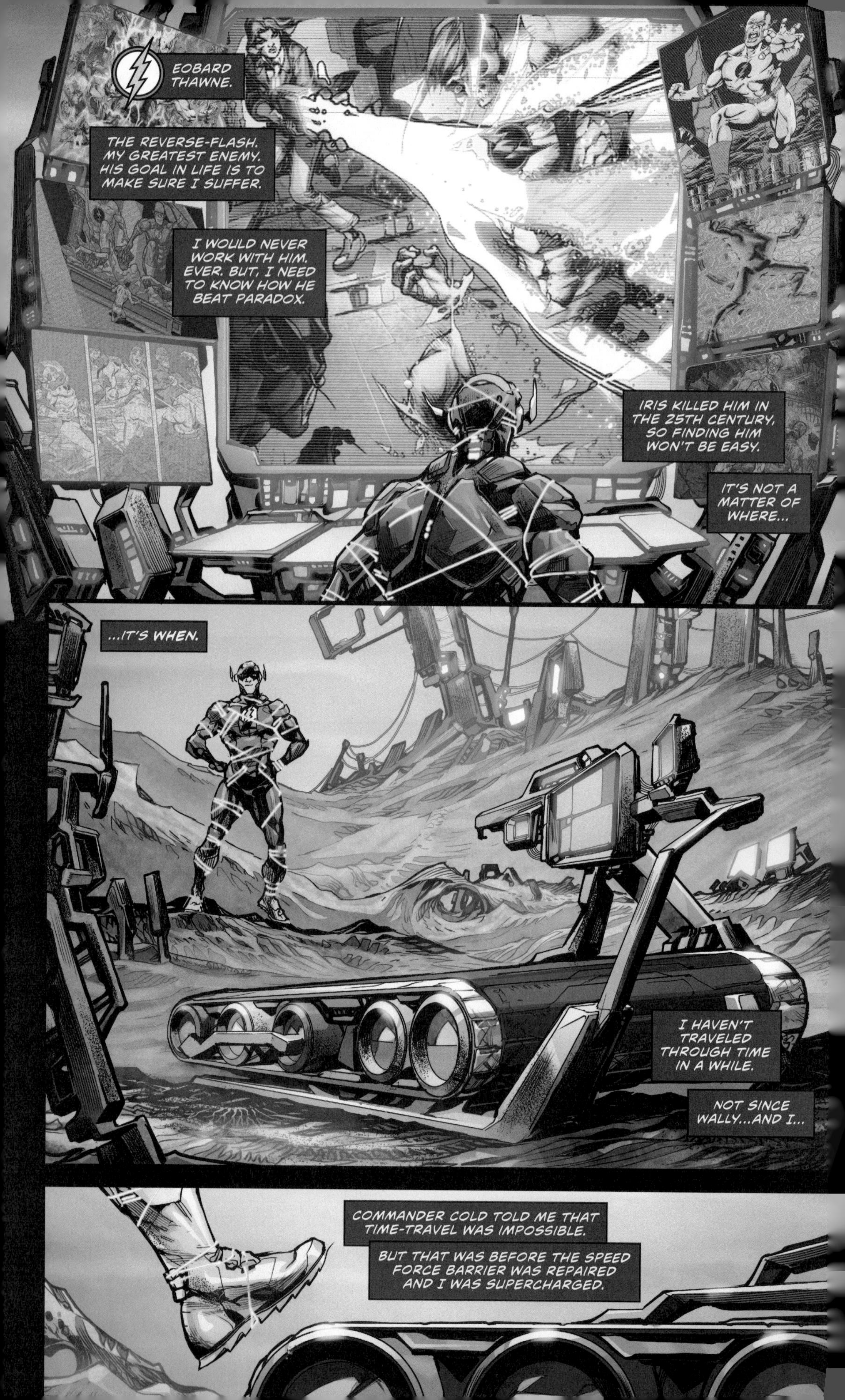
EOBARD THAWNE.
THE REVERSE-FLASH. MY GREATEST ENEMY. HIS GOAL IN LIFE IS TO MAKE SURE I SUFFER.
I WOULD NEVER WORK WITH HIM. EVER. BUT, I NEED TO KNOW HOW HE BEAT PARADOX.
IRIS KILLED HIM IN THE 25TH CENTURY, SO FINDING HIM WON'T BE EASY.
IT'S NOT A MATTER OF WHERE...
...IT'S WHEN.
I HAVEN'T TRAVELED THROUGH TIME IN A WHILE.
NOT SINCE WALLY...AND I...
COMMANDER COLD TOLD ME THAT TIME-TRAVEL WAS IMPOSSIBLE.
BUT THAT WAS BEFORE THE SPEED FORCE BARRIER WAS REPAIRED AND I WAS SUPERCHARGED.

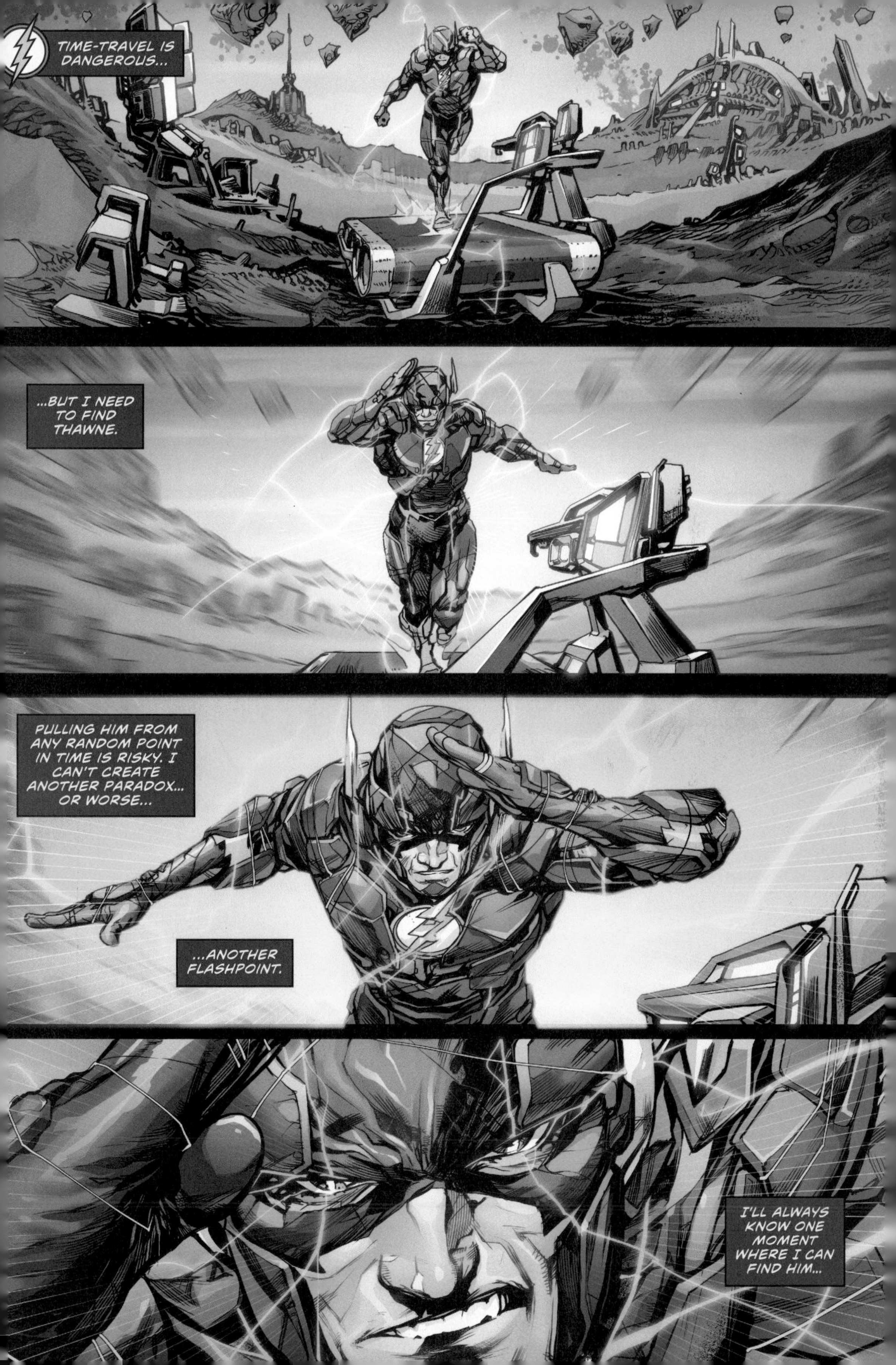
TIME-TRAVEL IS DANGEROUS...
...BUT I NEED TO FIND THAWNE.
PULLING HIM FROM ANY RANDOM POINT IN TIME IS RISKY. I CAN'T CREATE ANOTHER PARADOX... OR WORSE...
...ANOTHER FLASHPOINT.
I'LL ALWAYS KNOW ONE MOMENT WHERE I CAN FIND HIM...

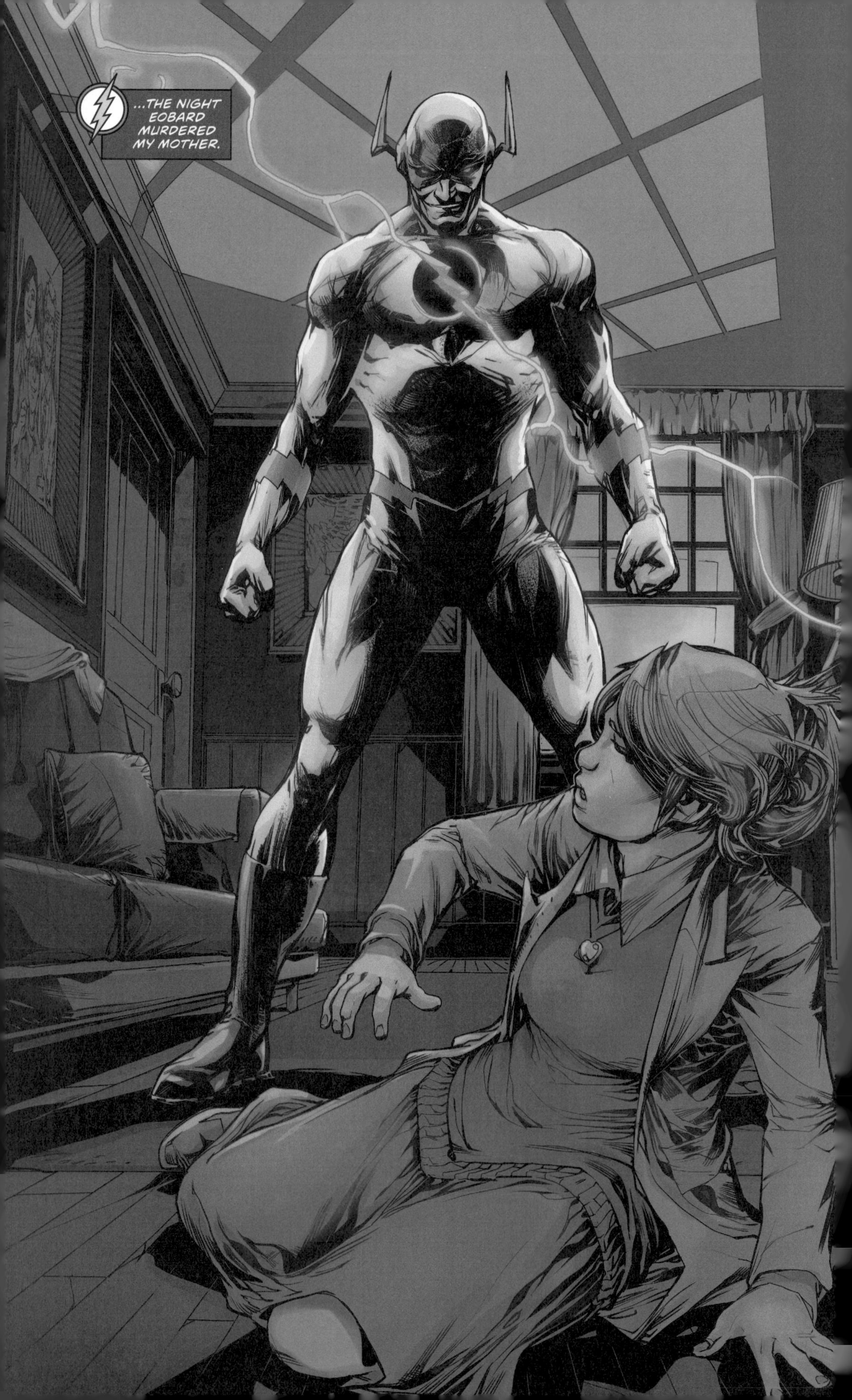
...THE NIGHT EOBARD MURDERED MY MOTHER.

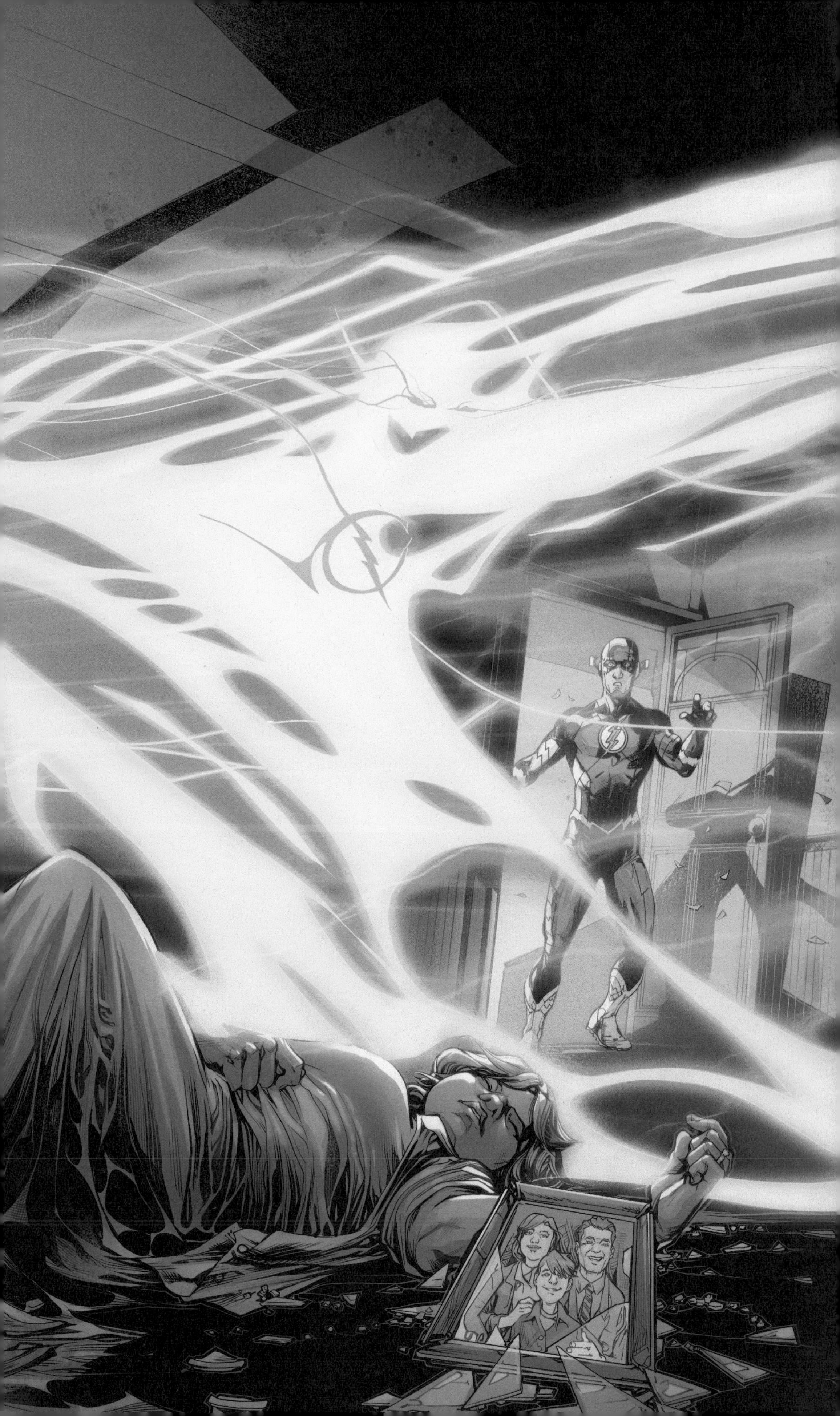

The Flash **#753** variant cover by JUNGGEUN YOON

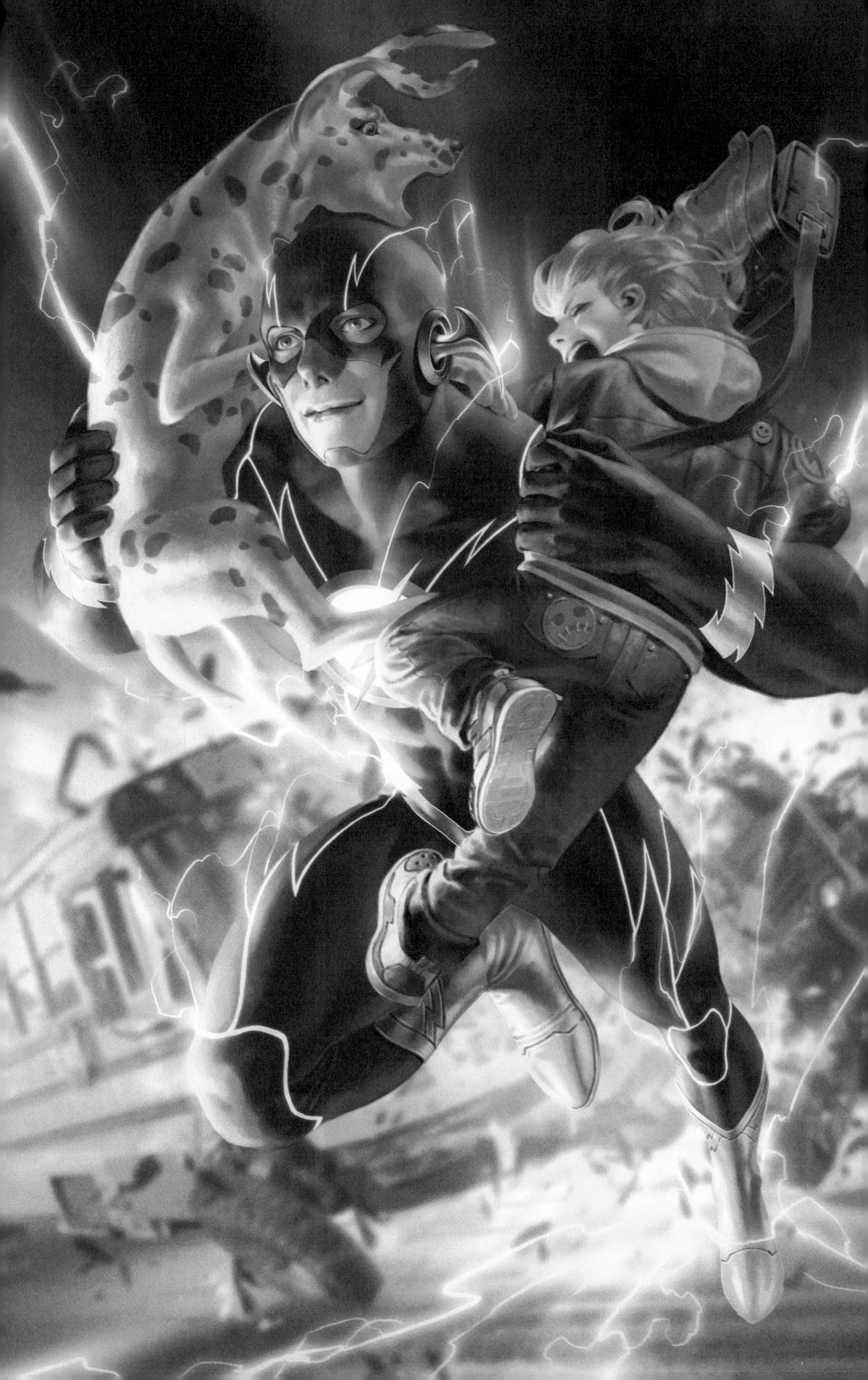

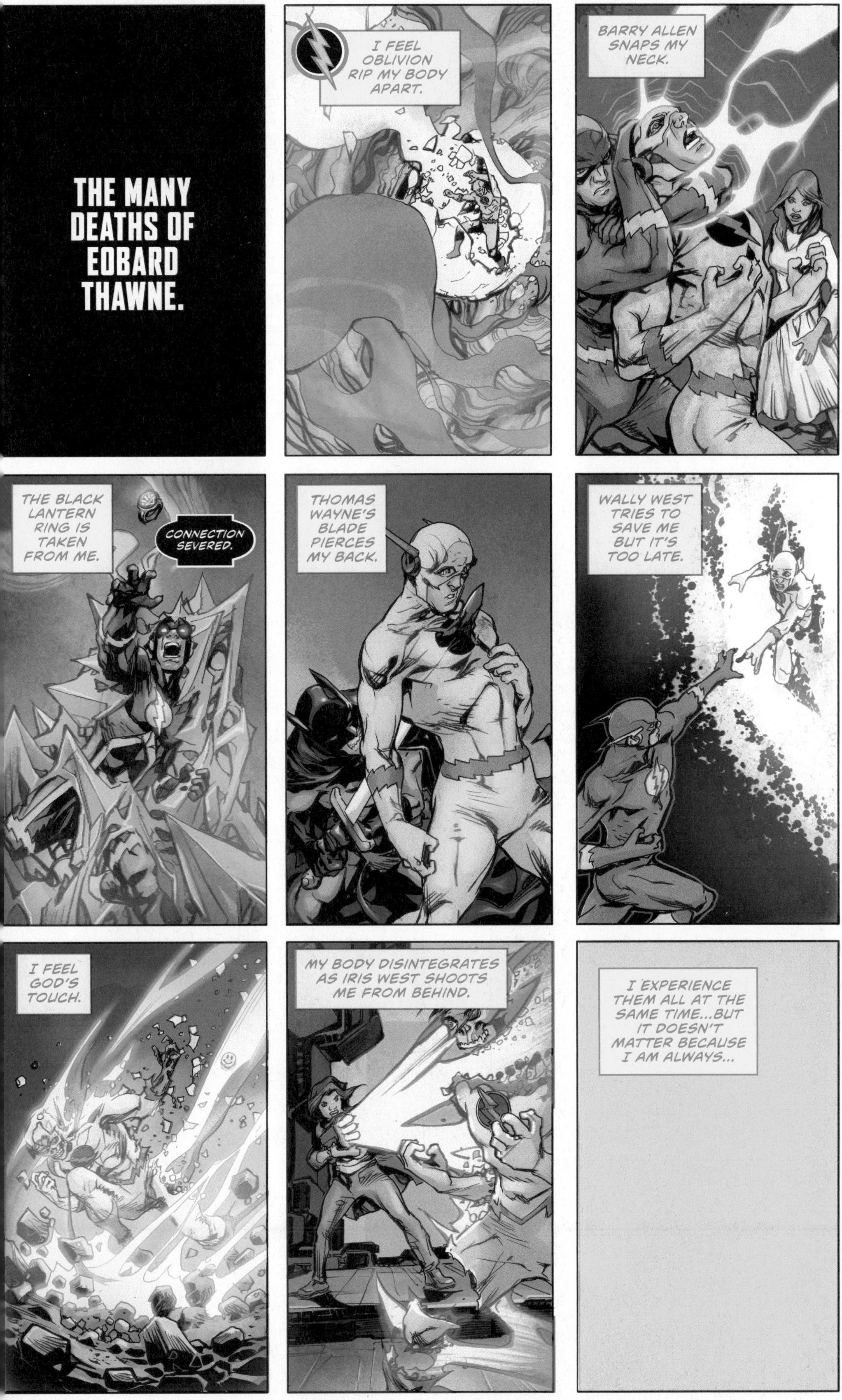
THE MANY DEATHS OF EOBARD THAWNE.
I FEEL OBLIVION RIP MY BODY APART.
BARRY ALLEN SNAPS MY NECK.
THE BLACK LANTERN RING IS TAKEN FROM ME.
CONNECTION SEVERED.
THOMAS WAYNE'S BLADE PIERCES MY BACK.
WALLY WEST TRIES TO SAVE ME BUT IT'S TOO LATE.
I FEEL GOD'S TOUCH.
MY BODY DISINTEGRATES AS IRIS WEST SHOOTS ME FROM BEHIND.
I EXPERIENCE THEM ALL AT THE SAME TIME...BUT IT DOESN'T MATTER BECAUSE I AM ALWAYS...

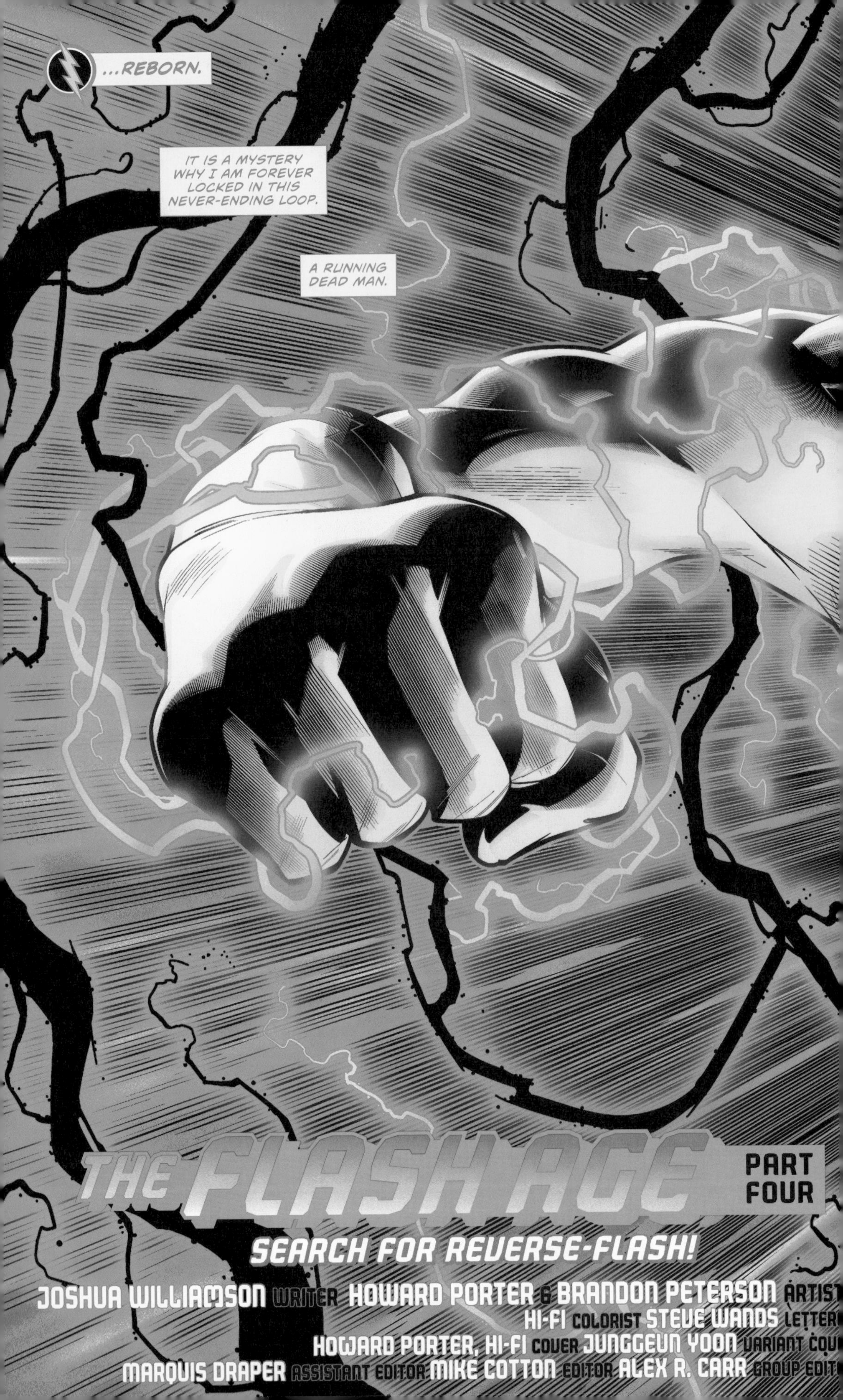
...REBORN.
IT IS A MYSTERY WHY I AM FOREVER LOCKED IN THIS NEVER-ENDING LOOP.
A RUNNING DEAD MAN.
THE FLASH AGE
PART FOUR
SEARCH FOR REVERSE-FLASH!
JOSHUA WILLIAMSON WRITER HOWARD PORTER & BRANDON PETERSON ARTIST
HI-FI COLORIST STEVE WANDS LETTER
HOWARD PORTER, HI-FI COVER JUNGGEUN YOON VARIANT COV
MARQUIS DRAPER ASSISTANT EDITOR MIKE COTTON EDITOR ALEX R. CARR GROUP EDIT

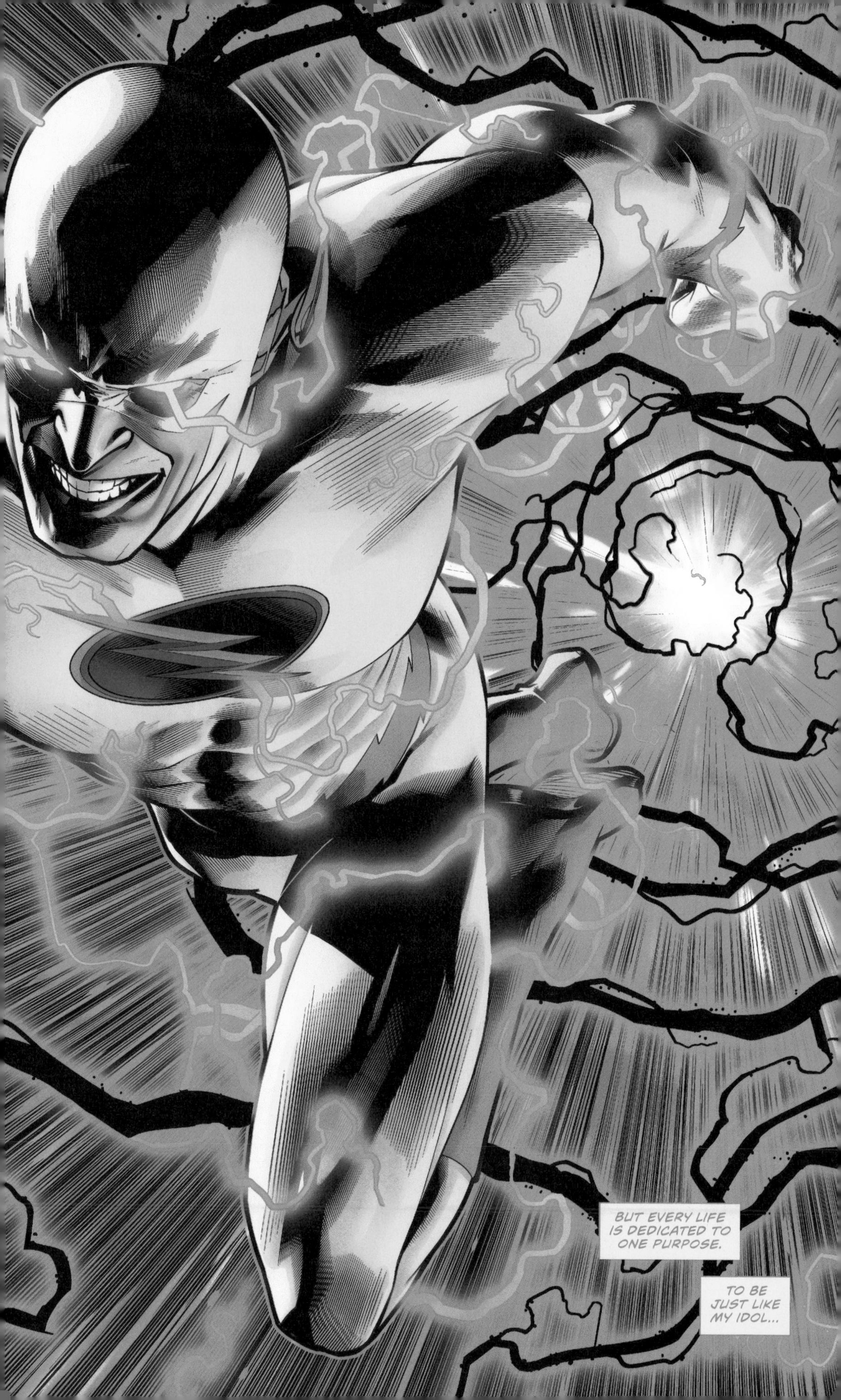
BUT EVERY LIFE IS DEDICATED TO ONE PURPOSE.
TO BE JUST LIKE MY IDOL...

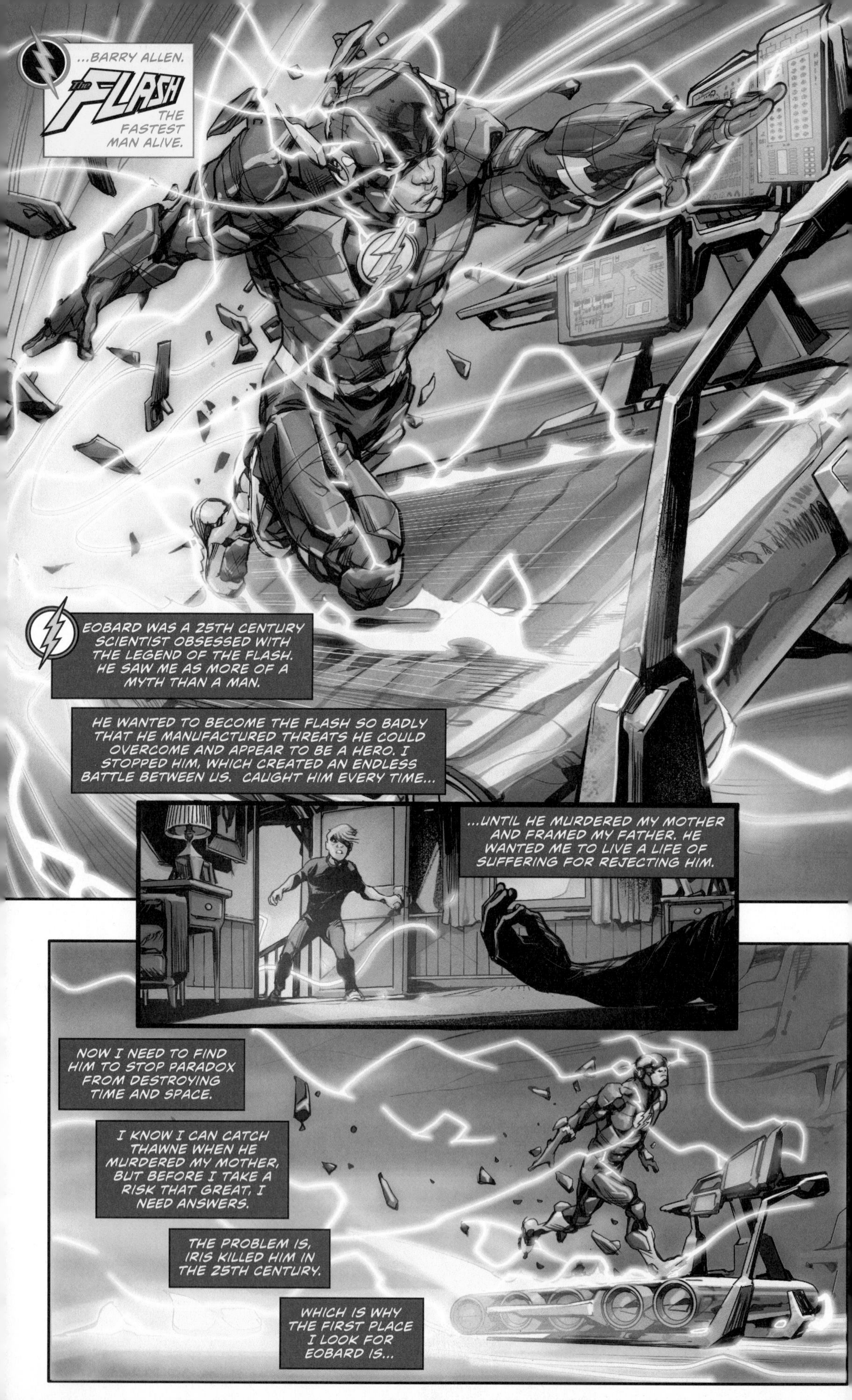
...BARRY ALLEN.
THE FLASH
THE FASTEST MAN ALIVE.
EOBARD WAS A 25TH CENTURY SCIENTIST OBSESSED WITH THE LEGEND OF THE FLASH. HE SAW ME AS MORE OF A MYTH THAN A MAN.
HE WANTED TO BECOME THE FLASH SO BADLY THAT HE MANUFACTURED THREATS HE COULD OVERCOME AND APPEAR TO BE A HERO. I STOPPED HIM, WHICH CREATED AN ENDLESS BATTLE BETWEEN US. CAUGHT HIM EVERY TIME...
...UNTIL HE MURDERED MY MOTHER AND FRAMED MY FATHER. HE WANTED ME TO LIVE A LIFE OF SUFFERING FOR REJECTING HIM.
NOW I NEED TO FIND HIM TO STOP PARADOX FROM DESTROYING TIME AND SPACE.
I KNOW I CAN CATCH THAWNE WHEN HE MURDERED MY MOTHER, BUT BEFORE I TAKE A RISK THAT GREAT, I NEED ANSWERS.
THE PROBLEM IS, IRIS KILLED HIM IN THE 25TH CENTURY.
WHICH IS WHY THE FIRST PLACE I LOOK FOR EOBARD IS...

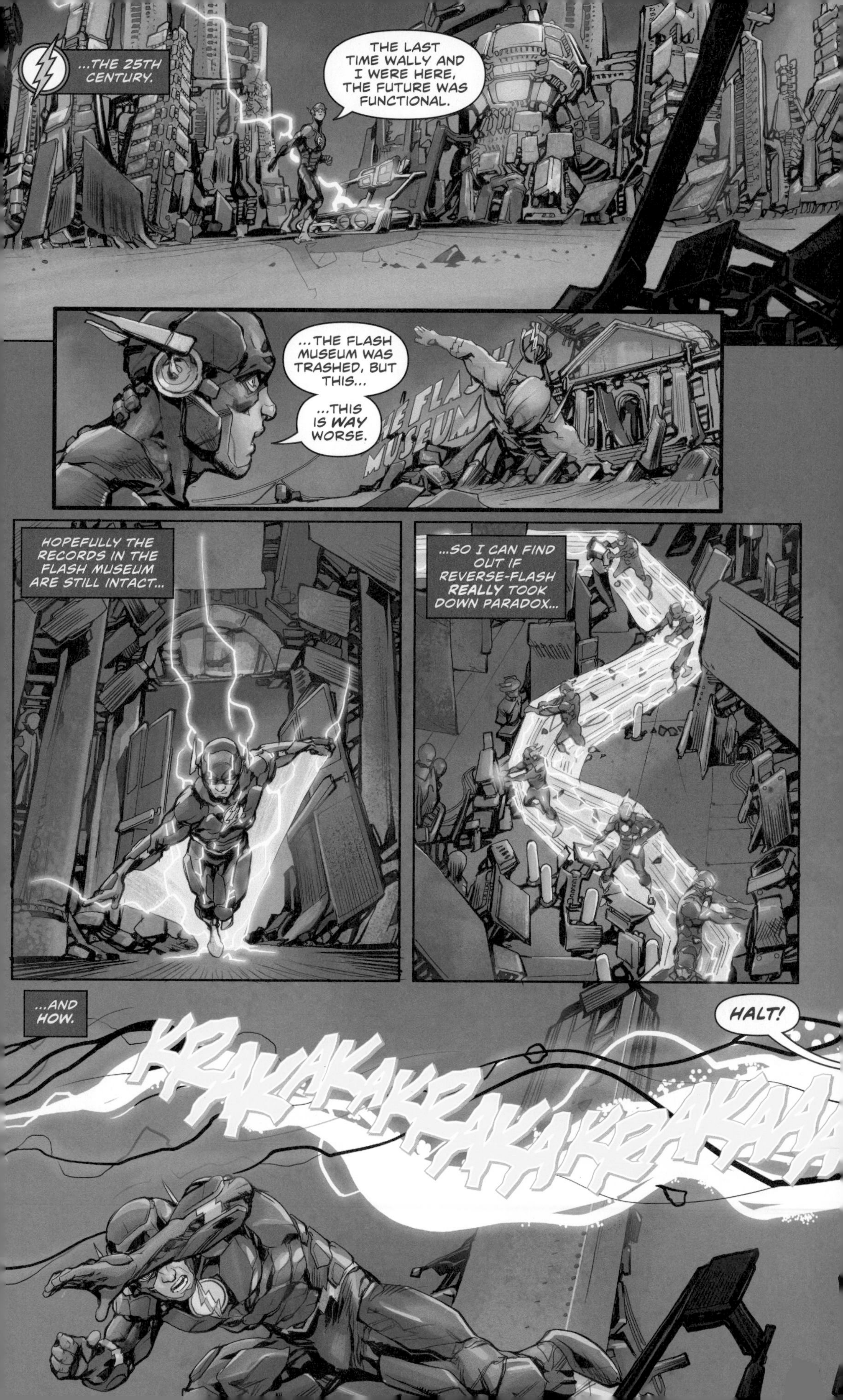
...THE 25TH CENTURY.
THE LAST TIME WALLY AND I WERE HERE, THE FUTURE WAS FUNCTIONAL.
...THE FLASH MUSEUM WAS TRASHED, BUT THIS...
...THIS IS WAY WORSE.
THE FLASH MUSEUM
HOPEFULLY THE RECORDS IN THE FLASH MUSEUM ARE STILL INTACT...
...SO I CAN FIND OUT IF REVERSE-FLASH REALLY TOOK DOWN PARADOX...
...AND HOW.
HALT!
KRAKAKAKRAKAKRAKAAA

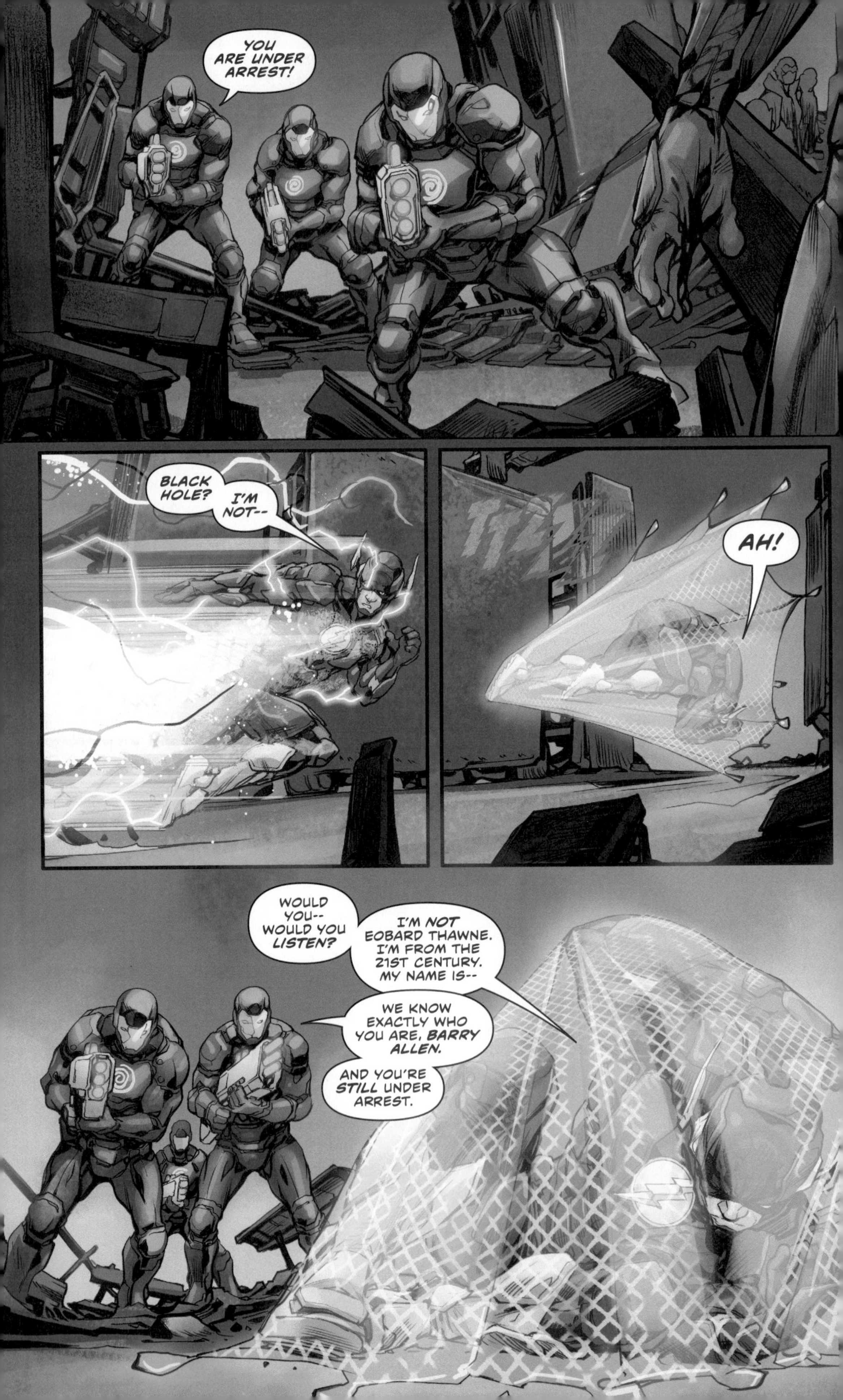

YOU ARE UNDER ARREST!
BLACK HOLE?
I'M NOT--
AH!
WOULD YOU-- WOULD YOU LISTEN?
I'M NOT EOBARD THAWNE. I'M FROM THE 21ST CENTURY. MY NAME IS--
WE KNOW EXACTLY WHO YOU ARE, BARRY ALLEN.
AND YOU'RE STILL UNDER ARREST.

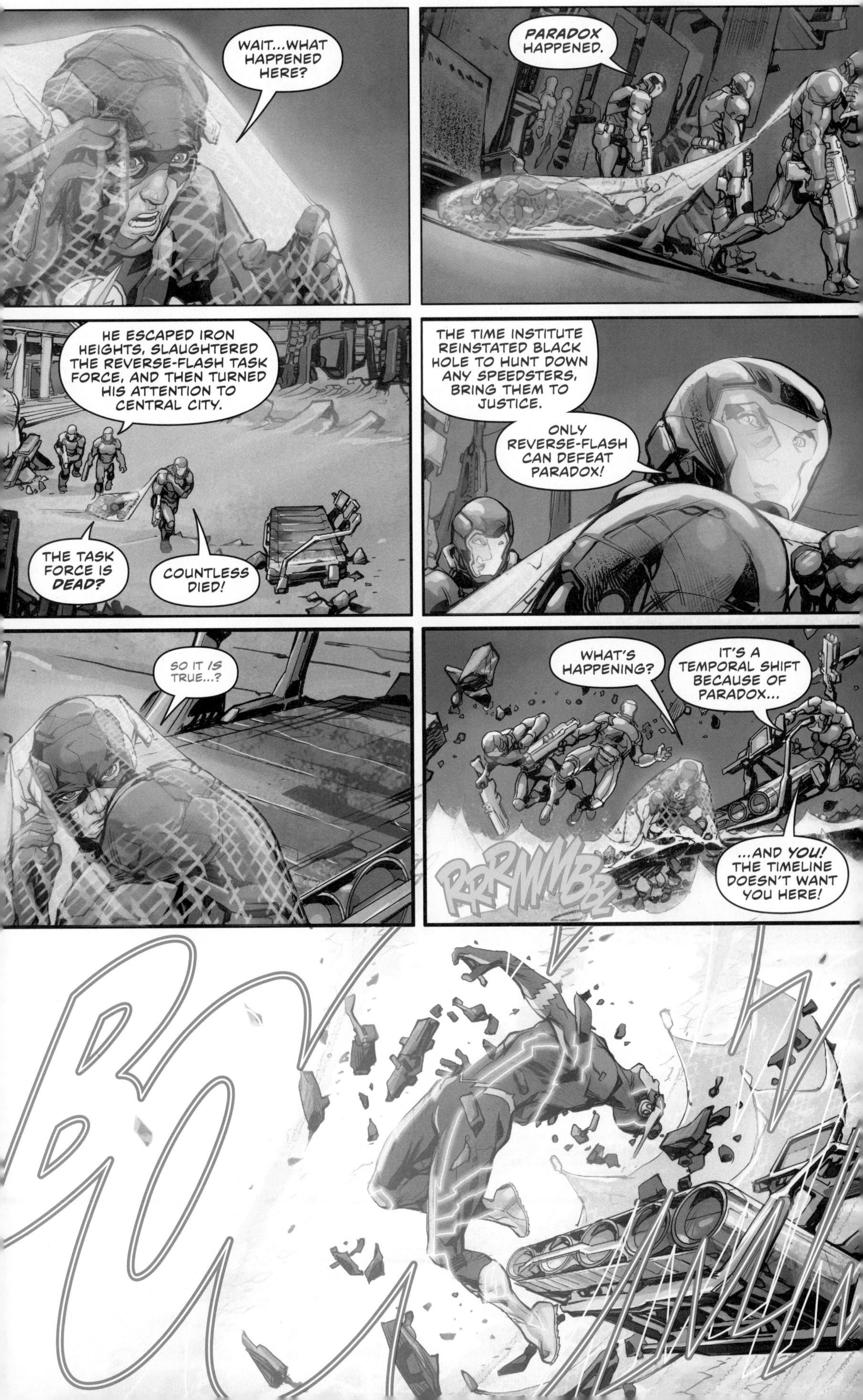
WAIT...WHAT HAPPENED HERE?
PARADOX HAPPENED.
HE ESCAPED IRON HEIGHTS, SLAUGHTERED THE REVERSE-FLASH TASK FORCE, AND THEN TURNED HIS ATTENTION TO CENTRAL CITY.
THE TASK FORCE IS DEAD?
COUNTLESS DIED!
THE TIME INSTITUTE REINSTATED BLACK HOLE TO HUNT DOWN ANY SPEEDSTERS, BRING THEM TO JUSTICE.
ONLY REVERSE-FLASH CAN DEFEAT PARADOX!
SO IT IS TRUE...?
WHAT'S HAPPENING?
IT'S A TEMPORAL SHIFT BECAUSE OF PARADOX...
...AND YOU! THE TIMELINE DOESN'T WANT YOU HERE!
RRRMMBBL

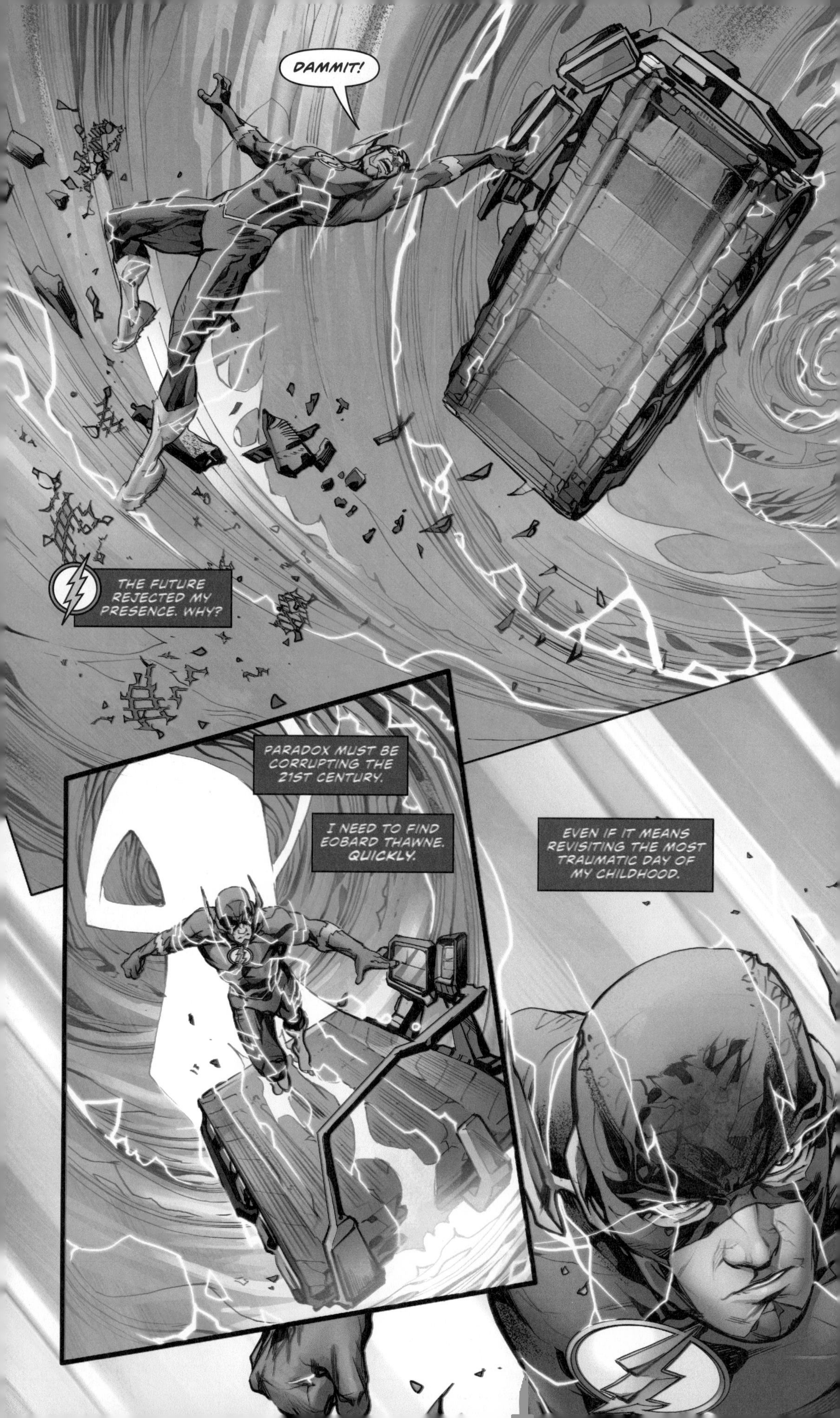
DAMMIT!
THE FUTURE REJECTED MY PRESENCE. WHY?
PARADOX MUST BE CORRUPTING THE 21ST CENTURY.
I NEED TO FIND EOBARD THAWNE. QUICKLY.
EVEN IF IT MEANS REVISITING THE MOST TRAUMATIC DAY OF MY CHILDHOOD.

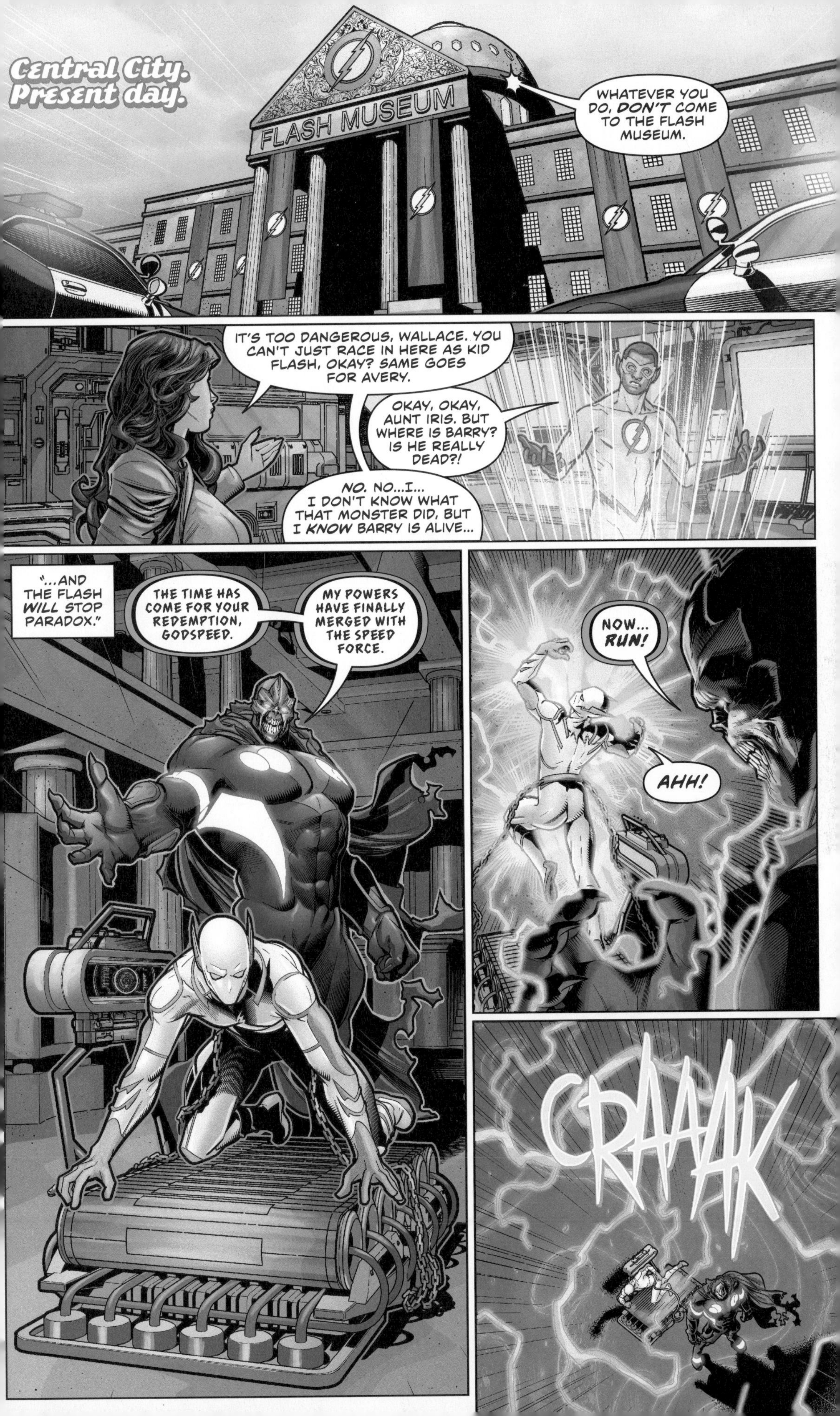
Central City. Present day.
FLASH MUSEUM
WHATEVER YOU DO, DON'T COME TO THE FLASH MUSEUM.
IT'S TOO DANGEROUS, WALLACE. YOU CAN'T JUST RACE IN HERE AS KID FLASH, OKAY? SAME GOES FOR AVERY.
OKAY, OKAY, AUNT IRIS. BUT WHERE IS BARRY? IS HE REALLY DEAD?!
NO. NO...I... I DON'T KNOW WHAT THAT MONSTER DID, BUT I KNOW BARRY IS ALIVE...
"...AND THE FLASH WILL STOP PARADOX."
THE TIME HAS COME FOR YOUR REDEMPTION, GODSPEED.
MY POWERS HAVE FINALLY MERGED WITH THE SPEED FORCE.
NOW... RUN!
AHH!
CRAAAK

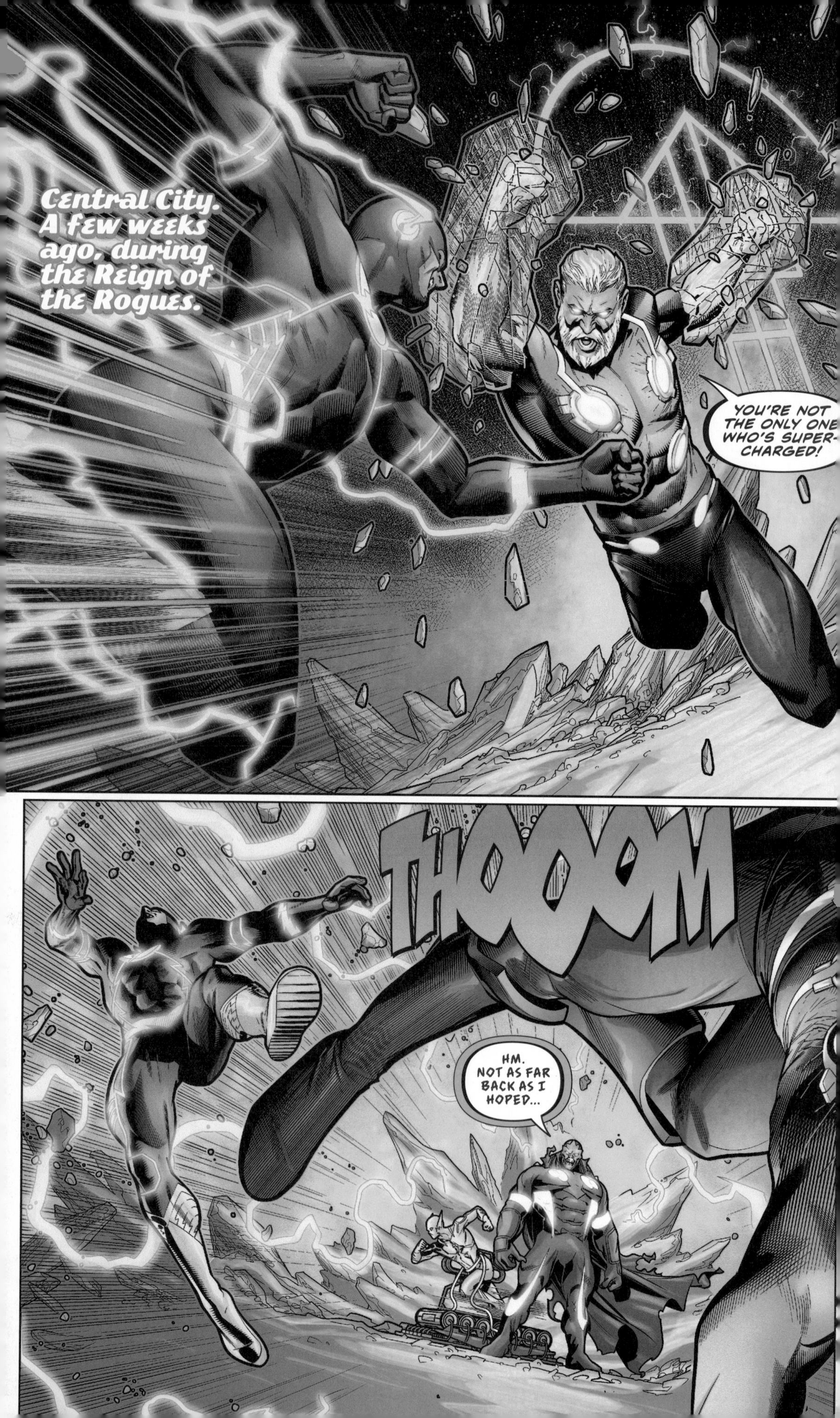
Central City. A few weeks ago, during the Reign of the Rogues.
YOU'RE NOT THE ONLY ONE WHO'S SUPER-CHARGED!
THOOOM
HM. NOT AS FAR BACK AS I HOPED...

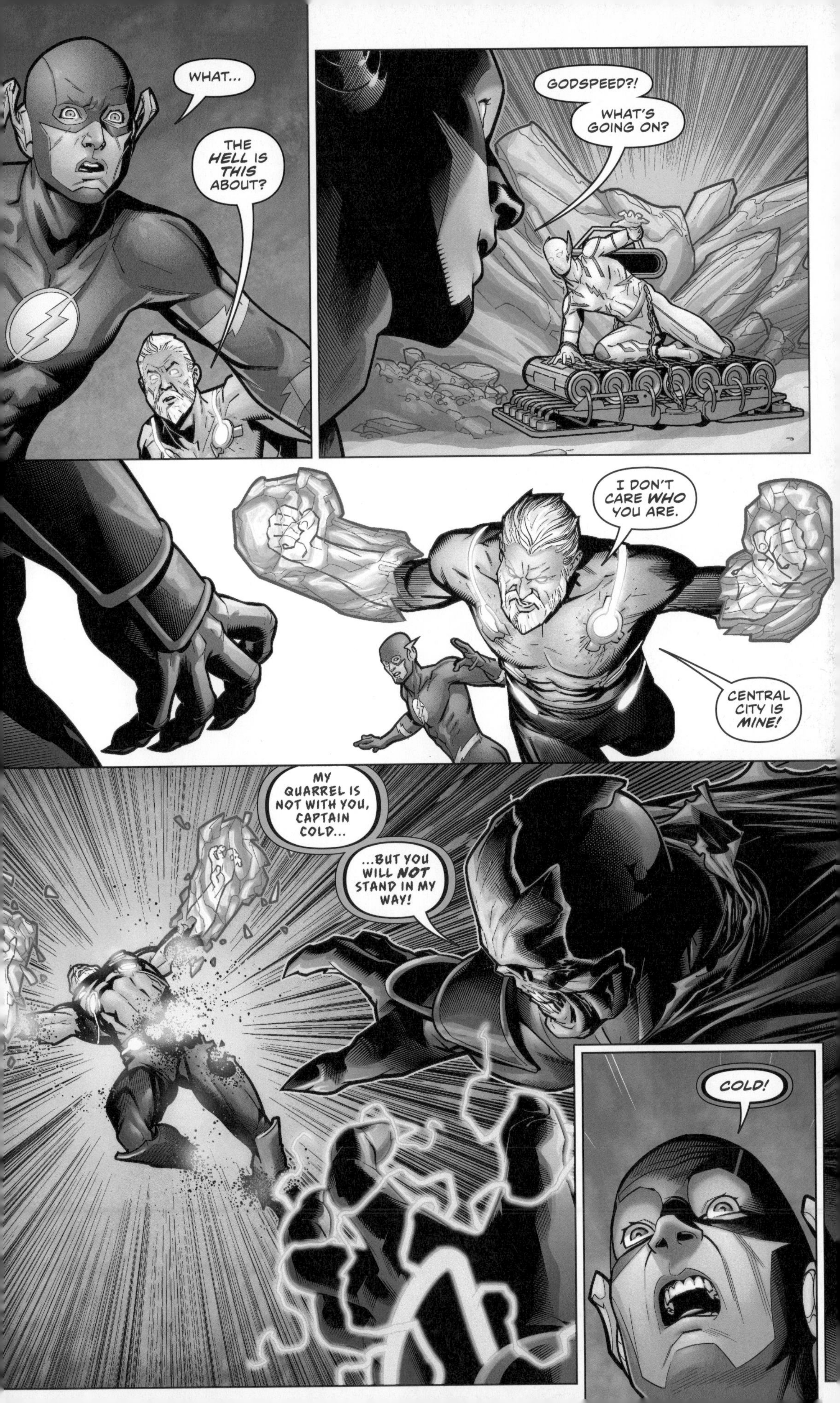
WHAT...
THE HELL IS THIS ABOUT?
GODSPEED?!
WHAT'S GOING ON?
I DON'T CARE WHO YOU ARE.
CENTRAL CITY IS MINE!
MY QUARREL IS NOT WITH YOU, CAPTAIN COLD...
...BUT YOU WILL NOT STAND IN MY WAY!
COLD!

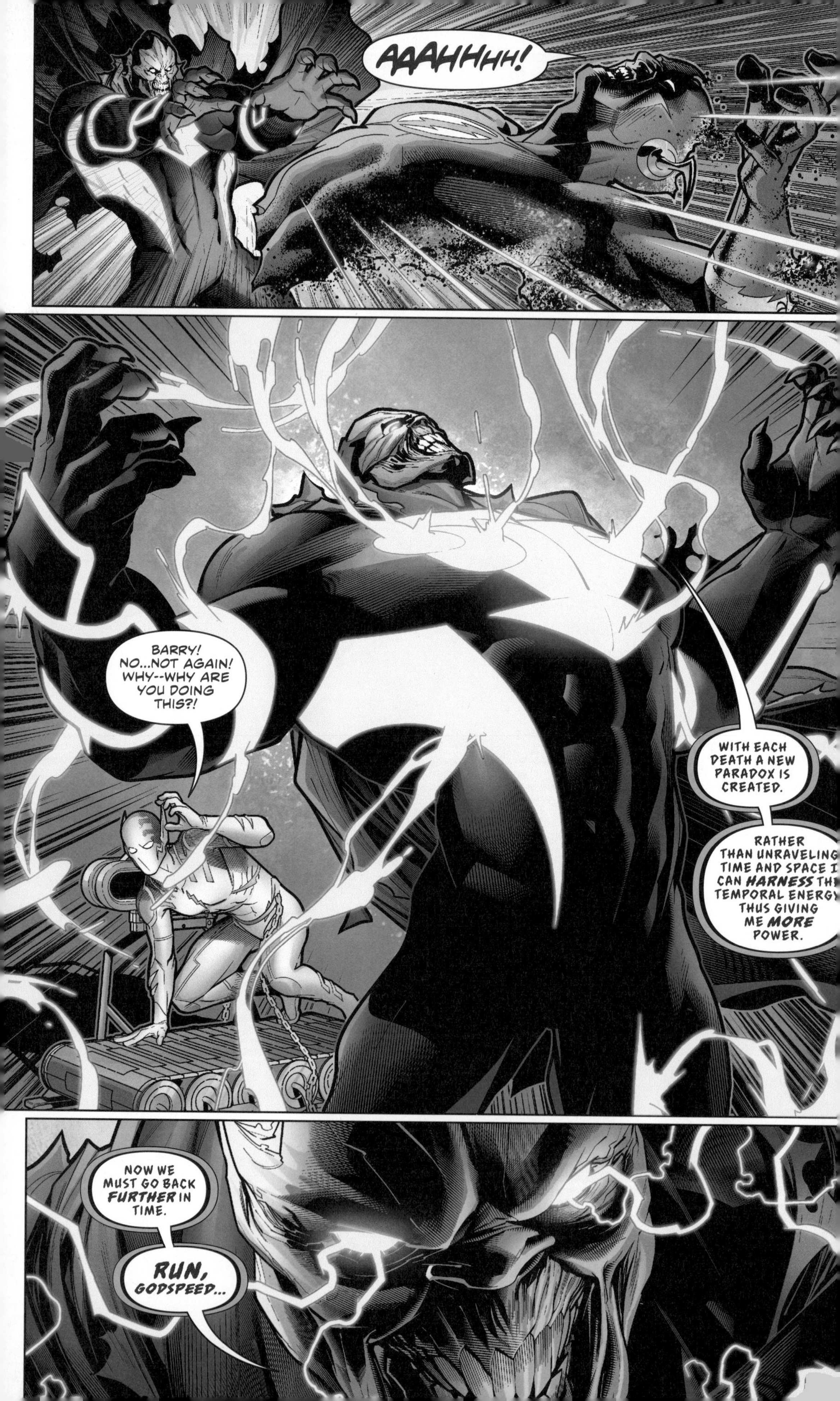

AAAHHHH!
BARRY! NO...NOT AGAIN! WHY--WHY ARE YOU DOING THIS?!
WITH EACH DEATH A NEW PARADOX IS CREATED.
RATHER THAN UNRAVELING TIME AND SPACE I CAN HARNESS TH TEMPORAL ENERGY THUS GIVING ME MORE POWER.
NOW WE MUST GO BACK FURTHER IN TIME.
RUN, GODSPEED...

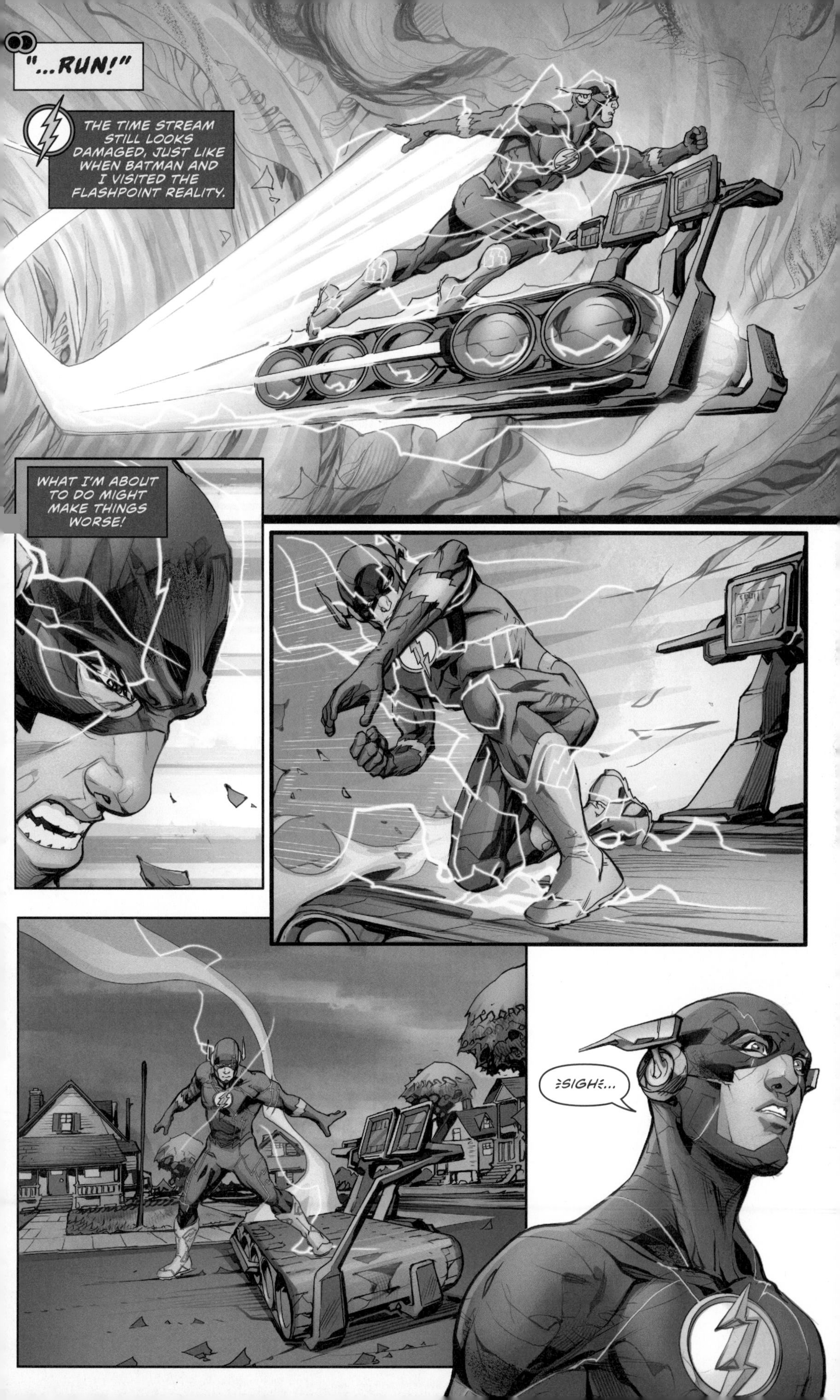
"...RUN!"
THE TIME STREAM STILL LOOKS DAMAGED, JUST LIKE WHEN BATMAN AND I VISITED THE FLASHPOINT REALITY.
WHAT I'M ABOUT TO DO MIGHT MAKE THINGS WORSE!
SIGH...

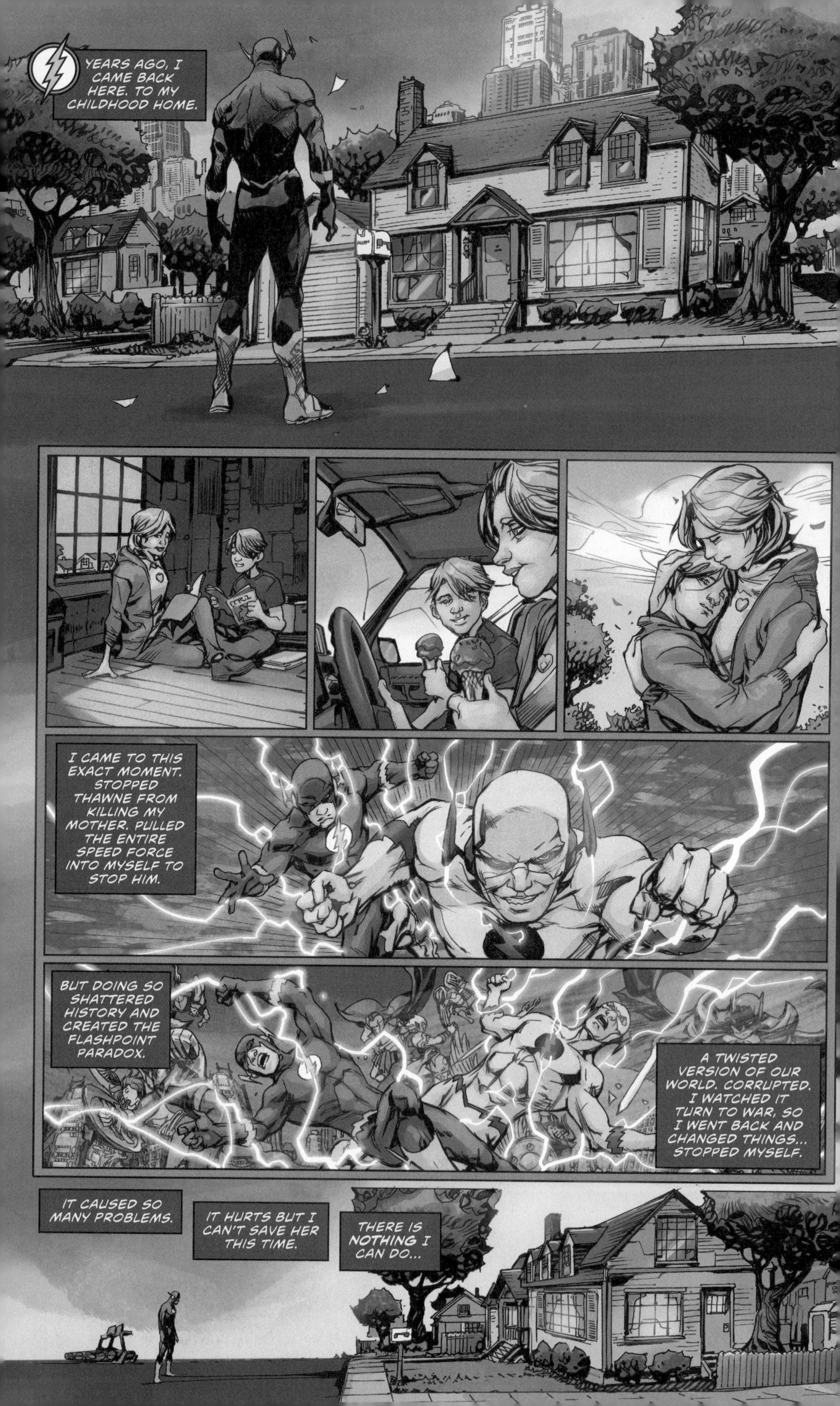
YEARS AGO, I CAME BACK HERE. TO MY CHILDHOOD HOME.
I CAME TO THIS EXACT MOMENT. STOPPED THAWNE FROM KILLING MY MOTHER. PULLED THE ENTIRE SPEED FORCE INTO MYSELF TO STOP HIM.
BUT DOING SO SHATTERED HISTORY AND CREATED THE FLASHPOINT PARADOX.
A TWISTED VERSION OF OUR WORLD. CORRUPTED. I WATCHED IT TURN TO WAR, SO I WENT BACK AND CHANGED THINGS... STOPPED MYSELF.
IT CAUSED SO MANY PROBLEMS.
IT HURTS BUT I CAN'T SAVE HER THIS TIME.
THERE IS NOTHING I CAN DO...

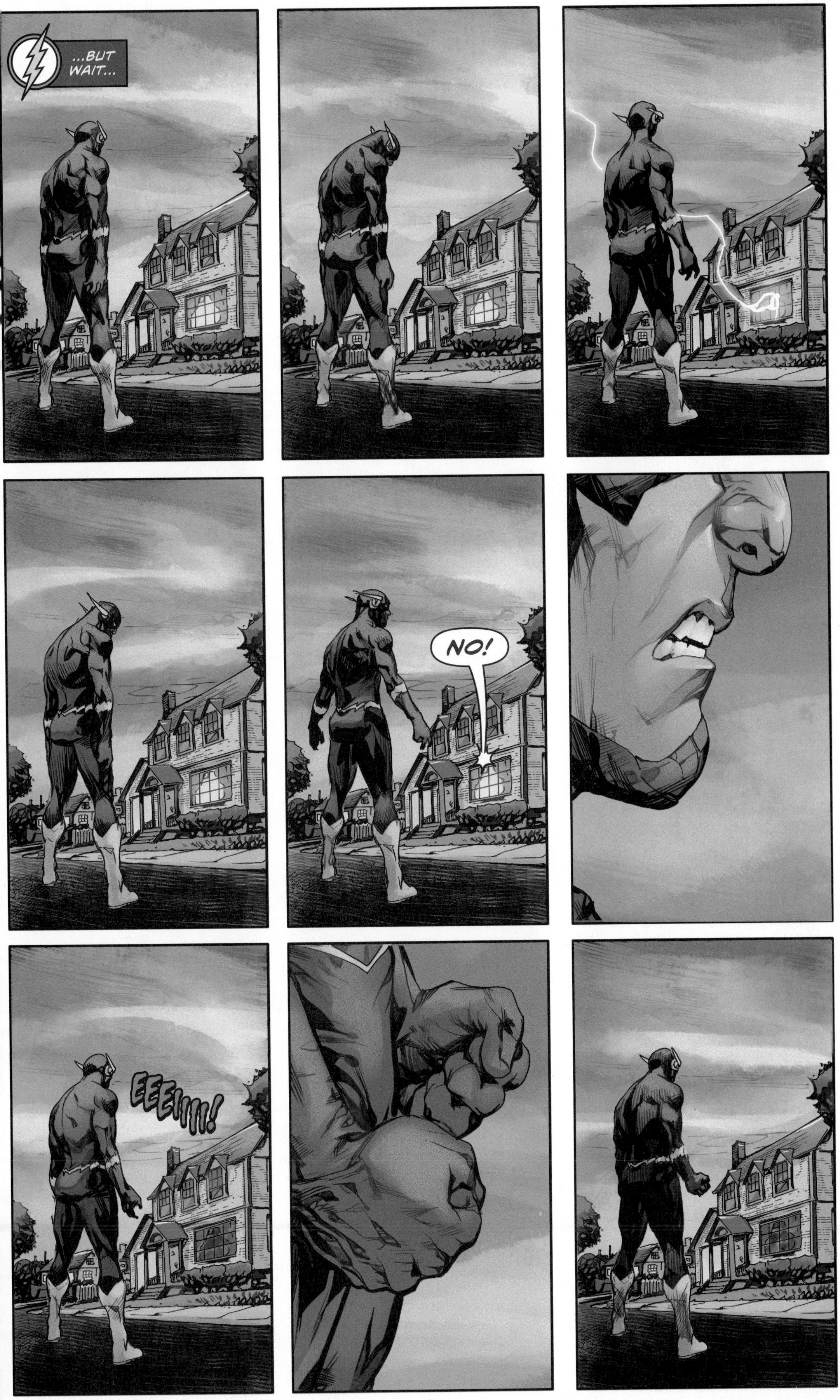
...BUT WAIT...
NO!
EEEIIIII!

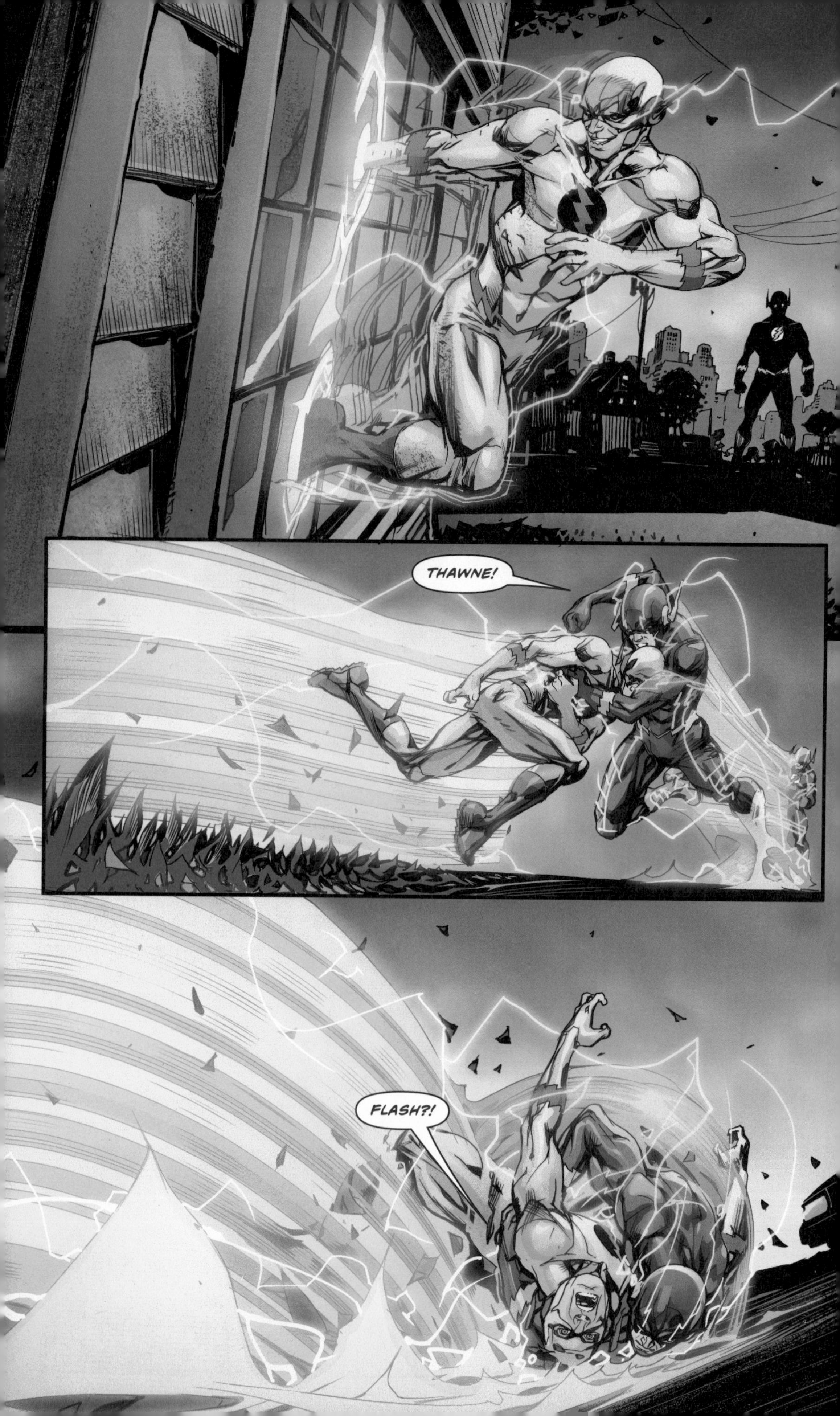
THAWNE!
FLASH?!

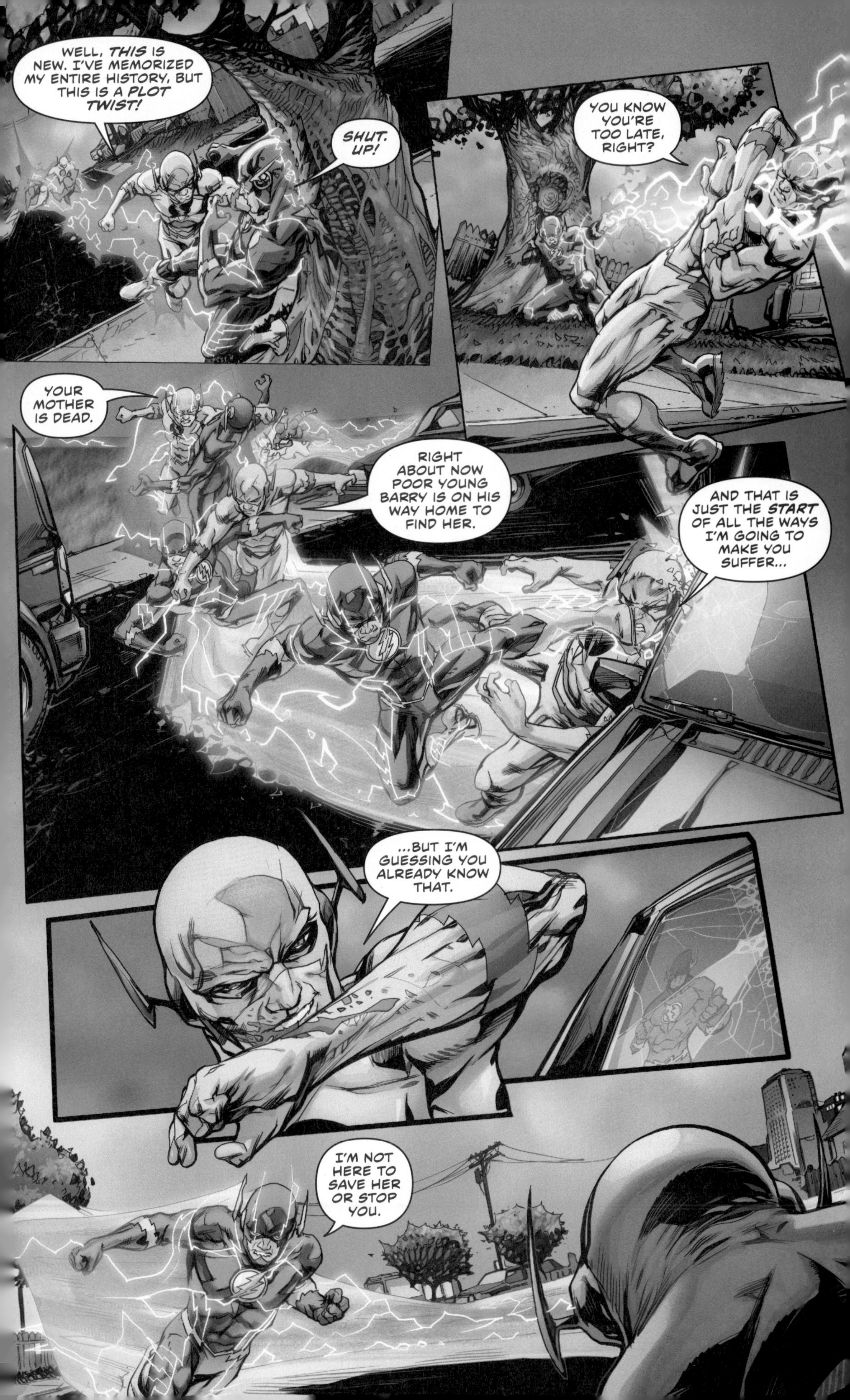
WELL, *THIS* IS NEW. I'VE MEMORIZED MY ENTIRE HISTORY, BUT THIS IS A *PLOT TWIST!*
SHUT. UP!
YOU KNOW YOU'RE TOO LATE, RIGHT?
YOUR MOTHER IS DEAD.
RIGHT ABOUT NOW POOR YOUNG BARRY IS ON HIS WAY HOME TO FIND HER.
AND THAT IS JUST THE *START* OF ALL THE WAYS I'M GOING TO MAKE YOU SUFFER...
...BUT I'M GUESSING YOU ALREADY KNOW THAT.
I'M NOT HERE TO SAVE HER OR STOP YOU.

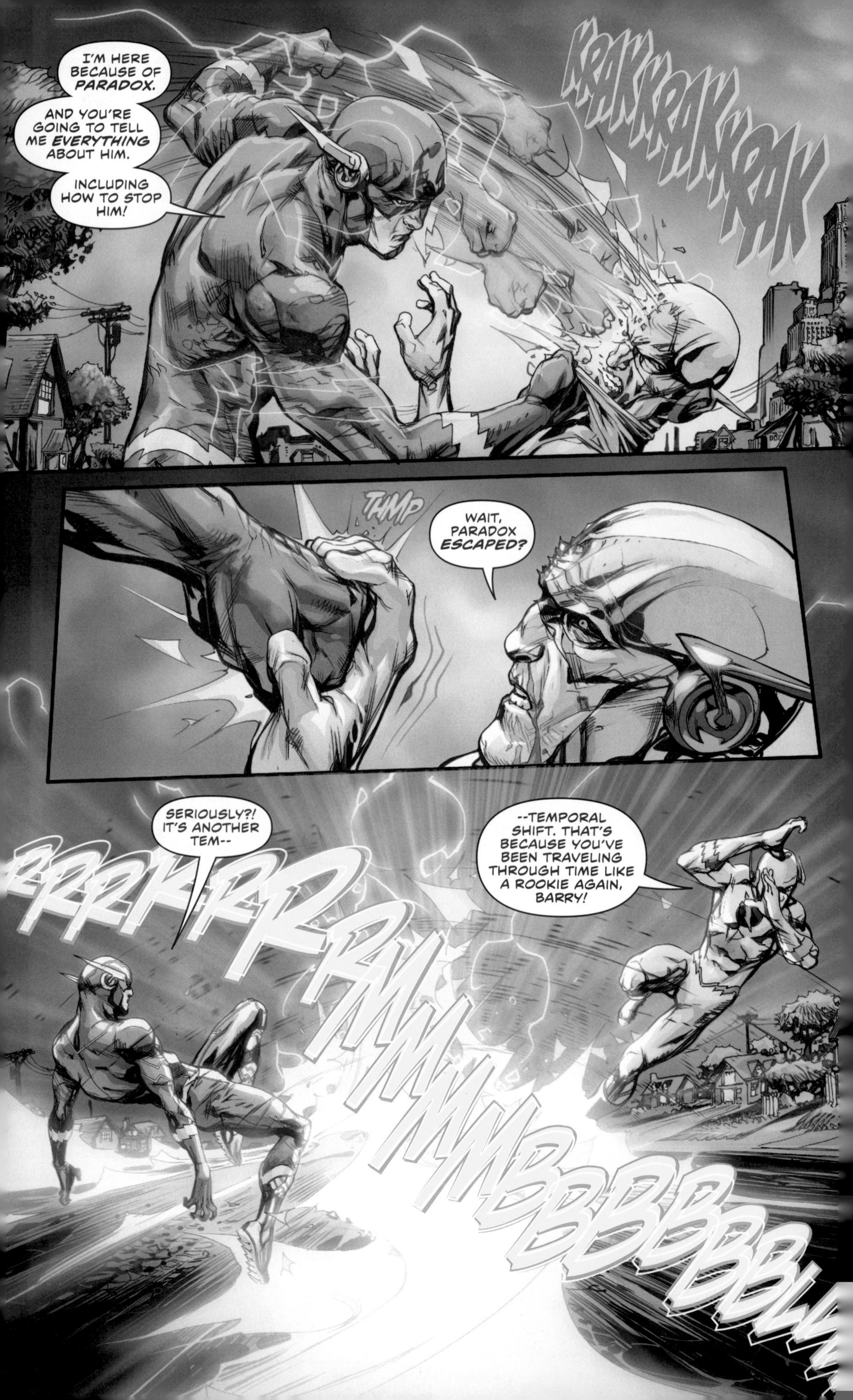
I'M HERE BECAUSE OF PARADOX.
AND YOU'RE GOING TO TELL ME EVERYTHING ABOUT HIM.
INCLUDING HOW TO STOP HIM!
KRAKKRAKKRAK
THMP
WAIT, PARADOX ESCAPED?
SERIOUSLY?! IT'S ANOTHER TEM--
--TEMPORAL SHIFT. THAT'S BECAUSE YOU'VE BEEN TRAVELING THROUGH TIME LIKE A ROOKIE AGAIN, BARRY!

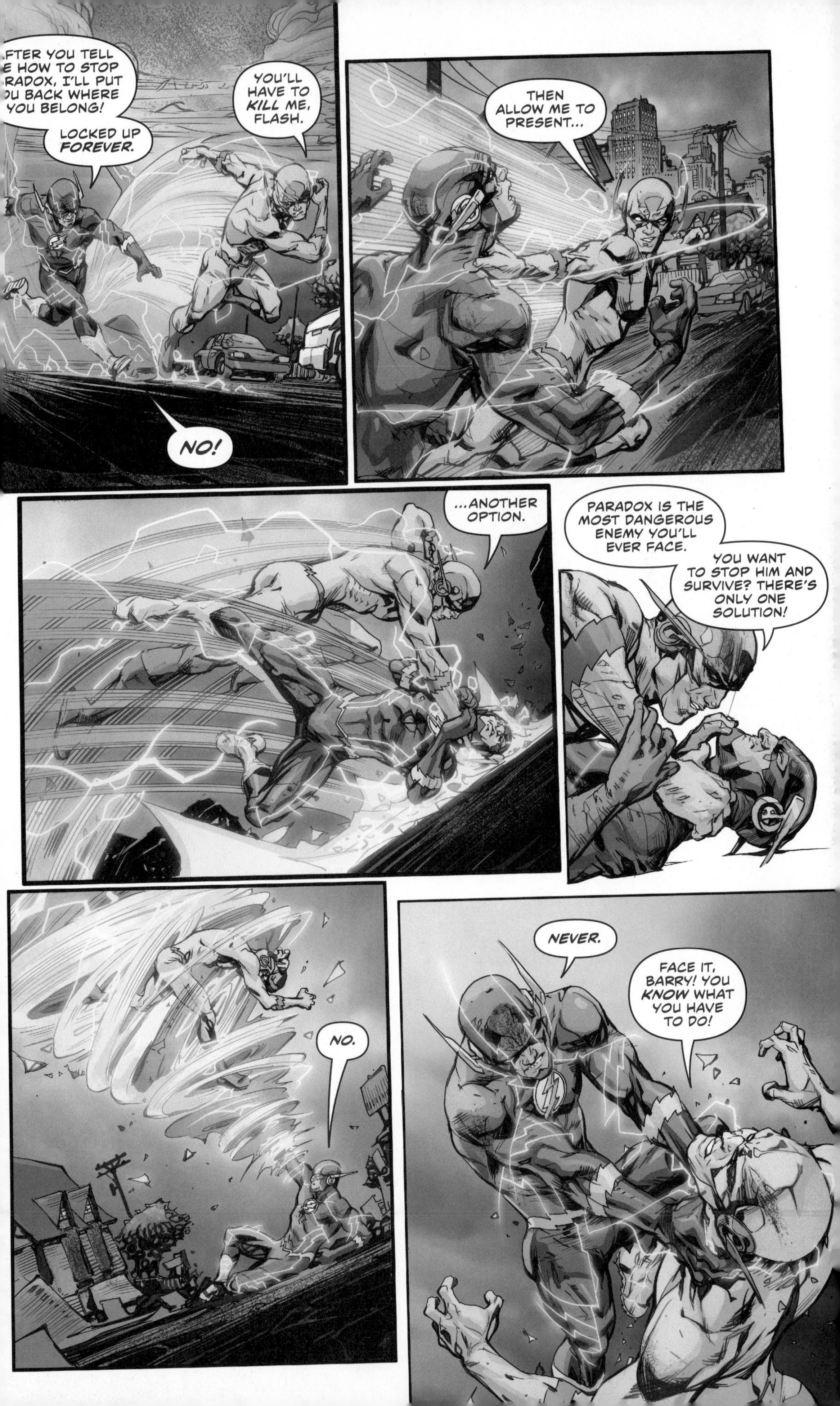

FTER YOU TELL E HOW TO STOP ARADOX, I'LL PUT U BACK WHERE YOU BELONG!
LOCKED UP FOREVER.
YOU'LL HAVE TO KILL ME, FLASH.
NO!
THEN ALLOW ME TO PRESENT...
...ANOTHER OPTION.
PARADOX IS THE MOST DANGEROUS ENEMY YOU'LL EVER FACE.
YOU WANT TO STOP HIM AND SURVIVE? THERE'S ONLY ONE SOLUTION!
NO.
NEVER.
FACE IT, BARRY! YOU KNOW WHAT YOU HAVE TO DO!

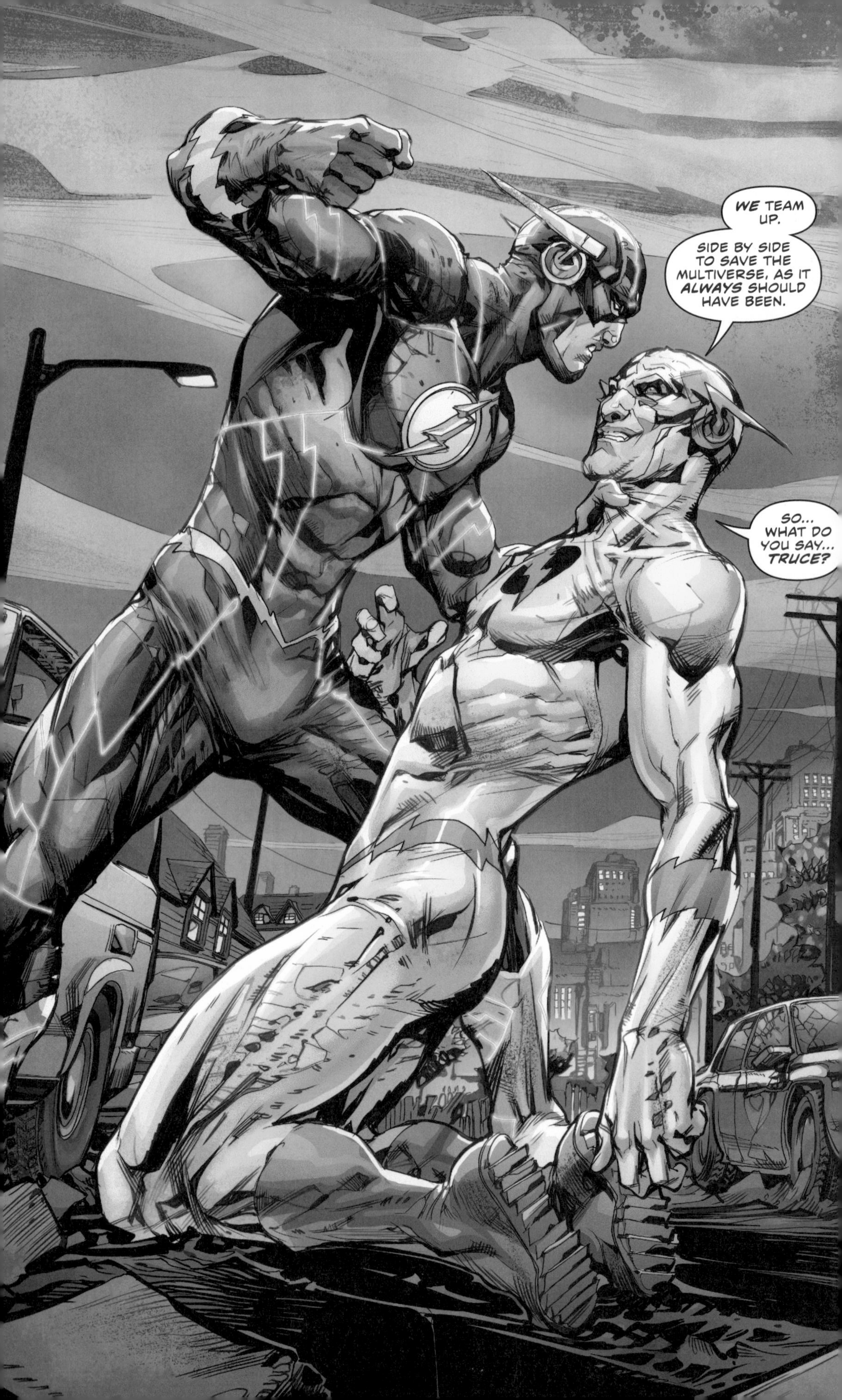
WE TEAM UP.
SIDE BY SIDE TO SAVE THE MULTIVERSE, AS IT ALWAYS SHOULD HAVE BEEN.
SO... WHAT DO YOU SAY... TRUCE?

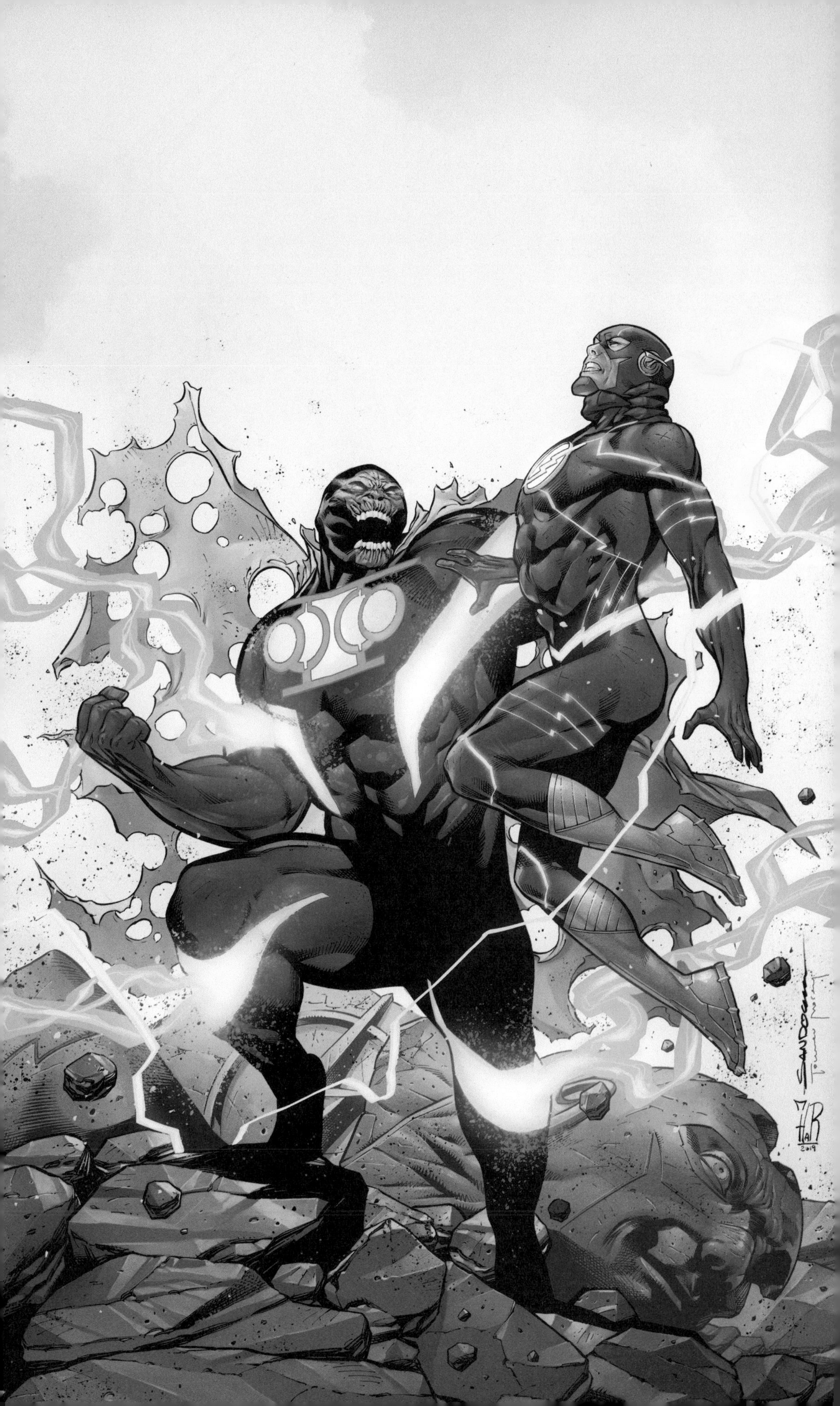

The Flash **#754** variant cover by RAFAEL GRAMPÁ

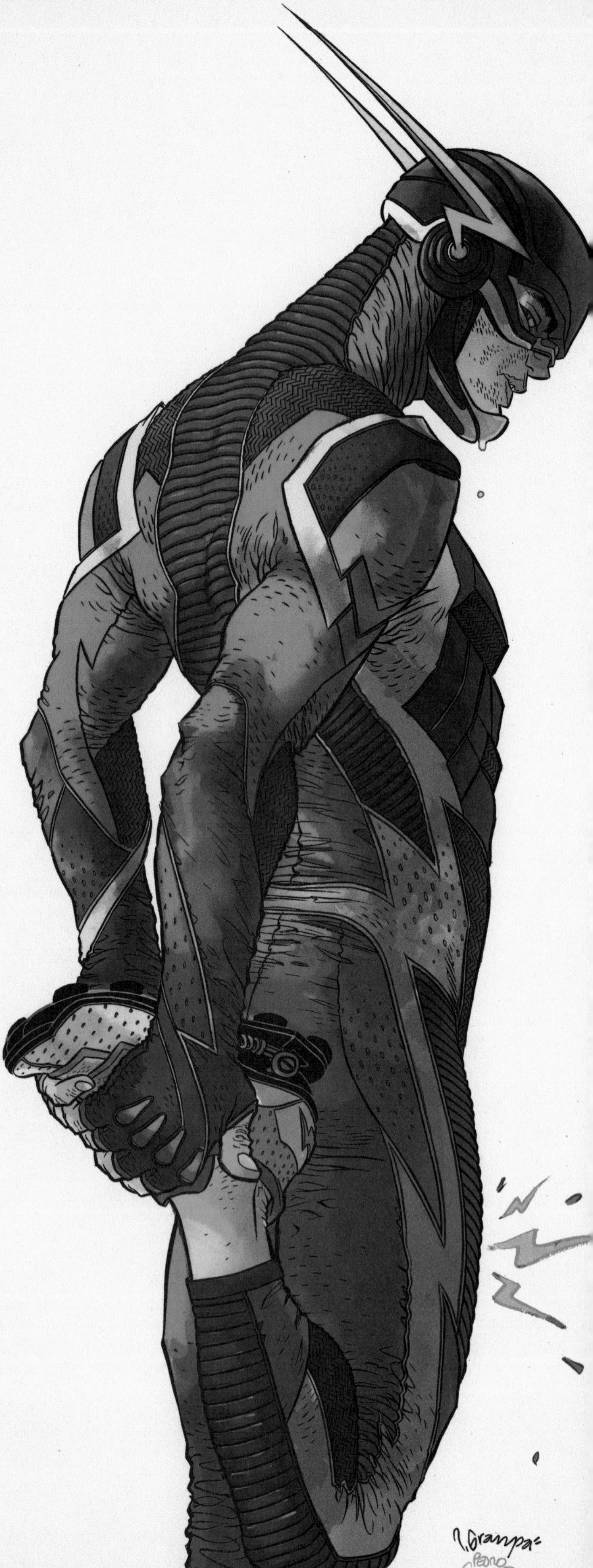

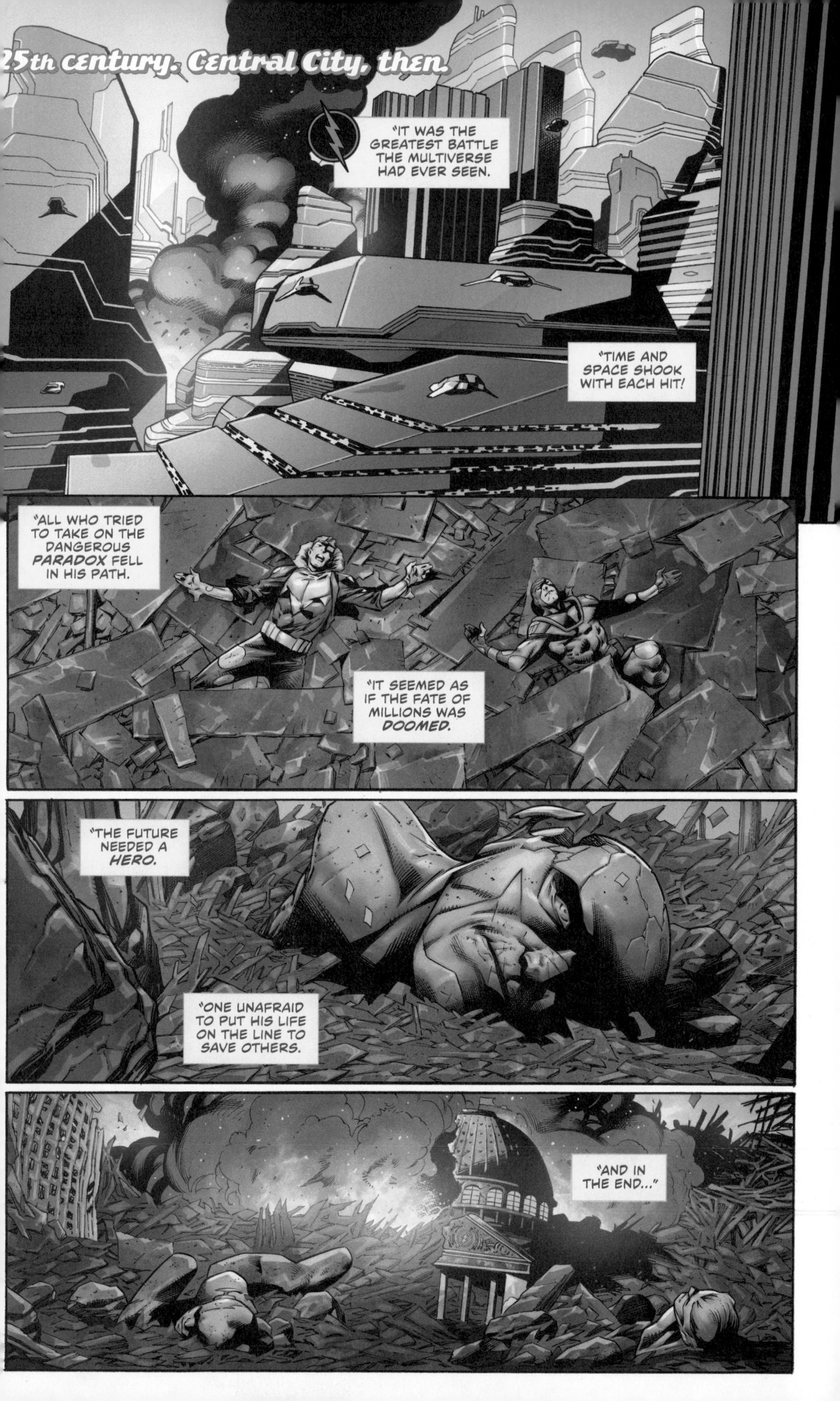
25th century. Central City, then.
"IT WAS THE GREATEST BATTLE THE MULTIVERSE HAD EVER SEEN.
"TIME AND SPACE SHOOK WITH EACH HIT!
"ALL WHO TRIED TO TAKE ON THE DANGEROUS *PARADOX* FELL IN HIS PATH.
"IT SEEMED AS IF THE FATE OF MILLIONS WAS *DOOMED*.
"THE FUTURE NEEDED A *HERO*.
"ONE UNAFRAID TO PUT HIS LIFE ON THE LINE TO SAVE OTHERS.
"AND IN THE END..."

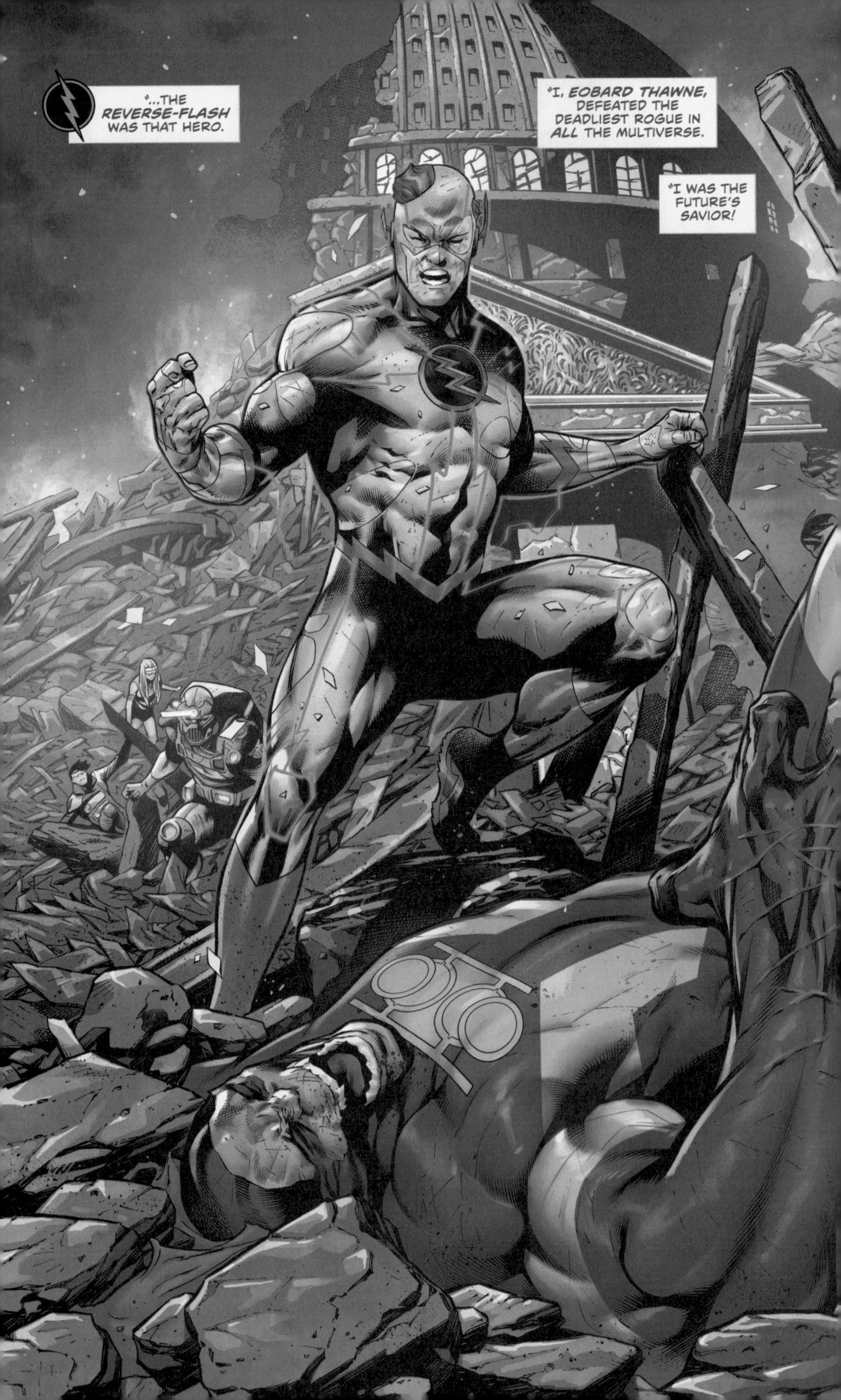
"...THE REVERSE-FLASH WAS THAT HERO.
"I, EOBARD THAWNE, DEFEATED THE DEADLIEST ROGUE IN ALL THE MULTIVERSE.
"I WAS THE FUTURE'S SAVIOR!

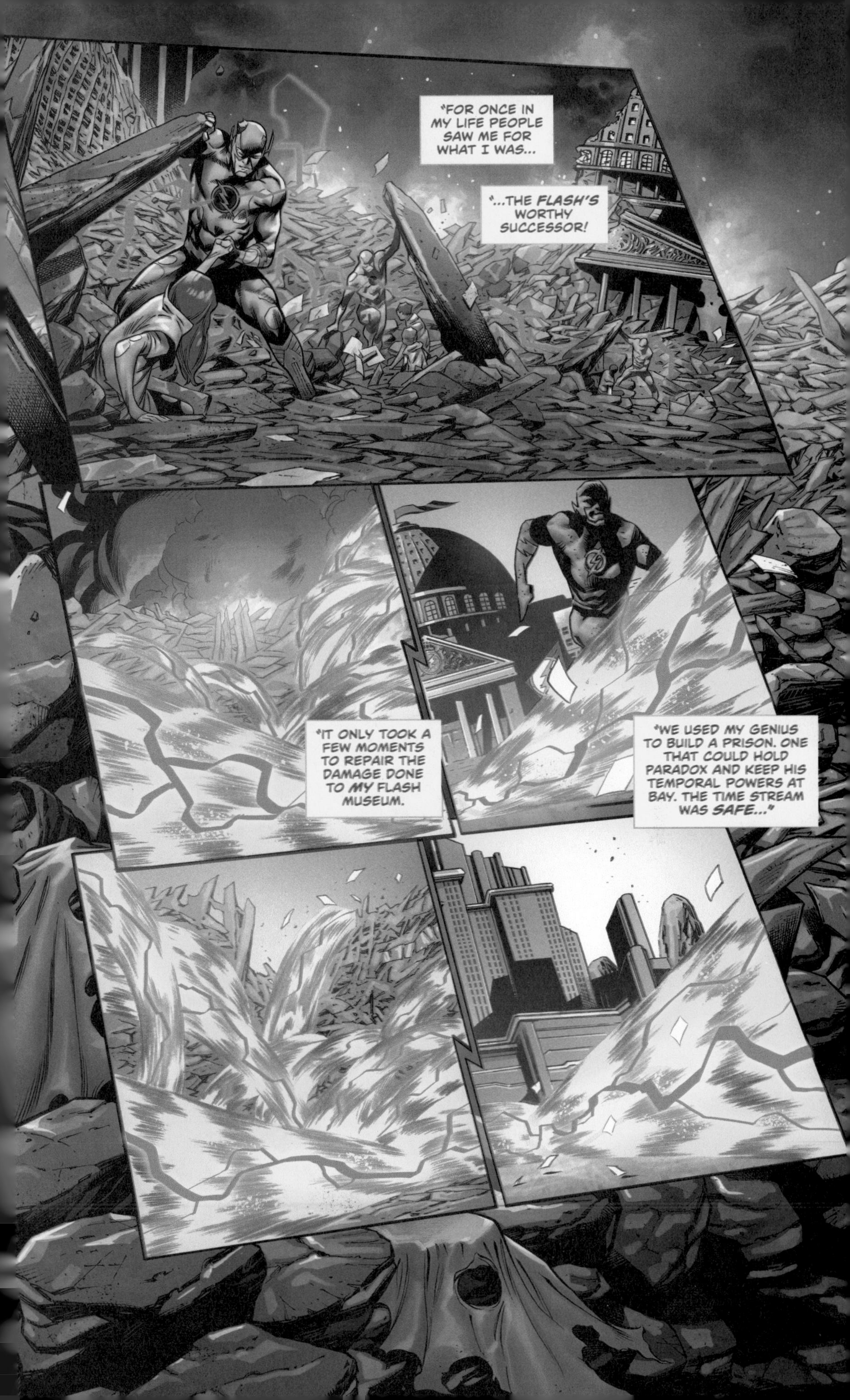
"FOR ONCE IN MY LIFE PEOPLE SAW ME FOR WHAT I WAS...
"...THE FLASH'S WORTHY SUCCESSOR!
"IT ONLY TOOK A FEW MOMENTS TO REPAIR THE DAMAGE DONE TO MY FLASH MUSEUM.
"WE USED MY GENIUS TO BUILD A PRISON. ONE THAT COULD HOLD PARADOX AND KEEP HIS TEMPORAL POWERS AT BAY. THE TIME STREAM WAS SAFE..."

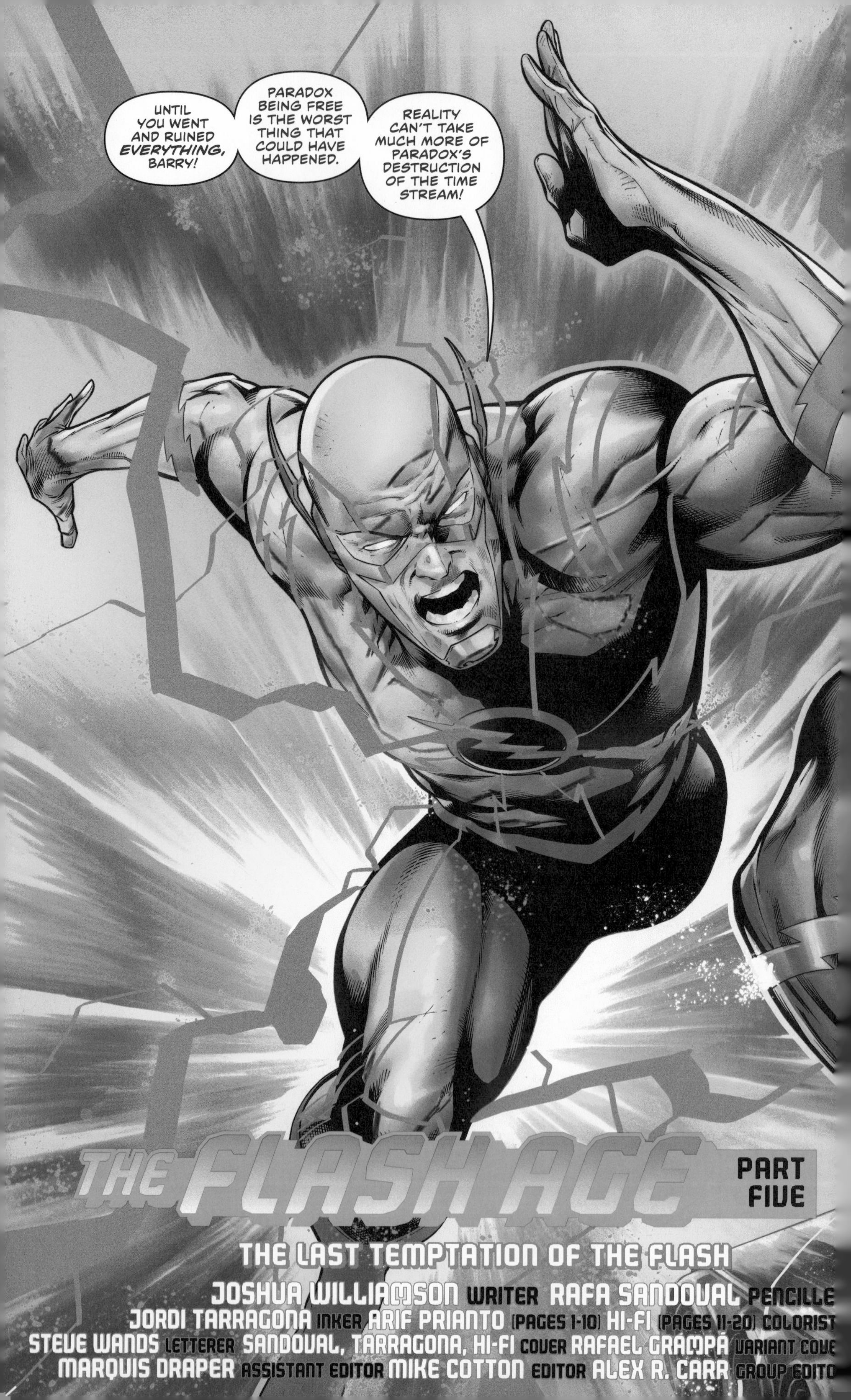
UNTIL YOU WENT AND RUINED EVERYTHING, BARRY!
PARADOX BEING FREE IS THE WORST THING THAT COULD HAVE HAPPENED.
REALITY CAN'T TAKE MUCH MORE OF PARADOX'S DESTRUCTION OF THE TIME STREAM!
THE FLASH AGE
PART FIVE
THE LAST TEMPTATION OF THE FLASH
JOSHUA WILLIAMSON WRITER RAFA SANDOVAL PENCILLE
JORDI TARRAGONA INKER ARIF PRIANTO (PAGES 1-10) HI-FI (PAGES 11-20) COLORIST
STEVE WANDS LETTERER SANDOVAL, TARRAGONA, HI-FI COVER RAFAEL GRAMPÁ VARIANT COVE
MARQUIS DRAPER ASSISTANT EDITOR MIKE COTTON EDITOR ALEX R. CARR GROUP EDITO

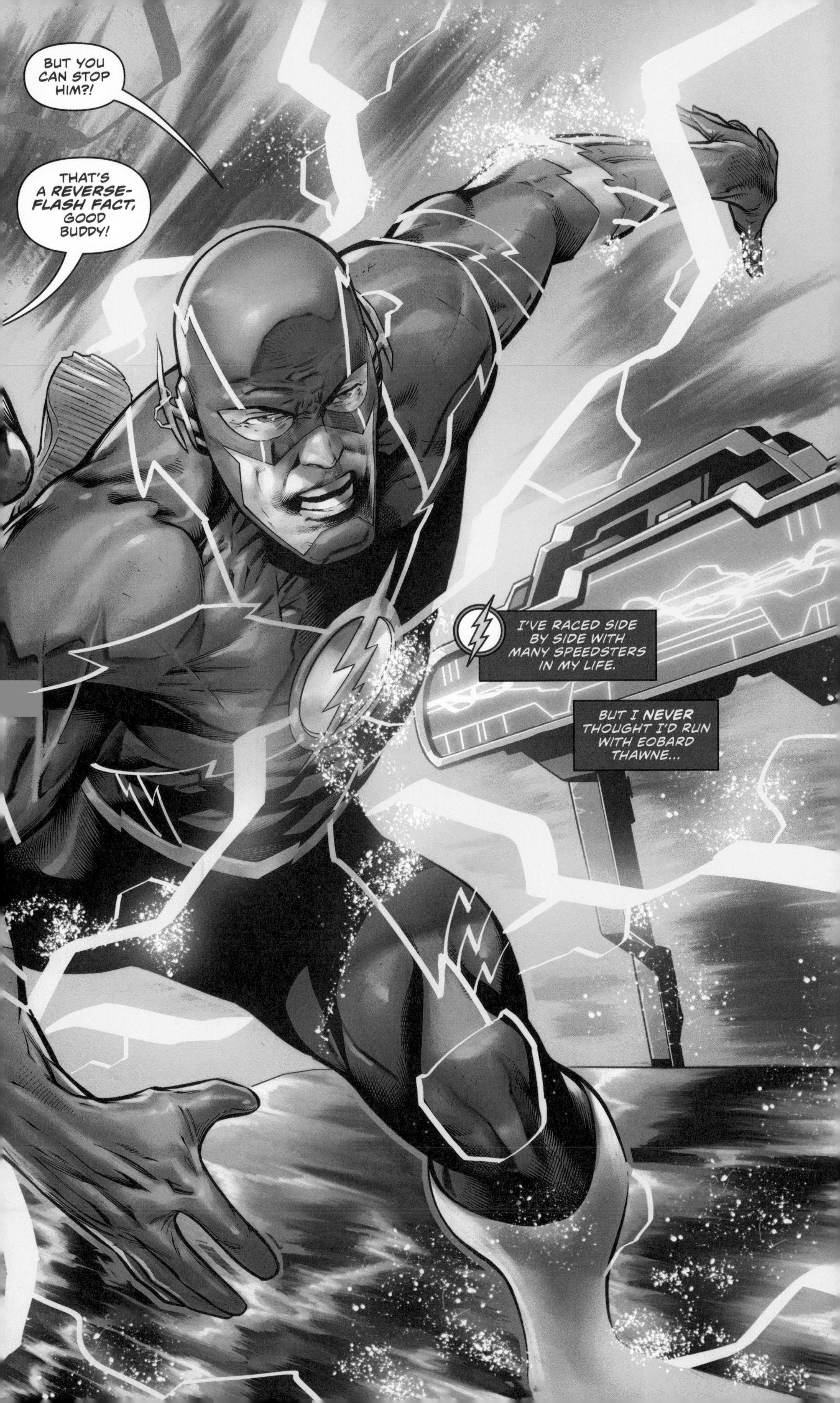

BUT YOU CAN STOP HIM?!
THAT'S A REVERSE-FLASH FACT, GOOD BUDDY!
I'VE RACED SIDE BY SIDE WITH MANY SPEEDSTERS IN MY LIFE.
BUT I NEVER THOUGHT I'D RUN WITH EOBARD THAWNE...

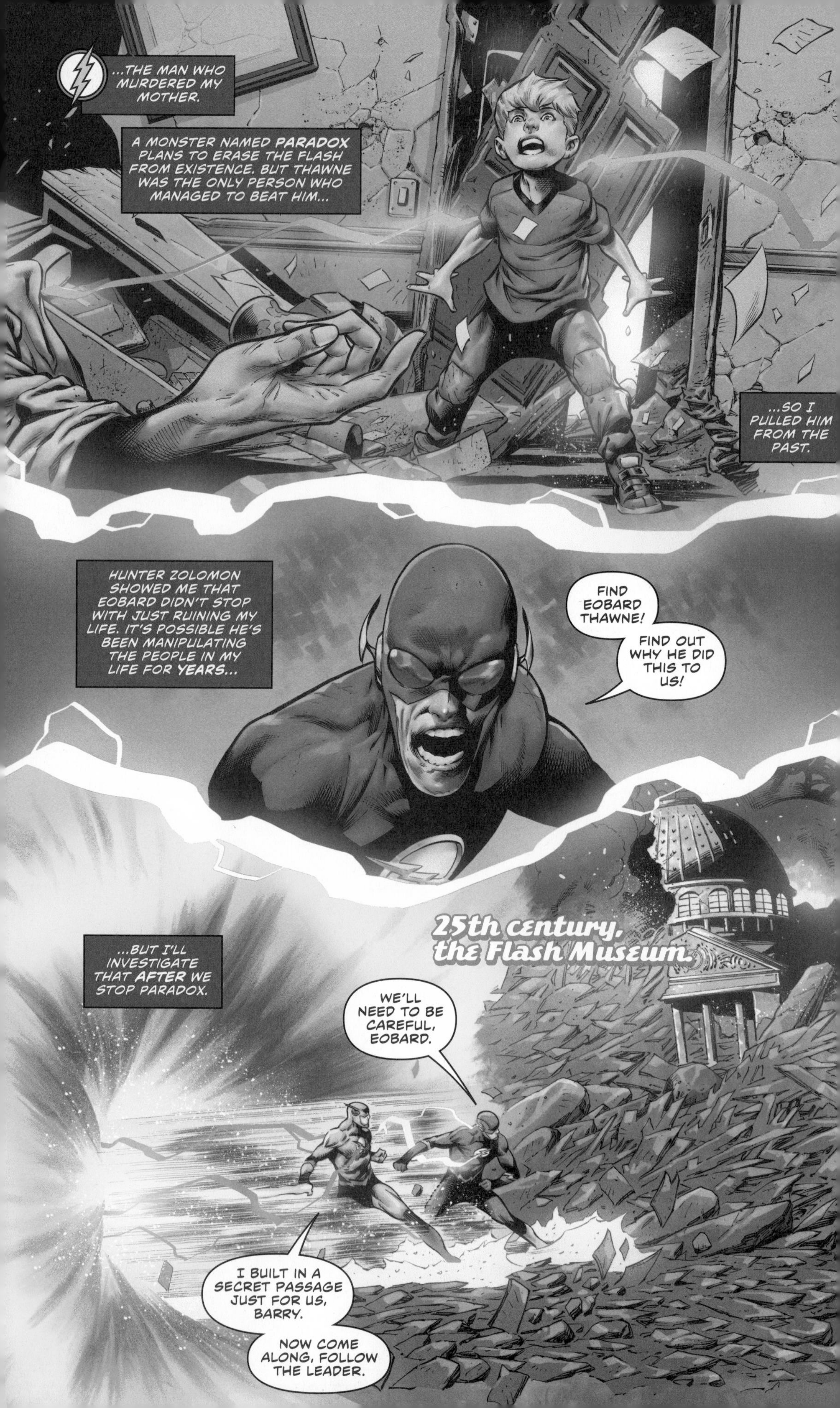
...THE MAN WHO MURDERED MY MOTHER.
A MONSTER NAMED PARADOX PLANS TO ERASE THE FLASH FROM EXISTENCE. BUT THAWNE WAS THE ONLY PERSON WHO MANAGED TO BEAT HIM...
...SO I PULLED HIM FROM THE PAST.
HUNTER ZOLOMON SHOWED ME THAT EOBARD DIDN'T STOP WITH JUST RUINING MY LIFE. IT'S POSSIBLE HE'S BEEN MANIPULATING THE PEOPLE IN MY LIFE FOR YEARS...
FIND EOBARD THAWNE!
FIND OUT WHY HE DID THIS TO US!
25th century, the Flash Museum.
...BUT I'LL INVESTIGATE THAT AFTER WE STOP PARADOX.
WE'LL NEED TO BE CAREFUL, EOBARD.
I BUILT IN A SECRET PASSAGE JUST FOR US, BARRY.
NOW COME ALONG, FOLLOW THE LEADER.

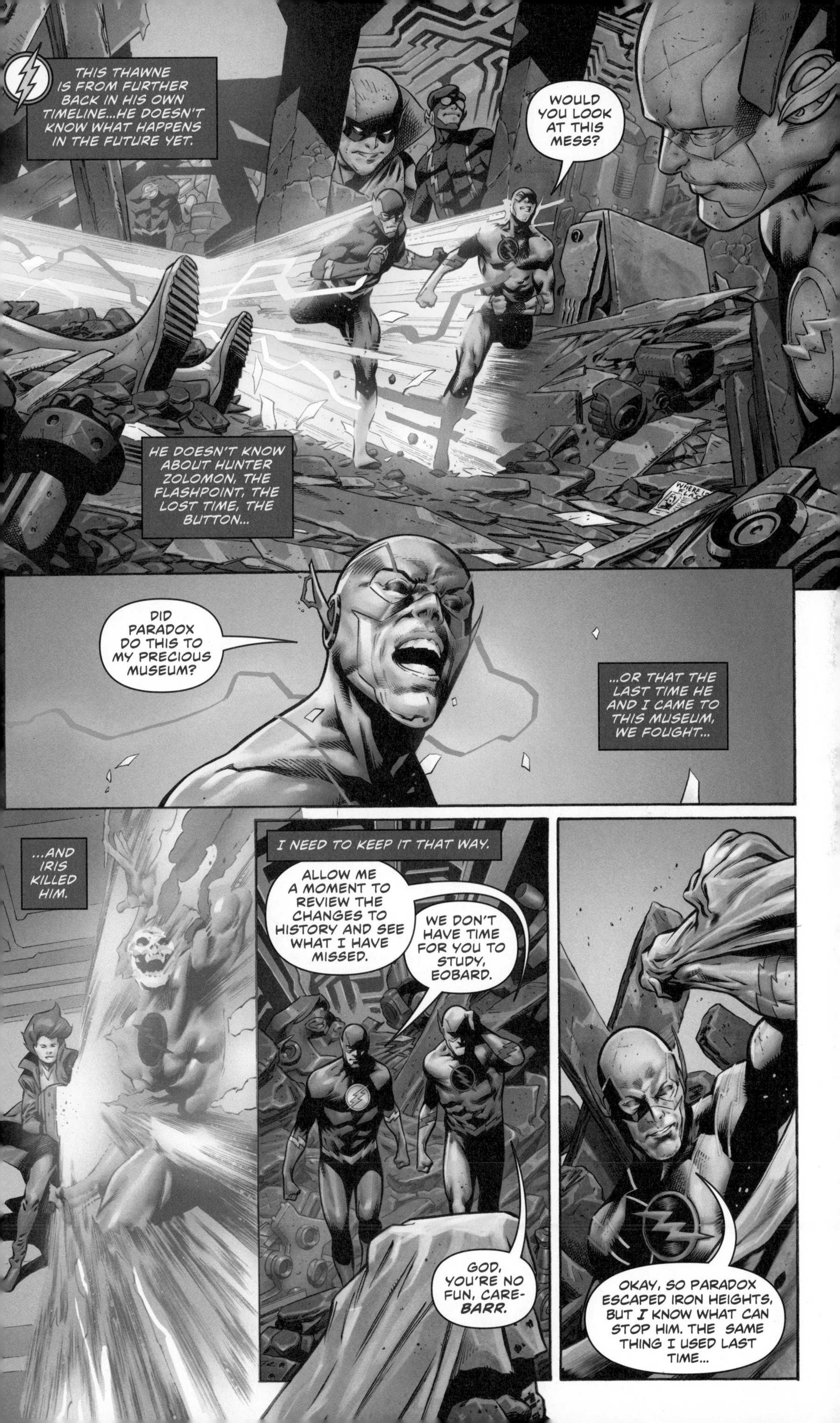
THIS THAWNE IS FROM FURTHER BACK IN HIS OWN TIMELINE...HE DOESN'T KNOW WHAT HAPPENS IN THE FUTURE YET.
WOULD YOU LOOK AT THIS MESS?
HE DOESN'T KNOW ABOUT HUNTER ZOLOMON, THE FLASHPOINT, THE LOST TIME, THE BUTTON...
DID PARADOX DO THIS TO MY PRECIOUS MUSEUM?
...OR THAT THE LAST TIME HE AND I CAME TO THIS MUSEUM, WE FOUGHT...
...AND IRIS KILLED HIM.
I NEED TO KEEP IT THAT WAY.
ALLOW ME A MOMENT TO REVIEW THE CHANGES TO HISTORY AND SEE WHAT I HAVE MISSED.
WE DON'T HAVE TIME FOR YOU TO STUDY, EOBARD.
GOD, YOU'RE NO FUN, CARE-BARR.
OKAY, SO PARADOX ESCAPED IRON HEIGHTS, BUT I KNOW WHAT CAN STOP HIM. THE SAME THING I USED LAST TIME...

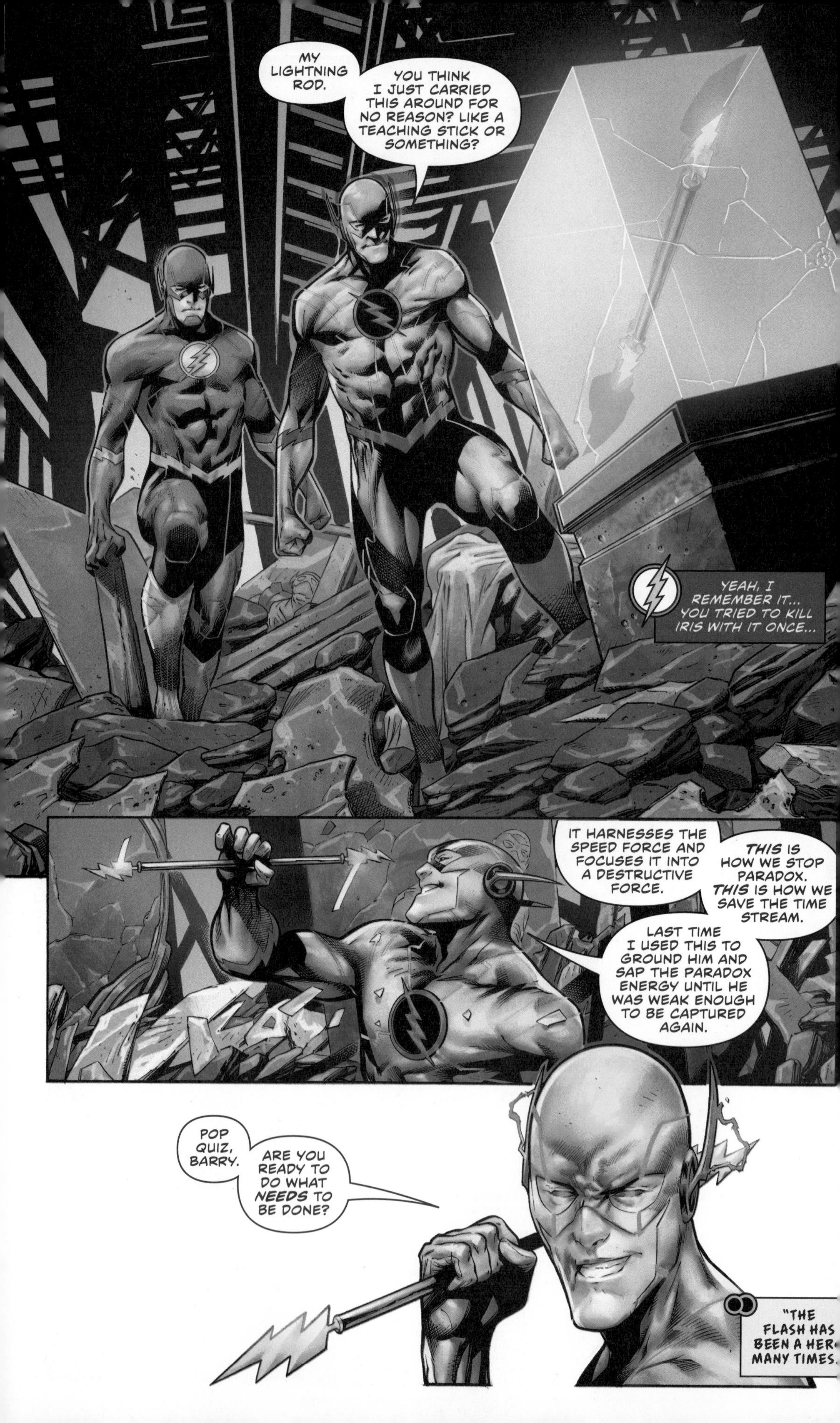
MY LIGHTNING ROD.
YOU THINK I JUST CARRIED THIS AROUND FOR NO REASON? LIKE A TEACHING STICK OR SOMETHING?
YEAH, I REMEMBER IT... YOU TRIED TO KILL IRIS WITH IT ONCE...
IT HARNESSES THE SPEED FORCE AND FOCUSES IT INTO A DESTRUCTIVE FORCE.
THIS IS HOW WE STOP PARADOX. THIS IS HOW WE SAVE THE TIME STREAM.
LAST TIME I USED THIS TO GROUND HIM AND SAP THE PARADOX ENERGY UNTIL HE WAS WEAK ENOUGH TO BE CAPTURED AGAIN.
POP QUIZ, BARRY.
ARE YOU READY TO DO WHAT NEEDS TO BE DONE?
"THE FLASH HAS BEEN A HER MANY TIMES.

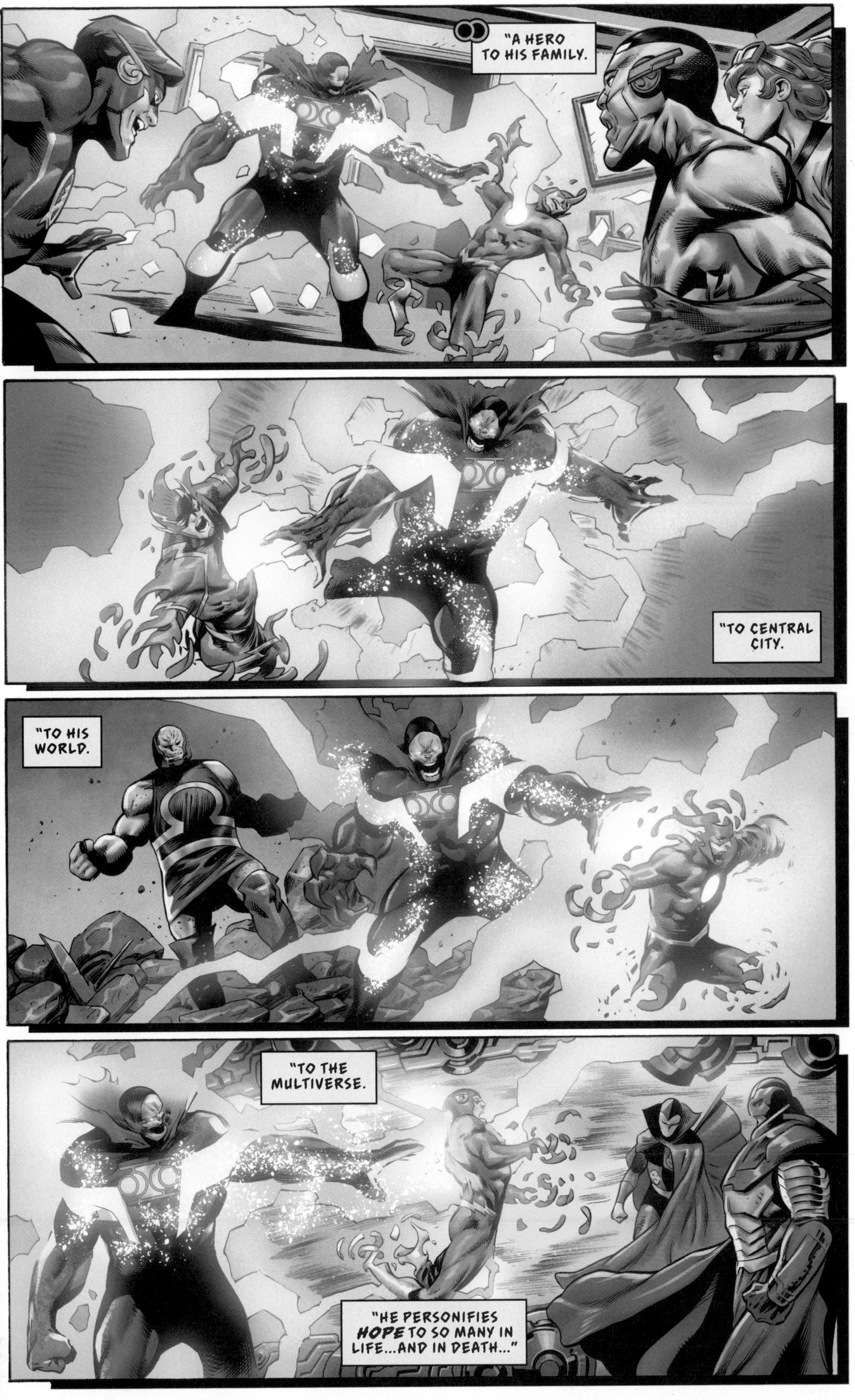
"A HERO TO HIS FAMILY.
"TO CENTRAL CITY.
"TO HIS WORLD.
"TO THE MULTIVERSE.
"HE PERSONIFIES HOPE TO SO MANY IN LIFE...AND IN DEATH..."

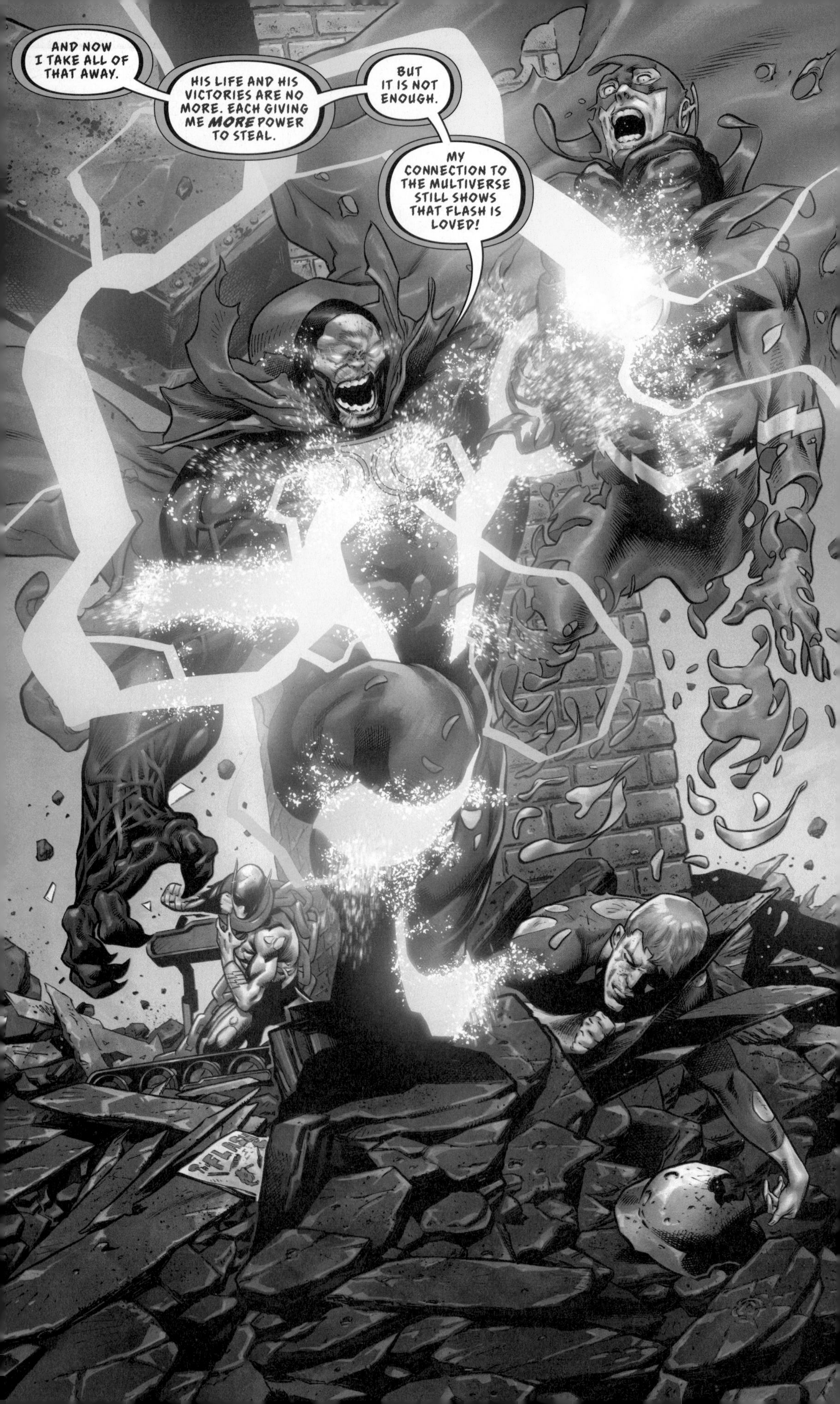
AND NOW I TAKE ALL OF THAT AWAY.
HIS LIFE AND HIS VICTORIES ARE NO MORE. EACH GIVING ME *MORE* POWER TO STEAL.
BUT IT IS NOT ENOUGH.
MY CONNECTION TO THE MULTIVERSE STILL SHOWS THAT FLASH IS LOVED!

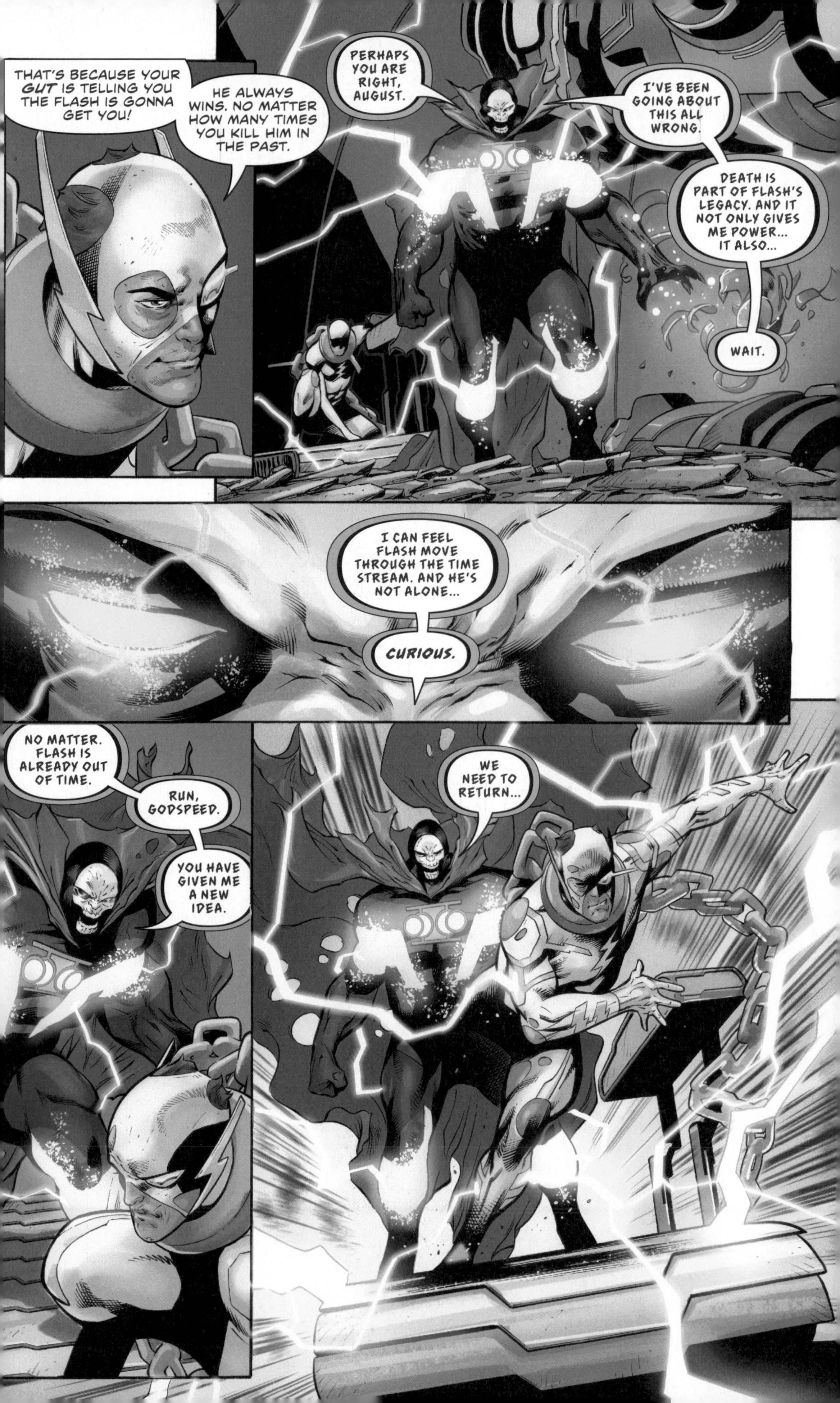
THAT'S BECAUSE YOUR GUT IS TELLING YOU THE FLASH IS GONNA GET YOU!
HE ALWAYS WINS. NO MATTER HOW MANY TIMES YOU KILL HIM IN THE PAST.
PERHAPS YOU ARE RIGHT, AUGUST.
I'VE BEEN GOING ABOUT THIS ALL WRONG.
DEATH IS PART OF FLASH'S LEGACY. AND IT NOT ONLY GIVES ME POWER... IT ALSO...
WAIT.
I CAN FEEL FLASH MOVE THROUGH THE TIME STREAM. AND HE'S NOT ALONE...
CURIOUS.
NO MATTER. FLASH IS ALREADY OUT OF TIME.
RUN, GODSPEED.
YOU HAVE GIVEN ME A NEW IDEA.
WE NEED TO RETURN...

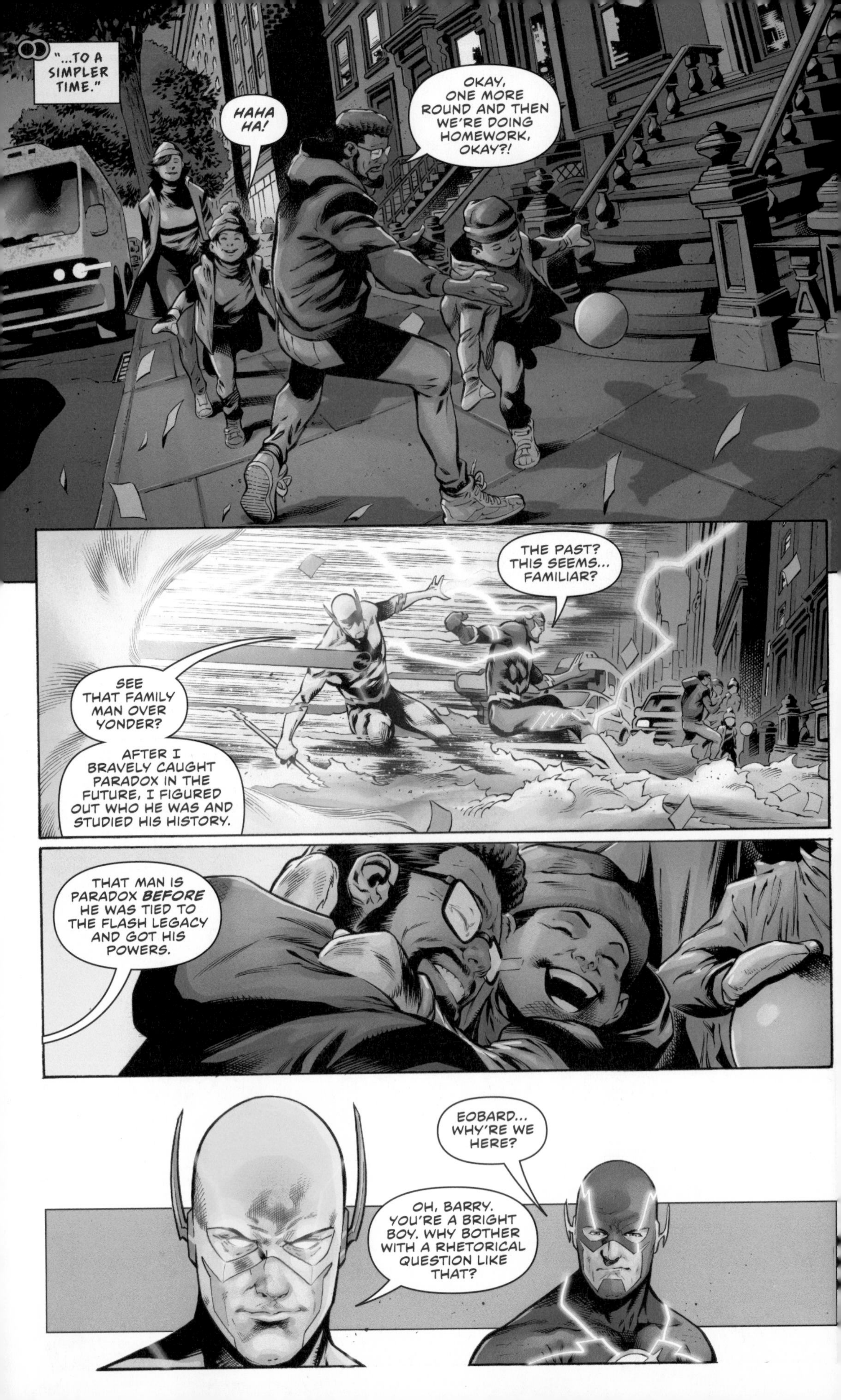

"...TO A SIMPLER TIME."
HAHA HA!
OKAY, ONE MORE ROUND AND THEN WE'RE DOING HOMEWORK, OKAY?!
THE PAST? THIS SEEMS... FAMILIAR?
SEE THAT FAMILY MAN OVER YONDER?
AFTER I BRAVELY CAUGHT PARADOX IN THE FUTURE, I FIGURED OUT WHO HE WAS AND STUDIED HIS HISTORY.
THAT MAN IS PARADOX BEFORE HE WAS TIED TO THE FLASH LEGACY AND GOT HIS POWERS.
EOBARD... WHY'RE WE HERE?
OH, BARRY. YOU'RE A BRIGHT BOY. WHY BOTHER WITH A RHETORICAL QUESTION LIKE THAT?

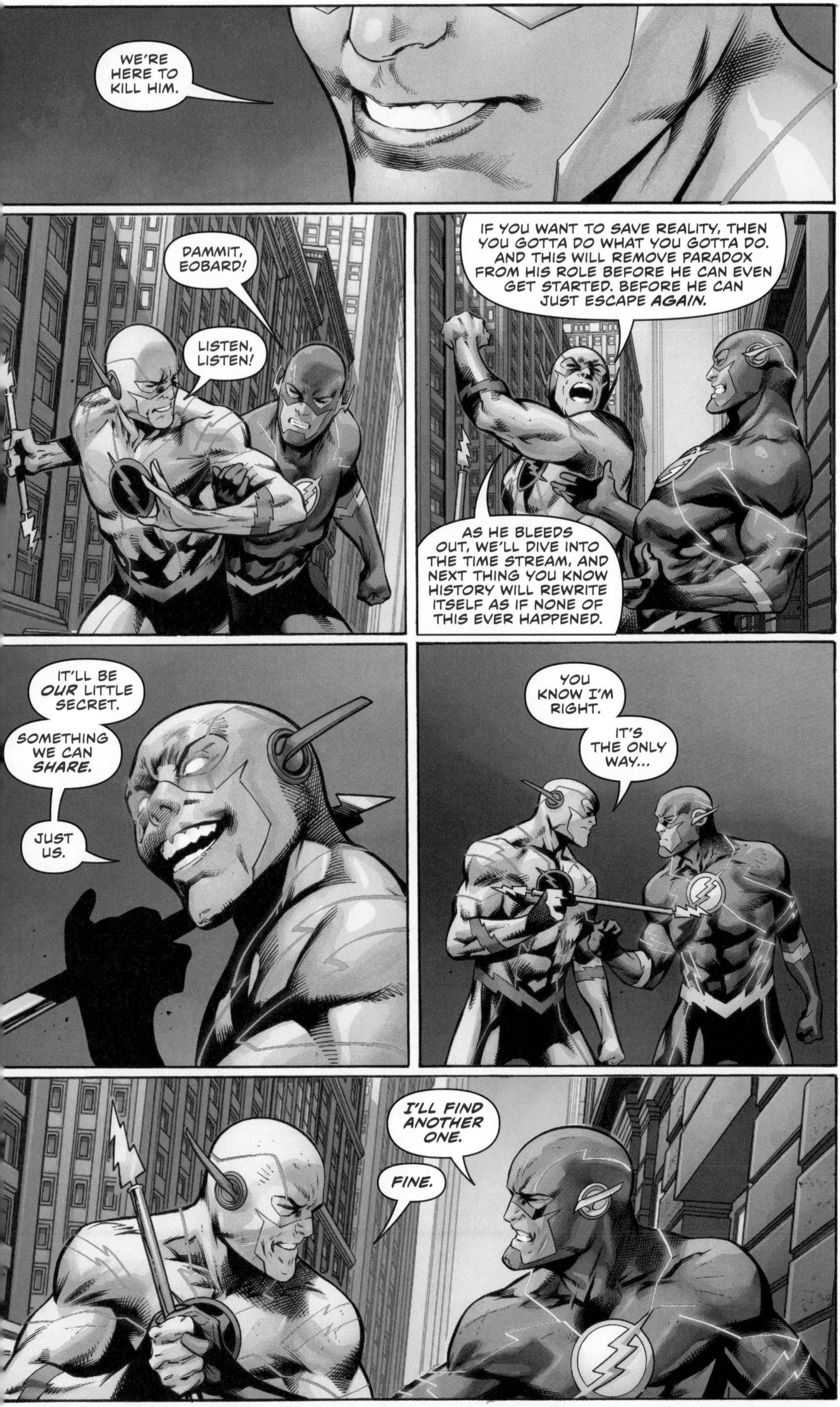
WE'RE HERE TO KILL HIM.
DAMMIT, EOBARD!
LISTEN, LISTEN!
IF YOU WANT TO SAVE REALITY, THEN YOU GOTTA DO WHAT YOU GOTTA DO. AND THIS WILL REMOVE PARADOX FROM HIS ROLE BEFORE HE CAN EVEN GET STARTED. BEFORE HE CAN JUST ESCAPE AGAIN.
AS HE BLEEDS OUT, WE'LL DIVE INTO THE TIME STREAM, AND NEXT THING YOU KNOW HISTORY WILL REWRITE ITSELF AS IF NONE OF THIS EVER HAPPENED.
IT'LL BE OUR LITTLE SECRET.
SOMETHING WE CAN SHARE.
JUST US.
YOU KNOW I'M RIGHT.
IT'S THE ONLY WAY...
I'LL FIND ANOTHER ONE.
FINE.

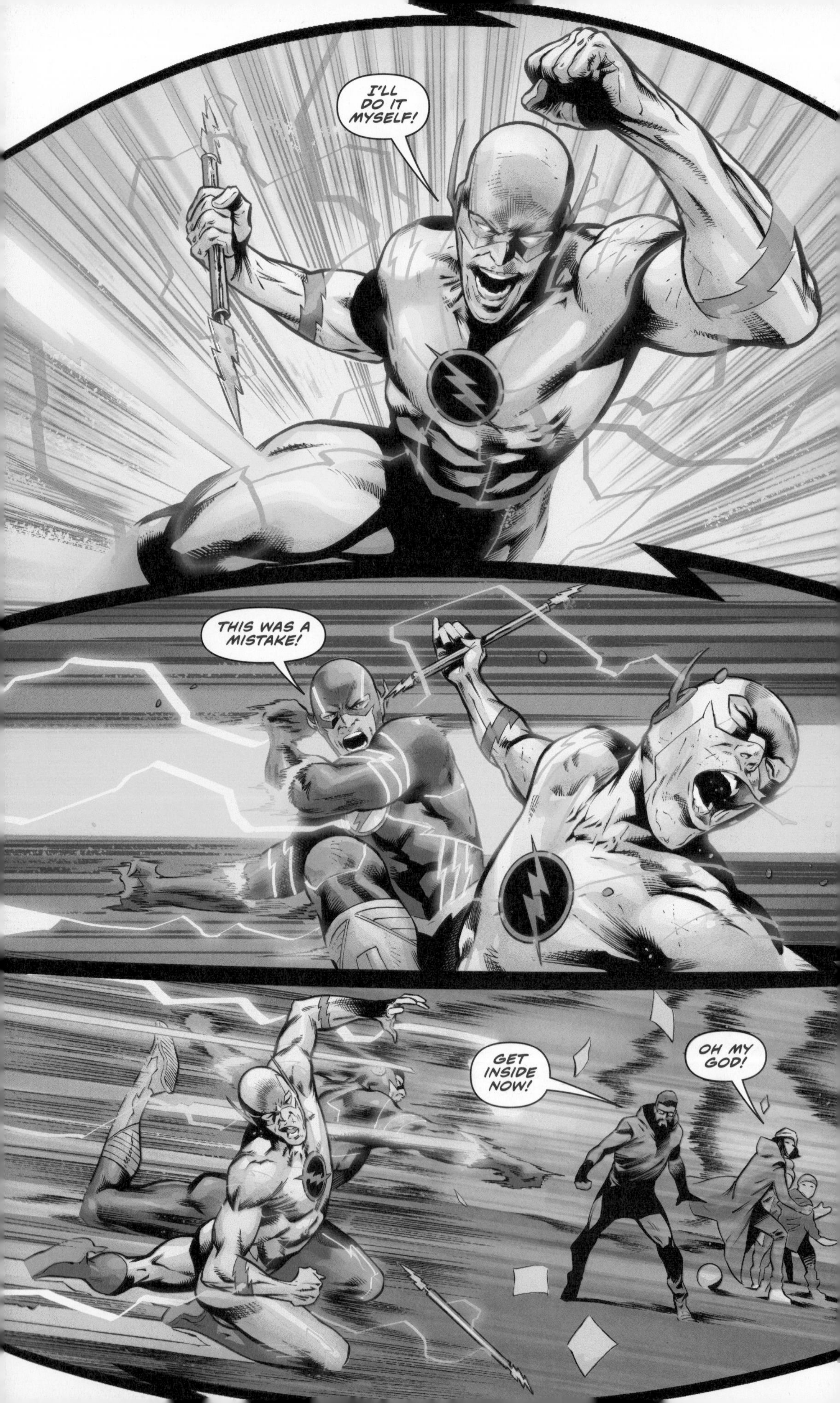
I'LL DO IT MYSELF!
THIS WAS A MISTAKE!
GET INSIDE NOW!
OH MY GOD!

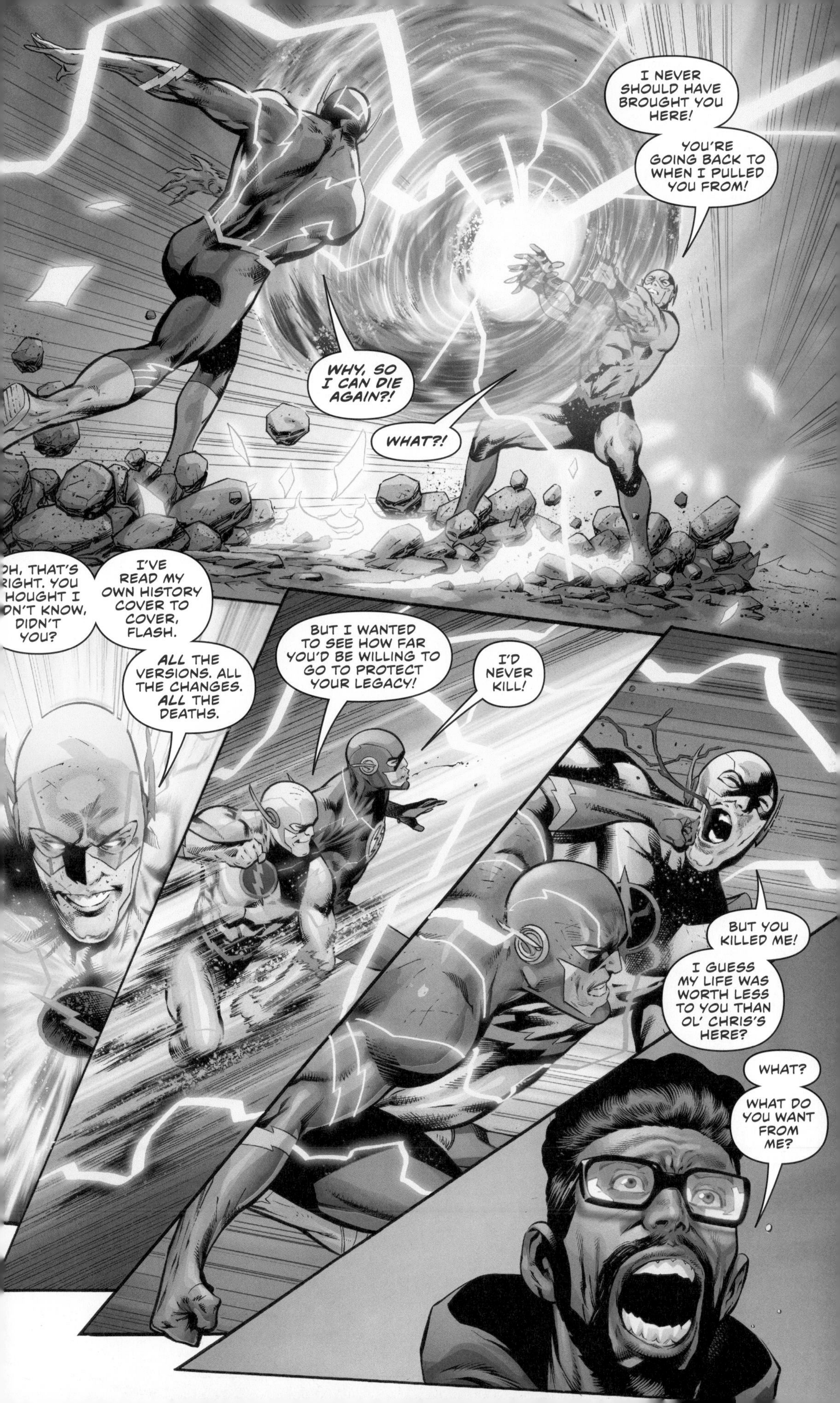
I NEVER SHOULD HAVE BROUGHT YOU HERE!
YOU'RE GOING BACK TO WHEN I PULLED YOU FROM!
WHY, SO I CAN DIE AGAIN?!
WHAT?!
OH, THAT'S RIGHT. YOU THOUGHT I DIDN'T KNOW, DIDN'T YOU?
I'VE READ MY OWN HISTORY COVER TO COVER, FLASH.
ALL THE VERSIONS. ALL THE CHANGES. ALL THE DEATHS.
BUT I WANTED TO SEE HOW FAR YOU'D BE WILLING TO GO TO PROTECT YOUR LEGACY!
I'D NEVER KILL!
BUT YOU KILLED ME!
I GUESS MY LIFE WAS WORTH LESS TO YOU THAN OL' CHRIS'S HERE?
WHAT?
WHAT DO YOU WANT FROM ME?

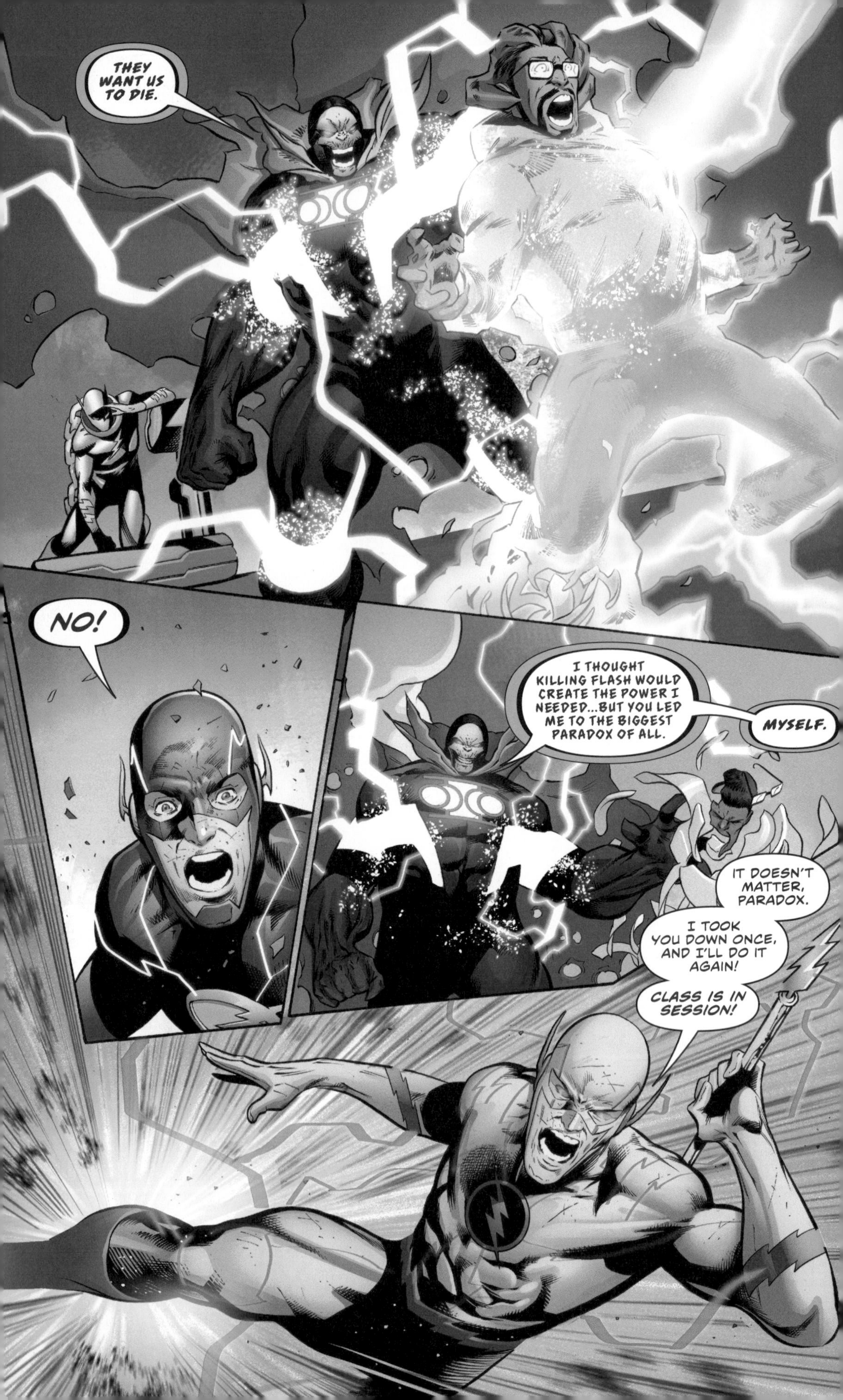
THEY WANT US TO DIE.
NO!
I THOUGHT KILLING FLASH WOULD CREATE THE POWER I NEEDED...BUT YOU LED ME TO THE BIGGEST PARADOX OF ALL.
MYSELF.
IT DOESN'T MATTER, PARADOX.
I TOOK YOU DOWN ONCE, AND I'LL DO IT AGAIN!
CLASS IS IN SESSION!

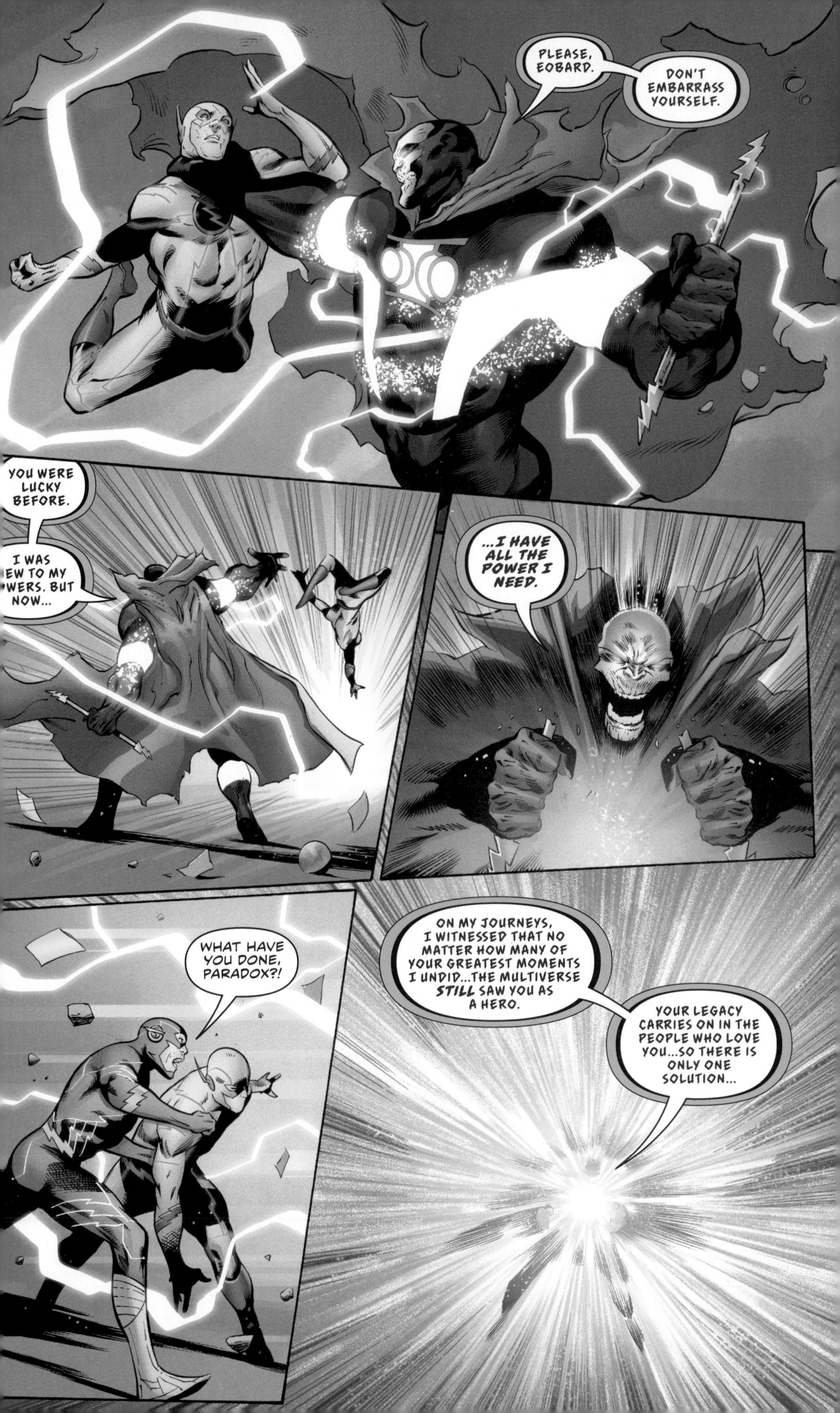
PLEASE, EOBARD.
DON'T EMBARRASS YOURSELF.
YOU WERE LUCKY BEFORE.
I WAS EW TO MY WERS. BUT NOW...
...I HAVE ALL THE POWER I NEED.
WHAT HAVE YOU DONE, PARADOX?!
ON MY JOURNEYS, I WITNESSED THAT NO MATTER HOW MANY OF YOUR GREATEST MOMENTS I UNDID...THE MULTIVERSE STILL SAW YOU AS A HERO.
YOUR LEGACY CARRIES ON IN THE PEOPLE WHO LOVE YOU...SO THERE IS ONLY ONE SOLUTION...

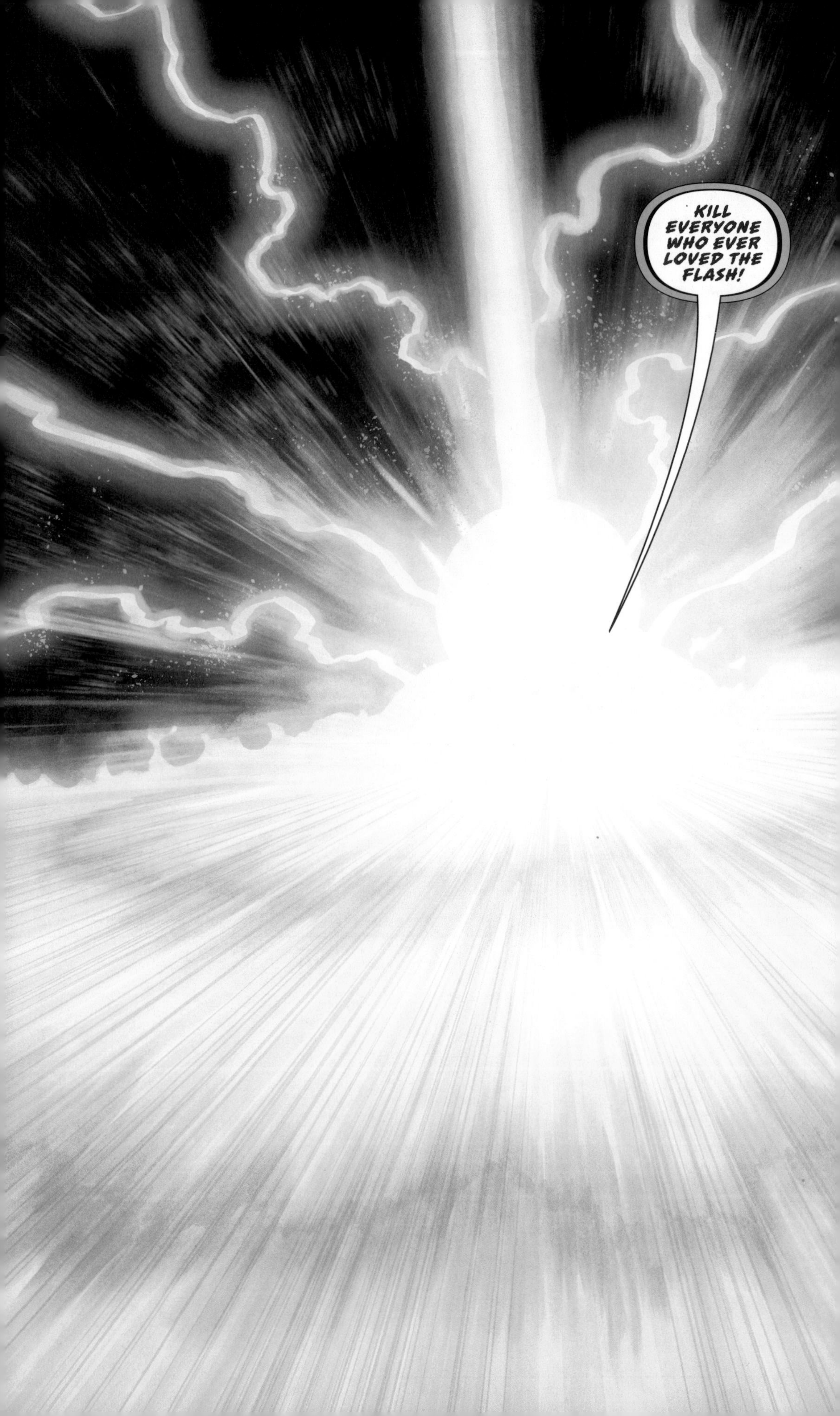
KILL EVERYONE WHO EVER LOVED THE FLASH!

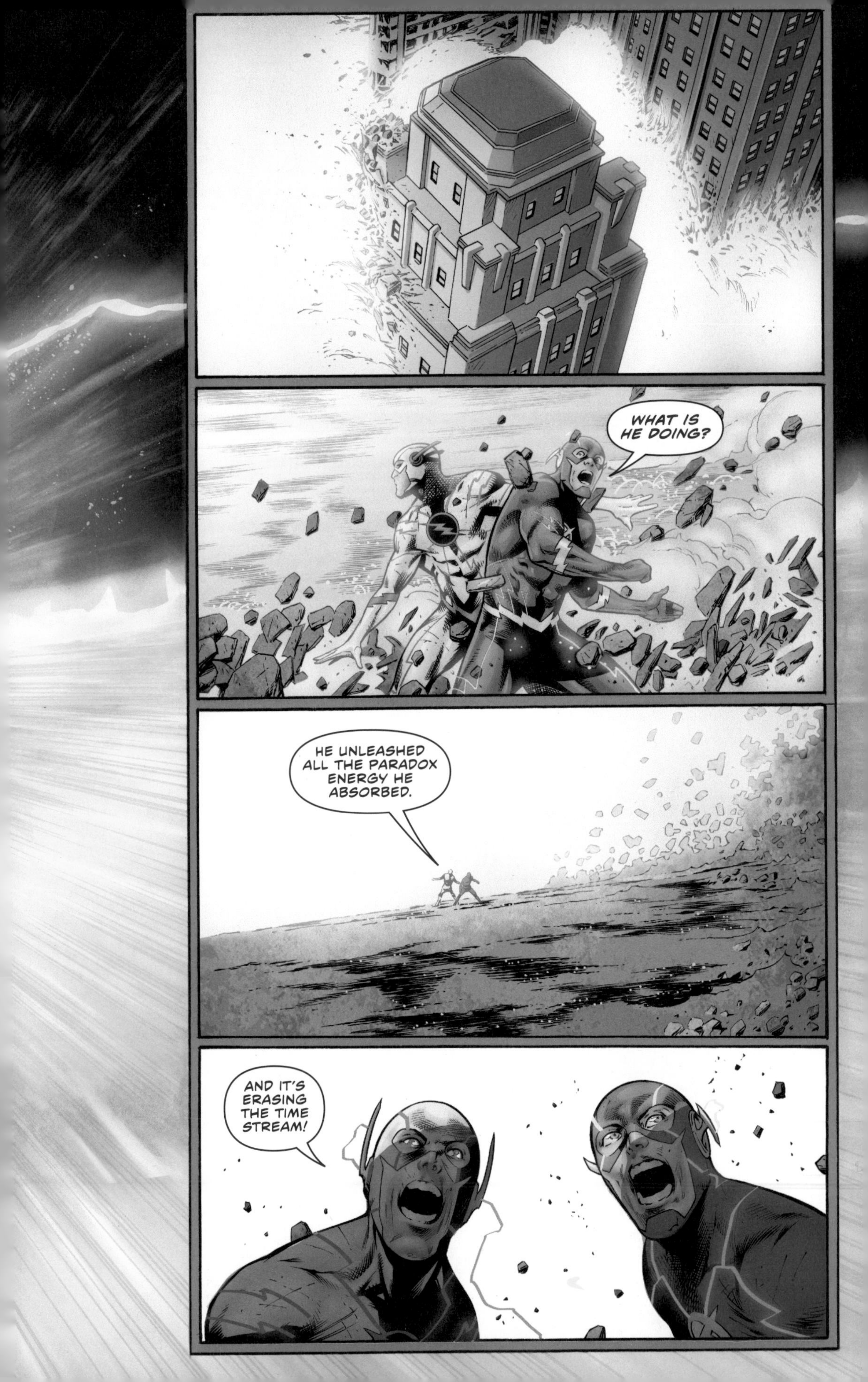
WHAT IS HE DOING?
HE UNLEASHED ALL THE PARADOX ENERGY HE ABSORBED.
AND IT'S ERASING THE TIME STREAM!

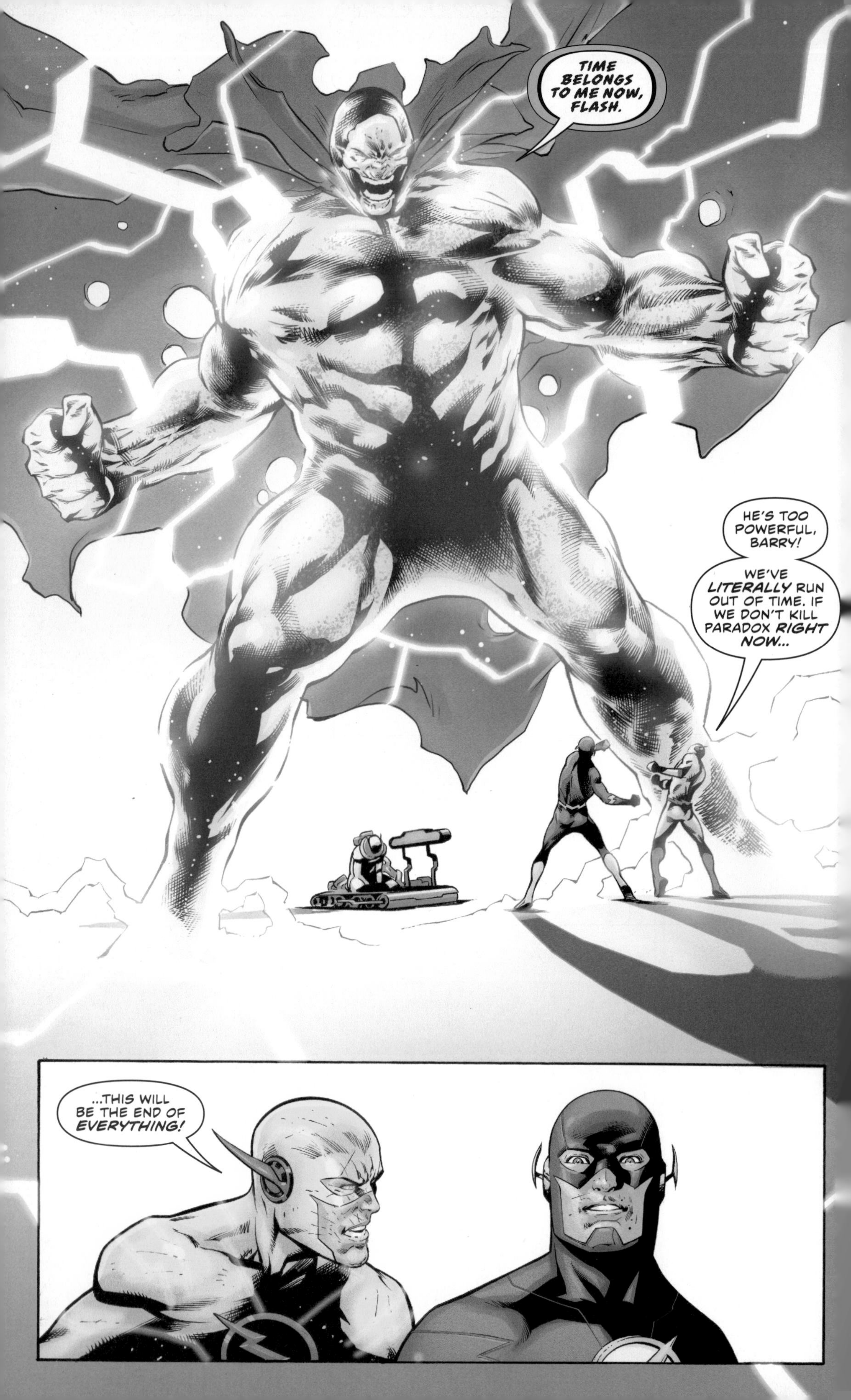

TIME BELONGS TO ME NOW, FLASH.
HE'S TOO POWERFUL, BARRY!
WE'VE *LITERALLY* RUN OUT OF TIME. IF WE DON'T KILL PARADOX *RIGHT NOW*...
...THIS WILL BE THE END OF *EVERYTHING!*

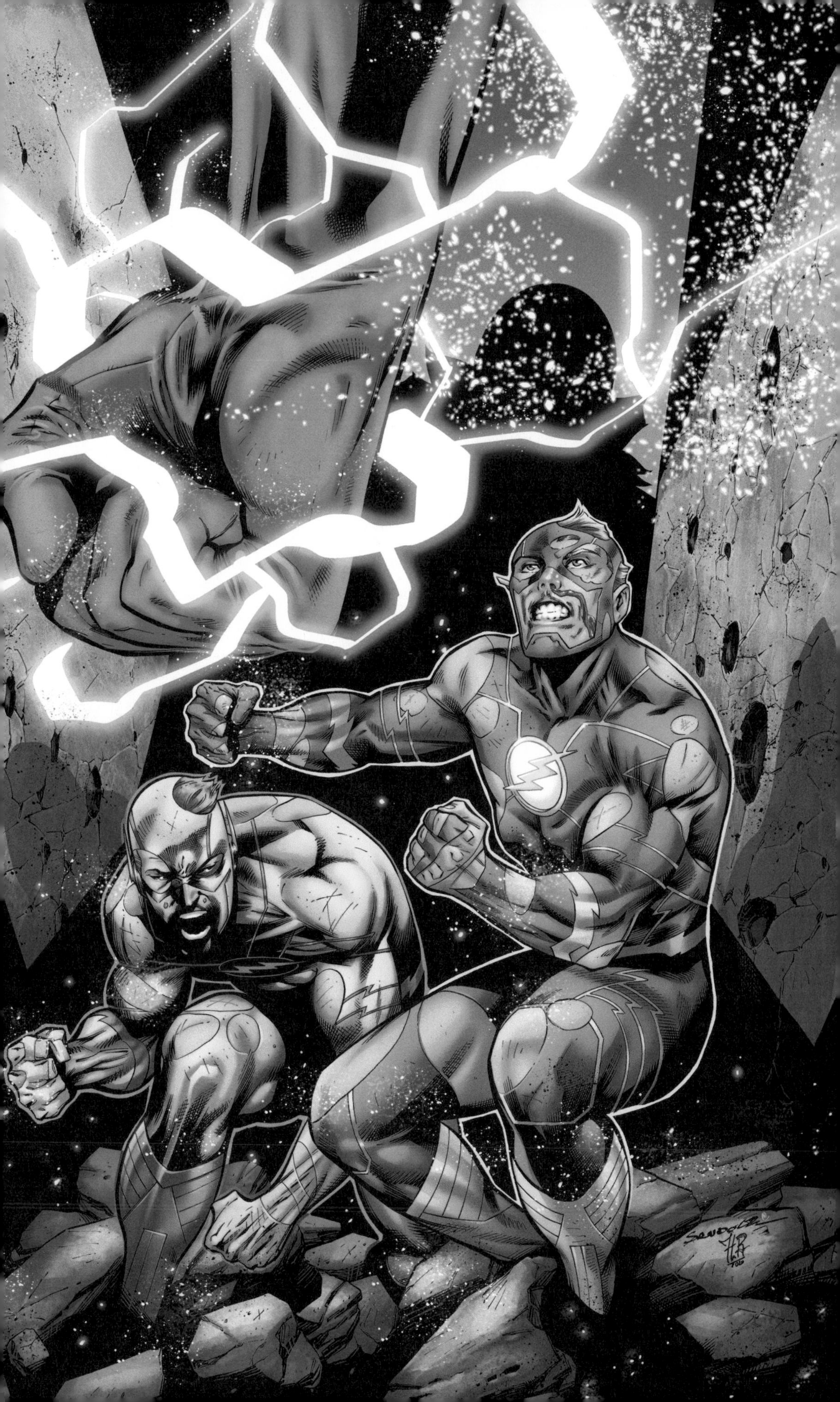

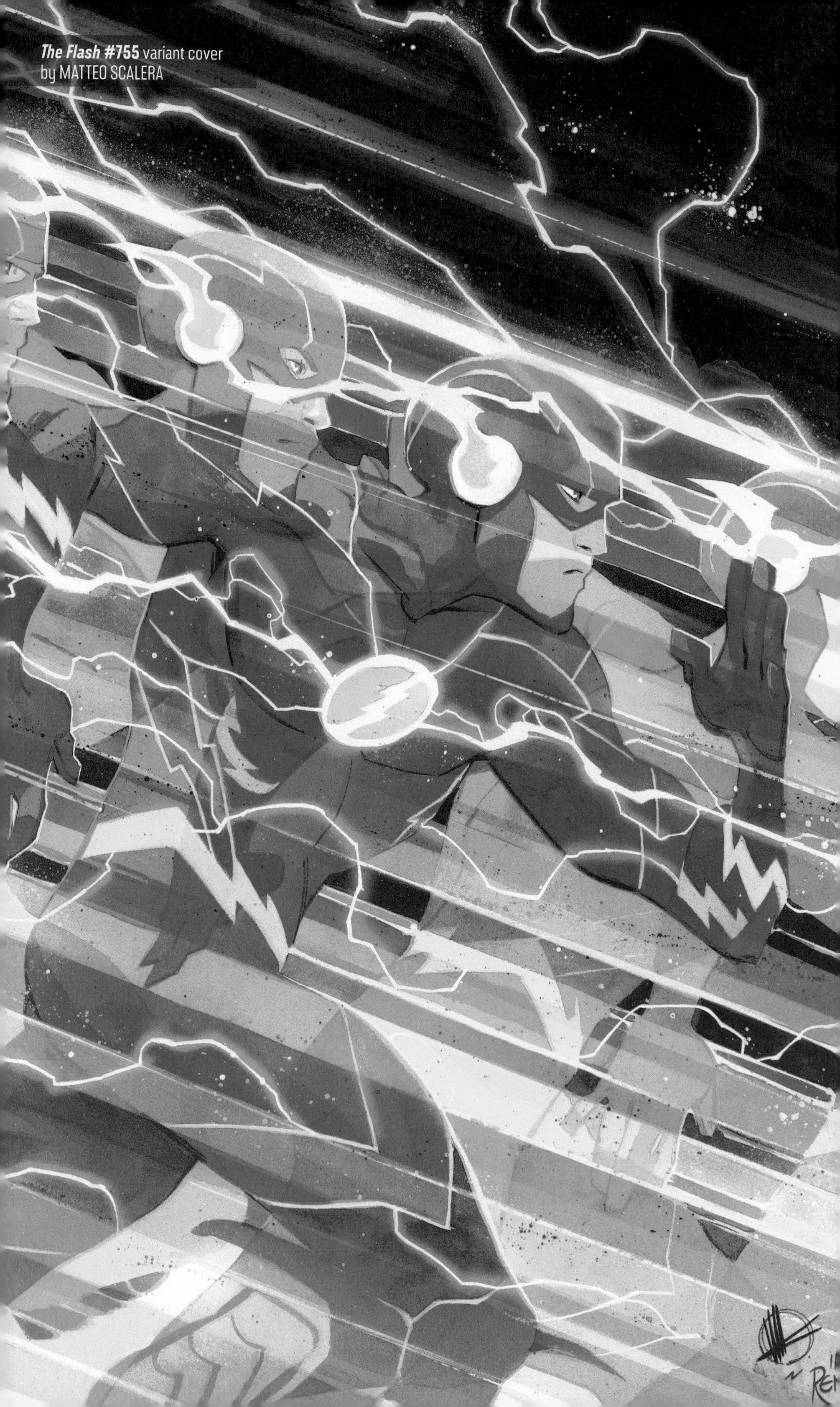

***The Flash* #755** variant cover
by MATTEO SCALERA

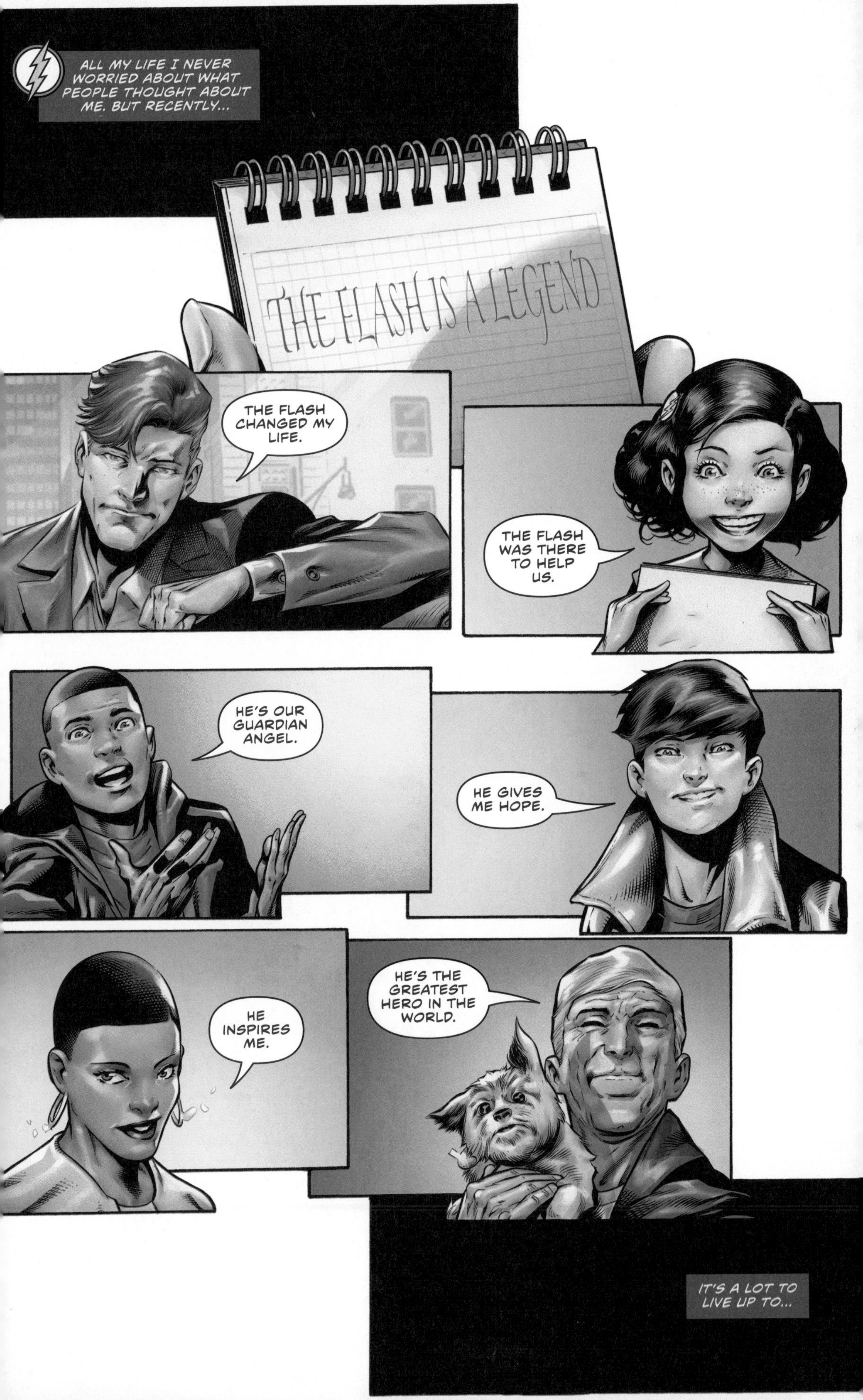
ALL MY LIFE I NEVER WORRIED ABOUT WHAT PEOPLE THOUGHT ABOUT ME. BUT RECENTLY...
THE FLASH IS A LEGEND
THE FLASH CHANGED MY LIFE.
THE FLASH WAS THERE TO HELP US.
HE'S OUR GUARDIAN ANGEL.
HE GIVES ME HOPE.
HE INSPIRES ME.
HE'S THE GREATEST HERO IN THE WORLD.
IT'S A LOT TO LIVE UP TO...

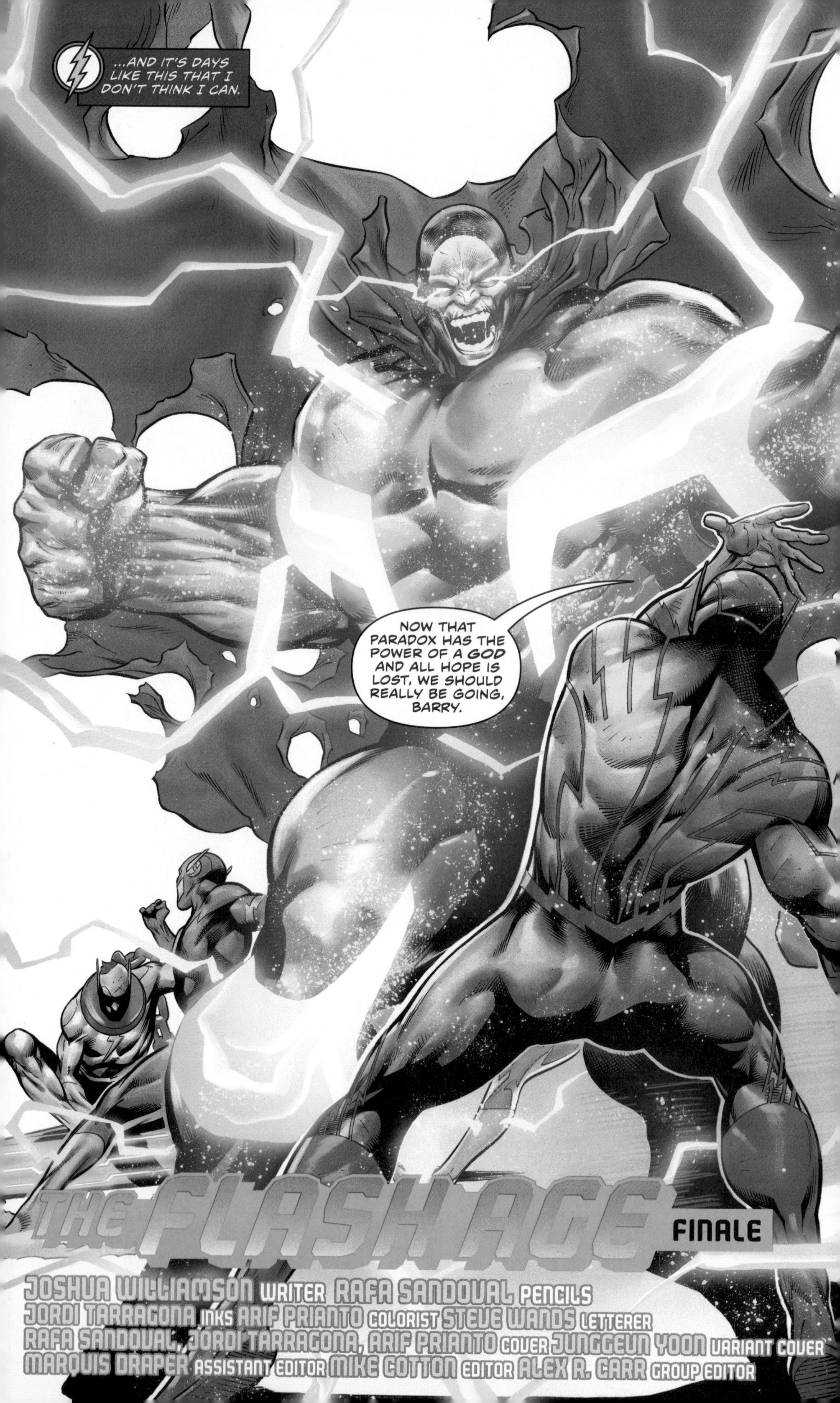
...AND IT'S DAYS LIKE THIS THAT I DON'T THINK I CAN.
NOW THAT PARADOX HAS THE POWER OF A GOD AND ALL HOPE IS LOST, WE SHOULD REALLY BE GOING, BARRY.
THE FLASH AGE FINALE
JOSHUA WILLIAMSON WRITER RAFA SANDOVAL PENCILS
JORDI TARRAGONA INKS ARIF PRIANTO COLORIST STEVE WANDS LETTERER
RAFA SANDOVAL, JORDI TARRAGONA, ARIF PRIANTO COVER JUNGGEUN YOON VARIANT COVER
MARQUIS DRAPER ASSISTANT EDITOR MIKE COTTON EDITOR ALEX R. CARR GROUP EDITOR

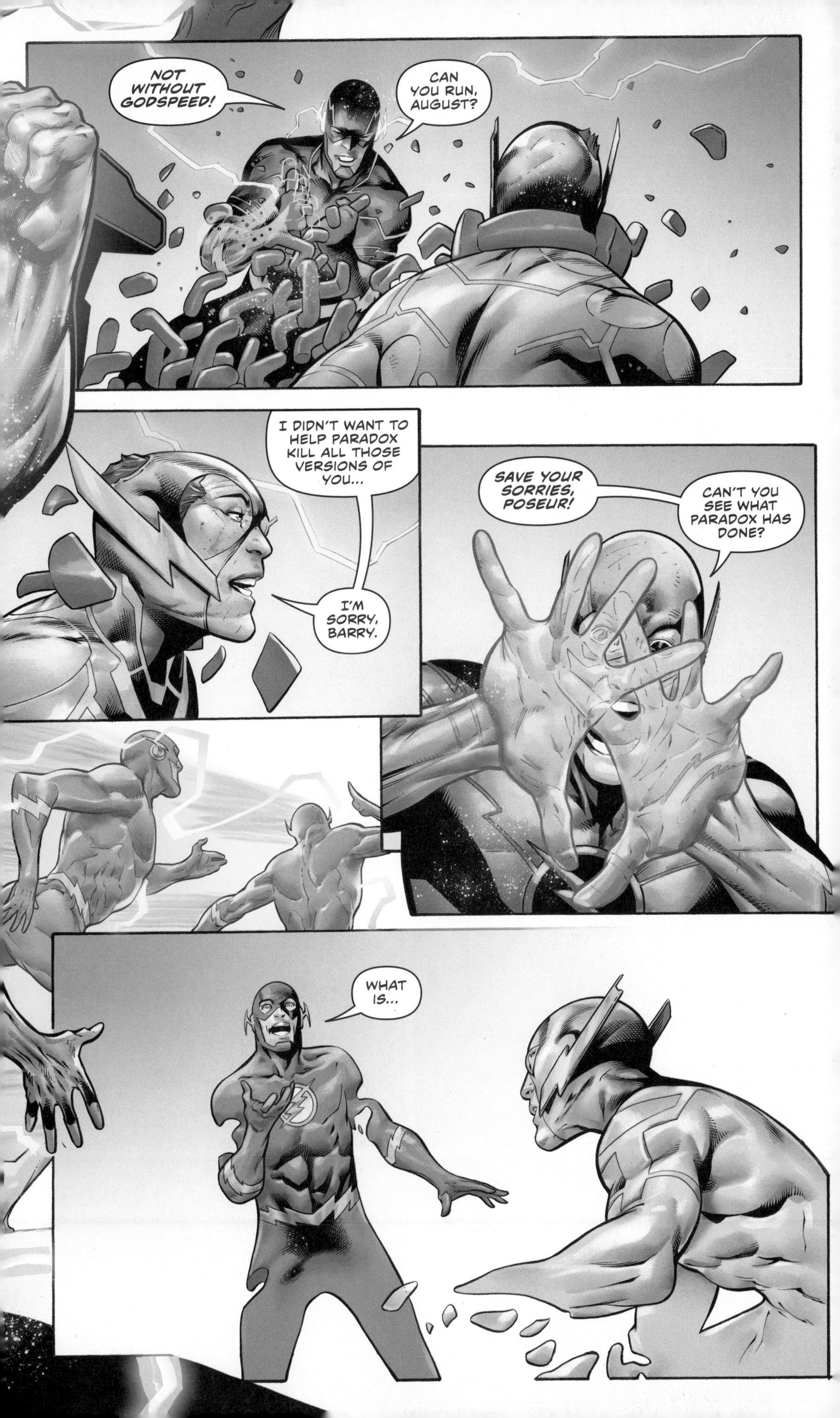
NOT WITHOUT GODSPEED!
CAN YOU RUN, AUGUST?
I DIDN'T WANT TO HELP PARADOX KILL ALL THOSE VERSIONS OF YOU...
I'M SORRY, BARRY.
SAVE YOUR SORRIES, POSEUR!
CAN'T YOU SEE WHAT PARADOX HAS DONE?
WHAT IS...

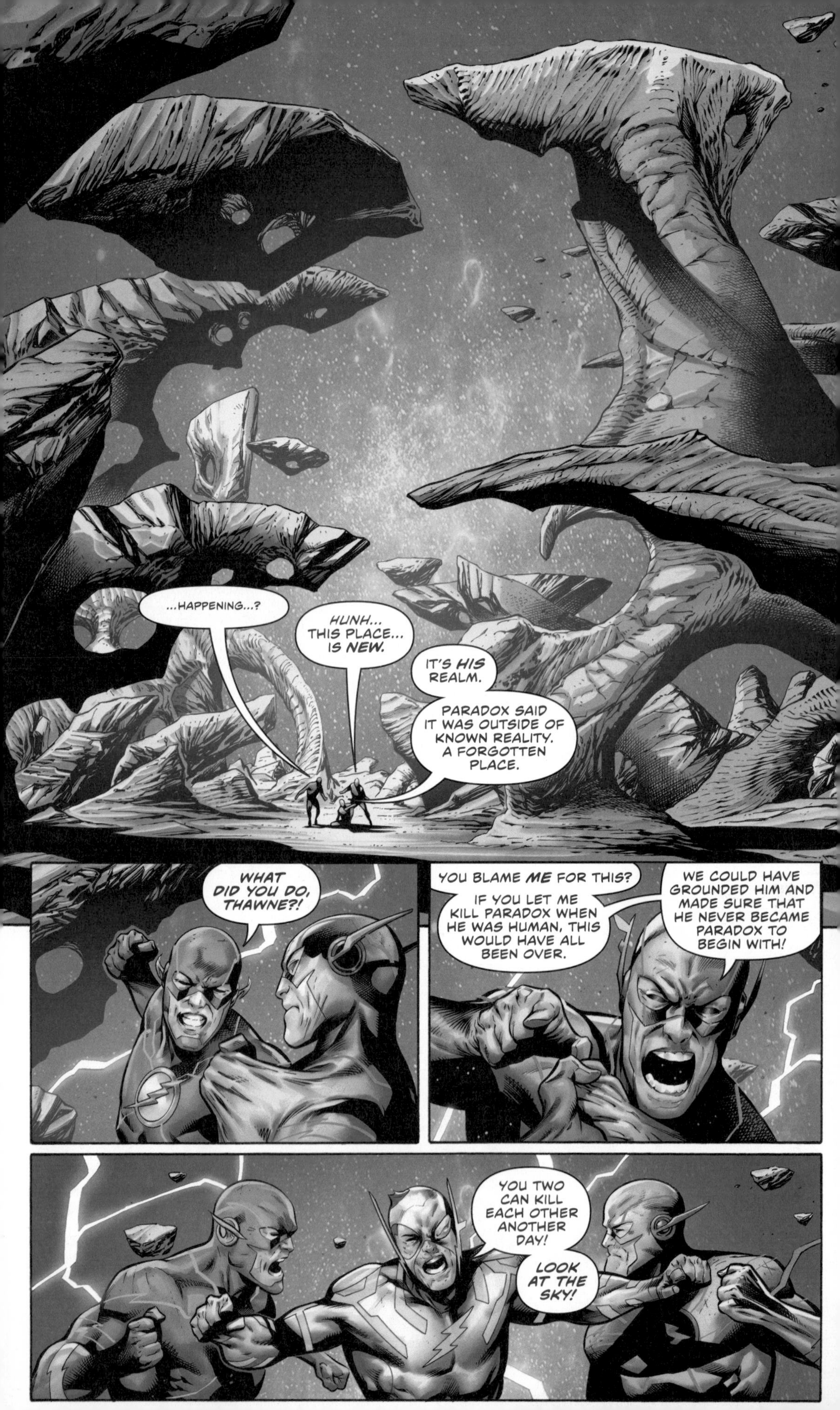
...HAPPENING...?
HUNH... THIS PLACE... IS NEW.
IT'S HIS REALM.
PARADOX SAID IT WAS OUTSIDE OF KNOWN REALITY. A FORGOTTEN PLACE.
WHAT DID YOU DO, THAWNE?!
YOU BLAME ME FOR THIS?
IF YOU LET ME KILL PARADOX WHEN HE WAS HUMAN, THIS WOULD HAVE ALL BEEN OVER.
WE COULD HAVE GROUNDED HIM AND MADE SURE THAT HE NEVER BECAME PARADOX TO BEGIN WITH!
YOU TWO CAN KILL EACH OTHER ANOTHER DAY!
LOOK AT THE SKY!

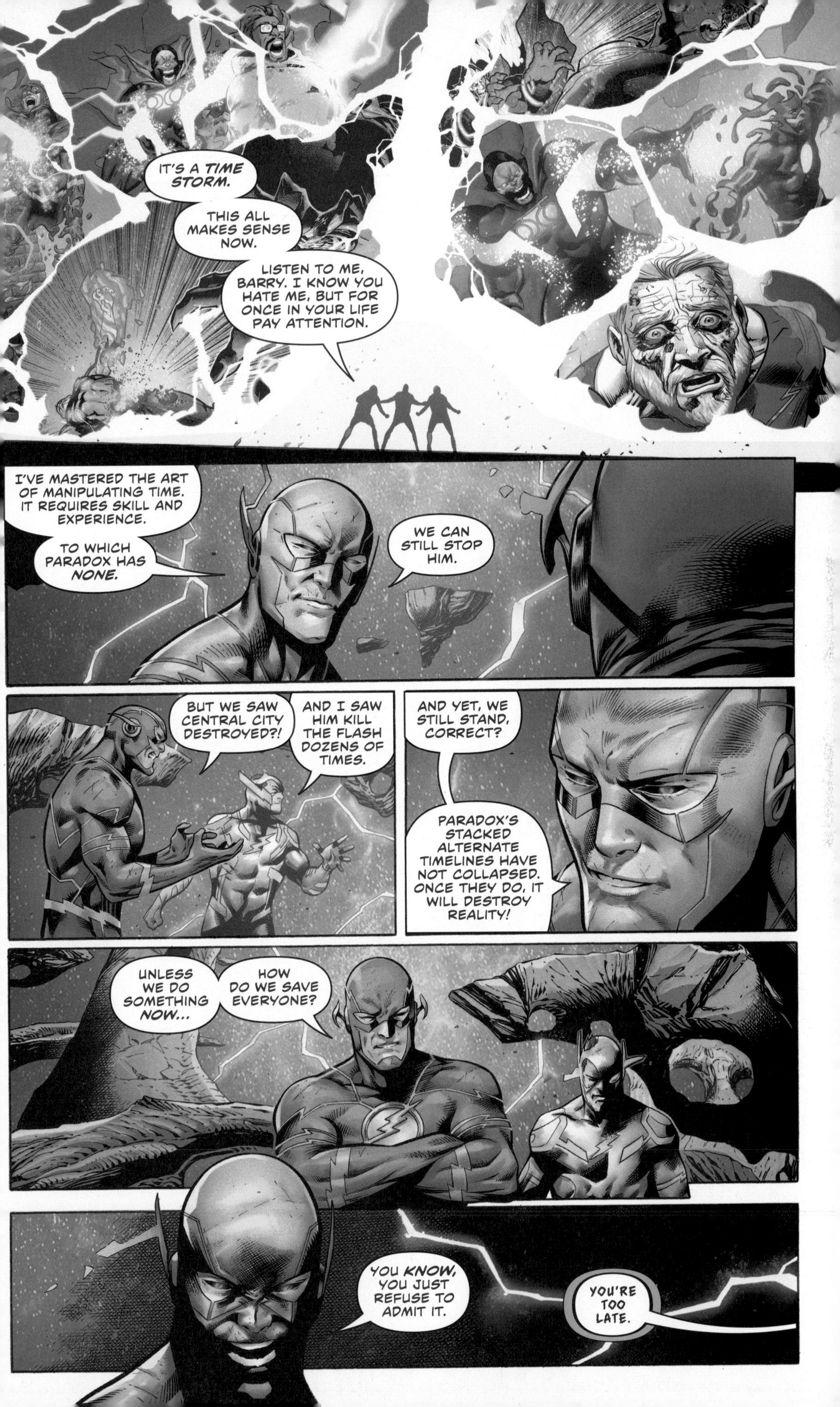

IT'S A *TIME STORM.*
THIS ALL MAKES SENSE NOW.
LISTEN TO ME, BARRY. I KNOW YOU HATE ME, BUT FOR ONCE IN YOUR LIFE PAY ATTENTION.
I'VE MASTERED THE ART OF MANIPULATING TIME. IT REQUIRES SKILL AND EXPERIENCE.
TO WHICH PARADOX HAS *NONE.*
WE CAN STILL STOP HIM.
BUT WE SAW CENTRAL CITY DESTROYED?!
AND I SAW HIM KILL THE FLASH DOZENS OF TIMES.
AND YET, WE STILL STAND, CORRECT?
PARADOX'S STACKED ALTERNATE TIMELINES HAVE NOT COLLAPSED. ONCE THEY DO, IT WILL DESTROY REALITY!
UNLESS WE DO SOMETHING *NOW...*
HOW DO WE SAVE EVERYONE?
YOU *KNOW,* YOU JUST REFUSE TO ADMIT IT.
YOU'RE TOO LATE.

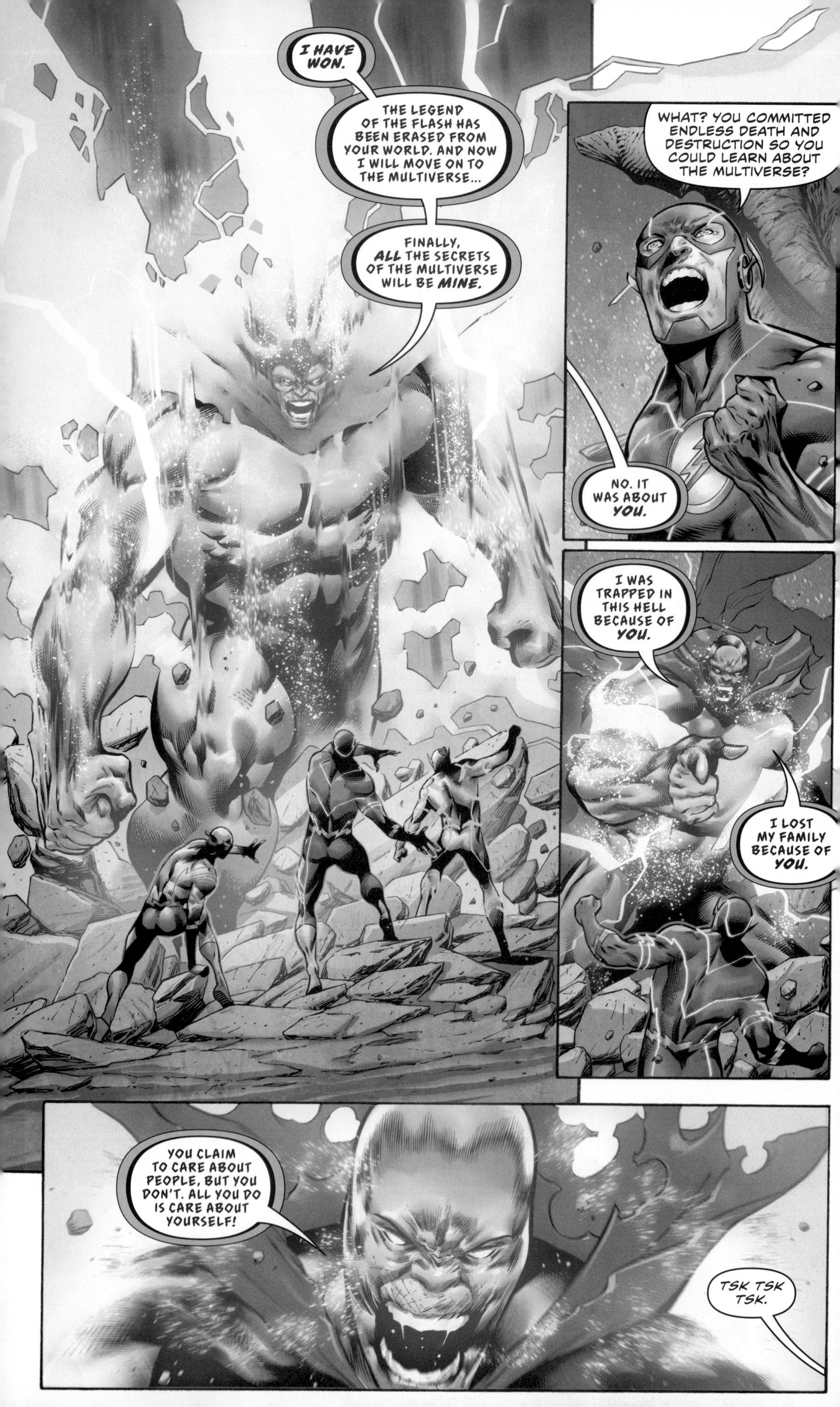
I HAVE WON.
THE LEGEND OF THE FLASH HAS BEEN ERASED FROM YOUR WORLD. AND NOW I WILL MOVE ON TO THE MULTIVERSE...
FINALLY, ALL THE SECRETS OF THE MULTIVERSE WILL BE MINE.
WHAT? YOU COMMITTED ENDLESS DEATH AND DESTRUCTION SO YOU COULD LEARN ABOUT THE MULTIVERSE?
NO. IT WAS ABOUT YOU.
I WAS TRAPPED IN THIS HELL BECAUSE OF YOU.
I LOST MY FAMILY BECAUSE OF YOU.
YOU CLAIM TO CARE ABOUT PEOPLE, BUT YOU DON'T. ALL YOU DO IS CARE ABOUT YOURSELF!
TSK TSK TSK.

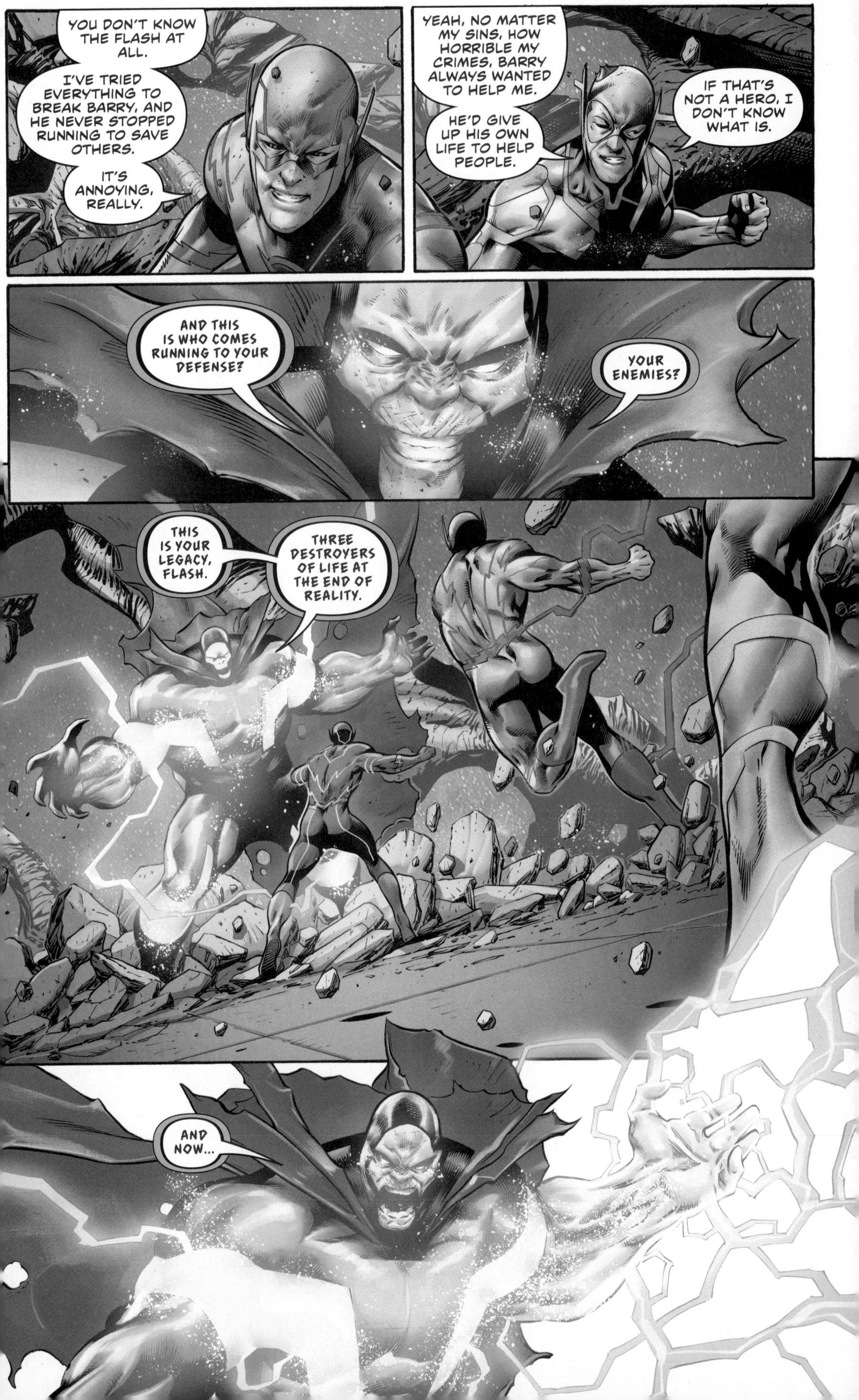
YOU DON'T KNOW THE FLASH AT ALL.
I'VE TRIED EVERYTHING TO BREAK BARRY, AND HE NEVER STOPPED RUNNING TO SAVE OTHERS.
IT'S ANNOYING, REALLY.
YEAH, NO MATTER MY SINS, HOW HORRIBLE MY CRIMES, BARRY ALWAYS WANTED TO HELP ME.
HE'D GIVE UP HIS OWN LIFE TO HELP PEOPLE.
IF THAT'S NOT A HERO, I DON'T KNOW WHAT IS.
AND THIS IS WHO COMES RUNNING TO YOUR DEFENSE?
YOUR ENEMIES?
THIS IS YOUR LEGACY, FLASH.
THREE DESTROYERS OF LIFE AT THE END OF REALITY.
AND NOW...

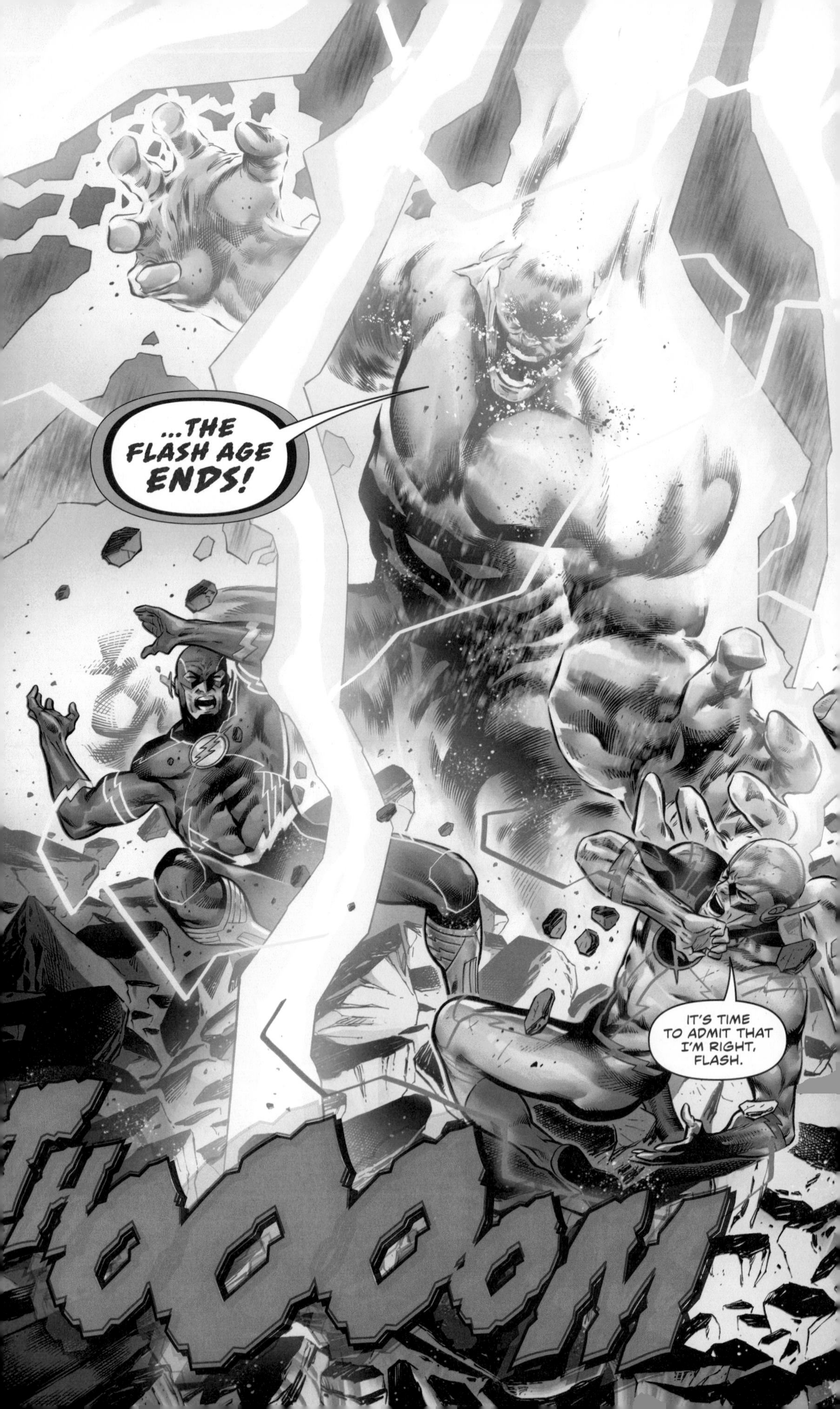

...THE FLASH AGE ENDS!
IT'S TIME TO ADMIT THAT I'M RIGHT, FLASH.
THOOOM

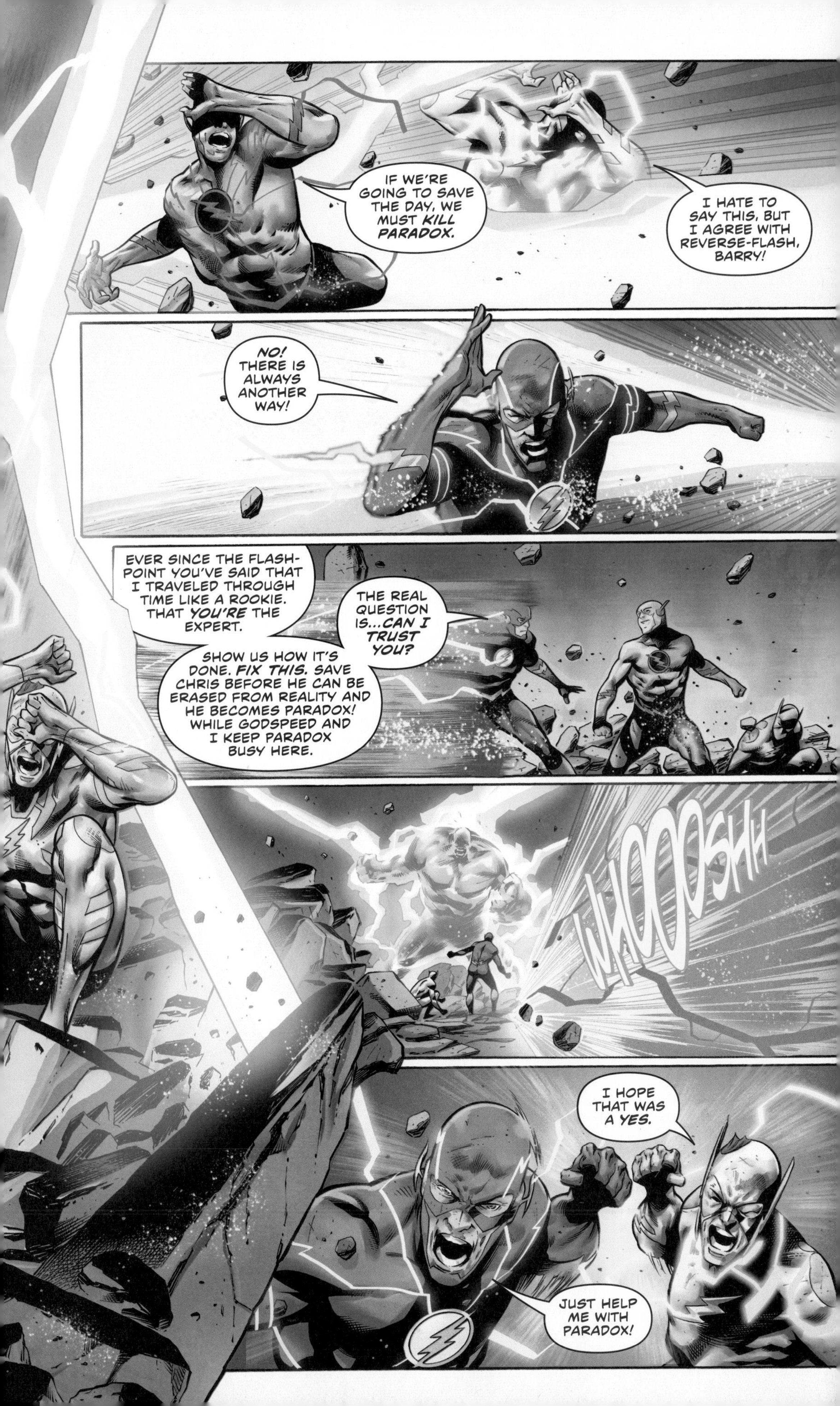

IF WE'RE GOING TO SAVE THE DAY, WE MUST *KILL PARADOX.*
I HATE TO SAY THIS, BUT I AGREE WITH REVERSE-FLASH, BARRY!
NO! THERE IS ALWAYS ANOTHER WAY!
EVER SINCE THE FLASH-POINT YOU'VE SAID THAT I TRAVELED THROUGH TIME LIKE A ROOKIE. THAT *YOU'RE* THE EXPERT.
SHOW US HOW IT'S DONE. *FIX THIS.* SAVE CHRIS BEFORE HE CAN BE ERASED FROM REALITY AND HE BECOMES PARADOX! WHILE GODSPEED AND I KEEP PARADOX BUSY HERE.
THE REAL QUESTION IS...*CAN I TRUST YOU?*
WHOOOSHH
I HOPE THAT WAS A *YES.*
JUST HELP ME WITH PARADOX!

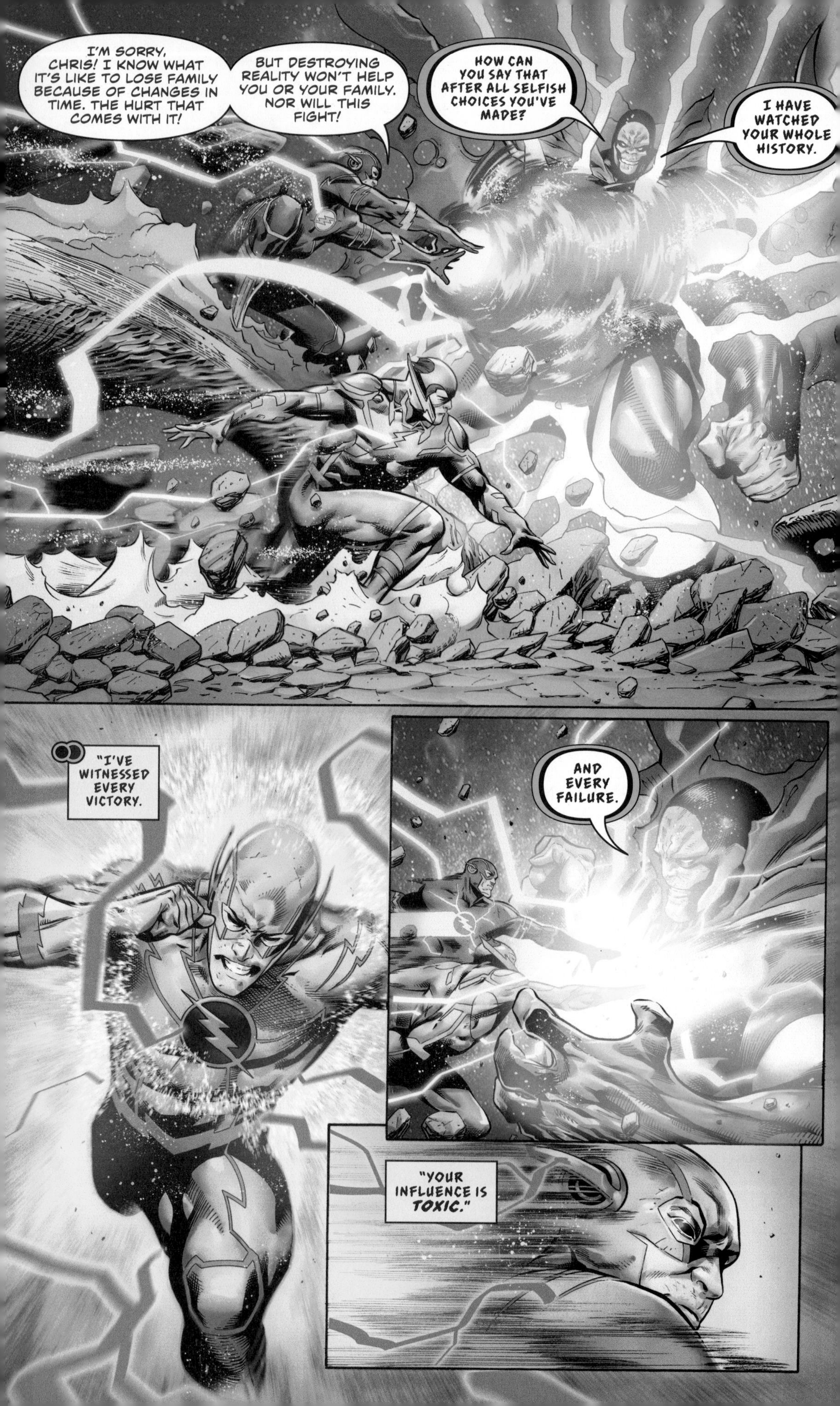
I'M SORRY, CHRIS! I KNOW WHAT IT'S LIKE TO LOSE FAMILY BECAUSE OF CHANGES IN TIME. THE HURT THAT COMES WITH IT!
BUT DESTROYING REALITY WON'T HELP YOU OR YOUR FAMILY. NOR WILL THIS FIGHT!
HOW CAN YOU SAY THAT AFTER ALL SELFISH CHOICES YOU'VE MADE?
I HAVE WATCHED YOUR WHOLE HISTORY.
"I'VE WITNESSED EVERY VICTORY.
AND EVERY FAILURE.
"YOUR INFLUENCE IS *TOXIC*."

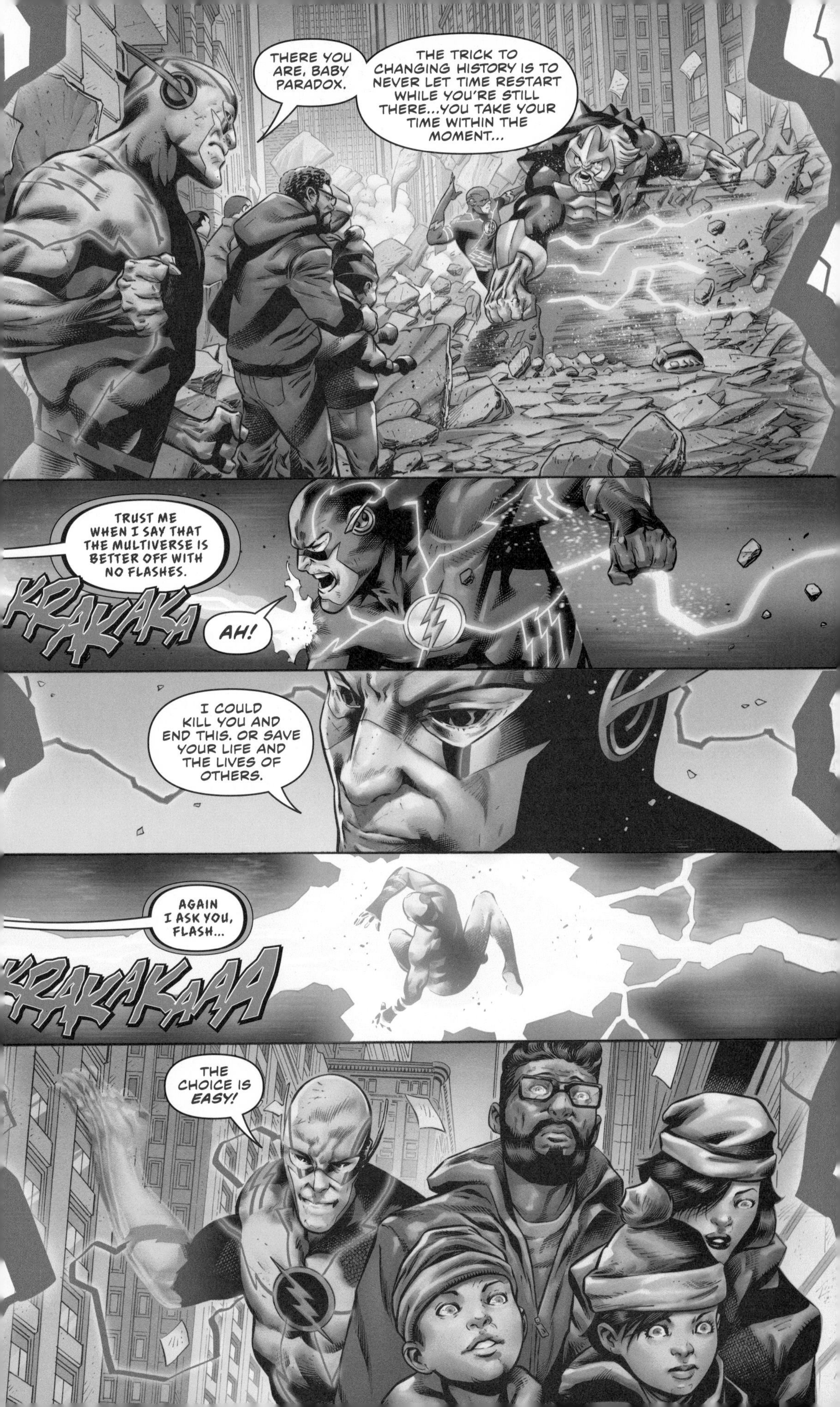
THERE YOU ARE, BABY PARADOX.
THE TRICK TO CHANGING HISTORY IS TO NEVER LET TIME RESTART WHILE YOU'RE STILL THERE...YOU TAKE YOUR TIME WITHIN THE MOMENT...
TRUST ME WHEN I SAY THAT THE MULTIVERSE IS BETTER OFF WITH NO FLASHES.
KRAKAKA
AH!
I COULD KILL YOU AND END THIS. OR SAVE YOUR LIFE AND THE LIVES OF OTHERS.
AGAIN I ASK YOU, FLASH...
KRAKAKAAA
THE CHOICE IS EASY!

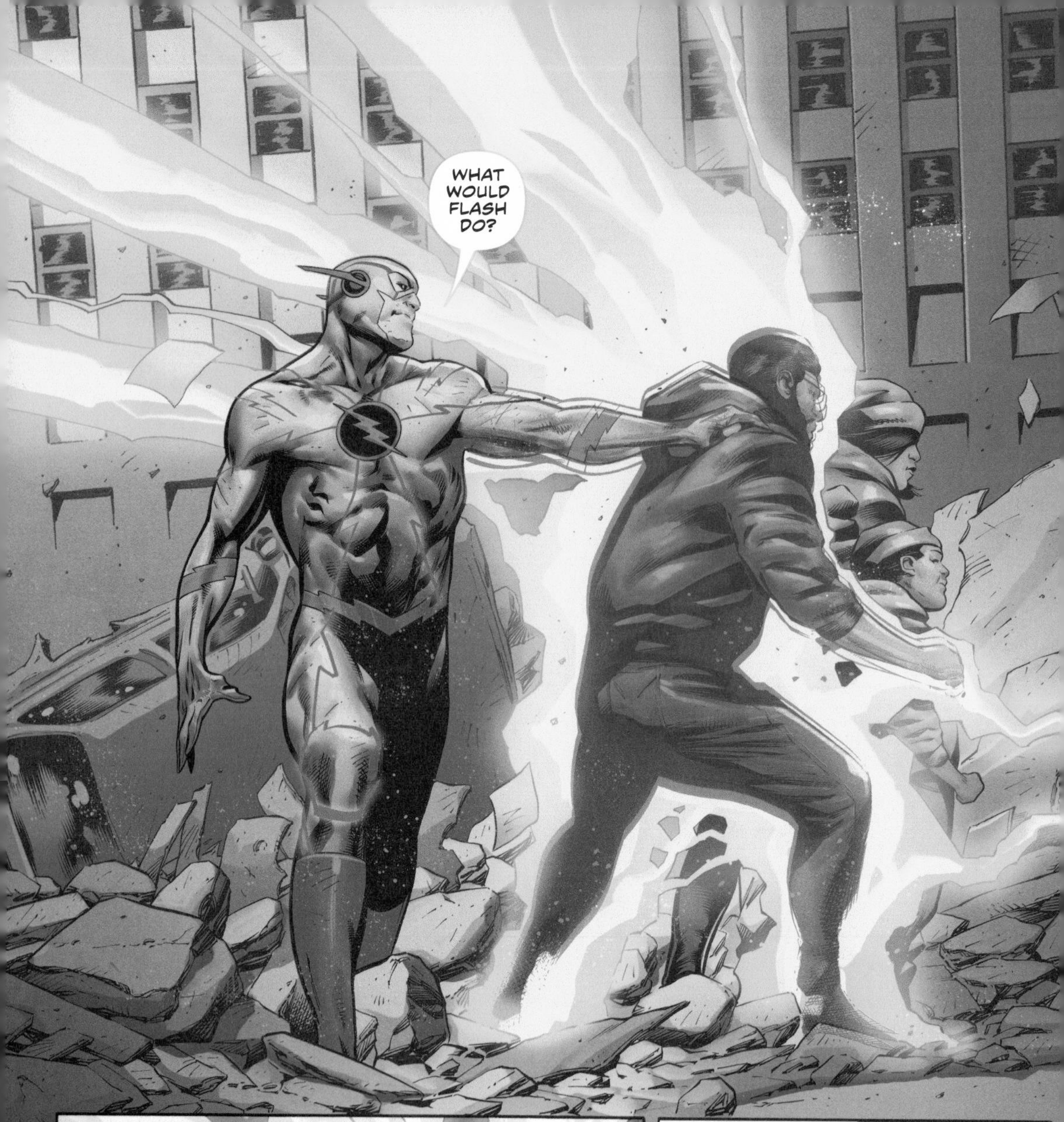
WHAT WOULD FLASH DO?

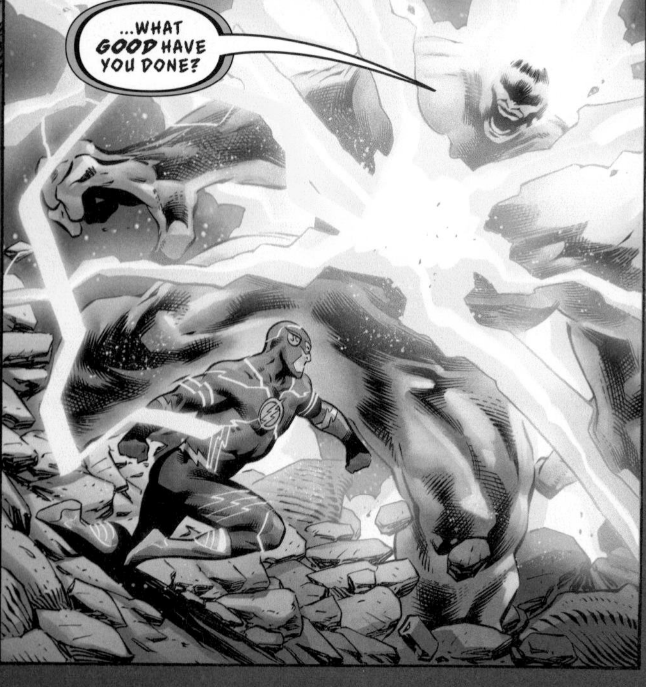
...WHAT GOOD HAVE YOU DONE?

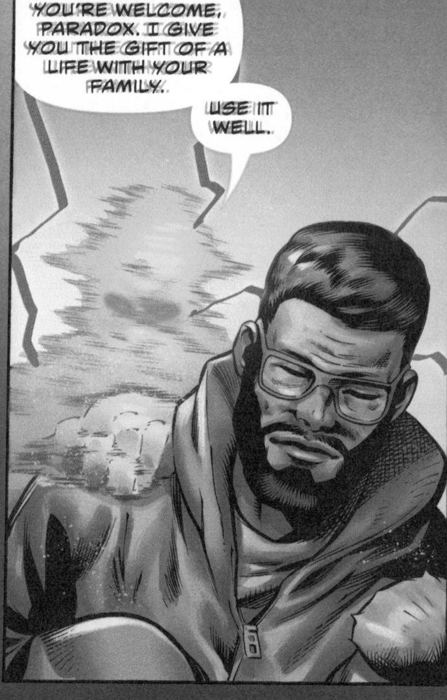
YOU'RE WELCOME, PARADOX. I GIVE YOU THE GIFT OF A LIFE WITH YOUR FAMILY.
USE IT WELL.

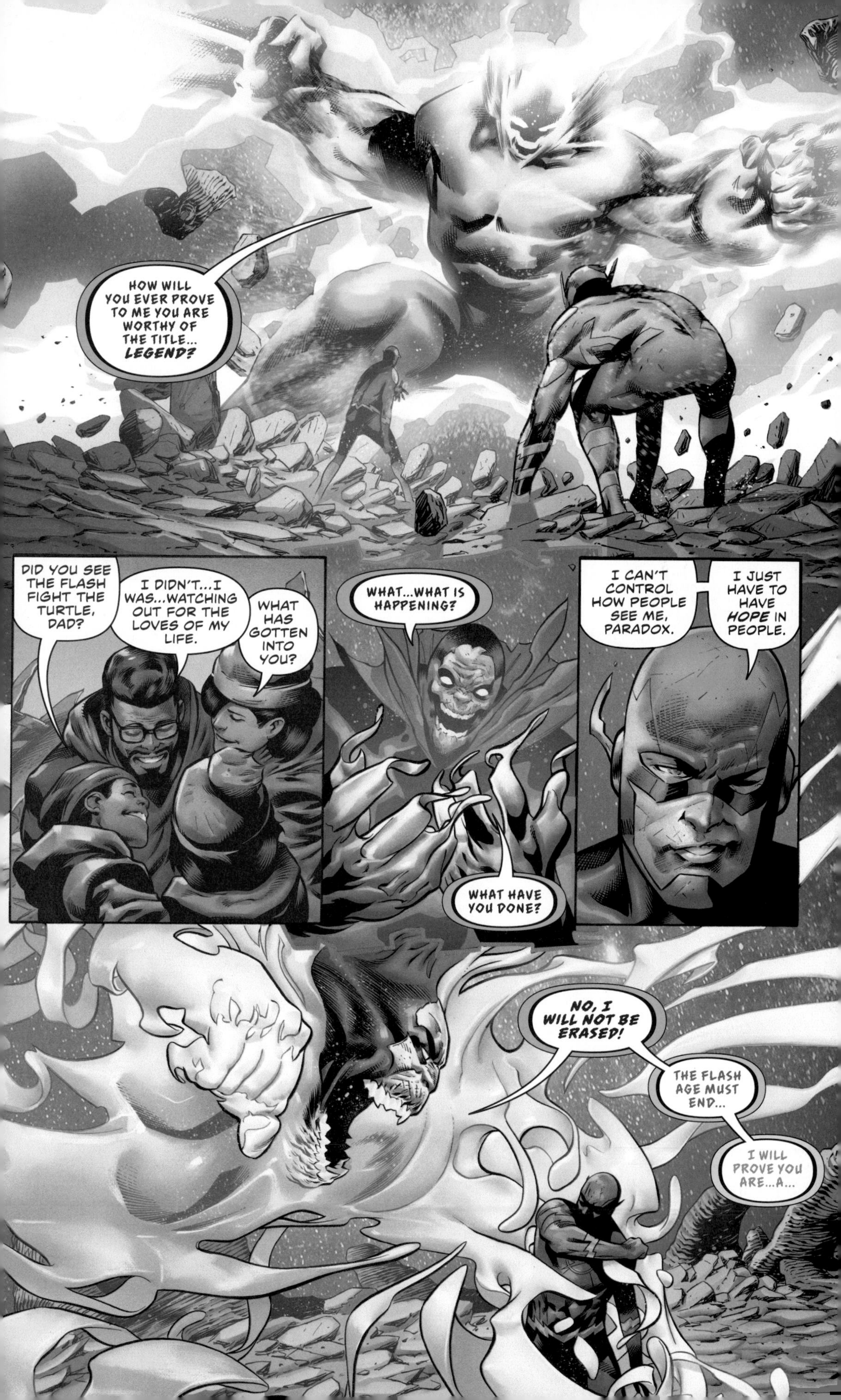
HOW WILL YOU EVER PROVE TO ME YOU ARE WORTHY OF THE TITLE... ***LEGEND?***
DID YOU SEE THE FLASH FIGHT THE TURTLE, DAD?
I DIDN'T...I WAS...WATCHING OUT FOR THE LOVES OF MY LIFE.
WHAT HAS GOTTEN INTO YOU?
WHAT...WHAT IS HAPPENING?
WHAT HAVE YOU DONE?
I CAN'T CONTROL HOW PEOPLE SEE ME, PARADOX.
I JUST HAVE TO HAVE ***HOPE*** IN PEOPLE.
NO, I WILL NOT BE ERASED!
THE FLASH AGE MUST END...
I WILL PROVE YOU ARE...A...

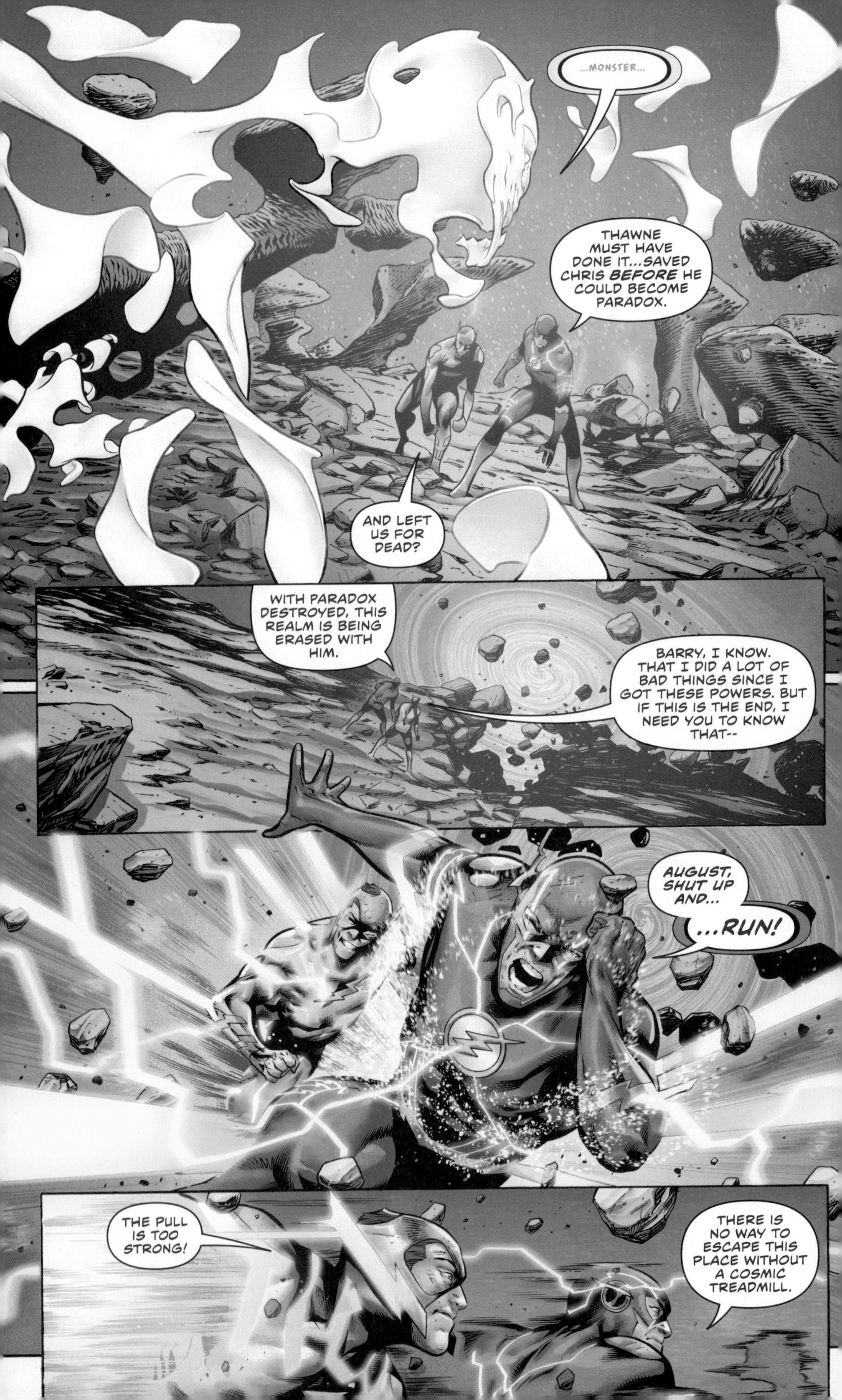
...MONSTER...
THAWNE MUST HAVE DONE IT...SAVED CHRIS BEFORE HE COULD BECOME PARADOX.
AND LEFT US FOR DEAD?
WITH PARADOX DESTROYED, THIS REALM IS BEING ERASED WITH HIM.
BARRY, I KNOW. THAT I DID A LOT OF BAD THINGS SINCE I GOT THESE POWERS. BUT IF THIS IS THE END, I NEED YOU TO KNOW THAT--
AUGUST, SHUT UP AND...
...RUN!
THE PULL IS TOO STRONG!
THERE IS NO WAY TO ESCAPE THIS PLACE WITHOUT A COSMIC TREADMILL.

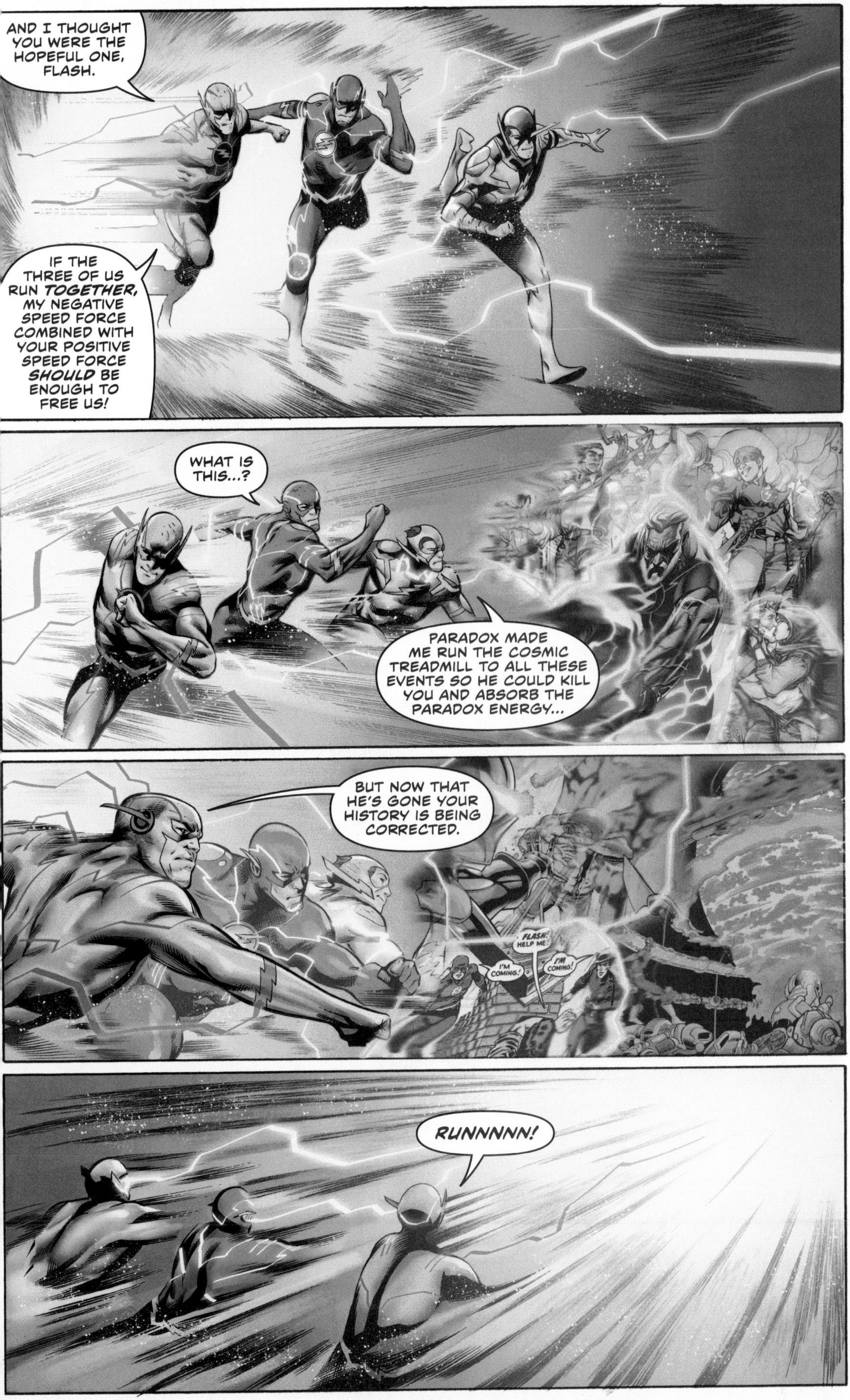
AND I THOUGHT YOU WERE THE HOPEFUL ONE, FLASH.
IF THE THREE OF US RUN *TOGETHER*, MY NEGATIVE SPEED FORCE COMBINED WITH YOUR POSITIVE SPEED FORCE *SHOULD* BE ENOUGH TO FREE US!
WHAT IS THIS...?
PARADOX MADE ME RUN THE COSMIC TREADMILL TO ALL THESE EVENTS SO HE COULD KILL YOU AND ABSORB THE PARADOX ENERGY...
BUT NOW THAT HE'S GONE YOUR HISTORY IS BEING CORRECTED.
FLASH! HELP ME!
I'M COMING!
I'M COMING!
RUNNNNN!

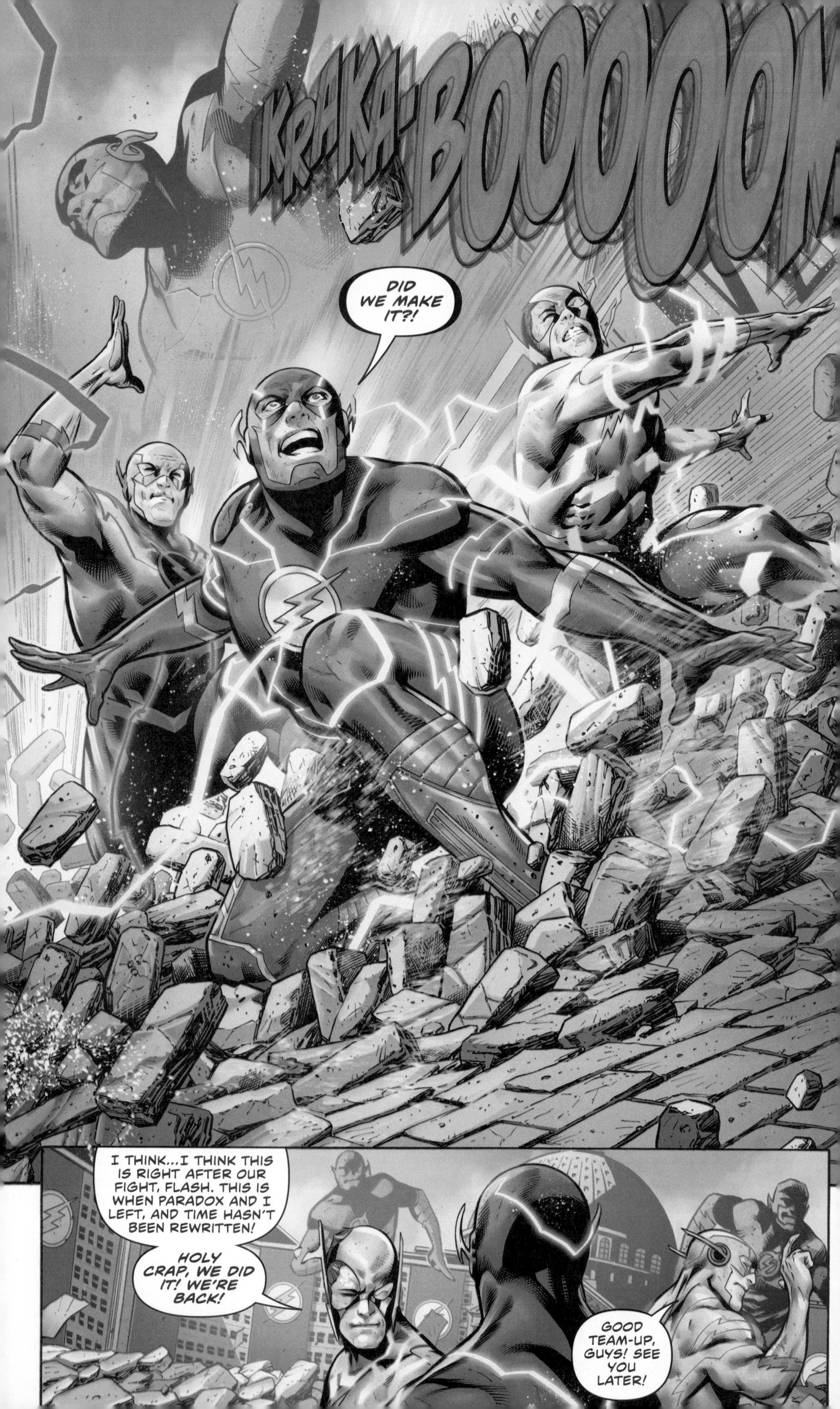
KRAKA-BOOOOOM
DID WE MAKE IT?!
I THINK...I THINK THIS IS RIGHT AFTER OUR FIGHT, FLASH. THIS IS WHEN PARADOX AND I LEFT, AND TIME HASN'T BEEN REWRITTEN!
HOLY CRAP, WE DID IT! WE'RE BACK!
GOOD TEAM-UP, GUYS! SEE YOU LATER!

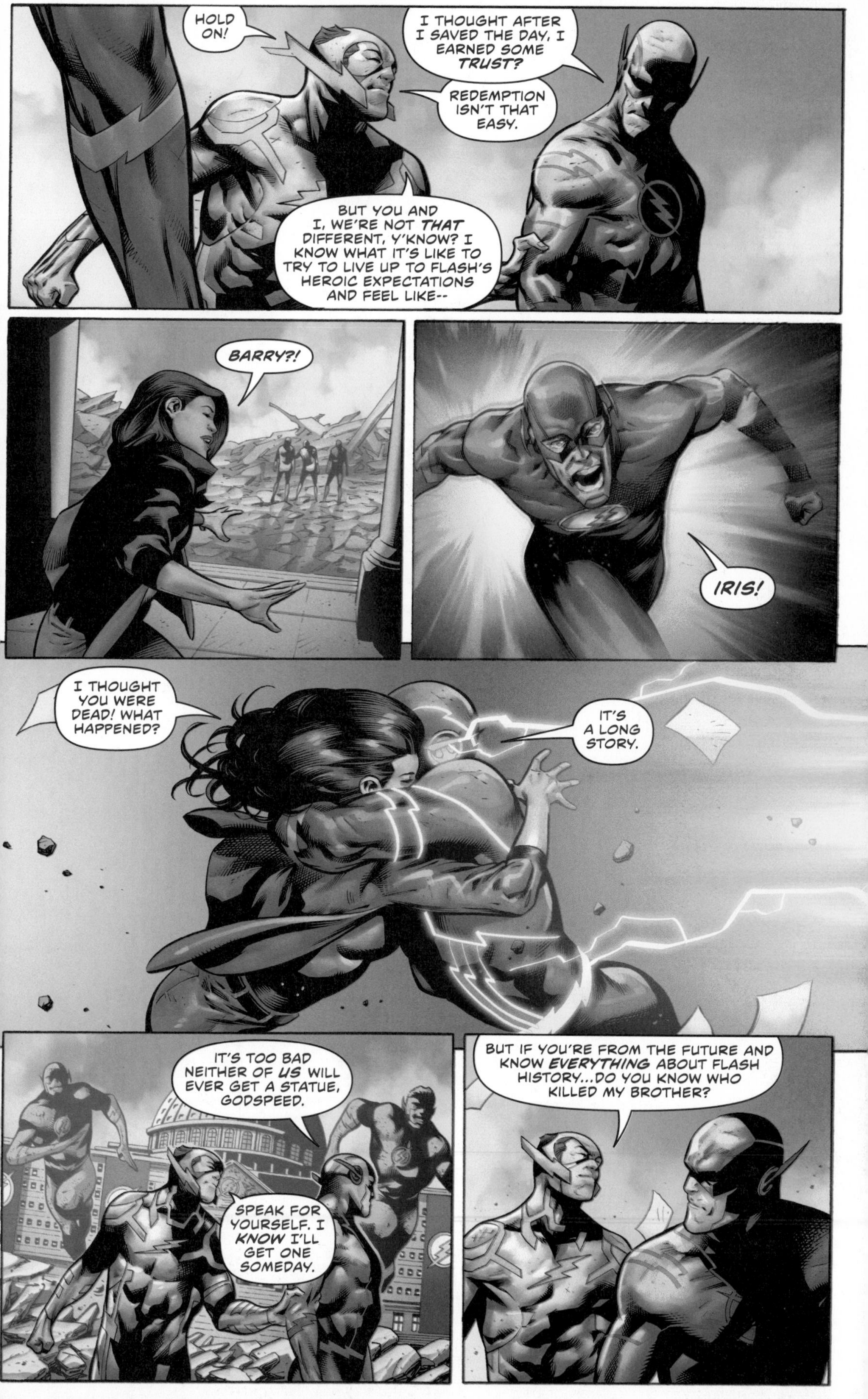
HOLD ON!
I THOUGHT AFTER I SAVED THE DAY, I EARNED SOME TRUST?
REDEMPTION ISN'T THAT EASY.
BUT YOU AND I, WE'RE NOT THAT DIFFERENT, Y'KNOW? I KNOW WHAT IT'S LIKE TO TRY TO LIVE UP TO FLASH'S HEROIC EXPECTATIONS AND FEEL LIKE--
BARRY?!
IRIS!
I THOUGHT YOU WERE DEAD! WHAT HAPPENED?
IT'S A LONG STORY.
IT'S TOO BAD NEITHER OF US WILL EVER GET A STATUE, GODSPEED.
SPEAK FOR YOURSELF. I KNOW I'LL GET ONE SOMEDAY.
BUT IF YOU'RE FROM THE FUTURE AND KNOW EVERYTHING ABOUT FLASH HISTORY...DO YOU KNOW WHO KILLED MY BROTHER?

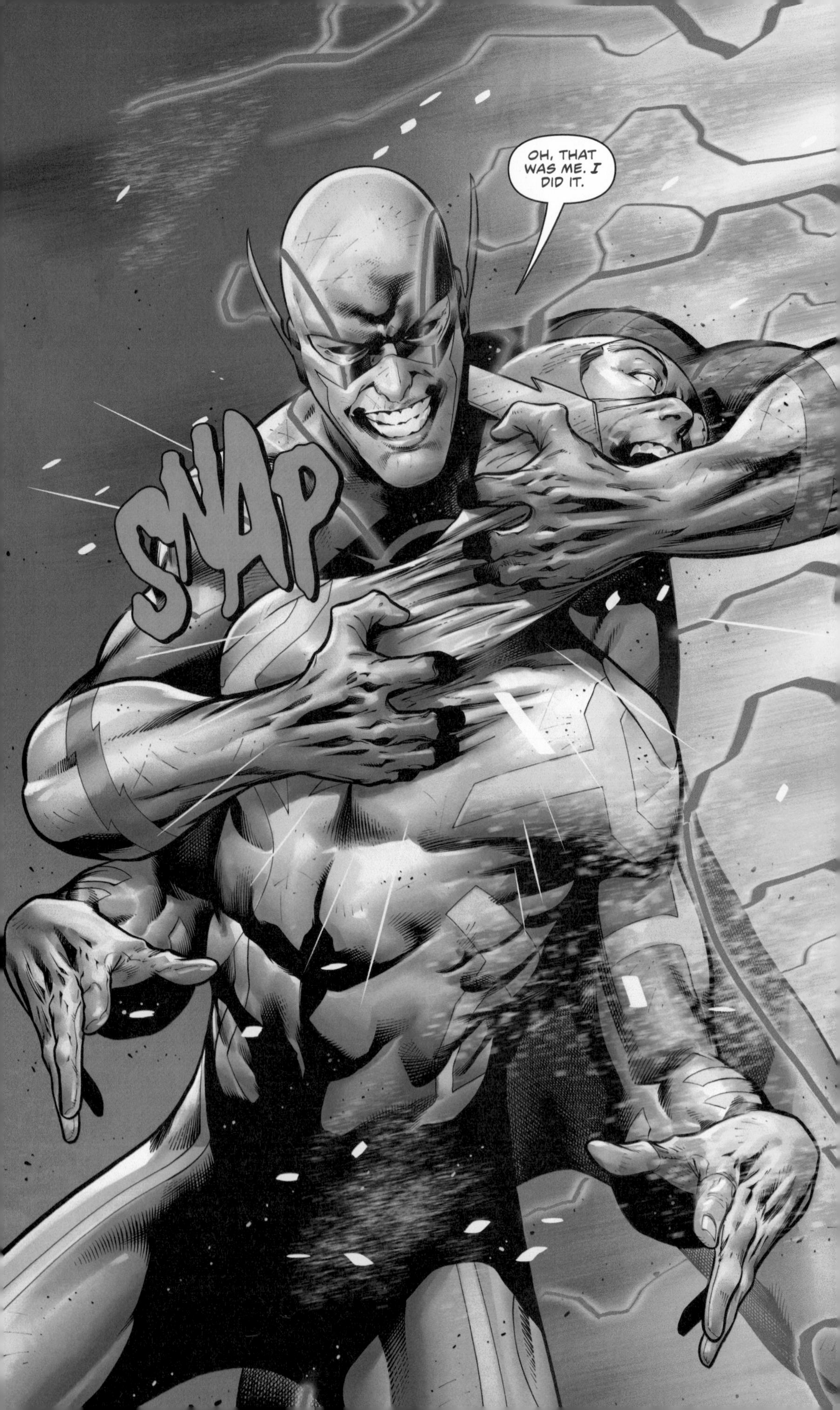
OH, THAT WAS ME. I DID IT.
SNAP

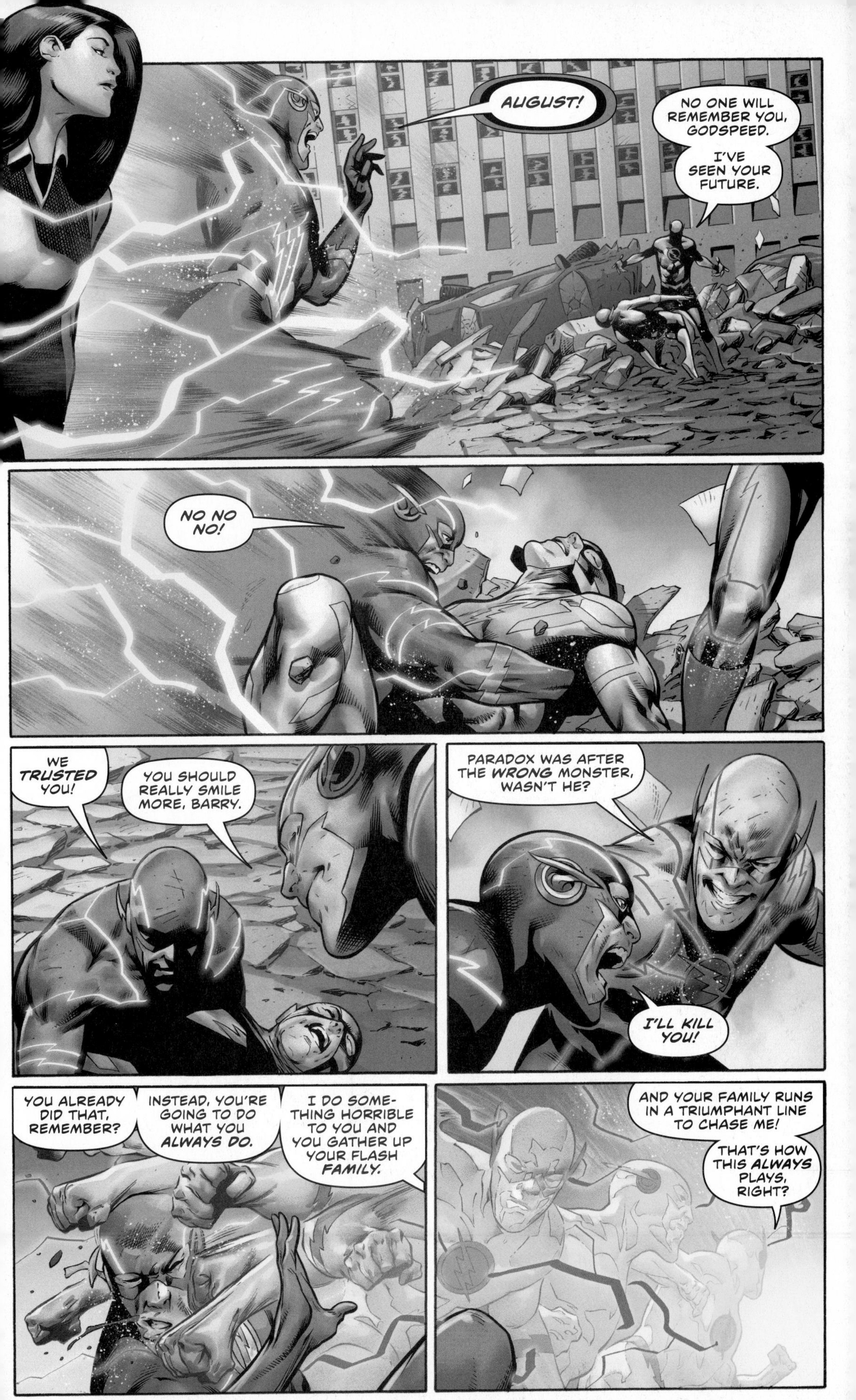
AUGUST!
NO ONE WILL REMEMBER YOU, GODSPEED.
I'VE SEEN YOUR FUTURE.
NO NO NO!
WE TRUSTED YOU!
YOU SHOULD REALLY SMILE MORE, BARRY.
PARADOX WAS AFTER THE WRONG MONSTER, WASN'T HE?
I'LL KILL YOU!
YOU ALREADY DID THAT, REMEMBER?
INSTEAD, YOU'RE GOING TO DO WHAT YOU ALWAYS DO.
I DO SOME-THING HORRIBLE TO YOU AND YOU GATHER UP YOUR FLASH FAMILY.
AND YOUR FAMILY RUNS IN A TRIUMPHANT LINE TO CHASE ME!
THAT'S HOW THIS ALWAYS PLAYS, RIGHT?

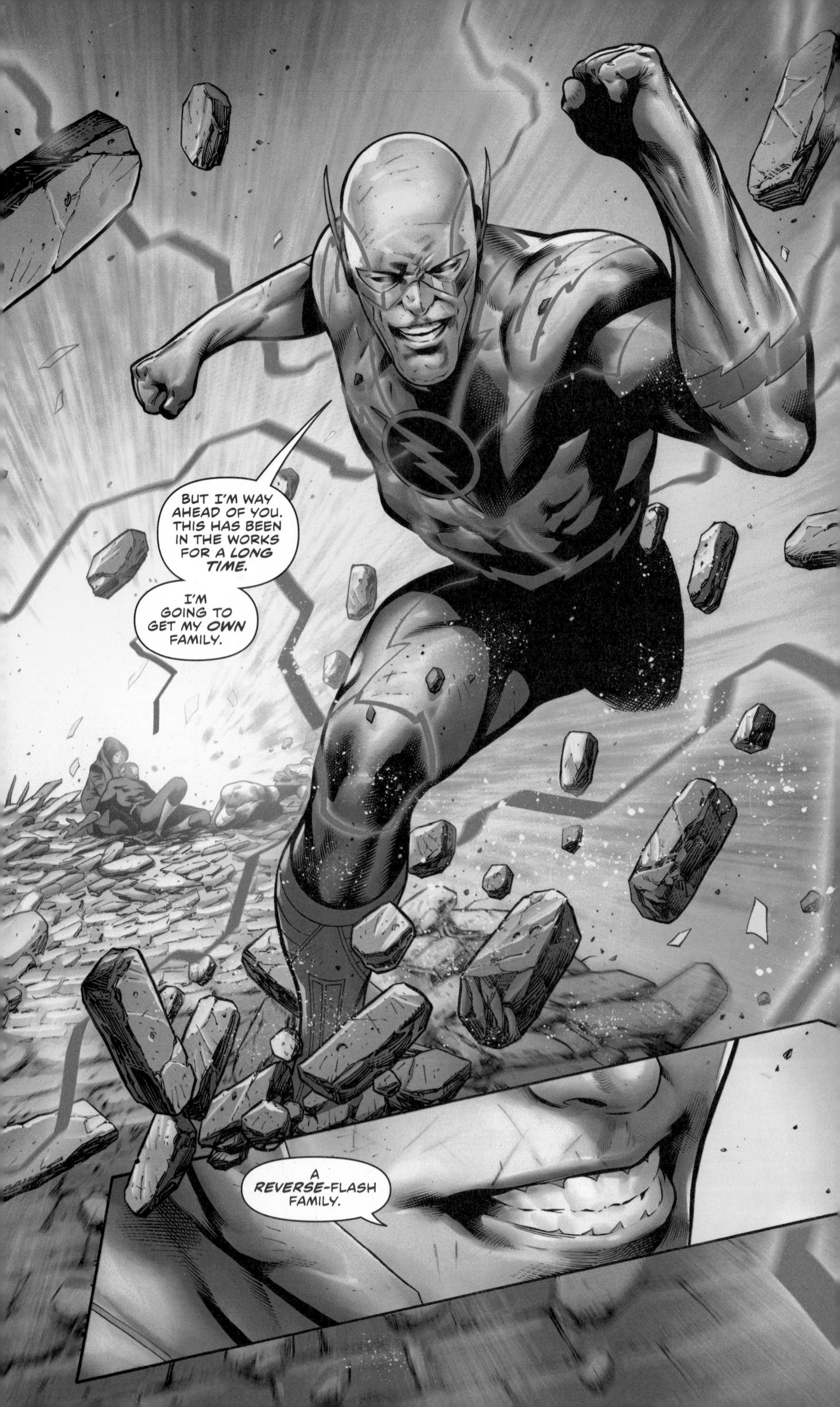
BUT I'M WAY AHEAD OF YOU. THIS HAS BEEN IN THE WORKS FOR A *LONG TIME.*
I'M GOING TO GET MY *OWN* FAMILY.
A *REVERSE*-FLASH FAMILY.